Conflict and Reconciliation

Studies in Methodism and Ecumenism in England
1740–1982

CONFLICT
AND RECONCILIATION

Studies in Methodism and Ecumenism in England
1740–1982

JOHN MUNSEY TURNER

EPWORTH PRESS

British Library Cataloguing-in-Publication Data available

7162 0410 X

First published 1985
by Epworth Press
Room 195, 1 Central Buildings
Westminster, London SW1

Phototypeset by Input Typesetting Ltd, London
and printed in Great Britain by
The Camelot Press Ltd
Southampton

For Hilary and Catherine

Contents

Foreword

The ecumenical movement in England has coped with recent disappointments by passing into a more reflective phase. Genuine unity needs to be rooted in deeper mutual understanding, a willingness to go back behind the pain of our present divisions and retell the story of who we are, and how we came to be, and why we felt so tragically impelled to go our separate ways. Then through the healing of memories, it becomes possible to start again.

John Turner here makes a notable contribution to this process. It is the story of a love-hate relationship between Methodism and the Church of England, a story he to some extent exemplifies in his own person. As a colleague at Queen's College, Birmingham, he left me in do doubt of his staunch Methodism, his fascination and fury with the Church of England, his commitment to ecumenism, and his determination to tell the truth as he saw it. Readers of this book will recognize the qualities, and will understand why generations of students, and not least Roman Catholic ordinands from St Mary's College, Oscott, valued his church history lectures so highly. The same trenchancy, forthrightness and mastery of detail come through on the printed page.

The story of two great churches in their relationship with each other ends in sad recrimination; yet not without hope. The truth remains that each needs the other; Methodism 'a society in search of the church'; and Anglicanism with its need of warmth, discipline, and lay commitment. This book can remind us of how much we have lost by our separation, and by God's grace may still regain.

John Ebor:

Bishopthorpe, York
29 January 1985

Preface

The seed thoughts of this study were sown by that great encourager of students, the late Norman Sykes, when I was reading history at St Catharine's College, Cambridge. As a theological student at Didsbury (now Wesley) College, Bristol, I wrote a dissertation on *Methodism and Anglicanism 1791–1850* for which I received the degree of MA from the University of Bristol in 1957. For clear and critical advice, I owe much to my supervisor at that time, the Revd Rupert E. Davies. Some material from this thesis is used in the earlier chapters of the book.

The teaching of church history to students of diverse confessions (including Roman Catholics at St Mary's College, Oscott) has shown the need to investigate the historical background of ecumenism and the causes of tensions which still exist. Such has been the pace of research since the 1950s that I have been able to do little more than offer a synthesis of the recent work of others. The second half of this book is the outcrop of work done for the second and third volumes of the *History of The Methodist Church in Great Britain* and ends with a chapter which is in the proper sense existential. I lived through the Anglican-Methodist negotiations as a circuit minister and interpret it from the grassroots rather than conference chamber. The Queen's College set up in its present form in 1970 is still the only fully ecumenical theological seminary in Great Britain, a laboratory of experiment in which I was privileged to participate for eleven years.

I do not claim total impartiality but hope to claim fairness and accuracy in what I have written, even if at times I have shamelessly plundered other people's ideas. The substance of this book was delivered as the Fernley-Hartley Lecture at the Methodist Conference in Plymouth in 1982. I am grateful for the honour of being thereby admitted to that long line of Methodists who have been stimulated to lecture and write for the Fernley-Hartley Trust.

I am greatly honoured by the kindness of the Archbishop of York, Dr John Habgood, in writing a Foreword. I am grateful also to Mrs S. Chambers and my wife for typing from my unique calligraphy and to my colleague, the Revd Michael J. Townsend for help with the proofs, also to the Revd Dr Alan Wilkinson for commenting on Chapter 8.

Halifax, 1984

Introduction

The historian of church relations in an ecumenical age finds himself in an exposed position. Theologians bid him bear in mind their goal of an organically united church. They exult, with William Temple, in the 'worldwide Christian fellowship as the great new fact of our era'.[1] Fellow historians[2] bid him remember, however, that schism may be a sign of life and warn him of the 'ecumenical end-product . . . a single denomination with impeccable Catholic order and no popular appeal at all'. At the same time some sociologists have suggested that 'ecumenicalism is always partly a response to adversity and numerical decline'[3] and it certainly is a paradox that it is sometimes the smaller rather than the larger church groups which vote positively for union schemes. There is a tendency for the ecumenically minded historian to smooth over past conflicts, finding syntheses which are the products of his wishes rather than his research. In contrast, any estimate of John Wesley's achievement might well begin with the late Dean Sykes' astringent comment. 'For although he touched religious life at many points both in this country and in the New World, and although it was his proud claim that the world was his parish, yet the principal result of his missionary labours was the foundation of a new society and the addition thereby of another to the divided members of Christ's Catholic Church. . . Thus the greatest religious figure of his age contributed more perhaps to the accentuating than to the healing of the divisions of the universal Church.'[4]

I shall begin by setting the Methodist Revival in its eighteenth-century setting, tracing the causes of its separation from the Church of England, comparing it sociologically with the contemporary Roman Catholic community. Then I will show its development from connexion or 'society' to a 'denomination', using that term in its modern sociological usage.[5] Increasingly during the period of the industrial revolution, the Church of England had to accept a role as one denomination in an increasingly pluralistic religious culture. The repeal of the Test and Corporation Acts in 1828, followed by Catholic Emancipation in 1829, marked the end of the 'one Church – one Commonwealth' dream; toleration was giving way to equality before the law. 'A free market in some opinions became a free market in all opinions.'[6]

The combination of militant dissent and latent secularization was bound to be painful to the established church. That church, too, was transformed in its theology and worship by the Oxford Movement and in its polity by the reforms initiated by Sir Robert Peel and Bishop Blomfield. I will seek to test the claim so frequently made[7] that it was the Oxford Movement, almost exclusively, which pushed Wesleyanism into the Free Church camp. It will be argued that it was a threatened but resurgent Anglicanism which clashed politically and socially with a Methodism past its peak of membership in relation to the population by 1840. Sociological pressures as much as the Oxford Movement exacerbated the old 'church' and 'chapel' cleavage, producing at times open and bitter conflict or sour isolationism.

If the Victorian age was a period of religious competitiveness, the twentieth century in England has been marked by new styles of co-operation, which have roots in the nineteenth century as well as in the secular atmosphere of the twentieth. I will briefly explore the role which Methodism has played in ecumenism from the later nineteenth century to the aftermath of the Anglican-Methodist conversations, when in 1972 a failure to secure a seventy-five per cent majority in the General Synod of the Church of England dashed the hopes of many in both churches that the division, so much regretted now, but clearly made inevitable in good faith by John Wesley, might be resolved. This failure was followed ten years later by the breakdown of the negotiations towards a Covenant of four churches due to a sufficiently large clerical veto in the General Synod.

Our story will reveal the variety of the English dissenting scene in which Methodism (even if some Methodists eschewed the name dissenter!) takes its place alongside the older Dissent, Roman Catholics and Quakers. Voltaire's ironic comment is apt enough. 'If there were in England only one religion, despotism would be feared; if there were two they would cut each other's throats but there are thirty and they live at peace happily.'[8] The role of Her Majesty's loyal religious opposition needs exploring in comparison with Germany or France, where the lack of a viable insurgent style of Christianity has had incalculable political consequences, not least a polarity between clerical and anti-clerical elements. Church history must not be abstracted from the society in which it takes place. 'Docetism' is the besetting sin of theologians! The rise of population, industrialization, secularization are the backcloth against which we can detect the aspirations of Anglican and dissenter alike to glorify the God in whom they believed, and which ought not to be forgotten, if we concentrate here on the last great conflict between 'church' and 'chapel' and moves towards its reconciliation.

1

Eighteenth-Century Background

The early history of Methodism is almost unintelligible without some knowledge of the trends in English life in the eighteenth century, the world of the Age of Reason and the Age of Revival, which both diverge and curiously run together, so that Jonathan Edwards, in America, could preach sermons like 'sinners in the hand of an angry God' and propound the philosophy of John Locke with equal conviction. Wesley was in many ways a man of his age and more influenced by contemporary thinking than has usually been thought to be the case,[1] so that he can at the same time appeal to 'men of reason and religion', yet in his identification with the poor, he reveals himself as prone to what a Voltaire or Montesquieu would dismiss as superstition. A far more accurate picture of the eighteenth-century church can now be painted following the work of Norman Sykes[2] and others who have corrected the exaggerated picture of the indolence of the Hanoverian Church of England, which was far too convenient a background for the supporters of either Methodism or the Oxford Movement.

Paul Hazard wrote of the period 1685 to 1775 as being that of the 'crisis of the European conscience'.[3] His thesis is broadly followed by Herbert Butterfield who showed the key role which the scientific revolution of the seventeenth century plays in the shaping of modern civilization. 'For my part, I should like to cry from the housetops that the publication of Newton's *Principia* in 1687 is a turning point in history for peoples to whom the Renaissance and Reformation can hardly mean anything at all – people among whom the battle of Waterloo could hardly be calculated to produce an echo.'[4] The thinking of Newton and Locke was leading to a totally different way of looking at God, Nature and Man, even if these views were the prerogative of a very small élite. Sectarian conflict and intolerance had wearied many with orthodox Christianity. New ways to God were being sought.

The Cambridge Platonists,[5] while giving due place to experience as a factor in religion, saw reason or the spirit of man as 'the candle of the Lord' striving to avoid the fanaticisms of Laudian and Puritan alike. Their influence was greatest on the school of churchmen who came to be called latitudinarian. They wished, while remaining orthodox, to reconcile Christian revelation with the new world picture which natural science was making plain. Newton's universe seemed to some – if not to Newton himself, whose religious views smacked of a previous age – to have little to do with the divine decrees or the anti-Christ.[6] God could be seen clearly enough in Nature and in the reason in every man:

> Nature and Nature's laws lay hid in night.
> God said 'Let Newton be' and all was light.

'By the middle of the seventeenth century we stand on the threshold of the modern world. The issues which occupied men's minds and the spirit in which they were debated carry us from an atmosphere still predominantly mediaeval to one which is essentially modern . . . Questions emerged which still command our interest. We still discuss the place of reason, the nature of authority, the character of the universe and we do so in the spirit which first appeared in the latter part of the seventeenth century.'[7]

There were those who, in the light of the new cosmology moved from Christianity into deism, replacing God the Father by the supreme architect of a mechanical universe. Others remained orthodox but highly rationalistic in their approach to faith. John Locke in 1795 wrote *The Reasonableness of Christianity*, to be followed next year by the deistic Toland's *Christianity Not Mysterious*. 'Locke's deity . . . is that of the contemporary reconcilers of science and religion such as Glanvill or Boyle and that of the eighteenth century as a whole – a Deity to be approached by demonstration, and whose existence, proclaimed by the spacious firmament on high, is as well attested as any proof in Euclid . . . Newton's great machine needed a mechanic and religion was prepared ahead with that which could serve the purpose.'[8] Orderliness, law and regularity were the watchwords of the day. Whether the sceptic was convinced is another matter.[9]

The deist anticipated many of the questions later asked by critical biblical scholars. Joseph Butler's *Analogy of Religion* (1736) showed the necessity of revelation but perhaps rational argument was not the way to turn the deist's flank. Butler, too, lacked, as did his opponents, any idea of religious development or historical criticism. Perhaps it was inevitable that the religion of Puritanism should change into the rational religion of Locke and Toland. In Christian history there often exists a questioning, questing spirit alongside a more imaginative quest for experience. In the eighteenth century reason and enthusiasm. Butler and Wesley lived in uneasy tension.

The deist might ignore the Christian revelation, the latitudinarian churchmen could not, but were careful to show opponents that revelation was not opposed to the natural revelation in vogue but underwrote it. Grace sustained reason. What God, after the gift of reason, had left man without, he gave by way of revelation. Their theology stressed the fatherhood of God and man's duty of benevolence to his fellows. Good works were far more important to Burnet, Tillotson and Tenison than were the lesser points of orthodoxy. The congregations of the Church of England were induced diligently to pursue 'the Whole Duty of Man'[10] and were assured that 'His Commandments were not grievous'. Christianity was a matter of social control. It offered ample rewards to the prudent in this life and in the next. For the reprobate there was Newgate here and no doubt some condign punishment hereafter. Churchmanship in the eighteenth century was seen by many as a complement of citizenship. What Simon Patrick[11] had called the 'virtuous mediocrity ... between the meretricious gaudiness of the Church of Rome and the squalid sluttery of fanatic converticles' had been eulogized in the days of Charles II when Joseph Glanvill had said:

By the blessing of God we enjoy a Constitution Apostolical in its Doctrine; Primitive in its Government; decent in its ceremonies; grave and pious in its liturgy; we have the Scriptures, the Creeds, the Sacraments, the main Ordinances and Duties of the first and purest times; we are freed from the Idolatries, Superstitions and other corruptions of the Roman Church on this hand; and clear from the vanities and Enthusiasms that have overspread some Protestants on that; our church hath rejected the painted bravery of the one; and provided against the sordid slovenliness of the other.

Was this the *via media* with grass beginning to grow on it, for lack of feet to tread it with real conviction?

Religion may have appeared to be in retreat in what has been called the period of the 'great secularization'[12] but benevolence was by no means moribund – enough to make G. F. A. Best and G. V. Bennett[13] point to signs of religious renewal. Certainly this was a period of projects and societies. Religious societies of pious layfolk, with diminishing clerical direction, had flourished for some time, paralleling and influenced by similar groups in German Pietism. The Society for the Reformation of Manners tried to put down vice by a system of 'informing'. The SPCK pursued the same aim by education, linking with the widespread Charity School Movement[14] which combined a clearly expressed aim of social control with genuine humanitarianism. The kindred SPG sought to pursue its work overseas. Here was a rich field where

> One, driven by strong benevolence of soul
> Shall fly, like Oglethorpe, from pole to pole.[15]

While there was much that was worthy in the life of the period, there was also a fearful complacency in the face of evil which the 'rationalists with a nostalgia for religion' had no means of overcoming.[16]

The Revolution of 1688–9 might appear to have ended the constitutional conflicts of the seventeenth century, but the agonizing problem of the source of authority in church and state remained. The 'rage of party' during the time of Queen Anne soured relationships in church and state alike. 'The churchmen had sowed discord and now they reaped pastoral ineffectiveness.'[17]

The virtual end of the convocations as sounding boards of clerical and episcopal opinion followed the loss of much of the Church of England's Puritan wing in 1662 and the loss of the Non-Jurors in 1690. Anglican claims to comprehensiveness were severely challenged. There was no clerical assembly to debate the problem of Methodism when it arose, though the factiousness of some of the members of the convocations before 1717 make it a moot point whether it would have grappled adequately with such a problem.[18] In 1725 the threat of Jacobitism had largely receded, the Whigs were in control of the machinery of state and church. Robert Walpole encouraged a damping down of conflict 'in an age of ideological torpor, when any religion charge there was left in politics could be expertly defused by the greatest bomb disposal expert English public life has known'.[19] This worked to the disadvantage of Dissent. Enthusiasm of any kind was anathema to the educated élite. The world of Queen Anne architecture and Pope's couplets could salute another Augustan age across a sea of superstition and barbarism.

All, however, was not well within the Establishment. The church's organization was ill-suited to meet the needs of a new epoch. The abuses were the legacy of mediaeval anomalies, which had survived the Reformation, as well as Tudor and Stuart plunderings. Few of the bishops were like the much-abused cripple Benjamin Hoadly who never set foot in his diocese of Bangor,[20] nor were the majority of clergy idle worldlings, but the church was no longer able to cater for the mass of the baptized. Bishops were claimed by politics and London – they were, after all, voting officers of the state. Clergy, of whom there was a surplus, eked out meagre stipends and the old problems of pluralism and non-residence were still common. At the time of the creation of Queen Anne's Bounty, 5,597 benefices were worth under £50 per annum.[21] Of these 2,122 were worth under £30 and 1,200 paid under £20. As late as 1810, 3,398 livings were returned as less than £150 with 1,061 of these worth less than £50 and a further 1,726 less than £100. On average, at any one time, over 1,000 parishes were simply unattended. Certainly by 1740 habits of indifference stretching back several generations had become embedded in the structures of many local communities. The parson tended to be dependent on the squire, a dependence which was often economic, though it was also a social and cultural alliance. The clergyman and the gentry both pursued the 'gentleman ideal' with a growing similarity of outlook and life-style.[22]

The parish system was a legacy of mediaeval conditions and population. New parishes could not be created save by private Act of Parliament – a cumbrous procedure.[23] Vested interests would look askance at change. Services were plain. Holy Communion was celebrated on an average four times a year in rural areas, monthly in towns,[24] though it is too facile to judge this by Tractarian standards. In the new urban areas which were beginning to grow in this pre-industrial revolution period, the church hardly touched the mass of the population at all. For instance, the pattern of settlement of the Shropshire coalfield created great difficulties for the territorial parish. 'Mining and iron-making villages grew up with complete disregard for established ecclesiastical boundaries and remote from parish churches.'[25] In this area, too, non-residence, pluralism and clerical poverty exacerbated the problems of the church, as was the case elsewhere. Throughout the expanding industrial North and the Black Country the Church of England's parochial machinery was totally inadequate. The much larger northern parishes (there were only 70 parishes in Lancashire and 193 in the West Riding of Yorkshire compared with 731 in Norfolk and 510 in Suffolk) originating in Celtic monasticism, were to prove the seedbeds of Methodism.[26]

In pre-industrial England, religion provided the nearest approach to overt class attitudes with a kind of 'sandwich' – Anglicans on top and bottom and Protestant dissenters in the middle. In the old society, dissent flourished in precisely those groups which both wished to and could afford to be somewhat independent of the paternal hierarchy. It was the middling groups of society who could afford the luxury of dissent. When dependency in the parishes begins to break down, dissent could be a possibility much lower in the social scale. If the Establishment was failing to grapple with rising population, dissent tended to introversion which hampered those with a wider mission. Since 1689, and more particularly since 1714 when the Schism Act proved a dead letter, the former 'old denominations' had been able to worship without fear. 'The laity

had made good their superiority in the national church. Some laymen
more precariously, but as it proved permanently, had also established
their right to live outside its bounds; an age of religious plurality had
begun.' With freedom there could creep in not only complacency but
a tendency for dissenters to filter back into the Church of England,
though there was also a good deal of what Doddridge called a 'secret
strength' even in the weaker southern and western counties and
much more deep, personal piety than was once thought the case.[27]

The plurality certainly meant a blurring of boundaries. M. R.
Watts,[28] using the 'Evans MS' figures and other sources, has shown
that in England in 1718 there were about 338,120 Protestant
dissenting 'hearers' with 637 Presbyterian congregations, 203 Independent and 536 Baptist groups. This represents 6.21 per cent of the
population. Roman Catholics, in this period, are estimated to number
80,000 out of a population in England and Wales of 5,500,000.
Doctrinal controversies divided many dissenting congregations, with
a tendency among Presbyterians for minister and congregation
to espouse a theological liberalism which was not conducive to
evangelistic activity. Puritan elect had become intellectual élite;
what G. F. Nuttall[29] calls the 'Arminianism of the head' of rational
dissent was very significantly more intellectualist than previous
styles. Despite the proper emphasis to be placed on the works of
Watts, Doddridge and the dissenting academics, orthodox Dissent
was somewhat static.[30] Hay Colligan's often quoted opinion that
the 'most depressing twenty years in English Christianity in the
eighteenth century were those between 1730 and 1750'[31] has some
weight, but it ignores the underground fires already smouldering
and the beginnings of overt revival.

Yet between 1715 and 1772, scarcely a new Independent church
was founded. Not a few vanished. It was the churches which
preserved their orthodoxy intact that tended to be influenced by and
to influence the Evangelical Revival which can be seen as a renewal
of the old Puritan emphases in a new setting, though the revival of
religion was not at first to blossom in Dissent but in the Church of
England.

If the eighteenth century was the age of reason and laicization or
secularization, it was also the time of the flowering of a renewal of
the 'religion of the heart' which was an international phenomenon
embracing Pietism in Germany, the great awakening in America,
Anglican evangelicalism and the Methodism of John Wesley and his
followers. Wesley must be seen in a rich context of revival for 'simple
chronology disposes of the stereotype of the whole Revival as a chain-
reaction from the Aldersgate Street experience and of John Wesley
as a solitary Moses striking the rock of petrified Anglicanism to

release a sudden stream of revival.'[32] Pietism (like Quietism in French Roman Catholicism) was a reaction against purely intellectual ways of approaching God and has complex interactions with the political situation in Germany after the Peace of Westphalia of 1648. Despite the influence of the Halle Faculty of Theology, it lacked the critical tools effectively to undermine rationalism and finally capitulated to it in German university circles. Yet it brought into the churches an intensified study of the Bible, a greater emphasis than in orthodox Lutheranism on the priesthood of the laity, a stress on the devotional aspects of theology with a style of spirituality which assumed doctrinal orthodoxy, concentrating on the more experiential modes of religious expression, not least in preaching. If the great Reformers had affirmed the centrality of word and sacrament and discipline in the life of the church, it was the contribution of the Pietist, Moravian and Evangelical to stress the fundamental importance of the Christian cell, the small company of Christians meeting for prayer, Bible study and mutual edification.[33]

England had its own unobtrusive Anglican style of Pietism in the religious societies[34] which provided high-church, devout, respectable recruits for the later revival. Wesley was to incorporate much of the emphasis of the societies into his system – concern for pastoral care, the endeavour to do good and to foster more personal religion, concern for education, missions and Bible study. His societies avoided the clerical condescension of the earlier groups. In an interesting way, too, the *Unitas Fratrum*, or Moravians, seemed peculiarly suited to attract high-churchmen and to make more palatable doctrines which might otherwise have been dismissed brusquely as enthusiasm or worse.

Calvinist evangelicalism had other origins – isolated groups of Anglicans experiencing conversion and perhaps releasing hidden and suppressed streams of Puritanism. This renewal was well under way before Wesley's 'heart-warming' experience of May 1738. The type of revival associated with these groups, unlike the more close-knit groups cohering around Wesley, was often spontaneous and individualistic, pursued by men who, unknown to each other, launched out on their own.[36] George Whitefield emerged as the charismatic leader, though without Wesley's autocratic powers of organization. Cross-fertilization followed in the next generation.

These movements were like tributaries flowing into a common stream, each stressing those doctrines of the Holy Spirit and the cross which the Age of Reason had pushed to the periphery of spirituality.[37] The interaction between them – often hostile – is part of a reaction to the 'citizen-churchmen' synthesis which was now breaking down, as well as to rationalism. There was a coincidence of dissenting evangelicalism with the breakdown of the older styles of dependency system and modes of social control which Harold Perkin[38] saw as crucial to any understanding of the role of Methodism in this period. Social change and revival alike were combining to produce the conditions in which England's second largest dissenting group was to grow.

So in the early eighteenth century there was a somewhat declining Dissent, an established church not able any longer to claim a monopoly of religious activity but with signs of renewal in the societies and an evangelical clergy which was to prevent the period from being entirely a religious disaster. Dissent began to gather steam again after 1770 with a growth of itinerancy and a period of evangelistic expansion and consolidation which might be called popular ecumenism. Certainly the rise of popular evangelicalism was to give English Dissent a broader base in the artisan groups, a clientèle not unlike that of Methodism, to which we must now turn. We shall analyse the interaction between Wesley, the Church of England and nascent evangelicalism. Wesley was to work out a theology and a practical method, not in donnish isolation but in the ceaseless activity of a people's theologian.

2

The Separation of Methodism from the Church of England – The Role of John Wesley

'I look upon all the world as my parish,' wrote John Wesley in 1739, probably to John Clayton, one of the Oxford Methodists who had criticized him for preaching in other men's parishes.[1] The sentiment was later echoed by George Whitefield.[2] Wesley's reply to his critic contains a clear statement of fundamental principles which were to underlie much of his future conduct:

> If by Catholic principles you mean any other than scriptural, they weigh nothing with me. I allow no rule, whether of faith or practice, than the Holy Scripture, but on scriptural principles I do not think it hard to justify whatever I do. God in scriptures commands me according to my power, to instruct the ignorant, reform the wicked, confirm the virtuous. Man forbids me to do this in another's parish; that in an effect to do it at all: seeing I have no parish of my own nor probably ever shall.

Wesley's view of church order is typified here. Methodism was for him to be defined in terms of mission, witness and nurture.

Not long afterwards, his principles were tested in the famous second interview with Jospeh Butler, of which Wesley's manuscript journal has survived.[3] Butler, referring to Whitefield said, 'Sir, the pretending to extraordinary revelations and gifts of the Holy Ghost is a horrid thing, a very horrid thing.' More bluntly he continued, 'You have no business here. You are not commissioned to preach in this diocese. Therefore I advise you to go hence.' Wesley's reply contained the same basic argument which he had used in the letter to Clayton. 'As to my preaching here, a dispensation of the gospel is committed to me, and woe is me if I preach not the gospel, wheresoever I am in the habitable world. Your lordship knows, being ordained a priest, by the commission then received I am a priest of the Church Universal. And being ordained a Fellow of a College, I was not limited to any particular cure, but have an indeterminate commission to preach the Word of God to any part of the Church of England.' Wesley's secondary argument about the 'indeterminate commission' by virtue of his ordination on the title of his college fellowship may be based on an erroneous deduction from the 'freedom from particular cure' granted by such a fellowship. It is a puzzling fact that Wesley did not apply for a formal licence from the University of Oxford to preach throughout the Church of England, which would have made unnecessary the obtaining of a licence from Butler or any other diocesan.[4]

Be that as it may, Wesley's principle of obedience to the gospel determined his conduct after 24 May 1738 and determined in great measure the steps which caused from the Methodist side the breach with the Church of England. In the interview with Butler it is possible to see a clash not only of eighteenth century and what could be called 'Pauline Christianity', but a theology of stability and order and a theology motivated by mission.

> The everlasting problem of message and structure, faith and organization, was solved astonishingly early and with a remarkable awareness of its goal, so that its emphasis upon a strong union and mutual responsibility, its combination of authority and obedience in a necessarily limited fellowship differed not only in degree but also in kind from both the Anglican tradition and the Church Orders of the Lutheran Reformation and stood nearer those early Christian congregations which were under Pauline influence.[5]

Martin Schmidt's summary is accurate as far as it goes, but the tragedy of this meeting of great men was that, as Dean Church put it, Butler anticipated 'before Wesley all that was deepest and truest in the Methodist appeal to the heart . . . When he comes to speak on this side of religion, in his sermons on the love of God, he is not afraid of soaring as high as the loftiest flight of contemplative devotion.' Methodist preachers, despite the three interviews, were bidden to read Butler for a century or more after them!

The mission of Wesley led to the creation of a 'connexion' – a new phenomenon in ecclesiastical typology, neither sect nor denomination. The policy of unlimited mission was, in the end, to involve holding clerically unauthorized services, the creation of new fellowships and societies outside the parish system, the erection ultimately of separate buildings for worship and the meeting of the Methodist societies, the appointment of officers in the Methodist societies like local preachers, stewards, class leaders with the itinerant preachers rapidly forming a highly mobile order, the registration of Methodist preaching places as dissenting places of worship, setting up the legal court of Conference and legal devices to secure continuity like the Model Deed of 1763 and the Deed of Declaration of 1784, the provision of a church constitution for the Methodists of the USA, the ordination of ministers for American Methodism, the provision of a revised Prayer Book for America and Great Britain, the ordination of ministers to serve in Scotland and England.[6]

The development of this complex system begins in the relationship of the Methodist societies with the religious societies which had flourished in England since the time of the later Stuarts. One facet of that complicated matter concerns us here, the relation between the Methodist societies and the parish. John Wesley's societies, unlike those of Horneck, Woodward and Samuel Wesley, were never under episcopal supervision. Neither the authorities nor Wesley ever sought it. Overton and Relton are therefore correct in stating, 'It is impossible not to come to the conclusion that from the very first the Wesleyan Movement, so far as it concerned organization, never was and never could have been a Church movement.'[7] While we must not exaggerate the role of the clergy in organizing societies, it is clearly the case that the 'biggest single cause of the schism was the pattern of the Wesleyan Societies. In the eighteenth century the societary nature of Wesleyanism made the split inevitable.'[8]

Samuel Walker, of Truro, who ran his own evangelical parish society, urged Wesley several times to abandon the extra-parochial itinerancy and societies outside the pastoral care of the parish minister, considering them both a serious breach of church order – the beginning of a continuous disagreement between Methodists and most Anglican evangelicals. Wesley's reply states his position clearly:

> At present I apprehend those, and those only to separate from the church who either renounce her fundamental doctrines or refuse to join in her public worship. As yet we have done neither; nor have we taken one step farther than we were convinced was our bounden duty. It is from a full conviction of this that we preached 'abroad', prayed *extempore*, formed societies and permitted preachers who were not episcopally ordained. And were we pushed on this side, were there no alternative allowed, we should judge it our bounden duty rather wholly to separate from the church than to give up any of these points. Therefore if we cannot stop a separation without stopping lay preachers, the case is perfectly clear – we cannot stop at all.[9]

Wesley was perfectly aware of his departure from recognized churchmanship and found himself soon in great difficulty, as did Charles Simeon at Holy Trinity Cambridge, before the Act of 1812 granted freedom from the Clarendon Code, when he omitted prayers from his Friday night meetings, so as not to contravene the provisions of the Conventicle Act.[10]

Much confusion concerning John Wesley's position in the Church of England and the relationship of Methodism with the Establishment after 1791 can be avoided if it is realized that Wesley had a clear idea of what separation meant for him and for the Methodists. His view was consistent and yet not entirely compatible with his churchmanship. Tyerman's epithet that he 'lived and died a hearty but inconsistent churchman'[11] is a not inappropriate comment. The letter to Samuel Walker,[12] already quoted, gives the clue. In 1766 the same point was made at Conference in the form of the typical dialogue:[13]

> Q. Are we dissenters? A. We are irregular. 1. By calling sinners to repentance in all places of God's dominion. 2. By frequently using extempore prayer. Yet we are not Dissenters in the only sense which our laws acknowledge: namely persons who believe that it is sinful to attend the service of the church, for we do attend it at all opportunities. We will not, dare not, separate from the church for the reasons given several years ago. We are not seceders, nor do we bear any resemblance to them.

At the Conference of 1755 and several times subsequently, notably in the *Reasons against separation from the Church of England* (1758),[14] Wesley maintained that it was not 'expedient' to separate from the Establishment. To Adam he wrote in October 1755: 'We will not go out; if we are thrust out, well . . .'[15] Adam and Walker accused Wesley of causing a separation by the use of lay preachers and the holding of irregular services.[16] Their notion of separation clearly included not only refusing to join in public worship and 'renouncing fundamental doctrines' but 'any action contrary to the order and discipline of the church'. Lay preachers, said Walker to Charles Wesley,[17] are contrary to the constitution of the Church of England and their use tantamount to separation. Discipline and order remained a stumbling block to many evangelicals. The 'eloquent convert' was for long an acute evangelical problem. Wesley clearly would not stop lay preaching for that would mean the end of the spreading of the gospel. 'Soul-damning clergymen lay me under more difficulty than soul-saving laymen!'[18] Itinerancy likewise was good for people, thought Wesley. 'I know that were I to preach one whole year in one place, I would preach both myself and most of my congregations to sleep.'[19] On Wesley's theory there was no separation; on Walker's there was. We can only conclude that Wesley was endeavouring to have the best of the church-world and the

Methodist-world, his actions being justified only on his own principle of the primacy of the gospel – and of the nature of separation.

Wesley maintained the same position throughout his ministry. Many times he reiterated his loyalty to the Church of England and warned against separation.[20] Thus in March 1787 he could say to Samuel Bardsley: 'I still think when the Methodists leave the Church of England, God will leave them. Every year more and more of the clergy are convinced of the truth and grow well-attested towards us. It would be contrary to all common sense, as well as to good conscience to make a separation *now.*' To Henry Moore he said: 'I am a Church of England man and as I said fifty years ago, so I say still, in the Church I will live and die, unless I am thrust out' (6 May 1788).[21] Wesley's manifesto of December 1789 is on the same theme.[22] He outlines his love for the Church of England, 'the most scriptural national church in the world' and his love for the Book of Common Prayer. He concludes: 'I never had any design of separating from the Church . . . Nevertheless, in spite of all that I can do, many of them will separate from it, although I am apt to think, not one half, perhaps not one third of them. They will be so injudicious as to form a separate party. In flat opposition to them, I declare once more that I live and die a member of the Church of England and that none who regard my judgment or advice will ever separate from it.'

There can be no doubt of Wesley's loyalty to the church as he thought it existed – this is made clear in all his polemics against both his learned and his scurrilous opponents. His doctrine of the meaning of the Church of England is perhaps best summed up in a letter to his brother Charles of August 1785.[23] 'What is the Church of England? It is not all the people of England. Papists and Dissenters are no part thereof. It is not all the people of England except Papists and Dissenters. Then we should have a glorious Church indeed! No, according to our Twentieth article a particular church is a congregation of faithful people . . . among whom the word of God is preached and the sacraments duly administered.' Here is a logical definition containing both the essence and the properties of a church which are faith, evangelism and nurture. Wesley was sure of his loyalty to the 'catholic church, the whole body of men endued with faith, working by love, dispersed over the whole earth'. He was sure the Methodists were not schismatics, for schism was for him *within* the church not *from* the church. This is an Anglican stance which became overladen by the 'branch theory' in the Tractarian era – but which emerged again, firstly from Anglo-Catholic writers like T. A. Lacey at about the time of the First World War and later in more liberal theologians like A. C. Headlam, O. C. Quick and S. L.

Greenslade. It is clearly the theology behind the Church of South India and the Churches' Unity Commission in the 1970s.

There is also the long tradition of what Calamy once called 'charity to the church', occasional conformity for other than political purposes. This was an unwillingness to separate totally from the Establishment, however deserving it might be of criticism. The tradition was taken over by many Methodists in Wesley's time and was common in the early part of the nineteenth century. Thus in John Ross's Exeter Returns of 1779 the Vicar of Launceston mentioned 'a conventicle belonging to the sect called Methodist, but as they, at times, frequent the parish church, I suppose they can't properly be called dissenters'. As late as 1821 the Vicar of Bridgerule said of the Methodists in his parish, 'They all attend church as the House of God and more regularly than those who have no such meetings.' In the same diocese of Exeter, though, there were signs of a feeling that the semi-separatist Methodists represented a social threat. In 1806 an address to the Primate said: 'Their locomotive ministry is unquestionably dangerous to the state, in so much as it deprives the state of that great source of protection against the mischief that arises from a knowledge of the individual who is commissioned to teach . . . I see in this county a regular *propaganda societas* under the Methodist protection.'[24] Loyalty to the church was often rebutted, also clearly pockets of genuine dissent swept by Wesley into his connexion tended to be more Donatist in their attitudes. It is important not to forget the popular styles of Methodism, which were never as Wesleyan as some interpretations of Methodism have assumed.

For all his loyalty Wesley came to realize that the ultimate result of his actions would be a separate Methodist Church and planned accordingly. 'A kind of separation,' he stated, in *Thoughts on Separation* (1758), 'has already taken place and will inevitably spread, though by slow degrees.' For good or ill, Wesley stamped his character and beliefs on Methodism in a way comparable with Ignatius Loyola and the Jesuits or William Booth and the Salvation Army, though a rider might be to advise a distinction being made between the 'order' of itinerant preachers and the much more heterogeneous laity. Too often Wesley has been torn out of his eighteenth-century context and set alongside Newman or Pusey rather than Hoadly, Butler, Secker, Warburton, Watson and Paley, whose ecclesiology was much closer to that of Wesley than it was to the Tractarians. Wesley's pragmatism was typical of his age. 'What is the end of an ecclesiastical order? Is it not to bring souls from the power of Satan to God and to build them up in His fear and love? Order, then, is so far valuable as it answers these ends and if it answers them not, it is nothing worth' (Letter to 'John Smith', 25 June 1746).[25]

In practice Wesley's concept of mission soon ran into legal difficulties. As early as October 1738 the Wesleys approached Edmund Gibson, Bishop of London, asking his opinion on the relationship of the Conventicle Act to the religious societies.[26] When the Bishop was asked, 'Are the religious societies conventicles?', he replied that he thought not, but referred the Wesleys to the 'acts and laws' saying 'he would determine nothing'. Gibson, no doubt, meant Canon 73 and the Conventicle Act of 1670. This statute was to be a thorn in Wesley's flesh for the rest of his life. Were the proceedings of the Methodist societies exercises of religion in accordance with the liturgy and practice of the Church of England? If not, the Act with its penalties applied to them and they could claim exemption only by claiming the protection of the Act of Toleration of 1689 which was tantamount to declaring themselves dissenters.

Wesley himself sought subtle means of evading this dilemma, but his followers had soon to take action to protect their lives and property from mob violence. Only by registering buildings and preachers under the Toleration Act could exemption be claimed from the Conventicle Act and the protection of the Riot Act of 1715 be invoked. As far as we know the first occasion on which a request for the registration of a Methodist meeting house occurred was in 1748 when the 'Room' at Bristol was registered as a Protestant meeting house.[27] Others followed in the 1750s. In 1759 there was a registration at the Archdeacon's Court at Lincoln of a Methodist preaching place as a meeting house for dissenters.[28] It is worthy of note that the itinerant preacher, George Tizard, described himself as the minister of a congregation claiming the full privileges of a dissenting minister. The first known example of a preacher's licence taken out by one of Wesley's preachers is dated 11 January 1758.[29]

Actions of this kind alarmed Charles Wesley who next year wrote to John Nelson, 'John, I love thee from my heart; yet rather than see thee a Dissenting minister, I wish to see thee smiling in thy coffin,'[30] and to William Grimshaw, the eccentric vicar of Haworth, 'Our preaching houses are mostly licensed and so are proper meeting-houses. Our preachers are mostly licensed and so are Dissenting ministers. They took out their licences as Protestant Dissenters.' Grimshaw threatened to withdraw his support from Methodism, since for him registration was separation. 'This licensing the preachers and preaching houses is a matter that I never expected to have seen or heard of among the Methodists . . . I am in connection and desire to continue so, but how can I do it consistently with my relationship to the Church of England? . . .' Grimshaw did not however sever his connexions. Charles Wesley had exaggerated the number of preachers licensed, but clearly the year 1760 was a crisis year in this matter – separation was narrowly averted.[31]

In 1763 Wesley laid down rules for the preachers in this matter.[32] 'Let all our Preachers go to Church, let all our people go constantly, receive the sacrament at every opportunity, warn all against niceness in learning, a great and prevailing evil, warn them likewise against despising the prayers of the Church, against calling our Society a Church or the Church, against calling our Preachers ministers, our houses meeting houses.[33] Call them plain preaching houses. Do not license them as such.' Preachers were to seek to be licensed 'not as a Dissenter but as a Methodist Preacher'. Wesley never seems to have realized the irregularity of the title 'Methodist Preacher' or that registration involved dissent, as Grimshaw with more logic saw clearly. Perhaps there were many more Methodists who were already thinking like Vincent Perronet in terms of a separate organization. Perronet, writing to Charles Wesley, on 6 July 1763, used the phrase 'It is undoubtedly a trying time for the poor Methodist Church.'[34]

The problem of the registration of Methodist buildings was brought to the judgment of the Court of King's Bench in 1766. The Justices of Derby had refused to register a Methodist preaching house, one of the reasons being that Methodists do not dissent from the Church of England but pretend only to observe her doctrines and disciplines with greater purity than their neighbours. King's Bench compelled the magistrates to register the Methodists as part of their duty but the judgment contained the warning that if the persons resorting to a registered meeting house did not bring themselves under the Toleration Act by taking the necessary oaths, such registering would not protect them from the penalties of the law.[35]

Wesley persisted in what seems an equivocal attitude towards registration, but the almost tragic nature of the dilemma is seen in a letter to Thomas Adam of Wintringham of 19 July 1768.[36] Adam had implied that the Methodists 'acted under a lie', professing themselves members of the Church while registering themselves as dissenters. Wesley pointed out that the greater part of the preachers were not licensed and those that are not as dissenters.

> I instance particularly . . . Thomas Adams and Thomas Drisco. When Thomas Adams desired a licence, one of the Justices said, 'Mr Adams, are you not of the Church of England? Why then do you desire a licence?' He answered, 'Sir, I am of the Church of England; yet I desire a licence that I may legally defend myself from the illegal violence of oppressive men.' When others applied

for a licence, the clerk or justice said, 'I will not license you but as Protestant Dissenters.' They replied, 'We are of the Church. We are not Dissenters, but if you call us so, we cannot help it.'

There were ninety chapels in England in 1769.[37] The number registered grew steadily. The whole process was given a jolt forward by the complete separation of the Countess of Huntingdon's Connexion from the Church of England, an event which affected Wesleyanism more than is realized.[38] In 1781 the Countess was compelled to register her chapel in Spa Fields despite her fancied favourable position as a Peeress of the Realm.[39] Her clerical helpers became either registered dissenting ministers or remained within the Establishment, resigning all links with the Countess, whose connexion ordained its own ministers. Wesley long pondered this action.[40] The idea of becoming a dissenter was abhorrent to him. Yet on 3 May 1787 he makes clear, after consulting Clulow his legal advisor, that it was safer to register all chapels and travelling preachers not as dissenters but simply 'preachers of the gospel'. Wesley continued this fiction to the end, though clearly these men were registered as dissenters, whatever evasion might be used for the satisfaction of his conscience.[41]

Wesley's desire to remain an Anglican and yet make use of the Toleration Act involved his followers in frequent squabbles with magistrates, many of whom were clergymen. Often the magistrates maintained that if the petitioners were Anglicans, then they would decline to be licensed, but if licensed should abandon the church.[42] The Anglican mind has always disliked 'charity towards the church'! It is all or nothing. Petty informing was common. The Conventicle Act was often enforced. Towards the end of his life, Wesley wrote two letters on the issue – one to a member of parliament, 'a real friend to religious liberty' – clearly William Wilberforce – the other to Sir George Pretyman (later known as Tomline), Bishop of Lincoln.[43] These letters illustrate the dilemma acutely. 'Now Sir, what can the Methodists do? They are liable to be ruined by the Conventicle Act, and yet they have no relief from the Act of Toleration. If this is not oppression, what is? . . . If you will speak a word to Pitt upon this matter you will much oblige.' He begs the Bishop to remember that Methodists in general are members of the Church of England. 'They hold all her doctrines, attend her services and partake of her sacraments. Do you ask, "Who drives them out of the Church?" . . . Your Lordship does . . . they desire a licence to worship God after their own conscience. Your Lordship refuses it and then punishes them for not having a licence! So your Lordship leaves them only this alternative – leave the Church or starve . . . O my Lord, for God's sake, for Christ's sake, for pity's sake, suffer the poor people to enjoy their religious as well as civil liberty.'

This was merely one of the problems of seeking legitimization of Methodism as a group of societies or connexion still retaining links with the Establishment. The development of an itinerant system into a close-knit connexion largely controlled by Wesley provided a major factor in the loosening of ties between the Church of England and Wesley. It was probably this, more than anything else, which prevented a closer liaison between the Wesleys and their contemporary evangelicals within the Church of England. Frank Baker[44] rightly sees the year 1749 as epochal in the coming of age of Methodism as a national entity, for by then a connexion was in existence which corresponded neither with Independency nor diocesan episcopacy nor Presbyterianism and which was beginning to offer a complete substitute for the parish church and its ministry, with its fasts and feasts corresponding to those to be found in English Catholicism.[45] Nothing illustrates this better than the long correspondence between Wesley and Walker of Truro which revolved around the itinerancy and the expediency of separation.[46] The creation of Conference in 1744 – the 'crown and sum of the Methodist system' – can be taken as an act of partial separation and in February 1784 that separation was taken a stage further with the Deed of Declaration which gave legal definition to Conference, setting up the Legal Hundred which ratified the decisions of Conference, establishing a pattern of continuity including a limitation of ministration in the chapels to those appointed by Conference on the principle of a three-year itinerancy, though this did not apply to ordained ministers of the Church of England.[47]

In 1784 there were more than three hundred meeting houses, many of them held under Wesley's Model Deed of 1763.[48] This deed required the trustees of chapels settled therein 'to permit such persons as shall be appointed at the Year Conference . . . and no other, to have and enjoy the premises, provided that they preach no other doctrines than is contained in Wesley's Notes upon the New Testament and his four volumes of sermons'. This provision marks off the Methodist preacher as one abiding by certain standards which were now granted the full recognition of the law. The equipment of the people's theologian was typically a book of exegesis and a collection of sermons!

Dr Whitehead, a contemporary of Wesley, called 1784 the 'grand climacterical year of Methodism'. More recently Professor Baker has stated that 'if ever there was a year when Wesley could be said to have irrevocably severed himself and Methodism from the Church of England, it was 1784'.[49] We must now test this statement. The 'climax' was largely the result of the situation in America. In 1782 the Methodist Societies in America had a membership of 11,785, mainly south of the 'Mason-Dixon' line where Anglican influence had been strongest.[50] During the War of Independence Methodism had been in jeopardy because of John Wesley's Toryism and opposition to the rebels. They had sought to be loyal to the Church of England. Priests were few and far between. 'Virginia,' said Samuel Wilberforce, 'had entered on the war with one hundred and sixty-four churches and chapels and ninety-one clergyman spread through the sixty-one countries.'[51] At the end of the war ninety-five parishes were 'extinct or forsaken', thirty-four were without ministerial service with only twenty-eight priests remaining. 'The flocks were scattered and divided, the pastors few, poor and suspected, their enemies dominant and fierce.'

Debate over the nature of episcopacy had been long and intense, for the inability of the church to prevail upon the state in the matter of American church government was of long standing.[52] This was surely a vital strand in the tangled skein of Wesley's actions. The possibility of going to Russia to procure a bishop was not overlooked.[53] By 1783 prejudice focussed upon Anglicanism brought about disestablishment in the six states in which the Church of England had been established by law. The total number of clergy was 155 in 1785 compared with 286 in 1774. American church life had produced a remarkable world where Episcopalian dissenters had resisted Congregationalist church tax and where Episcopalians were scandalized by the thought of bishops! It was in 1782 that William White, Rector of Christ Church and St Peter's Church Philadelphia, prepared a pamphlet called *The Case of the Episcopal Churches in the United States Considered*.[55] White wrote from a clearly distinguishable latitudinarian position, with strong overtones of Locke's political philosophy as well as echoes of Benjamin Hoadly. All denominations of Christians are on one level. They are voluntary associations of individuals for lawful and useful purposes. Parishes and dioceses are merely extensions of voluntary contract. White wanted a style of episcopacy in which any clergyman elevated to the office of bishop might continue to serve as a parish priest. In the emergency of the times, ordination by presbyters might be necessary. 'It will not be difficult to prove that a temporary departure from episcopacy would be warranted by her (Church of England) doctrines, by her practice and by the principle on which episcopal government is asserted.'[56] Necessity demanded it – Cranmer, Hooker, Whitgift, Ussher and Hoadly as well as the Marian exiles are cited in support. *The Case* was circulated in England as well as in America, and it would be odd if John Wesley's keen antennae had not picked up some echoes of it, though I can find no evidence that he read *The Case* and, indeed, later he failed to meet White when he had the opportunity.[57] White's scheme was not followed, and it was not until 17 November 1784 that a bishop was finally consecrated for the United States. The chosen candidate, Samuel Seabury, was consecrated by bishops of the Scottish non-juring episcopal church. English pulpits were closed to him. The first General Convention of the Protestant Episcopal Church opened on 27 September 1785 – and as an ironic footnote, White himself was consecrated Bishop of Pennsylvania at Lambeth on 4 February 1787.[58]

That was one side of the story. The other concerns the Methodists. During the war the Methodist folk were largely starved of the sacraments and came near, in 1779, to setting up their own presbytery to ordain men to preside at Holy Communion.[59] Wesley had approached Dr Lowth, Bishop of London, who had maintained jurisdiction in America, acting through resident ecclesiastical commissioners, to enquire whether he would ordain suitable men for America, but received the same rebuff as the American Anglicans had done. It must be remembered that Lowth was not a free agent in these matters but a servant of the state.[60] Wesley, like White, and from strikingly parallel principles, began to contemplate emergency action. In his Oxford days and for some time after his 'evangelical conversion', John Wesley held a version of what may be called the 'Catholic Anglican' doctrine of ministry and apostolic succession, though in the Minutes of the Conference of 1745 there is a view of church development which was significantly different.[61] Just as in his view of baptism, Wesley oscillates between a Catholic and Pietist viewpoint, so he appears to be ambivalent on matters of ministry. Robert Erskine was clearly an influence in modifying Wesley's complex views. In January 1746 Wesley read *An Inquiry into the Constitution, Discipline, Unity and Worship of the Primitive Church* (1691) by Peter King, who eventually became Lord Chancellor, and also later Edward Stillingfleet's celebrated *Irenicum* written just before the Restoration.

These two writings, both by men in their twenties, profoundly influenced Wesley's doctrine of the ministry.[62] He became convinced that the early church had nothing corresponding to monarchical episcopacy. Each congregation was independent. The episcopal form of government was not prescribed in the New Testament. 'I still believe the Episcopal form of government to be both scriptural and apostolical; I mean well agreeing with the practice and writing of the apostles. But that it is prescribed in scripture, I do not believe.'[63] Further – and vital to his future conduct – Wesley accepted King's observation that in the New Testament bishops and presbyters were fundamentally of the same order and that consequently presbyters could ordain. King, however, clearly saw them as different in *grade* or degree. Any ordination for him needed the bishop's permission. Wesley drew his own conclusions. 'Read Bishop Stillingfleet's *Irenicon* (sic) or any impartial history of the Ancient Church and I believe you will think as I do. I verily believe I have as good a right to ordain as to administer the Lord's Supper. But I do see abundance of reasons why I should not use that right, unless I am turned out of the Church.' Long before 1784 Wesley had reached the conclusion, succinctly summarized in the letter to his brother Charles of 17 August 1785, 'I firmly believe I am a scriptural *episcopos* as much as any man in England or in Europe, for the uninterrupted succession I know to be a fable which no man ever did or can prove.'[64]

Wesley's doctrine of the ministry has for long been obscured by polemical attempts to prove him to be either a forerunner of the Tractarians or a thorough going evangelical dissenter who had thrown off 'the grave clothes of ritualistic superstition', as J. H. Rigg, the Victorian Wesleyan maintained. Henry Bett's *Spirit of Methodism* (1937) continued the attempt to show that Wesley's whole attitude to the church, its authority, ministry and ordinances was purely pragmatic. Frank Baker can speak of 'his view of the church as a sacramental institution with an evangelical mission being slowly transformed into that of a missionary society performing sacramental functions, with the Church of England fulfilling the one task and the Methodist Societies the other', and can characterize Wesley as a 'doctrinally liberal iconoclast who had little use for many traditional beliefs and a somewhat low view of church, ministry and sacraments.'[65] Wesley's doctrine and practice must be seen in an eighteenth-century context. There are certain underlying principles which appear to have been constant in thinking and action from 1738 until his death.

The first is that the gospel and its needs determine church order. The second is that there is a clear distinction to be made between the preaching office and the administration of the sacraments. Thus the local and itinerant preachers were forbidden to preside at the sacraments. Repeated attempts were made by the preachers to secure Wesley's consent to their giving the sacraments to the Methodist people.[66] Wesley was charged with inconsistency. 'I do tolerate unordained persons in preaching the gospel, whereas I do not tolerate them in administering the sacraments . . . My principle (frequently declared) is this: I submit to every ordinance of man wherever I do not conceive there is an absolute necessity for acting contrary to it. Lay preaching is necessary else thousands of souls would perish. Lay administration, since it is not a matter of salvation, is not necessary.'[67]

Wesley's principle of 'no administration without ordination' was still maintained in the sermon on the ministerial office (the *Korah* sermon). J. H. Rigg rashly maintained that 'it was natural that some of his early predilections should have come back to him with passionate force . . . Now his calm judgment was enfeebled.' Contemporary evidence shows that it was no 'early predilection' but a life-long conviction.[68] Henry Moore wrote that 'he (Wesley) would never acknowledge any ministry that was not conferred in the scriptural, apostolic and ancient way of "laying on of hands" '. Moore remonstrated with Wesley about the *Korah* sermon, maintaining that there were many things stated that were not in 'the Book'. 'He looked earnestly at me, for some time, but not with displeasure. He made no reply and soon introduced another subject. I said no more. The man of one book would not dispute against it. I believe he saw his love to the church, from which he never deviated unnecessarily, had in this instance led him a little too far.'

A further principle of Wesley was that there was a succession in ministerial office, even if it was not that of the uninterrupted succession of the apostolic ministry. 'The fact is that Wesley's idea of succession was still in effect episcopal, not it is true the traditional and usually accepted view of episcopal succession, but in accordance with the belief that presbyters discharging their function as *episcopoi* had the right to ordain. When Wesley ordained it was as a presbyter exercising the inherent right of a New Testament *episcopos*.' J. E. Rattenbury came to the same conclusion. 'Wesley's ordinations were not in intention presbyterian; they were episcopal; they were given by a presbyter acting as a bishop, they were given by one who claimed to be, and for that reason gave them, a true New Testament bishop.'[69] Another way of interpreting the whole matter (often overlooked) is to see Wesley in this particular as very much in line with a liberal Anglican position stemming back to Richard Hooker,[70] who spoke of 'inevitable necessity' in relation to the Protestant Reformed churches, a view which can be traced through writers like Hoadly[71] (whom significantly Thomas Coke was reading on the boat to America in 1784) to contemporaries like Warburton, Paley and White in America. Wesley thus stands firmly in an Anglican tradition which has as much right to boast of its pedigree as that of the more Catholic view which was present but much overladen in the eighteenth century.

The theory can be seen as consistent. The practice appears less so and has about it anomalies which had serious consequences for the doctrine of the ministry in Methodism. A year before Wesley's ordinations the Countess of Huntingdon's Connexion held its first ordinations at Spa Fields Chapel. The claim was made that the ordinations were on the basis of the 'presbyter-bishop' theory to which Wesley himself subscribed. For Wesley the die was cast. The American Methodists needed a church constitution and they needed ministers; they should have both. Having broken its links with Great Britain, any ties with the established church were broken also which gave Wesley freedom to manoeuvre without disloyalty, a point often overlooked. It seems likely that the initiative in this matter came from Wesley himself and not from the inordinate ambition of Dr Thomas Coke, as L. Tyerman followed by A. B. Lawson suggest.[72] The upshot was that Thomas Coke, already a presbyter of the Church of England, was 'set apart' as 'superintendent' by John Wesley on 2 September 1784 at Bristol. Richard Whatcoat and Thomas Vasey, who had been ordained deacon on the previous day, were ordained presbyter by Wesley, Coke and James Creighton, another Anglican clerical assistant. The ordinations of Whatcoat and Vasey follow from Wesley's 'scriptural *episcopos*' theory but what was intended in the case of Coke? Whitehead put the problem: 'Dr Coke had the same right to ordain Wesley that Mr Wesley had to ordain Dr Coke', since both were presbyters.[73] When Wesley used the title 'superintendent', did he mean bishop? Just what did he mean by it? There is a dilemma here – either presbyters are bishops, in which case Coke needed no such consecration, or they are not in which case what right had Wesley to lay hands on Coke? This point assumes importance not only in the constitution of the American Methodist Church but also in English Methodism which effectively repudiated Wesley's theory and practice.

There have been many explanations of Wesley's action in setting aside Coke. Tyerman maintained that Coke magnified the whole affair to gain power and prestige. He hankered after a mitre. There is little evidence for this save for Coke's frequent indiscretions and naïvety, not least in his relationships with bishops and politicians. J. E. Rattenbury drew on Wesley's highly ambiguous subsequent correspondence with Coke and Asbury to conclude 'It is a delusion to assert that Wesley ever intended to give Dr Coke Episcopal orders. On his theory orders could only be given by those who had them and his orders were Presbyteral. He delegated to Dr Coke his own superintendency in America, quite aware, of course, that such a superintendency meant the exercise of Episcopal functions which in his opinion any Presbyter had a right to exercise if the "circumstances" made such activity necessary. Even Anglo-Catholics admit that Episcopacy was a function before it was an Order.'[74] Was Wesley merely delegating part of his huge pastoral responsibility to Coke and also Asbury? Was this a unique Wesleyan kind of *shaliach* theory no more tenable than the more famous one of Gregory Dix?

When Asbury and Coke began to call themselves 'bishops' rather than 'superintendents' Wesley rebuked them.[75] 'How can you, how dare you suffer yourselves to be called "bishops" rather than "superintendents"? . . . Men may call me a knave, or a fool, a rascal or scoundrel, and I am content; but they shall never by my consent call me a bishop! For my sake, for God's sake, for Christ's sake, put a full end to this! Let the Presbyterians do what they please, but let the Methodists know their calling better.' This curious and ambiguous statement – were American Presbyterians cocking a snook at Anglicans or emulating John Knox who wanted more and better and less prelatical bishops? – could well be a display of pique on Wesley's part. He had, in any case, in the Ordinal of 1784 clearly supplied the American Methodists with a style of episcopacy, if not the Anglican style. E. W. Thompson, followed by A. R. George[76] saw Wesley as an 'apostolic man' acting as the instrument of providence. John Kent has thrown doubt on this theory but even he uses the phrase 'great superintendent' of Wesley, which sounds episcopal enough. Wesley stated his intentions clearly in the letter to the American brethren which must be seen in terms of eighteenth-century views of church and state.

> . . . I was determined as little as possible to violate the established order of the National Church to which I belonged. But the case is widely different between England and North America. Here there are bishops who have a legal jurisdiction: in America there are none, neither any parish ministers . . . as our American brethren are now totally disentangled both from the state and from the English hierarchy, we dare not entangle them again with the one or the other. They are now at full liberty simply to follow the Scriptures and the Primitive Church, and we judge it best that they should stand fast in that liberty wherewith God has so strangely made them free . . .[77]

Wesley could apply not only his doctrine of providence but a Hookerlike doctrine of 'ineluctable necessity' and his belief that he was following the custom of the Alexandrian church in setting aside a 'superintendent'. His actions, however, apart from his theory, could and were interpreted as incompatible with loyalty to the contemporary Establishment. Apostolic boldness can appear as a flagrant breach of normal order. The person who said at the time, 'I wish that they had been asleep when they began this business of ordination; it is neither Episcopal nor Presbyterian but a mere hodge-podge of inconsistencies', may have been nearer the truth than those who are anxious to make Wesley's actions always logically consistent.[78]

The ordinations of 1784 were a link in the chain of actions leading to final separation. Charles Wesley was furious. He loathed the thought of separation, agreeing with Lord Mansfield[79] that 'ordination is separation'. He was full of gloomy foreboding of a 'new sect of presbyterians'. Some contemporary Anglican opinion was equally unfavourable. George Horne, Bishop of Norwich, in a charge to the clergy in 1791 said:

> We are informed that the liberties taken of late years against the ministry of the church have terminated in an attempt to begin a spurious episcopacy in America . . . Mr Wesley when questioned about this fact in his lifetime did not deny it but pleaded necessity to justify the measure . . . a fatal precedence if it should be followed. For if a presbyter can consecrate a bishop, we admit that a man may confer a power of which he is not himself possessed, as instead of the less being blessed by the greater, the greater is blessed by the less and the order of things is inverted.[80]

William Jones of Nayland, one of the leading 'Catholic' Anglican clergymen of the time, also issued a sharp criticism. 'In taking upon himself what no man can take, he could introduce in the issue more confusion than he would prevent.'[81] Jones, indeed, in 1795 called Methodism 'Christian godliness without Christian order'. Maybe there were few ripples on the Anglican sea because the whole matter was rather a hole-in-the-corner affair. There were after all no laity to shout 'he is worthy' at the consecration of Thomas Coke, a matter not overlooked by Asbury.[82] The same was true, also, of the consecration of Seabury by the Scots bishops.

Together with providing ordained ministers, Wesley provided the American Methodists with their own prayer book.[83] 'I have prepared a liturgy little differing from that of the Church of England (I think the best constituted National Church in the world).' Wesley's revision of the Prayer Book was certainly an act tending to separation. The reasons for his emendations – mainly omissions – have been variously interpreted. Tyerman spoke of a prayer book 'purged of popish and Calvinian errors'. H. Bett saw in it such emendations as any Protestant dissenter would make. 'In fact every single thing that has any trace of sacerdotalism or superstition is deleted.'[84] More recently the influence of the Savoy Presbyterians of the Restoration has been suggested, making Wesley a spiritual descendant of Baxter and Calamy.[85] Prayer book revisions of a more doctrinally liberal kind are also possible sources. Whatever may be the doctrinal motives of the changes, the practical demands of the American situation are sufficient warrant for many of Wesley's changes.[86] The major theological divergence from the 1662 Book is in the Ordinal where Wesley provides for the threefold order of 'Superintendents, Elders and Deacons', in some ways an ambiguous trimming between episcopacy and presbyterianism and in the order of communion and the daily offices where the absolution is turned into a petition. The Nicene Creed is omitted from the Communion rite. Confirmation is omitted – but that ordinance could hardly have been part of the American scene at all, with no resident bishop to administer it! Ordinations, too, had only been possible by a visit to England. Significant omissions (including the signation?) are made in the order for baptism, while several psalms 'highly improper from the mouths of a Christian congregation' are omitted from the Psalter.

Wesley's first ordinations were for the Methodists in the USA as was, at first, *The Sunday Service*. In 1785 he ordained John Pawson, Thomas Hanby and Joseph Taylor for Scotland.[87] The next year more preachers were ordained for Scotland and others for Antigua, Newfoundland and Nova Scotia. Wesley (as was the case with the USA) felt that this had nothing to do with the situation in England. This was the church-state argument again. He forbade Taylor and Hanby to wear the ministerial gown and bands south of the border. Wesley could point to early church precedents, but Hanby and Taylor were not convinced and presided at Holy Communion in England. Ronald Knox quipped that 'he had evolved a system of Gretna Green ordinations, which unlike Gretna Green marriages were not meant to have any effect south of the Tweed.' Wesley was, however, merely doing what the Establishment did in the same year, for in 1786 an Act of Parliament empowered the Primate to consecrate persons who were citizens *outside* His Majesty's Dominions, so long as these did exercise their respective offices *within* His Majesty's Dominions. American bishops or clergy visiting England were apparently treated as laymen, as women priests are now – at least they might not practise their ministry.[88]

As in America, the desire of the Methodist people for their own sacraments forced Wesley ultimately to ordain men for the ministry in England. Two matters need to be borne in mind – the fact that sacramental observance appears, by post-Tractarian standards, lax in contemporary Anglicanism. The other was the fact that some Methodists, following John Wesley's precepts and practice, desired frequent communions presided over by those who preached to them. Wesley urged them to go to their parish church for Holy Communion but they were often repelled from the Table and in any case many of them were quite strange to the parish church, its priest, its people and its worship. The meetings of 'society' for worship and fellowship were more than merely supplemental to what was often enough a very formal service in the parish church, nor was it easy for those gathered from practical paganism to feel at home in the church from which they had long been alienated. Conference stated in 1766 that 'our' worship presupposes public prayer like the sermons at the university . . . for it seldom has the four grand parts of public prayer: deprecation, petition, intercession and thanksgiving. Neither is it even on the Lord's Day concluded with the Lord's Supper.' This quickly became an anachronism. What Wesley called the 'prudential' means of grace were assuming a greater importance.[89]

There developed a duality about Methodist worship which was to have important consequences for the future. John Wesley or his Conference might issue their fiats, but the people, as a whole, had greater influence on the development of modes of worship after the first few years than has sometimes been realized. An element of Donatism was always present, which led to a denigration of the parish church among some Methodists. The monographs of J. E. Rattenbury, J. C. Bowmer and O. Borgen have stressed Wesley's sacramental thinking and his devotion to the eucharist. Some of the early Methodists shared Wesley's love of the sacraments, but from constant warnings that the people often neglect the sacrament we may conclude that many found satisfaction in the specifically Methodist exercises, especially the love feast. Samuel Bradburn wrote in 1792: 'Could you think much of the religion of a people who pretended great love for the blessed Jesus who shed his precious blood to redeem their souls if they neglected the dear memorials of his dying love? Is it not enough to make us ashamed to look God in the face, when we reflect upon the nature and importance of the Lord's Supper and consider how it is treated by many of the Methodists? Some are careless about it, others in a trifling spirit say they receive as the Quakers do.'[90]

The root of the problem was the natural desire of the folk to have the full means of grace in the chapels. Throughout their ministry the Wesleys communicated in parish churches when they could. Great crowds, unique at this time, were not infrequent.[91] In Bristol and London from an early period celebrations were held when ordained 'helpers' were present, in the Methodist preaching houses. After 1780 celebrations in Methodist chapels in the provinces became quite common. In 1755 and 1760[92] – frequently afterwards – Wesley was requested to allow the preachers to preside at the sacrament, but this request was refused. Methodist services were not officially to be held in church hours, making the novelty of evening worship common, facilitated after 1803 by the use of the incandescent gas mantle for lighting.[93] The rules about church hours were waived in certain circumstances such as when the minister was a 'notoriously evil man' or when he preached 'Arian or other pernicious doctrines' or when there were not churches in the town sufficient to contain half the people or where there was no church at all within two or three miles.[94] In Manchester at the end of the eighteenth century there was accommodation in the parochial churches for 11,000 out of 79,000 inhabitants. Between 1801 and 1851 the population increased from 125,911 to 515,581 and the number of Anglican churches from 23 to 56. The parish church of Halifax at this time covered the pastoral needs of what is now most of the Metropolitan Borough of Calderdale. In London the Establishment provided 15,000 seats for an estimated population of over a million. Figures may be disputed or exaggerated, spiritual neglect is not. Thus a style of 'Donatism' and social change combined to drive Methodism into independence.

Wesley, having conceded so much, finally ordained men for England.[95] On 6 August 1788 Alexander Mather was ordained deacon and on the next day superintendent. In February 1789 two more of Wesley's leading preachers – Thomas Rankin and Henry Moore were ordained firstly as deacons and then as elders.[96] Wesley's action in ordaining Mather as superintendent (did he receive the office of presbyter and the function of superintendent on the same day?) raised at once the problem of Wesley's plans for Methodism after his death. There had been a series of frustrations in the past which are pointers here.

By 1769 his proposed 'clerical union' of all evangelical clergymen had finally come to grief on the matter of irregularities in the parishes, despite theological agreement on original sin, justification by faith and holiness of heart and life.[97] The possible designation of John Fletcher as Wesley's successor[98] foundered with Fletcher's premature death, as had the scheme that Joseph Benson and Fletcher elaborated in 1775 for a Methodist 'presbytery' or 'Methodist Church of England' (the phrase was Fletcher's) subordinate to the established church.[99] It seems likely that Wesley contemplated a Methodist superintendency of Coke and Mather to lead Methodism after his death. Coke did not use his episcopal title in Britain, though Myles certainly calls Coke 'superintendent'. John Pawson made no bones about the matter: 'He foresaw that the Methodists would soon become a distinct body – he was deeply prejudiced against presbyterian, and as much in favour of episcopal government. In order, therefore, to preserve all that is valuable in the Church of England among the Methodists, he ordained Mr Mather and Dr Coke bishops. These he undoubtedly designed should ordain others. Mr Mather told us so at the Manchester Conference in 1791.'[100]

James Creighton, himself one of the clerical helpers, maintained in 1793 that Wesley repented of these ordinations, but there is paucity of evidence for this.[101] More difficult to dismiss is Bradburn's assertion in 1792 that Wesley asserted that after his death 'Methodists will be a regular Presbyterian Church'.[102] Bradburn claimed that 'his death would make us such – while he lived he was the Head, the Bishop. As soon as he died, his power died with him'. It may be that Bradburn was giving what were Wesley's fears as if they were Wesley's hopes. Looked at from the angle of subsequent events, Bradburn's pamphlet confirms rather than denies Pawson's statement.

More difficult to assess is a letter from Dublin dated 28 May 1794 which appears to be addressed to Bradburn by Joseph Bradford who was President of the Conference in 1795. He says, after an attack on Coke:

If Dr Coke, Messrs Bradburn and Moore have settled on it, there will be warm work. If Mr Wesley told Messrs Moore and Bradburn that he was determined that Methodism should after his decease become an Episcopal Church, he left the world with a lie in his mouth, which God forbid anyone, much less a Methodist preacher, should attempt to prove. I think I knew him as well as either of them and his mind upon these subjects and if I have any truth in me it was quite the reverse and I am sure I have as good reason to believe our late honoured Father as I can believe Mr Moore, Mr Bradburn or any other man.'

Bradford's letter shows that in the party conflict after 1791, each side tried to prove its beliefs and actions were in accord with 'our late honoured Father'. He may well have made incompatible prophecies about the fate of Methodism in the time immediately before his death. He had certainly uttered many forebodings about separation in the thirty years before it. We turn now to some of the underyling sociological factors in the separation and to a comparison between Methodism and the Catholic community.

3

Methodism, Catholicism and Patterns of Dissent

Methodism was felt by not a few to be a threat to social order in the eighteenth century, though its role can be seen to change later. It fits (as does Roman Catholicism) into a pattern of threat to social cohesion with squire and parson often enough combining with the aid of the mob still willing (at least before 1795) to play a docile rather than a subversive role.[1]

Opposition to Methodism can be divided into four styles – governmental, satirical, local and intellectual. Direct governmental opposition from Westminster was negligible. Dissent in this period had some measure of relief by Indemnity Acts (frequent though not annual) from the effect of penal legislation.[2] From 1779 subscription to the Thirty-Nine Articles was rescinded for dissenting ministers. Walpole had not been prepared to go further in repealing the Clarendon Code despite pressure, but his stance was one of tolerant indifference, the proper cynicism of a politique.[3] 'In 1760,' says J. H. Plumb, 'Methodism was easily the most highly organized body of opinion in the country, the most fervent, the most dynamic. Had it been bent on revolution in church or state, nothing could have stopped it. But then Methodism was not a religion of the poor but for the poor.' Plumb, no friend of Methodism, probably exaggerates its actual strength. Government did not see Methodism as dangerous, though parallels with contemporary Catholicism could be made. It was not mere scurrility which dubbed John Wesley a Jesuit. The mob could turn out at the behest not only of a Lord George Gordon but of a squirarchy enraged by religious enthusiasm.

There was opposition to Methodism from the satirist, the stage and the magazine. A. M. Lyles in *Methodism Mocked* has shown how widespread this was and how much of the fire was drawn by George Whitefield rather than John Wesley.[5] A good deal of this was harmless but opposition from the world of Beau Nash and the mechanics of Wednesbury were not wholly unconnected. Catcalls as well as duckings might do God service.[6] John Walsh has recently identified a number of elements in the local opposition.[7] Mob rioting was a common form of social protest or social celebration. Much of it had as its aim psychological humiliation rather than bodily hurt, though an early fatality was that of William Seward at Hay-on-Wye in 1741. Magistrates were often closely involved or indifferent. In 1780 one quarter of the 3,000 or more Justices of the Peace were clergymen, often enough dependent economically and socially on the squire.[8] The 'great vulgar' could stir up the small.[9] Methodism was more easily seen as a challenge to public order at local level. It had a highly organized nation-wide connexion in an age of decentralized government, the itinerants (like the vicars apostolic) had no local controls. 'The poor', to whom the itinerants appealed, were then organized. This could appear dangerous and divisive. Memories of the Civil War and the Commonwealth were not far beneath the surface. Methodism looked like Puritanism in a new dress. Clergymen saw themselves belittled beneath their noses and were often enough thought of as 'dumb dogs'. The preacher undermined patriarchal authority. Dissenters feared competition and also a reactionary backlash. Sometimes clearly it was the case of 'hired bands' operating on behalf of external interests[10] but just as probably it could be loyal lads annoyed at the way the local beauties ogled the preacher! Families could be split by the conversion of one of their numbers causing sometimes a clear and ominous social cleavage among working-class folk. So E. Welbourne,[11] speaks of the Methodists later in Durham, 'taking away from the pitman his dog, his fighting cock and his gun'. Prayer meetings would replace 'pay night frolics'. Clandestine class meetings and private love feasts brought similar rumours as those which plagued the early church. Wesley was thought to be a Jacobite or a crypto-papist or bribed by the Spaniards to raise a peasant army – after all some itinerants received horses at about the same time as their Roman counterparts.[12] This is the background to the matter of the registration of meeting houses.

Methodism rapidly increased its self-identity – persecution and pressure often increases this, reinforcing what Festinger has called 'cognitive dissonance'.[13] Parishes slowly learned to live with a duality of church and chapel, parson and preacher. When revolution threatened in the next generation, Methodists found themselves under pressure again but by then they had acquired a respectability which made William Cobbett mock at their conservatism and other-worldliness. Diminishing opposition was also a factor in Wesley's later years, bolstering his continued loyalty to the Church of England.

The fourth style of opposition was intellectual. Tucker, Gibson and Butler, 'John Smith', Warburton and Lavington, Porteus, Horne, Hurd and Douglas are, on any reckoning, a powerful opposition. Wesley was forced to reply to these critics and their strictures need to be taken more seriously than has usually been the case in Methodist historiography. Recently G. R. Cragg has edited Wesley's apologetic and in his earlier studies Martin Schmidt[14] has clearly outlined the gravamen of the charges against the Methodists.

> In spite of all their variations, the attacks from the Anglican side were all characterized by a great similarity. From all the writings, speeches and newspaper articles came the same complaints about 'enthusiasm', exaggerated piety, fanaticism, lust for power and tyranny, excessive austerity or unrestrained lawlessness, hypocrisy, disparagement of the regular church and its representatives and more than all, and running through all, threats to the peace of the church and disturbance of the public quiet. The memory of the Great Revolution a hundred years earlier was still living and it affected the whole controversy.[15]

Dean Tucker's early and astute attack[16] (he wrote at the behest of Bishop Butler, and was perhaps the most penetrating opponent of Wesley) disputed his concept of justification by faith. Both Bishop Gibson[17] and George Horne[18] saw it as the harbinger of moral carelessness and antinomianism – did not George Whitefield even scorn the 'Whole Duty of Man' as barely Christian? The empirical basis of Wesley's doctrine was disputed. 'Enthusiasm', defined by Gibson[19] as 'making inward, secret and sudden impulses the guides of their actions, resolutions and designs' was another constant charge. Assurance of salvation to Bishop Warburton[20] was a presumption that the Holy Spirit still operated as he had done in Apostolic times – a presumption indeed in the age of the Enlightenment.[21] Warburton, too, saw the dangers of what he thought to be a renewed Puritanism. George Lavington,[22] Bishop of Exeter, who called Ignatius Loyola 'that errant, shatter-brained visionary fanatic', linked Wesley with Montanism and *illuminati* of every age, not least the seventeenth century. The linkage with 'papists', however, was not as absurd as may seem. Lavington had to admit a common love for God and man and a passionate zeal to save souls, but would doubtless have agreed with John Green, later Bishop of Lincoln, who complained that 'Methodism removed Christianity from that basis of just and rational proof . . . that rock of evidence whereon it had stood for ages and set it down on the shaking sands of inward impulses which may be entirely fantastical.'[23]

Lavington scorned the doctrine of Christian perfection. Wesley's particular doctrine was attacked from all angles, not least that of the Calvinist wing of the Evangelicals. Perhaps Wesley sought, when advocating reconciliation, to make a molehill out of a mountain, since the doctrine of holiness was as important as the question of church order in splitting the evangelical movement.[24] Holiness was the truly Wesleyan emphasis and it was on this rock that the various attempts to unite Wesleyans and Anglicans came to grief. Church order was, however, in the long run crucial. Nowhere is this clearer than in the correspondence between Wesley and 'John Smith' (possibly the future Archbishop of Canterbury, Thomas Secker). In the last analysis Wesley could only point to converted tinners in Cornwall, keelmen in Newcastle, colliers in Kingwood and Stafford-shire as his apostolic justification.[25] There was a different view of the nature of the church at stake.

However much Wesley could point to Prayer Book, Articles and Homilies for support – his Calvinist opponents like A. M. Toplady could play precisely the same game with equal or greater force[26] – the ethos of Methodism ran counter to that of the Hanoverian age. Wesley's proper assertion of his orthodoxy went unheard and misunderstood in episcopal palaces where there was no common policy in dealing with the revival and where there was a natural fear of fanaticism and spurious humbugs, about whom Wesley could sometimes be naïve. Not untypical were Bishop Hurd of Norwich and Bishop Douglas of Carlisle who in his *Criterion*, directed against the Methodists, referred to the *Journals* of Wesley and Whitefield as writings 'already as much forgot as if they had never been published'. Readers were bidden to consult that excellent treatise *The Enthusiasm of Methodists and Papists Compar'd* in which 'the folly and absurdity of Methodism are so clearly pointed out, that it is amazing that so many who would neither be thought deficient in sense nor mistaken in their notion of religion, should still continue in this stage of superstitious enchantment'.[27]

There is the opening up here of a cultural cleavage which continued at least until the Education Act of 1870 – the world of the itinerant preacher and the world of the eighteenth-century prelate and their 'clerical subalterns' are poles apart as were the worlds described by Thomas Jackson[28] in his autobiography and that of the village parson and squire so well depicted in Woodforde or by Owen Chadwick in *Victorian Miniature*[29] and if the squire's daughter goes on preaching tours with the Methodist preacher, this merely underlines the point.

Who, in fact, were the early Methodists and where were they to be found? The sociology of early Methodism is ripe for full exploration.[30] There is clear evidence that the impact on the artisan group was out of proportion to its numbers in the whole population. The parallels with Lollardy and Puritanism are illuminating. If the 'industrious sort of people' were not originally drawn into the movement, many of the needy poor who were, became industrious.

The coincidence with urbanization is crucial. The representative townsman up to the middle of the nineteenth century was the tradesman, craftsman, small master and artisan – those who can later be called 'labour aristocrats' rather than the unskilled or semi-skilled labourer or the worker newly skilled in factory technique. Angus Buchanan has recently underlined the point made by W. J. Warner that this social group provided the lay leaders of Methodism and also the recruits to the early trade unions who had to battle for their standards against the unskilled immigrants from the country-side and Ireland. Methodism depended on the artisan and clearly recruited a larger constituency than the rest of Dissent from the artisan and manufacturing classes with local preachers forming a broader and more prosperous group compared with the itinerants – a pointer perhaps to future conflict, though Henry Bett was right to point out that 'with the exception of half a dozen of the earliest preachers who were soldiers, they (i.e. the itinerants) were nearly all from that social grade which lies between the working class and the middle class – skilled artisans, small tradesmen, small farmers, clerks, schoolmasters and the like – a class from which a great deal of what is best in English life has always come and which is certainly unjust and untrue to describe as the dregs of the nation'[31] which was the sneer of superior clerics.

The call of the Methodists was for simple pious lives removed from worldly pleasures and centred on home, chapel and business. The duty of hard work, the evils of luxury and extravagance, the virtues of foresight and thrift, moderation and self-discipline were instilled into ordinary church members, and provided an undergirding to the moral earnestness which was later to characterize Victorian England. The sociological consequence of becoming a Methodist could be a marginal move up the social scale, a feature in the twentieth century of Pentecostalism and 'black churches' in Britain. The 'sect' type of Christian grouping (Methodism, though technically a society or connexion, comes partially under this umbrella for sociological purposes) enables people with no stake in the wider community to feel a sense of status and belonging which could lead to wider hopes. Methodism thus fuelled the aspirations of the artisan groups.[32]

Methodism often, though not always, grew in the gaps of the parish system – the West Riding of Yorkshire, Cornwall, the Isle of Wight, for instance, where parishes were large, and certainly in Cornwall, a distance from new centres of population, were typical of the areas in which early Methodism thrived. Circuits with over a thousand members at the end of the eighteenth century were almost all to be found in grossly under-churched industrial towns, of which Leeds, Bradford and Halifax can be taken as normative examples.

The triangle formed by Halifax, Leeds and Sheffield was typical of the areas of swift growth and Methodist-parish ratio. Yorkshire, Staffordshire, Lancashire, Northumberland and Durham were strong centres of Methodism at the end of the eighteenth century.[33] The southern counties, except for Cornwall, Devon and Middlesex, continued to be a 'Methodist desert' well into the nineteenth century. Here, often enough, were the most effective Anglican parishes of the 'closed' style in which the squire was still dominant with all the sanctions this might involve in a tight system of social control.[34] The autobiographies of such typical Methodists as Thomas Jackson, Robert Newton and James Dixon reveal how very different was the lot of an itinerant in, for instance, Halifax or Wakefield compared with rural Herefordshire, where James Dixon was stationed in 1812. 'I believe that our circuit is the poorest circuit in all the kingdom and that there is less religion in the County of Hereford than there is in any other county.' This was an area where the Establishment was far from weak, very different from the large parishes of the West Riding. As John Walsh has put it:

> Methodism was able to enlarge and articulate existing cells of godliness and weave into a connexional system all kinds of little marginal outcrops and expatriates. Converts often had a traditional religious background. The ideal conditions for a new society would be that it be sited in a large, freehold parish well stocked with artisans or industrial workers or statutory freeholders with a number of leaderless, disgruntled Nonconformists ready to be woven into the Connexional system, with no parish clergymen (in 1743 out of a total of 836 parishes in the diocese of York 393 had non-resident incumbents and 315 were held by 'pluralists')[35] or a non-resident or immoral clergyman, near to good roads, close to older settlements, not far from the avuncular protection of a town society with an eloquent assistant preacher.

Even with all the circumstances ideally coinciding, a society might not thrive or become bedevilled by divisions. Even without all the favourable predisposing factors, spiritual revival could still occur. In the city of York, Methodism grew despite a congeries of parishes.

The recent assertion of E. P. Thompson[36] that Methodism acted as a repressive element in creating a non-revolutionary working-class consciousness is hardly applicable to eighteenth-century Methodism. Here rather was a society or connexion developing into a denomination which enabled artisans and others to express their sense of belonging outside the old dependency system.[37] It can be argued that the Wesleys' 'Arminianism of the heart' was a religious equivalent of the contemporary belief in freedom and liberty. It gave little men a prodigious sense of their importance before God – and this without any utopian sense of human perfectibility.[38] It can also be argued that with the breakdown of the older patriarchal social system and the partial abdication of the old ruling order[39] in some areas of the country with increasing parochial conflict on matters like enclosure or tithes, with a growing status for the clergy, Methodism provided a group system where the new outsiders could gain status, a sense of identity and importance.

In 1791 a second unified connexion had been created in England with 91,000 members to parallel the 80,000 Roman Catholics of the other connexion, if it can be called such. Both had links with the *Ecclesia Anglicana* but both can be seen as new growths bursting out of the older husk. Both were on the brink of rapid expansion as industrialization and rising population became the dominant feature of social change. To a sociological comparison between these two styles of dissent we now turn.

From time to time there appears a book which opens up a new historical perspective. Such a book was John Bossy's *The English Catholic Community 1570–1850* (1975). Bossy seeks to show how the English Catholic groups developed a kind of non-Protestant dissent from the middle of the reign of Elizabeth I. He draws heavily on social anthropological studies, such as those of Mary Douglas which ask how a dissident group organizes itself. He reveals how 'feasts and fasts' develop to express their group's interior stability and yet how many Catholics were also concerned to be seen as an integral part of wider society, even occasionally conforming to the worship of the parish church. Few of the gentry wanted to be branded as traitors after all.[40] There was at the same time a feeling of belonging to a communal group, sharing the same ultimate commitment – what the sociologists call a *Gemeinschaft*. There was also the need to participate in a wider society, the *Gesellschaft*. Catholics were constantly tempted to retreat into that ghetto in which John Henry Newman claims to have found them in 1845. It was Newman, too, in the Preface to the *Tracts for the Times* who said that 'Methodism and Popery are in different ways the refuge of those whom the church stint of the means of grace; they are the foster-mothers of abandoned children.' This in no way implies theological convergence.

How much have the foster-mothers in common? Such a comparison might give a new perspective to both Catholic and Methodist historiography despite the clear risk of exaggeration. The evidence clearly is more sociological than theological and the same comparisons should be made with 'orthodox dissent' also to be complete.

In the early years of Elizabeth's reign and even later, there were many 'church papists' not only loyal to Queen Elizabeth but maintaining links with what had become the Establishment. Those 'church Methodists' (or 'old planners' to use the technical term) who at Wesley's bidding, and later of their own volition, went to the parish church for matins and evensong and for the monthly or quarterly Lord's Supper – unless the parson repelled them or preached wholly unacceptable doctrine – were not dissimilar, though they were under no cruel penalties as were Elizabethan Catholics. This tradition continues through the nineteenth century though it became more difficult in a period of Anglican resurgence and triumphalism. It is a feature of English Dissent often misunderstood and disliked by Anglicans, later frowned upon by the Tractarians who, in the railway age, began to claim episcopal confirmation as a *sine qua non* of communion at Anglican Tables.[41] The tradition was not confined to Wesleyans either – the Protestant Methodists of Barnsley went to the parish church in the 1820s; Bible Christians were doing the same in the West Country.[42] There is a sense here of Dissent being in some measure parasitical on an Establishment which was there to be used – and of course, *had* to be used for weddings until 1836 and normally for burials unless there was a dissenting graveyard (there are many still open in the West Riding) or later civil burial ground.

Bossy shows how styles of what he calls 'seasonal conformity' developed in Catholicism – feasts and fasts including the mass, which were private events and included services without a priest, not unlike the lay-led services of early Methodism.[43] Methodism began to assume an independency when what John Wesley called its 'prudential' means of grace – preaching services, love feasts, class meetings, watchnights (normally at the full moon to avoid 'muggings') and the Covenant service began to assume supreme importance for ordinary people, many of whom were strangers to the parish church, its minister and its worship. The 'occasional conformists' and 'old planners' might have been those slightly higher up the social scale compared with the majority – a matter difficult to test. Certainly by 1795 when the *Plan of Pacification* permitted Methodist itinerant preachers to preside at Holy Communion, a full diet of 'feast and fast' was available. Methodism, like English Catholicism, developed its own style of celebrating seasons[44] which could appear deliberately in contrast to the means of grace of the parish church, but which were as much geared to money raising which is always a feature of Dissent, whether Catholic or Protestant. There was no Queen Anne's Bounty or Waterloo Money or Ecclesiastical Commission for the 'foster-mothers'. Social anthropologists are more likely to be sympathetic to 'Men's Weekends' and 'Women's Days' than recent generations of ministers who make little attempt to understand folk-religion. The rites of passage – baptism, marriage, burial – reveal also a community on the way to total separation. Catholics gradually evolved their own system – marriages without a priest were not infrequent before 1753. Methodism shows parallels here, though not a few Methodists deliberately sought the rites of passage in their parish churches, when it was no longer necessary to do so.[45] Wesleyanism was somewhat reluctant to make use of the Marriage Act of 1836, though by 1880 it was aligned with Dissent in the battle – and it can only be described as a battle – to allow dissenting ministers to conduct burials in the parish churchyard. Bishop Wordsworth of Lincoln saw it as a threat to the very political existence of the Church of England. One angry rector armed his flock with pitchforks to keep the dissenters out of the churchyard.[46] It is quite clear that some Anglicans saw in civic cemeteries a considerable loss of their revenue. The opening of the Kensal Green cemetery lost the Vicar of Paddington £200 a year.[47]

Catholicism, because of its doctrine of the church, tended to what we can call connexionalism with a key role given to the Vicars Apostolical before the restoration of the hierarchy in 1850 by Pius IX. This was a system quite different from the somewhat isolated pockets of Lollards, 'the secret multitude of true professors', as John Foxe called them or more independent congregations in the late sixteenth or seventeenth centuries. It was much more like the system which John Wesley developed. Clearly it was a national, indeed an international, as well as a regional organization which drew not a little governmental and local suspicion on Methodism as a state within a state, perhaps as potentially dangerous as the papists, though little action was taken until the early nineteenth century under the alarm of revolution.

Herbert Workman[48] showed that a comparison could be made between Wesley and St Francis, not least in his linkage of holiness and joy and his concern for the poor. Conference was suspiciously like a Chapter General. A comparison between the itinerants and St Dominic's 'order of preachers' is more to the point, for Wesley was surely much more of a Dominic than a Francis. Albert Outler, more recently, has shown parallels with the Anabaptist preachers. There are Puritan and Pietist precedents too, but there is clearly more than a whiff of the religious order about Wesley's rules for his preachers which has lingered even into the twentieth century. In the eighteenth century, comparison, too, can be made between the Wesleys and Alfonso Liguori (1696–1787). 'The heirs of the Counter-Reformation sometimes astound by likeness of behaviour to that found in the heirs of the Reformation.' Following Werner Stark,[49] Professor Owen Chadwick spots a parallel between the appeal of Wesley and

Whitefield to what he calls 'the people of England as distinct from the middle classes of England' and the appeal of Liguori and his Redemptorists to the people of Italy. Liguori on his donkey mimics unconsciously Wesley on his horse, popular hymnody matched that of Charles Wesley. 'The effects of a mission were dramatic. Men handed over pistol and daggers, women threw away low-cut dresses, young men offered themselves as ordinands or monks. After a mission by fourteen Redemptorists at Sarno, the taverns were deserted for ten years' – even John Fletcher at Madeley could hardly equal that.[50] Liguori certainly preached a style of assurance, though he also stressed sacramental devotion and the confessional. Astutely Professor Kent sees both Wesleyanism and Catholicism seeking to 'reconcile the Christian model of the perfect life with the growth of the bourgeois spirit'. Using diverse methods 'both reacted to the spiritual and intellectual isolation of the lower ranks of an excessively rigid, hierarchical society and both wanted to awaken in people a greater awareness of the importance of translating theology into human existence especially where the practice of holiness was concerned.' The Awakening was more than a pan-Protestant phenomenon.

There is something Franciscan about the privations of some of the early itinerants – Wesleyan and later Primitive Methodist, and their families. Certainly the Primitive Methodists threw up a ministry not *for* the poor but *of* the poor. Comparisons should be made not with increasingly affluent Anglican parsons with the gentry-style parsonages but with William Ullathorne (later to be the first Roman Catholic bishop of Birmingham) pioneering his mission in the poverty of Coventry, or Francis Martyn in Wolverhampton.[51] In the nineteenth century the new-style priest trained at Ushaw or at Oscott and the new-style Wesleyan minister trained at Hoxton, Didsbury or Richmond was a very different kind of 'professional' in a rapidly changing situation. Bunting's men, loyal to Conference, representing the greater church in the local situation, paralleled the new priests ministering to the Irish invasion, free from the power and patronage of the Catholic gentry.[52]

The role of the priest in the English Catholic community before 1850 involved a great deal of dependence on a friendly gentry. The number of priests in 1770 was about 400.[53] Wesley's itinerant preachers, who were mainly full-time lay agents, numbered at that time about 140, but the numbers of both groups were growing. It would be strange if they were not sometimes confused. Hogarth drew the Methodist preacher with fallen wig revealing friar's tonsure! Both represented a central organization and in the Catholic case an international one. Can one say that Methodist dissent comes of age when the itinerant preacher – literally itinerant and living off the land as it were – became rooted in a local community, acquiring rapidly many of the characteristics of the incumbent and the dissenting pastor – including bureaucratization! In the 1980s the incumbent is turning in rural areas into an itinerant without, often enough, the lay leadership which enabled the Methodist itinerant to be an 'episcopal' figure. The Catholic priests were at first itinerant (for obvious legal reasons). Being granted a horse was a sign of having arrived, followed, when this became legally possible, by the buying or building of presbyteries. The preacher's horse and house were signs of a more formal and settled status. Many an itinerant's wife in both Wesleyanism and Primitive Methodism had a hard struggle before the manse became a normality.[54] Itinerancy is much more a Catholic than a Protestant phenomenon with the celibate priest or monk expendable, having that *disponibilité* which can still describe a ministry available to the church's need.

Another area where Catholicism, Dissent and Methodism ran parallel is the great increase in both after about 1770. There were 80,000 Catholics in England in 1770, there were 750,000 in 1851.[55] The style of Catholic congregations changed from rural to urban. 'Congregations of labourers, handicraftsmen, tradesmen, the simply poor, their wives and children topped by a stratum of business and professional families replaced in the centre of the scene congregations of gentry, farmers, agricultural labourers and rural craftsmen.'[56] To these were added the masses of 'Erin's root-fed hordes'. Was the average Methodist congregation all that different with its above average numbers of 'labour aristocracy' as Clive Field and others have shown? How far did both groups reflect the aspirations rather than the despair of the new individual proletariat? Both groups also reflect the end of the pre-industrial 'dependency system'. Put crudely, more people could afford to be dissenters. The evidence seems to point to the conclusion that during the social upheavals of the first industrial age, both Catholicism and Methodism could seek and win the interest of people 'whose inherited assumptions had been upset, who had lost touch with the Church of England and who responded to anyone who proved from whatever point of view to be genuinely interested in their lives'.[57] The abandoned children found foster-mothers.

Another element worth consideration in this parallel between Catholicism and Methodism is that, as with all dissenting groups, it was found necessary to legitimize their property rights. Just as Wesley needed his Model Deed of 1763 with the registering of preaching houses for worship, so Catholics, when it was legal to do so, began this same process. The familiar pattern of trustees and trust deeds emerges with trustees responsible for receiving 'bench rents'.[58] Unseemly squabbles distinctly similar to those at Birstall and Bristol[59] occurred in late eighteenth-century Catholicism. A new middle-class laity was asserting its rights in both groups. When a Franciscan speaks of a 'pack of upstart purse proud puppies' seeking to influence John Milner in 1803,[60] we can compare them with those bourgeois West Riding trustees who put their great organ in the Brunswick Chapel in Leeds at the cost of £1,000 and a thousand members. The bid in Catholicism for clerical supremacy is paralleled, too, in Wesleyanism by what opponents readily saw as the self-conscious hierarchical tendencies of Jabez Bunting and his friends in Wesleyanism. As we shall see later, a new clerical self-consciousness marked both Evangelicalism and Anglo-Catholicism in the Church of England. This was to threaten dissenter, Catholic and Methodist alike before long.

The last parallel is in the field of education.[61] Wesleyan efforts to build its own primary system (and on a minor scale at 'senior' level with a growing public school system in some measure apeing the Woodard system) faltered after 1870. There were 912 Wesleyan schools at the peak of voluntary endeavour in 1873, backed by the powerful advocacy of J. H. Rigg. Cardinal Manning had a grander aim – the provision of Catholic education for every Catholic child. By 1900 there were 1,000 Catholic schools, and by 1975, 3,100. The parallels are closer in higher education. Both Wesleyans and Catholics were apprehensive about, if not openly hostile to, their young people going as students to Oxford or Cambridge when the removal of religious tests made it possible. Free from the protective sub-culture they might become agnostic or Anglican – a fear by no means entirely foolish. T. H. Green, the philosopher, indeed, said:

> The opening of the national universities to Nonconformists has been, in my judgment, an injury rather than a help to Nonconformists. You are sending up here, year by year, the sons of some of your best and wealthiest families; they are often altogether uninfluenced by the services of the church which they find here and not only drift away from Nonconformity, they drift away and lose all faith; and you are bound, as soon as you have secured the opening of the universities to your sons, to follow them here when you send them here, in order to defend and maintain their religious life and faith.

There was an element of the ghetto and shades of the papal 'Syllabus of Errors' of 1864 about some of the opposition. The antagonism between Newman and Manning represented different responses to the dilemma. The heroic but abortive attempts of both

Newman and Manning to establish at Dublin and Kensington purely Catholic centres of higher education typify this. The other response was the realization, firstly by the Wesleyans, that cultural isolation was impossible if not stultifying. The middle classes and dissenters of all types were pushing into secondary and higher education whatever hierarchies might proscribe. The stationing of the attractive and radical Hugh Price Hughes[62] at Oxford in 1881 was one sign that official Wesleyanism was aware of the dangers and possibilities. The more enduring sign was the establishment of the Leys School under W. F. Moulton in Cambridge in 1875[63] giving Methodism a clear institutional centre for student and don alike, of which Moulton's son, James Hope Moulton, Fellow of King's, was a symbol.

Catholicism reacted more slowly. The Pope was persuaded to reward Catholics so foolish as to allow their offspring to seek education at the older universities by deeming them guilty of heinous sin.[64] In February 1893, dressed in Cambridge gown and hood, Anatole von Hügel, curator of the archaeological museum in Cambridge, attended a papal audience, presenting a gift on behalf of Catholic Cambridge undergraduates – a species supposedly non-existent.[65] The Congregationalist Mansfield College and the Anglican Pusey House, both at Oxford, were cited as examples of religious centres fostering particular forms of doctrine and piety. Friedrich von Hügel, Anatole's brother, campaigned against the ultramontane demands of the hierarchy and when the ban was lifted, the Roman Catholics, with characteristic thoroughness, established chaplaincy centres like Campion Hall and St Edmund's House which have been models of pastoral care, with later chaplains of the calibre of Ronald Knox to staff them. Methodism, likewise, made careful chaplaincy provisions which were to bear fruit in the large Methodist societies of the 1930–60 period when the products of the 1870 and 1902 Education Acts were enabling their offspring to go to university or college in large numbers – very large numbers in comparison with the proportion of Methodists to the population. For a generation or so the Methodist societies and Catholic societies have often been the largest groups of Christian students outside the Christian Unions which represent undenominational conservative evangelicalism. The Catholic and Methodist chaplains begin with a clear constituency – those commended by local priests and ministers. The old connexionalism thus has its after-life in both churches.

The churches at the beginning of the nineteenth century were preparing for the 'age of religious boom' as E. R. Wickham has called it.[66] Roman Catholicism and Methodism were now in sociological terms denominations, as was the Church of England. Neither Methodism nor Roman Catholicism were trammelled by establishmentarian restrictions. Both had a missionary field and a missionary urge at home and abroad. Many similarities still remain – it is sheer Anglican pretentiousness to suggest that the Church of England is in some way a bridge between Catholicism and Methodism. The dissenter recognizes the dissenter in the other church, for there is a common background of restriction. By the middle of the twentieth century the Roman Catholic Church has become the foremost upholder of what can be called still the Nonconformist conscience, especially in matters concerned with human life, its origins and its demise and concern for the poor. The relationship of Methodism to Counter-Reformation and Catholic spirituality, despite Maximin Piette, Gordon Rupp, Jean Orcibal and Gordon Wakefield,[67] still awaits a full treatment, but I would hazard the guess that the whole 'mounting' of Methodist history within English Christianity may need radical revision in the light of John Bossy's novel definition of Nonconformity which I have tried to take seriously in this chapter.

It is also the case that ecumenical co-operation between the two 'foster-mothers' is a matter of recent years. In Wesley's day and certainly in the nineteenth century, Roman Catholicism was suspected by Methodists as being not only politically a menace but theologically heretical and dangerous. Indeed, as David Hempton has recently convincingly shown, 'Wesley's anti-Catholicism was one of his profound and enduring legacies to the 'Wesleyan connexion and the connexion's vigorous anti-Catholicism – in which it genuinely reflected its following – was a most important determinant of Wesleyan political attitudes during the nineteenth century.'[68]

4

The Theological Legacy of John Wesley

It is possible to speak of 'that line of seminal theologians that stretches from Paul, through Augustine, Luther, Calvin, the Federal theologians and on through Schleiermacher and Reinhold Niebuhr who have discovered their most profound theological insight in their attempts to bring the gospel pastorally to people.'[1] Into that company John Wesley can enter for he worked out his theology not so much in the 'groves of academe' but on horseback and in dialogue with friend and foe. Karl Barth spoke of 'irregular dogmatics'[2] by which he means a theological style closer than others to the actual preaching of the gospel – the commentary, the sermon and perhaps the hymn are cases of 'irregular dogmatics'. Wesley again is relevant here, for are not a commentary and a collection of sermons the standards of what an older generation of Methodists called 'our doctrines'. Were not the hymns of Charles Wesley the means by which plain people learned line by line and sang their creed?

Has John Wesley's basic stance any relevance to the ecumenical conversation of our day? There is always the difficulty here of a tendency to read back into Wesley (or anyone else) the ideas and preoccupations of a later age. Herbert Butterfield's salutary warning needs to be heeded. 'The primary assumption of all attempts to understand the men of the past must be the belief that we can to some degree enter into minds that are unlike our own . . . it is not for him to stress and magnify the similarities between one age and another and he is riding after a whole flock of misapprehensions if he begins to hunt for the present in the past. Rather it is his work to destroy those very analogies which he imagined to exist.'[3] Examples of what Butterfield warned against are found in attempts to align Wesley with fashionable theologies of liberation,[4] which would do best to stand on their own feet. Yet Wesley and the Evangelicals clearly did use the language of liberation, especially in the anti-slavery campaign. The Exodus story (so beloved of modern liberation theologies) was certainly a theme used by Wilberforce with vehemence. Wesley stands however in the long line of Christian conservatives which includes Augustine, Luther, Hooker, Burke,

Wilberforce, Shaftesbury and Newman whose concern for the poor was just as real, if expressed differently, as that of modern theologies of liberation, whose theologies emerge out of desperate concern for the oppressed and whom we ignore at our peril, however critical we may be of them. So we shall need to pay close attention to Wesley's context, heeding but not daunted by Butterfield.

Many have been the assessments of John Wesley. Bishop Warburton, a notable Anglican contemporary, said of him and of Ignatius Loyola: 'Where the two talents of Fraud and Fanaticism unite to furnish out the leader of a sect, great will be the success of his undertakings.'[5] In the 1930s Henry Bett maintained, following Herbert B. Workman and George Eayrs,[6] that by the primacy given to experience in Methodist thinking, Wesley carried the Reformation to its logical conclusion. 'The religious contribution of Methodism was the recovery of the evangelical witness and the evangelical experience.' Its theological contribution was to be seen in its assertion of the offer of free grace to all and its doctrine of holiness – limitless grace and limitless love are thus the keys to Methodist theology. Bett, clearly, saw Wesley as the precursor of Schleiermacher with his stress on the experiential and the religious self-consciousness which dominated Protestant theology for a century and may still be dominant.[7] At the same time as Bett, an American, George Croft Cell,[8] saw in Wesley's theological stance 'an original and unique synthesis of the protestant ethic of grace and the catholic ethic of holiness'. This we will examine later. We should see Wesley not as a great system builder – he was no Aquinas or Calvin – but rather as a folk theologian, the thinker whose *balance* and *stance*, if not the details of his approach, still may have contemporary relevance.

One traditional – though twentieth-century – way of setting out Wesley's stance has been what has been called the 'Epworth Quadrilateral' – all need to be saved, all can be saved, all can know they are saved, all can be saved to the uttermost.[9] Some Methodists may now find this statement somewhat slick or even glib, and might prefer to substitute for it an 'Epworth Triangle' – the priority of God's universal love; the need for a personal faith; no limitations can be put to God's grace in its effect on humanity given the limitations of living in a body in a fallen world.[10]

Firstly Wesley stresses the priority of God's universal love. This is where John Wesley ran full tilt at the Calvinist doctrine of double predestination. Like Calvin – for Wesley was in the clear Reformation tradition – he was in no doubt about mankind's sinful state. 'Wherein,' he asked in 1745, 'may we come to the very edge of Calvinism? In denying all natural free will and power antecedent to grace. But God will grant that grace to all.' This is the esence of

Arminianism or the doctrine of universal grace and the free movement of the Spirit one of the legacies of that 'radical Reformation' which alongside the traditions of Lutheranism and Calvinism was such a fruitful source of religious ideas. Wesley derived this indirectly, not from Arminius but through one side of his own Anglican tradition.[11] Arminius stated that the atonement was intended to be available for all, that people are incapable of saving faith without the Holy Spirit, that divine grace is indispensable for salvation but not irresistible and that it is not certain that all believers will persevere to the end. Mankind is dependent on grace, yet is still free.[12] A rich man bestows on a poor and famishing beggar alms by which he may be able to maintain himself and his family. Does it cease to be a pure gift, because the beggar stretches out his hand to receive it?[13] Wesley insisted on the total depravity of mankind due to the Fall, but also insisted that grace goes before as prevenient grace. Mankind is certainly dependent on God for salvation – a proper Reformed position – but also has personal responsibility. Prevenient grace offered to all enables all to turn to God and makes humans responsible for their own damnation if they reject the gospel. God creates in people the freedom to receive his grace.

Wesley tries to reconcile the Protestant tradition of justification by faith – 'being declared right by faith through grace alone' with an abandonment totally of the position that God predestines some to salvation and others to damnation. As W. R. Maltby put it:

> Our theological coat was cut to the figure of total depravity, but when it was tried on, it was found not to fit any kind of human nature. Accordingly we let out a seam in the back, as far as it would go, and the margin thus gained with the stitches still showing, we call prevenient grace . . . God loves this human life of ours, not only as a moralist, approving where it is good and disapproving where it is bad, but as a poet or artist loves it, because he cannot help loving a thing so strange, piteous and enthralling as the story of every human soul should be.[14]

This is the beginning of the healing which is salvation. Wesley is always looking forward to and back from his view of man as capable of being made whole by grace. Modern revivals of the idea of Christ as the head of the whole human family, 'the light that lighteth every man', are not far from Wesley's position. E. D. Maurice and Karl Rahner spring to mind at once. Wesley put forward a view of humanity which we can call 'an optimism of grace' (the phrase is Rondet's) as distinct from the shallow optimism of the Enlightenment, which believed mankind to be originally and fundamentally good and even perfectible, and the pessimistic view of the hyper-Calvinist type in the eighteenth century.[15]

Wesley's doctrine infuriated his extreme Calvinistic opponents like Augustus Montague Toplady, who could with one hand write 'Rock of Ages' and with the other call John Wesley 'a low and puny tadpole in divinity'. But Toplady was always underrated by Methodists. If grace is free, Toplady said, there is danger of either antinomianism or Pelagianism – why bother about law at all?[16] Antinomianism was Wesley's bogey also! No doubt there were Methodists at whom the finger could be pointed, but as we shall see, Wesley protected his flank well. So Wesley stressed the universality of God's love, a matter which rings through his brother's hymns.

> The morning breaks, the shadows flee,
> Pure universal love Thou art.
> To me, to all Thy mercies move,
> Thy nature and Thy name is love.[17]

This is what G. F. Nuttall has called 'an Arminianism of the heart' which was a precondition of missionary activity undertaken that all might be saved by the power of Christ.[18] Now, can this 'Arminianism of the heart' withstand the impact of the reality of God in other religions or the almost total eclipse of hell in the mainstream Christian tradition? The first was just over Wesley's horizon and it was on the agenda of *philosophes* and writers of the Enlightenment typified by Lessing's play *Nathan der Weise* with its clear assertion of plurality of religions, all seeking the light. Hell – though never overstressed by Wesley – was part of the apparatus of the people's theologian. Perhaps at its lowest we can say that Wesley's point has been taken only too well and that the danger now is of an uncritical universalism with judgment drained away.

The second side of the triangle is the necessity of a personal faith. Like Paul and Luther before him, Wesley put his stress on faith – sure trust in God on mankind's side, acceptance, pardon on God's side, and all gift, no merit whatsoever. This is what Wesley meant when he said that he had exchanged the 'faith of a servant' (doing all he could for God) for 'the faith of a son' (accepting what God in Christ could do for him). This is faith as hope, it is also faith as assurance, an assurance that we are pardoned by God. The assurance is not that we hope to be forgiven but that we *are* forgiven now. This is an assurance of pardon and of relationship – '*Abba*, Father' – never an assurance that we are worthy. Now here is a point where there are lurking dangers, for when one talks of assurance, there is a danger of subjectivism and the self-conscious style of arrogant piety that can go with it. For some time Wesley and his preachers asserted that unless a person has a conscious assurance of salvation, he is simply not pardoned by God at all. He came, however, to see the extravagance of this. 'When fifty years ago, my brother Charles and I, in the simplicity of our heart, told the good people of England that unless they knew their sins were forgiven they were under the wrath and curse of God, I marvel Melville, they did not stone us. The Methodists, I hope, know better now. We preach assurance as we always did, as a common privilege of the children of God, but we do not enforce it under the pain of damnation.'[19] The point I would stress here is the centrality of being put in right relationships with God by grace through faith. 'I think on justification just as I have done any time these seven and twenty years and just as Mr Calvin does. In this respect I do not differ from him an hair's breadth.'[20] Right relationships are the heart of the matter.

I know of no more stimulating recent discussion of this than that of the Czech J. M. Lochman's *Living Roots of the Reformation* (1979). Lochman just avoids the danger of reading back present ideas into the past. He reads the old doctrines forward rather than judges them from a neo-Marxist stance. He sees justification by faith as enabling us to see people in right standing with God, not as workers or performers. Faith is the way in which the comprehensive practice of the new life is made possible. Lochman, like Wesley, refuses to separate individual and corporate ethics. Cut off from justice, faith becomes sentimental. In a 'performing society' – capitalist or communist – we must look to faith again to enable us to value people. I would want to add that justification by faith might save us from the awful guilt-ridden 'frantic philanthropy' which seems to be a substitute for gospel these days. Our concern for others should stem not from our guilt about the supposed sins of our imperialist grandparents but from 'the wonder why such love for me'. Anything less can lead to pharasaic self-righteousness. This is a constant peril.

Recently Lesslie Newbigin suggests that so often we say:

> Theology must be done in a particular context. So we get the context and then get the guidelines and then begin to work out answers and end with a political programme which so often means law not gospel, for if you don't agree with the programme you are a reprobate! How much of our Christian talking about the problems of industry, of economic justice, of racial equality, produces only a paralysing sense of guilt or impotence or else the blind fanaticism of the crusader who can see no moral issue in the world except the one he has chosen to concentrate on.[21]

This is the preaching of the law. Another route is to begin with people put right with God by faith who know only too well the sin and cupidity in themselves and in all human institutions, who know full well that the 'realm of grace' and the realm of 'my station and its duties', to use the phrase of F. H. Bradley, much used by A. D. Lindsay (a twentieth-century reminting of Luther's two kingdoms theory) are separate and yet intertwine together. Such a person sees no hope of utopia but, knowing himself to be a sinner, goes out as 'Christ to his neighbour' (Luther again) with maximum flexibility.

On the whole area of Christian experience, woe betide any 'charismatic movement' which thinks more of feelings and experiences than of relationships, or more of the warmed heart than the one who warms the heart and activates the mind. John Fletcher was right when he said 'I build my faith not on my experience, though this increases, but on the revealed truth of God'[22] – yet at the same time Western Protestants have tended to starve the emotions, so that a renewal of a theology of experience ought not to have taken Methodists by surprise,[23] so long as we do not attempt to impose a stereotype on people's spiritual development. Much guilt has been suffered by Methodists in recent years over this matter and there are signs that this is still the case. For many of us assurance means that fear about life's meaning goes, to be replaced by the adventure of being thrust into it without any neatly packaged answers, but with the real eye-opener which is faith in Christ produced by the Holy Spirit who makes Jesus our contemporary.[24] We may prefer to use the traditional language which speaks of the Holy Spirit at work in us, witnessing that we are children of God.

The third side of the triangle is the belief in the limitlessness of God's grace. Wesley is never static in his thinking about the relationship of people with God. Repeatedly he asserted that Christian perfection, what God does in us and with us, is the key emphasis of the Methodists. The quest for holiness was inexorably bound up with saving faith. 'This doctrine is the grand deposition which God has lodged with the people called Methodists and for the sake of propagating this chiefly he appears to have raised us up.'[25] What did Wesley teach and what can it mean, if anything, to us now?

Firstly we can survey the sources of Wesley's teaching, presupposing the Bible as his primary source. The Anglican Reformers gave him the necessary undergirding of justification by faith. The Articles and Homilies of the Church of England were patient of an Arminian interpretation. From the Moravians came his clear assertion of the necessity of new birth and the assurance of faith, that Pietist stress which would prevent Methodism from ever acceding to a conception of escalator-like progress from womb to tomb. From the Anglicanism of the Caroline tradition, especially Jeremy Taylor and William Law (and also à Kempis) came the stress on the

Christian life as utter devotion to Christ. From the Eastern Fathers, especially Gregory of Nyssa, mediated to Wesley by 'Macarius the Egyptian' (his homilies are now known to be those of a fifth century Syrian monk) came the view of perfection (*teleiosis*) as the goal (*skopos*) of the Christian in this life. As Albert Outler has shown, the conception of perfection of the Eastern Fathers as a process rather than a state gave Wesley a spiritual vision rather different from that envisaged in some Roman spiritual theology. Likewise the tendency to static quietism and the idea of imputed rather than imparted righteousness of Zinzendorf and his friends are inadequate. Thus the ancient and Eastern tradition of holiness as disciplined love became fused in Wesley's mind with his own Anglican position of holiness as aspiring love producing what he felt was a distinctive contribution to Christian thinking.[26]

Wesley was concerned with the goal of Christian life, with the 'faith that works by love'. He saw perfection as a process and took as models not only Moravians but French Catholics like Jean Baptiste de Renty (1611–1649), a pupil of de Bérulle, the Oratorian. Professor Outler summarizes Wesley's view of perfection:

> It is the conscious certainty, in a present moment, of the fullness of one's love for God and neighbours as this love has been initiated and fulfilled by God's gifts of faith, hope and love. This is not a state but a dynamic process; saving faith is its beginning, sanctification is its proper climax. As faith is in order to love, so love is in order to goodness – and so also goodness is in order to blessedness. This complex pattern of means and ends is designed to unfold in the life process itself, and thus requires some sort of temporal interval for its fulfilment.[27]

Wesley saw the essence of perfection as perfect love for God and neighbour: this rather than any kind of sinlessness is his main emphasis. It is a gift to be received rather than something to be strained after, though Wesley greatly emphasized the means of grace – the sacraments, prayer and scripture as means to the end of perfect love. For the Reformers, perfection was perfection in faith, but to Wesley it was an inherent perfection in love and obedience, not sinless perfection. There are still tempers, infirmities and mistakes as well as constant temptations. Wesley carefully 'hedges his bets'. Perfect love means a 'restless, passionate, heartbreaking, consuming concern for other people'.[28] It was a social reference which saved Wesley from mere introverted Pietism with which some of his later followers can be charged. 'The Gospel of Christ knows of no religion but social, no holiness but social holiness.'[29] Gordon Rupp sees here a combination of the Pauline and Johannine elements in the Christian testimony when within the safe orbit of sovereign grace and pardoning love he insists on the power and good pleasure of the Father to fulfil in us his perfect will.[30] Rightly Wesley could say that he aspired after what he prayed for in the Collect for Purity of the Anglican rite. 'Cleanse the thoughts of our hearts by the inspiration of the Holy Spirit that we may perfectly love Thee and worthily magnify Thy Holy Name.' Wesley's doctrine is part of his rich teaching on the work of the Holy Spirit, though the doctrine of the Spirit is never obtrusive. His positive emphasis is part of Methodism's gift to the world church – this is an 'eschatology of love' with which Wesley balances the Reformed 'eschatology of faith'. Faith, vital throughout (Wesley never departs from the undergirding of *sola fide, sola gratia*) becomes the means of which love is the end. Faith is the hand-maid of love. It might be said that if the distinctive word of the Reformers is faith and the distinctive word of Catholic spirituality is love, the distinctive word of Wesley is 'faith working by love', the two inextricably bound together. This is a balanced assertion that, given the limitations inherent in existence in a body in a fallen world, we dare set no limit to what the grace of God can do for a person here and now.

What are the criticisms which can be made of the doctrine by Methodists and non-Methodists alike? I summarize them for convenience. Wesley operates on an inadequate or rather a confusing doctrine of sin.[31] His definition of sin as a 'wilful transgression of a known law' is dangerous since it ignores the unconscious drives of human nature. In our post-Freudian days we know well enough that our worst sins are those of which we are unconscious. Sin comes, in Wesley's view, to be seen almost like a rotten tooth which can be extracted by a celestial dentist. Sin surely is the self in wrong relationship with God. No one can say whether he or she is free from sin or not. In fairness to Wesley, he has also an Augustinian view of original sin and does not stress the negative aspect of perfection, but the ambiguities in this area are serious. Wesley's stress on consciousness of guilt can cause 'guilt feelings' rather than genuine guilt to assume a dominant role and lead to what E. B. Pusey called 'salvation by feeling', accusing Methodism of woeful inadequacy at this point.[32]

It is doubtful whether a view of perfection as instantaneous can be sustained – or the notion that the 'sanctified' can be conscious of being sanctified. This is a dangerous concept apt to encourage a pharasaic type of self-appraisal. P. T. Forsyth was surely right to say 'If we ever come to any such stage as conscious sinlessness, we would be placing ourselves alongside Christ, not at his feet . . . It is certain that the perfect man will be the last to know how perfect he is.'[33] The final sentence here is pertinent to Wesley in particular. Furthermore, on the instantaneous aspect of perfection, modern biblical scholarship does not appear to support Wesley. Vincent Taylor could say, 'There is no support in New Testament teaching for the view that sanctification is a sudden and miraculous gift of the Spirit in response to importunate prayer.'[34] Since Taylor wrote, much more analysis has been done on the New Testament texts and narratives and we need to ask now what really is the nature of what many are claiming as the 'baptism of the spirit'.[35] Clearly this is a deepening of faith and experience but not perfection in Wesley's sense of the word. Methodist tradition here is deeply divided. Two distinct emphases have lived in uneasy symbiosis since Wesley's time. One stream represented by Richard Watson and William Burt Pope stresses *growth* in holiness, the other stemming from Adam Clarke, receiving support from William Arthur and the teaching of Cook, Champness and Chadwick associated with Cliff College, stresses much more a clear moment of awareness usually called the 'second blessing'.[36] The interplay here between British and American emphases is fascinating – certainly there was a 'feedback' process whereby the Cliff College tradition used the American tradition rather more than that of Watson and Pope.[37]

The average English Methodist knows little of the mainstream tradition of Christian perfection unless he has heard it through the 'second blessing' tradition or in Charles Wesley's holiness hymns which are still sung. There has been an almost wanton neglect here despite the advocacy of Newton Flew and W. E. Sangster, though both were critics of the details of Wesley's position. The undergirding of the charismatic movement by a Catholic tradition of liturgy has meant, I think, that charismatics in the more Catholic communions have been able to make their contribution in a less threatened and paranoid manner than some of their contemporaries in Methodism. The dangers of introversion here parallel what we have noted in connection with assurance. Wesley, too, in implying that holiness on earth is necessary to reach heaven not only rules out further progress beyond death, but drives a dangerous wedge between the sacred and the secular if the idea is to be pursued that the world is only to be used, while God is to be enjoyed. This point was spotted by R. W. Dale in his brilliant analysis of the Evangelical Revival.[38] A world-converting holiness is needed which sees life in the light of the love of God and which recovers a delight in the world which God has given us. We would be right to see what Matthew Arnold would have called a 'philistine' element in one of Wesley's preachers, John Pawson, who burnt Wesley's annotated copy of Shakespeare as 'worthless lumber not tending to edification'.[39]

Wesley stressed 'faith working by love'. We rightly need to take up Wesley's stress on healing and see holiness, health and wholeness as bound up together. The relationship of individual holiness to the holiness of the church is another factor which cannot be ignored. Could this bring church and medicine, especially psychiatric medicine, into creative dialogue, which, despite pioneers like Guntrip, Weatherhead and Lake, is still in its infancy? Can Maslow have anything in common with Wesley or is the cultural distance too great for dialogue to be attempted? I suspect this is now the case.[40] I suspect, too, that David Martin's trenchant analysis of what liberal theology could lead to has largely come to pass. 'Conversion would become merged in notions like maturity; holiness would approximate to psychological health and Christian assurance to confidence. Sin is translatable into the terminology of alienation or neurosis. The peace of God may be either peace between nations or an unruffled temper. Grace can even be translated into moral and social graces. In sum "God" becomes a combination of an ideal society and the extrapolation of human potentiality and dominion: Durkheim and Feuerbach vindicated.' Wesley's doctrine is basically individualist even if he always stressed its social aspect and the need for growth in a group setting which does latch on to a good deal of modern thinking.[41]

What then is left after the critical comments? Putting it positively, we can derive from the doctrine a goal for living. The goal is perfect love. So often it is true of Christians that they are content with spiritual mediocrity. We have in Wesley's teaching an incentive for living in the work of the Holy Spirit that is intended for all Christians. Wesley would have nothing to do with that 'double standard' which has always been both the blessing and the bane of Catholic spirituality. Love is seen as the characteristic of the Christian. Wesley's doctrinal stance is compatible with the insight also of group dynamics studies and *Gestalt* psychology and the stress on the healing of the whole person which could bring church and medicine into creative dialogue, which we would be most foolish if we thought this in any way a Methodist monopoly. We have to ask of any community: 'Is it producing whole, healthy people or maimed, stunted people?'

Recently J. G. Davies in *Every Day God* (1973) has set up a new 'model' of holiness. Holiness is linked with *shalom*, a totality including a harmonious community with openness as its characteristic. As each person realizes his or her potentialities and approaches nearer to his or her human perfection and maturity, he or she is approaching the condition of Christ and finding the holy. Such a movement is centred on the service of our neighbours. Davies points to such exemplars of 'worldly holiness' as Dag Hammarskjöld, Camillo

Torres, revolutionary priest, and Danilo Dolci identifying with the poor of Sicily. This is to find the Holy God in the midst of life. Here certainly is a development of one side of the matter; the Wesleyan emphasis would supply the element of grace largely lacking in Davies.

A new style of thinking, now emerging from the Catholic tradition, may prove more penetrating. This is the concept of the 'second journey' which follows on the integration of the 'first journey' of childhood, puberty, adolescence and early adulthood with its frequent high endeavour and motivation. Wesley himself in his utter devotion to Christ (the faith of a servant) is a good example. The 'breaking' process in Georgia leads to the 'Aldersgate experience' and the subsequent energies and spiritual productivity of the 'second journey'. For many, bereavement or break-up of marriage or a decision which cannot be put off, loss or change of job, may be factors in the beginning of a 'second journey'. Wesley's doctrine of perfection with its combination of *process* and *crisis* can be re-interpreted in the light of this new insight of what can happen spiritually to what we could call the 'Nicodemus' generation needing to begin anew, though it could be linked with justification also. Contemporary 'Third World' Methodism is striving, too, to develop a new style of holiness which is corporate rather than individualistic, stressing justice as well as freedom and peace. The fact that Methodism in the developing nations wishes to explore Wesley more deeply gives some hope that the stream has not yet dried up.[42]

Wesley drew on rich resources of Eastern Christianity and Counter-Reformation spirituality as well as on Protestantism. It has been claimed that he produced an 'original and unique synthesis of a Protestant ethic of grace and the Catholic ethic of holiness'. This might suggest a hodge-podge of Catholic doctrine and Protestant spirituality. Wesley, indeed, like Marx, was more than a synthesizer. He brought back to Protestantism a dominating concern for holiness and the restoration of moral aspiration to a central place in the life of the believer.[43] This is not a mongrel blend of Protestantism and Catholicism but rather a genuine 'Catholic evangelicalism'. It is of no little significance that holiness was in the last analysis the dominant concern of the Tractarians. 'Holiness without which no man can see the Lord' was almost the slogan of John Henry Newman. The tragedy was that a rather narrow Methodism which had lost much of Wesley's rich sacramentalism met an aggressive high Anglicanism with neither side exploring together the concept of 'acceptance' and the Catholic ethic of holiness. There is still much ground to explore here. Modern Anglo-Catholics, quite unconsciously, are on a track similar to classical Wesleyanism.

St Thomas Aquinas spoke of '*fides caritate formata*' – 'faith formed by love' – and assumed that God cannot receive mankind into fellowship with himself unless people merit it by fulfilling his law.[44] God infuses his love into us before accepting us. In other words, for Thomas, mankind must be sanctified, made fit, by some means or other if he is to be justified in the sight of a God who is himself just and holy. Wesley begins with humanity as it is. 'It is not a saint but a sinner who is forgiven and under the notion of a sinner.' He preached not 'faith formed by love' but 'love formed by faith', sanctification flowing out of justification. Holiness does not mean beginning as a saint (except in the New Testament sense) and excluding sinners, but accepting sinners with a view to making them saints in the fullest sense of the word. This is not far from that 'activism in grace' which H. O. Evennett saw as the hallmark of the spirituality of the Counter Reformation. A comparison between the views of Contarini at Ratisbon in 1541, the Canons of the Council of Trent and John Wesley reveal striking similarities, even if Wesley would have shuffled the Tridentine pack of theological cards somewhat differently. The same could be said *mutatis mutandis* of John Henry Newman's *Lectures on Justification* which, despite their Aristotelian logic, are nearer to the teaching of William Burt Pope than meets the eye.[45] It is perhaps significant that a recent study of the concept of righteousness in Paul by J. A. Ziesler,[46] a New Zealand Methodist scholar, points to the possibility that when Paul speaks of righteousness verbally – i.e. to be made right or just – he is talking in terms of relationships, acceptance by God, but that when he is talking of righteousness as a noun, he is thinking of change, moral change. Maybe this is what Wesley was straining after and where the link between Methodist spirituality and Catholic thinking can begin to be made.

Lastly, what of John Wesley as Christian conservative? Wesley made no pretensions to being a politician, though he emitted a stream of political pamphlets! In stance he was conservative, which at his time in economic thinking meant an adoption not of the new style *laissez-faire* market economies of Adam Smith and Ricardo, but an espousal of the older mercantalism.[47] Classical Christian conservatism bears little resemblance to that guyed by Daniel Jenkins as defending the prosperity of the previous generation.[48] The stress is on human imperfection, on corporate continuity and tradition, an organic view of the state or of politics, an Augustinianism which characterized both Luther and Wesley, though what Rondet and Rupp called 'optimism of grace' showed Wesley's mutation of it as more synergistic, a matter taken up by Bernard Semmel, who sees Wesleyanism as keying in with the democratic ideas described by R. R. Palmer[49] as emanating from America at this time. If Luther shows Christ and culture 'in paradox', to use Richard Niebuhr's categories, Wesley can be seen as a 'transformer' of culture. Clearly Wesley's appeal to the aspiring is important here and may give a clue to subsequent Methodist political philosophy. Wesley's politics were realistic, not utopian, stemming from his Toryism which has to be seen as in opposition to dominant Whig groups in his time, a matter often overlooked,[50] though since Namier it has not been possible to speak in terms of the modern party system when defining eighteenth-century political terminology. It was Wilberforce (to whom Wesley's last letter on slavery was sent, with its thrust at racism which denied the validity of a black man's oath against a white man's – 'What villainy is this?' said Wesley) and the seventh Earl of Shaftesbury who did more for the poor than most Whigs and Liberals until T. H. Green gave liberalism a philosophy of moderate collectivism and a new utilitarianism which led to a crusade for social justice under Lloyd George. Conservation of nationhood is another Conservative characteristic – there is not a little of that in Wesley as in Burke, though Wesley can combine eulogies of the King with scepticism about an established church, a kind of latter-day non-juring spirit, if not directed at the monarchy.

Wesley was an autocrat without the humbug of condescension or *noblesse oblige*. He could at times be called a Tory radical, save that his style was hardly that of Disraeli! He was an opponent of revolution, American or French, and at the same time a friend of the poor who were helped by neither. He was a man who could traipse for hours in the London snow collecting for charity, who gave almost all his wealth away, having a horror of capital accumulation or luxurious living. 'The undeserving poor' got far more support from him than do the 'undeserving rich' whom he lambasts as wastrels. The poor gave Wesley a welcome and an audience. He saw them as receptive and humble with hidden talents which Methodism was able to awaken. As John Walsh has recently put it, 'In Wesley's hands the denunciatory side of the Protestant work ethic is directed against the rich and not the poor.'[51]

His economics may seem naïve now but he disclaimed political acumen and did not consider himself a politician.[52] In a strange way he was both a man of the Age of Reason and yet in touch with the mixture of magic and Christianity which made for popular religion. He somehow straddled the world of rich and poor, a stance which was taken up years later by one of the greatest Methodists since Wesley, John Scott Lidgett (1854–1953)[53] who lived in comparative poverty for decades in the Bermondsey Settlement in the East End of London while active in several spheres at once – ecumenism, university education, LCC politics (he led the Progressives, i.e.

Liberals), journalism and national education from 1902 to 1944. Lidgett combined Wesley's intense personal teaching with the broader theology of F. D. Maurice. Wesley's legacy to Methodism in general – for Lidgett was somewhat exceptional – was of a style of politics which we may call moralistic – seizing on moral issues and bringing them before the nation, though as Henry Rack, John Kent and others have shown, rarely changing the mood of politics unless larger groups in society agreed with the stance taken.[54] If Hugh Price Hughes and Henry Carter are taken as the characteristically activist ministerial Methodists, Robert Perks and Arthur Henderson can be seen as characteristic lay Methodists immersed in politics, espousing on the one hand Liberal imperialism and on the other international idealism.

To summarize a complex matter. Wesley's religious legacy was a basic quadrilateral of Bible, tradition, religious experience and reason.[55] If the Bible is isolated from all else, bibliolatry follows which was never characteristic of Wesley even if he called himself 'a man of one book'. If tradition is isolated, a wooden conservatism can follow but Wesley avoided that with his principle of the priority of the gospel. If religious experience is overstressed, the *Schwärmerei* takes over which Wesley would never allow, even if he was naïve sometimes about other people's experiences. The danger of the charismatic emphasis is that subjectivism always lurking beneath the surface of the Methodist sub-culture which has always been an uneasy fellowship of revivalist and churchman. Yet if reason is over-stressed, the dry arid 'Arminianism of the head' results against which Wesley was in full attack! The balance may yet be Methodism's contribution to the world church, A balance in which a concern for the needs of the world can combine with a proper concern for the evangelization and salvation of the individual which was at the heart of Wesley's theology and practice and is more than an 'antique drum' which his latter-day followers ritually beat when aroused. The irony of Wesley's quadrilateral is that fundamentally it is the theology of Richard Hooker. It is the pure milk of later Reformed Anglicanism which Wesley always claimed to espouse. The tragedy of modern Methodism is that it was ready to share its inheritance with its old mother but her younger Anglo-Catholic sons still shut the door against her and somehow she has to brood over the treasures alone.

5

From Connexion to Denomination –
Two Case Studies: Wesleyanism 1791–1850
and Primitive Methodism 1807–1932

Much historical and sociological research on the morphology of sect groups has been done since Max Weber first propounded a dichotomy of church and sect, followed by Ernst Troeltsch's threefold division of sects, churches, spirituals and mystics. Church can easily become norm, if you support it, or denigrated Establishment, if you don't; sect can be seen too easily as aberration, enthusiastic coterie or genuine carrier of faith.[1] Typologies have become highly complex like those of H. Becker and J. M. Yinger, who subdivides into universal church (Methodism is ranked here), *ecclesia*, denomination, established sects (e.g. the Salvation Army), sects and cults. Bryan Wilson propounded a useful sevenfold categorization of sects. More recently the development of sect into denomination has become central in sociological and historical analysis of which an outstanding recent example is the work of Elizabeth Isichei on the Quakers. She modifies Becker's statement that 'denominations are simply sects in an advanced stage of development and adjustment to each other and to the secular world'. The need clearly is for detailed analysis of particular development.[2]

Liston Pope in *Millhands and Preachers*[3] itemized twenty-one indices in the transition or development. Wesleyanism and Primitive Methodism can be measured against them. This is Pope's 'control' or model: (1) from membership of the propertyless to membership of property owners; (2) from economic poverty to economic wealth, as shown by the value of church property and ministerial salaries; (3) from the cultural periphery to the cultural centre of the community; (4) from renunciation of or indifference to the prevailing culture and society to affirmation of it; (5) from personal to institutional religion; (6) from non-co-operation with or ridicule of established religious institutions to co-operation with them; (7) from suspicion of rival sects to disdain and pity for all sects; (8) from a moral community excluding unworthy members to a social institution embracing all who are socially compatible within it; (9) from an unprofessionalized part-time ministry to a full-time ministry; (10) from a psychology of persecution to a psychology of success and dominance; (11) from voluntary, confessional membership to ritualized membership (such as previous membership of another acceptable denomination or socialization by the denomination itself); (12) from being predominantly concerned with adult members to equal concern with children; (13) from emphasis on evangelism and conversion to emphasis on religious education; (14) from emphasis on death and a future in the next world to emphasis on life and a future in this life; (15) from adherence to strict biblical standards such as tithing and non-resistance to acceptance of general cultural standards of religious obligation; (16) from a high degree of congregational participation in services to delegation of responsibility to a small minority; (17) from fervour and activity in worship to restraint and passivity; (18) from a comparatively large number of religious services to a programme of regular services at stated intervals (evidence of the compartmentalization and institutionalization of the religious style); (19) from reliance on spontaneity in worship and administration to a fixed order of service and administrative procedure; (20) from use of hymns derived from folk music to slower, more stately hymns derived from a remote liturgical tradition; (21) from emphasis on religion in the home to delegation to church officers and organizations.

Pope's indices are far from being totally satisfactory criteria but to place Wesleyanism and Primitive Methodism alongside them spotlights distinct differences, not least in constituency. Pope's first index presupposes Richard Niebuhr's claim that a sect is a religious group which rejects the social environment in which it exists and takes its rise in the religious revolts of the poor. Wesleyanism, as we have seen, made its appeal basically to artisans. Primitive Methodism appealed often to a somewhat lower stratum of the population. In each case 'respectable' poor would tend to rise in the social scale when imbued with the virtues of thrift, frugality and earnestness. Wesleyanism certainly built on a large scale as did all the later Methodist groups, but ministerial stipends were always modest, touching only £250 per annum by 1932. Primitive Methodist itinerant preachers were near their proletarian roots and remained comparatively poorly paid. Wesleyanism, however, began in the university and was never without its cultured élites and 'cousinhoods'. Primitive Methodism's development from Hugh Bourne and William Clowes to Arthur S. Peake is much more akin to Pope's 'model' here, though Methodism has never been at the cultural centre.

Wesley is probably rightly characterized as a 'transformer' of culture by Richard Niebuhr.[4] Wesleyanism has never been aligned with a 'Christ against culture' mentality and it could be said in the latter part of the nineteenth century to have embodied the *mores* of a section of the middle class seeking to impose their culture on others. This is one element in the Nonconformist conscience. Primitive Methodism was culturally more monochrome and could more easily be identified with social *malaise* such as that often called the 'revolt of the field'. The tension which Pope stresses between personal and institutional religion was prevalent in Methodism from its origins. There has always been an uneasy symbiosis of churchman and revivalist. Primitive Methodism was more resistant to hierarchical control and more local in its style than the more centralized Wesleyanism which split on this very issue. Ridicule of established order was never a Wesleyan characteristic, despite Wesley's principle of the gospel overriding church order, but some of the early Methodists were clearly more Donatist or exclusive than Wesley himself. There was, from above, always resistance to any attempt to increase the distance between Wesleyanism and the Church of England, despite the pressures impelling it into the Free Church camp. Primitive Methodism was always more a genuinely dissenting group with few Anglican corpuscles in its bloodstream. Wesleyanism always had a more 'churchly' look about it; the other Methodist groups were seen as rivals, then somewhat reluctantly as allies within one confessional family. Neither Wesleyanism nor Primitive Methodism were ever sectarian in the sense that the society was thought wholly exclusive. Rejection from it was never tantamount to excommunication from the wider church. The prolonged Victorian controversies over the class meeting as a test of membership revealed the impact of a wider social group impinging on Methodism.[5] It can also be seen as a sign of a latent secularization. Clearly the stress was moving from evangelism to nurture and socialization in both groups.[6]

The change from an amateur to a professional full-time ministry is as true of the Church of England as it is of Wesleyanism. The eighteenth-century parson developed into the professional priest. The development from itinerant preacher to localized circuit minister is a parallel development, with institutions for ministerial training to match it. By 1820 Wesleyanism was claiming to be a stabilizing force in English society even if only as a form of self-defence. Primitive Methodists felt themselves to be 'everywhere spoken against' in their early days and hardly ever enjoyed the fleshpots of power. What Pope calls 'ritualized membership' was certainly becoming common in early Victorian Wesleyanism. By 1837 the Wesleyans were stressing infant baptism, though revivalism was never without its supporters. Primitive Methodism, though it had its 'high-churchmen', was never sacramental at any deep level – membership could be a very casual matter. A feature of Wesleyanism after 1830 was a greater concern for children, with Sunday schools changing their role from social control to the Christian nurture of Methodist families – a sign of lack of expansion like the changes in the class meeting from evangelism to fellowship.

Methodism was never wholly otherworldly or millenarian, but a glance at the *Methodist Magazine* in its various styles illustrates a slow transition. Hell has moved off the scene by the 1870s. Methodism never demanded tithing or even total abstinence of its members (Primitive Methodism was more solidly behind the temperance banner) but again a transition of style can be traced. 'Christian stewardship' is rather far removed from the 'rules of society'. On styles of worship, Pope's model does not readily fit. Wesley combined 'instituted' with 'prudential' means of grace though there were always Wesleyans who preferred the latter and felt that the instituted liturgical modes were 'unmethodist'. The issue was clearer in Primitive Methodism, where there was no overt Anglican element. The transition here was from a charismatic-revivalist style to one which could look like an over-dominance of the preacher. Hymn singing and music always played a larger role in Methodist congregational participation than in most other religious groups. Was there a shift from fervour and activity in worship to restraint and passivity? Again there was much plurality in Methodism from the beginning, ranging from the charismatic to stately liturgy in some of the principal urban chapels. The institutionalization of services occurred very early on also. The phenomenon of the 'preaching plan' which so baffles or irritates other churches because of its long-term time budgeting, was to be found in every Methodist group including the tiniest minor schisms.

Methodism inherited a dual tradition of worship and was always comparatively highly organized, though the period of Jabez Bunting produced an even more centralized constitutional procedure, which was paralleled much later in Primitive Methodism. In that communion, too, official service books were a comparatively late phenomenon, though hymn books (as is often the case in the English Free Churches) always produced a measure of liturgical uniformity. Pope's mention of hymnody is quite misleading, since he confuses hymns and tunes. The matter is complex in Methodism. Early tunes included Handelian styles like 'Gopsal' and 'Jericho Tune' as well as more florid styles. Charles Wesley's hymns provided a staple of rich content from the beginning. Hymns 'lined out' by the preachers clearly taught doctrine – *lex orandi* very much became *lex credendi*.

Wesley's hymns also had an amazing variety of metre and language. In Primitive Methodism the development from the Dow-Bourne books to the book edited by John Flesher in 1853 was certainly a move from a revivalist to a more broadly based hymnody. Pope's last point does not shed much light on Methodism which in all its forms has attracted people from artisans to folk somewhat higher up the social scale by giving scope for office to a largish number in any one congregation.

Pope's analysis, though helpful, is not easily applicable to Wesleyanism. It is more applicable to Primitive Methodism which reflected revivalism much more than other styles of Methodism save for the Bible Christians in the West Country. The concept of the denomination[7] can certainly be applied to Wesleyanism. David Martin sees it as 'His Majesty's loyal religious opposition always out of office'. This is a fair analogy until it becomes clear that the established church also becomes one denomination among many in the nineteenth century despite the anachronisms and panoplies of prestige. This is certainly the case after 1829, by which date both Dissent and Catholicism were free of mere toleration and moving towards equality before the law. Methodism fits uneasily into sociological typologies. Joachim Wach, more perceptively, saw it as an example of the *'ecclesiola in ecclesia'*, comparing it fruitfully with Pietism.[8] This is not far from the mark. Michael Hill, elaborating on Wach, sees elements of the 'religious order' about early Methodism, a matter to which, with regret at its non-consummation, E. B. Pusey referred in 1862. The idea of Methodism as a kind of misplaced ecclesiastical 'province' has been adumbrated also recently.[9] It bears a distinct resemblance to the plan which Fletcher formulated. This seems a pipe dream in an eighteenth-century context. If a sect is a religious group which rejects the social environment in which it exists, then that definition fits neither Methodism nor orthodox dissent in England. 'The history of Methodism together with that of the Congregationalists, and to some extent the Baptists, begins in a "spiritual brotherhood" or Holy Club which in turn becomes *ecclesiola in ecclesia* and finally a denomination, but at no point approximates to a sect.'[10] I would modify this to state that Methodism began as a society which may be defined as a 'group of earnest believers who are determined to improve the quality of the spiritual life by a regular spiritual discipline and to invite others to share it with them without any repudiation of fellowship with those who live the Christian life in a different manner.'[11] This definition is a little ideal, since it does not take into account the tendency to what we have called Donatism in any élite religious group, but it is reasonably accurate. The societies coalesce into a connexion which has a more centralized base.

There were a plurality of connexions in the eighteenth century of which that cohering around John Wesley as 'charismatic leader', to use the Weberian concept, was by far the largest but certainly not unique. Connexion can develop into denomination within a generation or two. I use the word 'development' precisely here rather than evolution to avoid the 'fallacy of origins' and the view of some that the subsequent evolution leads to mere religious coral reefs, 'burnt out shells of once burning personal religiosity',[12] though the bleak, barren, empty chapels of West Yorkshire and Lancashire make even that statement not ridiculous. To explore the development of a connexion into a denomination is to explore the self-identity of a religious group, a style of research now being applied to the early church.[13] We shall look firstly at Wesleyanism and then Primitive Methodism where the pattern can be seen in a much more sharply defined shape, almost classical in form, a development from the charismatic leadership of a William Clowes to the cool scholarship tipped with evangelical warmth of Arthur Samuel Peake, with a 'routinization of charisma' which has the air almost of inevitability about it.

When Wesley died on 2 March 1792, he left behind a connexion of 72,476 members with many more adherents and supporters. The term 'connexion' which we have clearly differentiated from 'sect' or 'society' can be defined as 'a number of societies who have agreed to unite themselves in a common bond of doctrine and discipline, under a common code of regulations and usages and under a common government'.[14] As such, Methodism was already largely independent of the Church of England, but the connexion was with Wesley himself. What would happen now? Where would *episcopē* or oversight lie? How was the problem of leadership to be resolved? What was to be the relationship of preachers and people? What was to be the relationship of the connexion, and the individuals who comprised it, with the Church of England?

The problems must be seen in their context of a rising population, urbanization, fluctuating social discontent, and the impact of the French Revolution after which nothing in politics or religion would ever be the same again. While it is difficult to obtain accurate population figures before the census of 1801, it is clear that the population had increased from about 5,000,000 to 9,000,000 in England and Wales in the eighteenth century and was to reach 18,000,000 by 1851. In 1750 there had been only two cities in Britain with more than 50,000 inhabitants – London and Edinburgh. In 1801 there were already eight, in 1851 twenty-nine. By this time more Britons lived in towns than in the country and almost one-third of them lived in towns of over 50,000 inhabitants. No change in human life since the beginning of civilization has been as profound as the coming of industrialization. In 1700 the five most populous counties are believed to have been Middlesex, Somerset, Gloucestershire, Wiltshire and Northamptonshire. In 1800 they were Middlesex, Lancashire, the West Riding of Yorkshire, Staffordshire and Warwickshire.[15] The cotton towns grew fastest – the parish of Manchester increased in population from 125,911 in 1801 to 515,581 in 1851. Then there was growth in the 'iron' towns, then the centres of the woollen industry. Bradford grew from 13,264 inhabitants in 1801, to 103,378 in 1851 to 288,458 in 1911. An important factor was the rapid settlement of dense working-class populations outside the narrow limits of the existing towns. We have already noted that early Methodism became strongest in industrial areas. From 1791 to 1815 the number of members increased from 72,476 to 181,709, with the greatest strength in Yorkshire, Lancashire, Staffordshire, County Durham, Northumberland, Middlesex and Cornwall. In 1800 Wesleyanism represented 0.85 per cent of the population; by 1830 it was 1.53 per cent of the population.[16]

It was in the new industrial areas that the established church was at its most weak and ineffective and was generally to remain so until after the Napoleonic Wars, if not until the reforming legislation under Peel. The much more flexible organization of Methodism was to provide religious services for multitudes who were not reached in any way by the Church of England. 'Where the national church required an Act of Parliament, a grant of money, an educated gentleman and a crop of lawyers, the Methodists required only a friendly barn and a zealous preacher – at least for a beginning.'[17] In many, though not all, areas where Methodism achieved its greatest results, the accommodation in the parish church was totally inadequate, even with the often disregarded system of proprietary chapels. In 1815 the Province of York still had only 2,000 parishes compared with 10,000 in the Province of Canterbury. In Manchester there were still only 56 churches when the population was 515,581. In Liverpool the total church accommodation amounted to about 21,000 seats for a population of 94,000; a little later in Oldham the figures were 1,700 for 18,000, in Stockport 2,000 for 33,393, in Walsall 700 for 9,389. In the woollen towns the same picture can be drawn. In 1837 the Vicar of Leeds was still pastorally responsible for a population of some 125,000 people with a chapelry system which had proved unworkable even in the eighteenth century. 'There is little doubt that Methodism owed its early and substantial success in Leeds to the weakness of the Anglican chapelry system and the lack of

Anglican churches in the rapidly growing areas of the town.' Bradford was very similar. Between 1800 and 1840 only three Anglican churches were built as the population boomed from 13,264 to 66,715. In 1851 Bradford had the third-highest proportion of Nonconformists in the urban areas of England. The situation in London was hardly better. The Duke of Portland compelled the parish of Marylebone, with a population of 40,000, to be content with a village church. Earl Stanhope maintained that 4,000,000 people in England had no means of attending church.[18]

With revolution in the air, local magnates were alarmed. In 1792 the Mayor of Liverpool wrote to the Home Office urging the government to build churches in the numerous villages that had sprung up with the growth of manufactures, giving his reasons as not the advantages of spiritual exercises but the danger of leaving these places to the Methodists. 'For, Sir, in all these places are nothing but Methodist and other meeting houses and as the people in the country are in general disposed to go to some place of worship on the Sunday they go to these because there is none other; and thus the youth of the country are trained up under the instruction of a set of men whom I think we have of late too much reason to imagine are inimical to our happy constitution.' One of the factors justifying the grant in 1818 for the building of churches was this very argument, with which we shall be concerned later. There seems little doubt that the lack of provision for worship for multitudes of the new populations of the towns was a cardinal factor in the increasing separation of Methodism from the Church of England which occurred in the years 1791–95 and afterwards.[19] This can often enough be added to the element of Donatism or exaggerated strictness which tended to characterize the connexion, to many of whose members the Church of England was lax and even sub-Christian, a matter which angered not a few Anglicans who feared sectarianism.[20]

The Methodists after Wesley's death sought to follow his footsteps but quickly took divergent paths, each group believing itself to be in the true Wesleyan succession. On 30 March 1791, after his death, a number of prominent preachers met in Halifax to discuss the future of the connexion. Their views were printed and distributed throughout the circuits of Methodism – the first of a host of suggestions and counter-suggestions. They boldly faced the key problem – How was the government of Methodism to be carried on? 'There appear to be but two ways – either to appoint another "King in Israel" or to be governed by the Conference Plan, by forming ourselves into Committees'. They proposed an annual President of Conference, a series of committees with a president – the embryo of districts and district chairmen. Similar meetings were held elsewhere, notably at Bristol and Birmingham, with similar conclusions, though the laymen of Cornwall meeting at Redruth on 14 July highly disapproved of the proposals for dividing the kingdom into districts, conceiving that it would be injurious to Methodism. They also proposed far-reaching changes in the local constitution for the Methodist Societies, urging that much more power be placed in the hands of society stewards, chosen not by the preachers but the people. These two resolutions illustrate the tension in Methodism on the subject of internal church government and are portents of a conflict which was to divide the connexion again and again from 1797 onwards. Final *episcopē* or oversight had clearly resided in Wesley himself. With the adoption of the 'Halifax Scheme' in the Conference of 1791, *episcopē* was transferred to the Conference, or more strictly to the Legal Hundred. There were to be 'no more Kings in Israel'; instead, in the curious phrase of the time, the Conference was to be 'the living Wesley'.[21]

Bound up with the internal problem of leadership was the relation of preacher and people which involved presidency at the sacraments and ultimately relationship with the Establishment. Discussion of the matter began in the circuits after Wesley's death. One group of Methodists, representative mainly of the more wealthy laymen, was strongly opposed to any widening of the gulf between the connexion and the Establishment with which they had strong social links. Their views were typified by resolutions issued by eighteen laymen of Hull, dated 4 May 1791. Their point is made clearly: 'We are well convinced that the usefulness of the Methodists has been and will be greatly increased by their continuance in Connexion with the Church of England; and we believe, as did the late Mr Wesley, those of them who separate from the Church of England will dwindle away into a dry, dull, separate party. We cannot consent to have the sacraments administered among us by the Methodist preachers nor to have the preaching in the Methodist chapels during the hours of divine service in the church.' Similar resolutions were adopted at Bristol and Birmingham and circulated throughout the connexion at the behest of Joseph Benson, one of the more conservative of the preachers, and at Sheffield when the preachers attested that they knew no person in the circuit who did not entertain the same views.

Replies came from laymen at Birmingham who did not approve of Benson's action, and from Newcastle-on-Tyne – where a young preacher named Alexander Kilham was beginning to exert a powerful influence. Challenging the Hull laymen, the Newcastle Methodists wrote: 'You brethren at Hull have ministers in the church, which perhaps exceed all others for purity and uprightness of conduct; (probably a reference to Joseph Milner) but do your pious ministers prevent profligate sinners from approaching the altar? Do they resolve they shall not share in the ordinance till they are at least reformed in their outward conduct? . . . Let us ask, do you believe in your heart, your preachers are called of God, to the work of the Ministry?' This pamphlet, not without Donatist overtones, represents the party of separation among Methodists, many of whom would echo Kilham's sentiments.

> It appears that our being closely united to the Established Church is founded on reasons not justifiable from the scriptures. It is more honourable to attend service at the church than to worship among the Dissenters! It takes away a good deal of the scandal of the Cross. It may be advantageous to our business in the world . . . Our being connected so closely with the church cannot be looked on in any other light than a specious trimming between God and the world. We never met with any arguments for our continuing closely united with the church but what are political – or in other words sold under sin.

Kilham's rather bitter words underline the tendency of some of the more wealthy members of the connexion to favour the Establishment rather than Dissent, but some of the separatists were sacramentalists and some wished for an episcopal system.[22]

The majority of Methodists preferred a more empirical middle way and their counsels prevailed at the Manchester Conference of 1791. William Thompson, then at Halifax, who had no aspirations to power and adhered to neither of the extreme groups, was elected President. Conference agreed to a policy of 'no change' on the sacramental issue. Thompson had expressed his opinions to Joseph Benson at Birmingham[23] just before Conference, advising him to 'stick to the old plan'. 'Do what you are doing now. If you preach in church hours or "without book" or baptize, go on so doing.' Conference adopted an ambiguous resolution – 'We engage to follow strictly the plan which Mr Wesley left us.' As William Myles[24] pointed out, 'This answer was variously interpreted according to the wishes of the two parties already mentioned.' No doubt Joseph Benson and the laymen of Hull could interpret the 'old plan' to mean close liaison with the Church of England, others like John Pawson could say, 'Not so, our "old plan" has been to follow the openings of Providence.'[25] Some of the preachers ordained by Wesley continued to administer the sacraments and more ordinations at district level took place. In this manner three of the preachers were ordained at the Newcastle District Meeting and three others at Manchester, including Bradburn. Ordinations certainly continued and it can be argued that Conference sought to control them rather than forbid them.[26]

The Conference of 1791 had achieved a false peace by shelving vital issues. In the circuits the issue could not be so easily set aside. Debate became furious. At a united meeting of the Leeds, Wakefield, Sheffield, Birstall, Dewsbury, Bradford and other circuits it was unanimously agreed in May 1792 'not to separate from the church'. About a month later the preachers belonging to the Leicester, Northampton, Nottingham and Derby District came to a similar conclusion, resolving to 'remain in the present situation with regard to the Established Church'. The Stockton preachers concurred, not so those of Newcastle who wished 'full liberty to receive the sacrament among themselves or at church, or wherever they can most to their satisfaction'. They would not be deprived of the Lord's Supper.[27]

Disturbance was growing as was social discontent – the London Conference was hard pressed to find some agreement. Another interim solution was found by the apostolic precedent of drawing lots! Adam Clarke, standing on a table, drew the lot. 'You shall not give the sacrament this year.' Ordinations were forbidden 'without the consent of Conference first obtained . . . The Lord's Supper shall not be administered by any person among our societies in England and Ireland for the ensuing year on any consideration, except in London.'[28] The lofty aims of the 1792 Conference were not fulfilled. Events moved towards a crisis. 'I am well satisfied,' said John Pawson, the President of the Conference, 'that except liberty is given to those preachers and those societies who wish to have the sacrament, we shall have a division both among the preachers and people.'[29] Bristol became the focal point of division.[30]

On 26 August 1792 the new chapel at Portland Street was opened. At the request of the trustees the preachers for the day, Samuel Bradburn and Thomas Roberts, read matins in gowns, bands and surplices, an assuming of clerical dress which angered the local incumbent, the Revd W. E. Edwards of Westbury-on-Trym. This, to him, was 'unwarranted usurpation . . . Your design is obvious, you make the form of our establishment an allurement to procure a congregation . . . You are dissenters according to the strictest sense and meaning of the expression.' Bradburn – very much a Methodist radical – replied swiftly. Edwards' letter is described as 'thinly disguised malevolence' and this 'from an awakened clergyman, truly justified'. The note of pique there disguises the frequent inability of Methodists to see that Evangelicals regarded them as unnecessary, if there was an Evangelical around! Bradburn makes it clear that at Portland Street there is a communion table and a burial ground and that 'we shall certainly baptize the children of our people who desire it. We shan't marry (i.e. solemnize matrimony). We do not consider you when thus employed in a religious capacity, but an officer of the state.' This is not only a very old Puritan sentiment, but Bradburn seemed unaware that dissenting marriages would not be legal at this time, unless Jews or Quakers were involved. 'In everything that relates to the office of minister of Jesus Christ, I consider myself as standing on equal ground with you.' Bradburn admits Edwards' charge of dissent and claims to be a dissenting minister presumably on the basis of his ordination in 1792.

Bradburn soon afterwards wrote another pamphlet of considerable importance which contains a clear statement of the various viewpoints of the time.[31] In typical Wesleyan manner Bradburn defines separation as staying away from the parish church altogether, though he considers Dr Coke virtually left the church by becoming an itinerant preacher. He then summarizes the views of those who think the Methodists are 'church people' – they do not disapprove of the hierarchical constitution of the church which was one prime cause of early dissent, they have no scruples regarding manner of worship, they believe all the doctrines of the church as contained in the Book of Common Prayer, the Creeds, the Articles and the Homilies; they have no objection to canon law; and their practice makes them good churchmen. The views of the dissenters are then presented. Methodist preaching places are licensed as dissenting places of worship; the preachers are licensed as dissenting preachers; the preachers are not under any episcopal control, the service is often in church hours and is either of a dissenting type or is one in which a prayer book is used containing an un-Anglican ordinal; finally Methodists often speak against the church. 'Methodists in connexion with the late Mr John Wesley are in general . . . on the side of the Established Church, in their constitution or church government they are mild presbyterians . . . some of them regularly go to church in (what are called) canonical hours, others occasionally conform, as many other dissenters do, in receiving the Lord's Supper and many thousands of them are simply hearers of their own preachers and seldom go anywhere else.' Then follows an amazingly sane and liberal scheme for what can only be called 're-union' of Methodism with the Church of England, which bears a close resemblance to that of Fletcher of Madeley and which has as its cardinal point a proposed ordination of all preachers of over seven years' standing. If the bishops will not agree to this, then if Methodists are still to call themselves 'church people', they must shut up their places of worship in church hours and go to church or cease to call themselves 'church people'. He concludes, 'I give it as my opinion that while all the Methodists who choose it, go to church, and all who do not, have full liberty to receive the ordinances from their own preachers under the direction and control of the Conference, the Connexion will stand as part of the Church of Christ on the rock of ages, and the gates of hell shall not prevail against it.'

This kind of thinking commended itself to many, but the 'church party' was still strong and eager to maintain its own interpretation of the 'old plan'. Benson was in Birmingham[32] when the mob was hot for 'Church and King'. Thomas Coke, earlier, gloomily feared 'a bloody summer and a headless king' as more than a mere republican toast.[33] Joseph Entwistle (1767–1841) passing through Manchester in the summer of 1792 saw on the one hand democrats carrying an effigy of Pitt as if he were Guy Fawkes, while patriots boozed gloomily in the inns singing the National Anthem.[34] If Methodism remained politically quietist, the events in political life influenced its decision-making quite clearly.

The 'Church Party' can be said to have gained a Pyrrhic victory at the Leeds Conference in 1793[35] when resolutions were passed forbidding preachers to wear clerical attire or use the title, the Reverend, '*towards each other*'. The distinction between 'ordained and unordained men shall cease', a phrase of curious ambiguity. The Pastoral Address (6 August 1793) made clear the Conference regulations on the sacraments. 'We find that we have no alternative but to comply with their requisition, i.e. the request of the people for the sacraments, or else entirely to lose them . . . O brethren, we hate putting away, especially those who are members of the mystical body of Christ and our dearly beloved brethren . . . The sacrament of the Lord's Supper shall not be administered by the preachers in any part of the Connexion, except where the whole society is unanimous for it, and will not be contented without it, and in even these few exempt societies, it shall be administered as far as possible in the evening only and according to the form of the Church of England. For we could not bear that the sacrament which was instituted by our Lord as a bond of peace and union should become a bone of contention. It is the people who have fixed us in this further deviation from our union to the Church of England.' The resolutions were carried by eighty-six votes to forty-eight.

For long Methodist historians have variously interpreted the significance of these decisions. George Smith[36] says 'the jealous advocates of the old plan saw it as a decisive defeat' while those 'who as they termed it were struggling to liberty of conscience, found it a very unsatisfactory measure' since one person could inhibit the sacrament being held in any particular chapel. Smith seems correct in part of his interpretation since the sacrament could now be given in a society unanimously in favour. This was a breach in the 'Church

Methodists' ' dyke but the decisions about ministerial dress and ordination were 'church party' rather than separatist measures. Samuel Bradburn certainly thought so when he wrote to Alexander Kilham on 12 December 1793. 'I really believe the little interruption we met with will do us good. Do not destroy your gown and bands, nor suppose they are for ever done with . . . We must have a Methodist constitution or plan of discipline explained and we shall in due time.'[37]

A. W. Harrison, echoing a sentiment of Atmore at the time, interpreted the phrase about 'distinctions between ordained and unordained men' to mean that 'it was a sufficient ordination for any of the preachers when he was received into full connexion by Conference'.[38] This is a plausible view, which found considerable favour from 1795 onwards, but would appear to be contradicted by the pastoral addresses. One of these addresses, dated 8 August 1793, was a reply to a printed letter sent from the trustees of the New Room and Guinea Street, Bristol, who complained about departure from the 'old plan'. The circular letter of Conference claimed not to have separated from the 'old plan'. 'We are determined to remain in connexion with the Church of England. We have no desire of making our societies separate churches. We have never sanctioned ordination in England, either in this Conference or in any other, in any degree or even attempted to do it.' The 'Church Methodist' voice speaks here a word of re-assurance to the trustees, and there is no trace of the theory of 'virtual ordination'. But the clichés of both parties are embedded in the Conference statements.[39]

A. R. George[40] has shown how, at this time, the idea began to spread (despite the 1793 resolutions) that reception into full connexion was 'virtual ordination'. Atmore certainly thought so. William Thompson in a letter to Benson of 1795[41] says, 'It is proposed that the Methodist preachers shall have nothing to do with ordination of any kind, because their being four years upon trial . . . and their being received at Conference by their senior brethren giving them the right hand of fellowship is a full proof that they are called of God to the work of the ministry which we believe to be scriptural ordination.' This was to be combined with 'simplicity and plainness' with no titles or distinctive attire. Thompson's conception of the meaning of 'reception into full connexion' was certainly not that of John Wesley. The travelling preachers were developing through a form of what might be called lay agency – unordained preachers allowed to administer sacraments – to the Wesleyan ministry of the time of Jabez Bunting. The change was almost complete by the time of Richard Watson,[42] the apologist and theologian of the Wesleyanism of the early nineteenth century. Watson, writing in 1831 in his *Life of Wesley* implies that Wesley's admission of a man to preach was 'virtual ordination' or, as he put it, 'true ordination'. Watson suggests that it would have been an improvement had there been the imposition of hands as a gesture towards 'the usage of the majority of the churches'. Watson's arguments, like that of Thompson much earlier, would seem to be a slightly anachronistic defence of the practice of 'virtual ordination' arising from the 1793 resolution abolishing distinctions between 'ordained' and 'unordained' preachers. A Wesleyan ministry was developing in which practice was to precede theory, utility to precede theology in direct contrast to the more doctrinaire usages of orthodox Dissent in England, in which a theology of church and ministry arose before the gathering of the saints in separation from the Establishment. The constitution of the separated Wesleyan church, like Topsy, 'just growed', but contained early on in its bloodstream a doctrine of ministry which still owed much to John Wesley (even if it muddled his legacy) and not a little to the Puritan conceptions of a Baxter or a Doddridge. The process is a fine illustration of how a denomination, in the end, requires and acquires a full time professional ministry.

If the Conference of 1793 did not entirely satisfy either the 'Church Methodists' or people like Bradburn, it did not satisfy Thomas Coke or Alexander Mather.[43] We have already quoted John Pawson's letter on what he considered to be Wesley's intentions. Mather and Coke he considered 'bishops who could ordain others . . . I sincerely wish that Dr Coke and Mr Mather may be allowed to be what they are – bishops; that they ordain two others chosen by the Conference and that these four have the government of the Connexion placed in their hands for one year, each superintending his respective District being stationed in London, Bristol, Leeds and Newcastle . . . We must have ordination among us at any rate.' These points emerged clearly at a meeting of eight of the leading preachers, in private, in an inn at Lichfield on 1 April (so says Bradburn) 1794. The eight were Coke, Mather, Taylor, Pawson, Bradburn, Moore, Clarke and Rogers. Coke, with the example of the United States in his mind, proposed that he should confer presbyter's orders on the unordained men present (so much for 'virtual ordination') but the counsels of Moore and Mather prevailed and it was decided to submit the ideas to Conference. Adam Clarke's Minutes show that the group desired 'no avowed separation from the Church of England', but that the sacrament of the Lord's Supper shall be administered if a majority of the society desire it (unless a majority of the trustees are against it), that there shall be an order of superintendents. 'These Superintendents shall ordain preachers admitted into full connexion as deacon and elder. The Superintendents should each supervise a 'general division'. Tactlessly, six out of the eight proposed as superintendents were present at Lichfield which sealed the fate of the scheme!

The Conference which met at Bristol in 1794 was not a happy one. It is noticeable that Coke was still not elected President. The Lichfield proposals were rejected as 'tending to create invidious and unhallowed distinctions among brethren'.[44] At this Conference the power of the trustees of the local chapels began to assert itself again and added the tension between connexional and local control of chapels and preachers to the conflicts over sacrament and separation. A delegation of trustees met at Bristol to decide on the pressing of their claims before Conference which followed the 'old plan'. A powerful challenge was thus offered to Conference with a demand that the concessions regarding the sacrament in 1793 be withdrawn. Joseph Benson moved that 'the Conference do confirm and ratify the declarations of last year respecting the sacrament'. A letter replying to the Trustees drew an answer earnestly repeated 'that ordination, the administration of the sacrament, burying the dead, be laid aside'. A committee was appointed to make reconciliation. Considerable concessions were made in a circular letter of 8 August 1794 signed by the President and Secretary.[45] These concessions upheld the 1793 decisions laying down that the sacrament of the Lord's Supper was not to be administered 'where the union and concord of the societies can be preserved without it'. The preachers will not perform the office of baptism 'except for the desirable ends of love and concord' even if this sacrament had been administered by preachers before Wesley's death. A clear distinction is made between stewards and itinerant preachers, who determine membership, appoint stewards and times of service. Trustees were confirmed in their power over property.

A. W. Harrison[46] who applies the 'virtual ordination' theory to decisions of the Conference, calls them 'the low water mark of concession to the Church Methodists' though, in fact, some of the resolutions go further towards complete separation. In 1793 a society had to express unanimity; now the much looser phrase 'the desirable ends of love and concord' was applied. It is possible to see in the 1794 decisions another cautious compromise and an attempt to please both sides. 'If the church connexion was to retain any substance the trustees would have to fight for it as the partisans of established institutions were fighting elsewhere.'[47] The battle was joined at Bristol.[48] Of over one hundred places where Holy Communion might be administered, five were in Bristol. Two large chapels were not on the list – Wesley's Room in the Broadmead and the daughter chapel in Guinea Street. The trustees were strongly in favour of the 'old plan' and went to the parish church for communion.

At Portland Street Chapel the sacrament of the Lord's Supper had been celebrated during Conference and on 11 August[49] Henry Moore (ordained by Wesley) assisted Dr Coke in administering the elements. The trustees of the New Room gave notice that he had no authority to preach there.[50] This was a challenge to the whole connexional system, even if they could claim provocation. Moore went to the new Room, and was denied the pulpit. He took the majority of the congregation to Portland Street after making a statement of intent.[51] The trustees felt sure of their ground owing to the loosely drawn up trust deeds of their chapels and the anticipated arrival of a sympathetic superintendent, Joseph Benson, who with Rodda and Vasey would be expected to support them. The people, supported by Dr Coke and Jonathan Crowther, rallied to Moore's support. Shortly afterwards Ebenezer Chapel, Old King Street, was erected, within yards of the New Room, virtually superseding it.[52]

The action of the trustees was followed by the kind of pamphlet warfare typical of the eighteenth century.[53] Moore presented his own case, pointing out that Wesley had trouble with these same trustees. He had wide support including Coke and Bradburn. Coke, with some extravagance, praised God that 'Trustee tyranny is at an end in Bristol. The people would not submit themselves to these men if we would.'[54] Charges and counter-charges were made – the people at Portland Street retaliating upon the New Room trustees by forbidding Joseph Benson their pulpit. Attempts at compromise failed – even though Portland Street were prepared for a 'lay preacher' (an interesting refutation of the 'virtual ordination' theory) to administer communion only if the society were unanimous.[55] The trustees demanded an extraordinary session of Conference, a proposal instantly scotched by John Pawson and Thomas Hanby in a circular letter. The connexion was now stirred – trustees in Stockport and Manchester supporting their fellows at the New Room and being answered by trustees and local preachers at Liverpool and Leeds. A pamphlet with the title, *Considerations on a Separation of Methodists from the Established Church*, appeared at the time stating as a principle that Methodist preachers are not clergymen, but laymen and that Methodism was a 'society' not a church.[56] The action of the separatist party was tantamount to the setting up of rival altars. Jonathan Crowther answered this charge in January 1795 in *The Crisis of Methodism*, suggesting that Alexander Knox was the writer of the *Considerations*. Crowther maintained that many Methodists had never been Anglicans.

It is not and never has been from mere admiration of the hierarchy but on the ground of usefulness that the Methodists . . . still continue in the church. Our call is not to prop up human establishments nor yet to pull them down, but to go about doing good. We must not call out 'the Church', 'the Church' like those who cried out 'Great is Diana of the Ephesians'. I do not believe that there will ever be a total absolute separation of the Methodists from the Established Church of England, so long as that Church shall endure. Some say that to administer the sacrament will make the preachers proud – surely to preach the gospel and to fill the office of ambassador from God to man must be a work of far greater importance and real dignity than sprinkling a little water on a child or distributing a little bread and wine.

With the connexion divided in this way and social discontent also at a climax,[57] it seemed that the Conference of 1795 at Manchester would be the stormiest since Wesley's death. Joseph Bradford, a moderate, was elected president. Fasting and prayer marked the first day. The next day a committee of nine preachers was chosen by ballot and instructed to draw up a plan to bring peace to the distracted connexion. The preachers elected a committee representing differing viewpoints[58] which produced a plan, which, with the alteration of only one article, the Conference passed unanimously.[59] It was then submitted to the assembled trustees who approved it with a large majority, adding suggestions. This *Plan of Pacification* ensured peace throughout the connexion on the sacramental issue.[60]

In the provisions of the *Plan*, it was laid down that the 'Sacrament of the Lord's Supper shall not be administered in any chapel except the majority of the trustees of that chapel on the one hand and the majority of the stewards and leaders belonging to the chapel (as the best qualified to give the sense of the people) on the other hand allow of it.'[61] Conference sanction was also to be given. The same strictures applied to baptism, burial and service in church hours. Holy Communion was to be administered only by those authorized by Conference and was intended, like baptism, 'for the members of our own society'. The 'open table' was a much later conception. The service should take place on Sunday evenings, except where the majority of stewards and leaders desire it in church hours. 'It shall never be administered on those Sundays in which it is administered in the parochial church.' The form of the service in England should be 'that of the Established Church with hymns, extempore prayer and exhortation'. If there was to be a service in church hours then either the service of the established church, 'our venerable father's abridgment', or at least the lessons appointed by the calendar were to be read. This was not complete separation, but it was the major step in that direction. The innovation was the Sunday evening Communion service. T. H. Barratt was right in saying 'Wesley's wonderful morning sacramental service was forgotten. All this was done out of deference to the Church of England. But the Methodists have paid a sad price for the pathetic loyalty of their fathers to their old unkindly mother'[62] – nevertheless evening services were clearly sociologically suited to many of those forming the Methodist Societies. Adam Clarke, writing in 1816, said, 'The Methodists in England have incomparably more grace and more stability since the introduction of the sacrament than before. But the four years of partial prohibition, followed by the restrictions of 1795, created a tradition which went far to annul the teaching and example of John Wesley, sowing seeds of which the harvest is still being reaped.' There is truth in that statement, even in the mid-1980s.

The second part of the *Plan* was concerned with discipline and in particular the powers of trustees and Conference. 'The appointment of preachers shall remain solely with the Conference; and no trustee or number of trustees shall expel or exclude from their chapel or chapels any preachers so appointed.' Moral or doctrinal charges or disputes about a preacher's abilities could be heard by a proper District court presided over by the District Chairman. The Legal Hundred were confirmed in their Conference powers. Any official disturbing the peace of a Society could be expelled after due process. Connexionalism was upheld.

Such was the solution of what we can call the connexional problem. W. R. Ward sees this as a means by which the bulk of the Methodist community could move into practical dissent[63] and consummated the defeat of the struggles of the lay aristocracy of the connexion in the great urban centres of London, Bristol, Birmingham, Liverpool, Manchester, Leeds, Halifax and Newcastle to bolster up the church against the anti-establishment torrent of the rank and file. The *Plan of Pacification* was set out in an atmosphere in which the mobs were no longer firmly for 'Church and King' marking a shift to the left under popular pressure, but the shift was not too great. The views of Alexander Kilham did not prevail. Lessening of popular discontent enabled the connexion to assign Kilham to expulsion.[64] 'If peace with the government could be had at the price of jettisoning Kilham, that price was never to be lower than in 1796.' The *Form of Discipline* of 1797[65] completed the creation of Wesleyanism as a distinct denomination, though the pressures and storms of social tension were by no means assuaged by the secession of Kilham and the beginning of the New Connexion in 1797. Yet even in Bristol the breach was healed. In October 1800 the trustees who had fought

Moore handed over Guinea Street and in August 1808 the New Room itself, to the trustees of the chapel of Old King Street who accepted all the financial liabilities and sold the New Room to the Baptists. Thus ended the dispute which at first threatened no less than the division of the whole connexion.[66]

Perhaps this stage of the separation of Methodism from the Church of England is best summarized in a long letter written on 16 June 1829 by Adam Clarke (1762–1832) to Humphrey Sandwith (1792–1874), the surgeon of Bridlington. Clarke had been a preacher in the connexion for fifty years. 'I ever found many people in most places of the Connexion very weary of not having the sacrament of the Lord's Supper administered in our own chapels by our own preachers.' Clarke gently chides Charles Wesley for threatening damnation to those who would not go to the parish church, but clearly blames the preachers and 'several leading opulent men' for the delay in full sacramental observance. He is clear that the *Plan of Pacification* was the 'result of the well ascertained wants of the societies'. The alternative would have been the 'annihilation' of the societies. 'Methodism has brought many into the church and taken none out of it. We hold all its doctrines and proclaim and defend their purity and excellence everywhere – use the same baptism and eucharist and the same form as the church does; and we have been under God the means of a great moral change even in the church itself. If they who have been so much helped by us have not grace or dignity or spirit to acknowledge it, that is their fault – we thank God, take courage and keep on in the even tenor of our way.'[67]

Not all Methodists were as eirenic as Clarke; many Anglicans were not flattered by imitation. Conference had espoused virtual separation, but even if Conference had crossed the river, many were still on the other side and others longed to swim back again. In Halifax, for instance, John Pawson had begun to preside at the Holy Communion but Samuel Waterhouse presented a petition against this, signed by one hundred and twenty members and five leaders. He withdrew, subsequently, to the parish church, though he was still an occasional 'hearer' and held love feasts 'after the Methodist fashion at his own house'.

The fluid undenominationalism of eighteenth-century revival had not entirely frozen into denominational blocks. While a great number of societies took advantage of the *Plan of Pacification*, in Bradford the Methodists still processed for a time out of their Octagonal Chapel, preacher at the head, for Morning Prayer and until 1810 received the monthly sacrament.[68] John Crosse, the Vicar, was a man in the Grimshaw-Venn tradition of co-operation. This was just before a spurt of Methodist expansion giving them 3,568 members in Bradford

in 1841 compared with 694 in 1781. Joseph Sutcliffe claimed that in
the East Riding ten years passed from Wesley's death to the time
when a single Methodist was prepared to receive either of the
sacraments from his own preacher. Anomalies like the Anglican
'chapel of ease' at Stainland, near Halifax, where the pulpit was
supplied by the Wesleyans, a kind of joint church venture continuing
until 1838, paralleled the more famous situation at Madeley.[69] In
'high Wesleyanism' the change came slowly. Jabez Bunting was the
first preacher without Anglican orders to read prayers at Wesley's
Chapel. Not until 1826, when Henry Moore presided at Holy
Communion, was such a preacher permitted to preside at the
sacraments. For another generation there were those who saw
Wesleyanism as a possible bridge between orthodox Dissent and the
Establishment, but neither dissenters nor Anglicans were particularly interested in this conception. Methodist loyalty to the state
church was rarely received with gratitude. The connexion itself, even
if rent by discord until 1857 over *episcopē*, was not in disorder over
its fundamental gospel. 'Its evangelical Arminianism gave it a great
source of unity by setting a convenient barrier between itself and
other dissenting groups who were either evangelical but Calvinist
(like the orthodox independent) or Arminian but Socinian like many
of the presbyterians.' Wesleyanism was becoming a denomination.[70]

Detailed chronology can now be abandoned for bird's eye survey.
During the nineteenth century Wesleyanism continued its development into a fully fledged denomination.[71] Its ministry developed
from an extraordinary mission to a settled pastorate. The itinerant
system, designed for pure evangelism, enabled it to act as a shuttle
weaving a close knit community which came self-consciously to call
itself 'the Body'. As we have seen, the theory of 'virtual ordination'
was conceived to give the itinerant preachers the status of regular
ministers.[72] By 1818 it was the custom to grant to the itinerants the
title of the 'Reverend'. Conference, which after Wesley's death
forbade such a title, preferring the suffix 'preacher of the gospel', was
later in the century to fight a successful lawsuit to obtain the right
to the title on the tombstone of a minister's daughter.[73] Ordination
by the laying on of hands was introduced firstly for those proceeding
to the mission field and, following prolonged debate, for all in 1836
– a symbolic proclamation of conscious maturity. Since our concern
here is with relationships with Anglicanism, we have no need to
do more than briefly summarize the influence of Jabez Bunting
(1779–1858) on Wesleyanism.[74] As the representative leader of many
of the ministers and the wealthier laymen, typified by James Wood of
Manchester and Gilyard Scarth of Leeds, he forged a denominational
system with centralized government and a committee structure with

scope for powerful laymen. The organization of the Missionary Society as a great international charity and the creation of the Theological Institution (1834) were the most notable of Bunting's achievements. The use of the Centenary Fund of 1839 which amounted to £216,000 showed Bunting's priorities – the Wesleyan Theological Institution (£70,000), the Wesleyan Missionary Society (£40,000), the Trust of Wesleyan Chapels, the support of aged ministers and ministers' widows, Wesleyan education and the British and Foreign Bible Society. As we shall see later, a large denomination cannot avoid close contact with government, not only on moral issues like slavery or public order, but on issues of foreign policy and education also.

In what opponents glibly called the 'Buntingite' system, the ordained ministry was to play a leading role. New superintendent was to be more than old priest writ large! To expect an immature ministry to withstand the pressures of revivalism, Sunday schools often independent of ministerial control and open as W. R. Ward says to 'gusts of popular radicalism' and to laymen who wanted more local control and less clericalization, was to expect too much. Battles between locals and cosmopolitans can be expected as a denomination develops. The clash between high and low Methodism, recently so well outlined by W. R. Ward, in his editing of the Bunting correspondence, John Kent, John Bowmer and David Gowland, is a feature of this conflict which has erupted in Methodism at every major crisis. Too much weight was thrust on an immature ministry. A tradition of authority cannot easily be created in three or four decades. It might have been claimed that the 'living John Wesley is the brethren in full connexion' but the laity claimed a larger share in government. The minister came to derive his authority in later Victorian years more from his personal gifts than from his ordination. This particular tension has never been fully resolved in Methodism.

The sacraments for long tended to be overshadowed by the worship of the society – love feasts and class meetings meant more to some Methodists than the Holy Communion. The Anglican parentage of Methodism is most clearly seen, nevertheless, in the mode in which Holy Communion was conducted. The society-connexion tension with the concept of a denomination is to be seen, however, in the definition of membership. Membership of the church in the post-imperial West has been clearly through baptism followed normally by some rite of 'confirmation', even if that ordinance is a 'rite in search of a meaning' and often unused as in America.[75] Membership of a Methodist society was technically recognized when the person had been placed on 'class book' and had accepted the rules of membership. Exclusion from the society was certainly not tantamount to excommunication. As a society grows and new generations come into it, its membership basis approximates more to that of the denomination. Concentration on the nurture of the next generation assumes as much importance as the conversion of adults. Education is seen as part of evangelism which points to an inability to enlarge the boundaries of the sub-culture. Thus in 1837 Conference urged parents to 'consecrate their children under the bond of the covenant in his visible church in baptism. By baptism you place your children within the pale of the church . . . they are grafted into the glory of Christ's disciples.' In 1846, it was urged that 'catechumen classes' be set up and by 1878 Junior Society classes were to be created for the training of new members. 'All possible impressiveness is to be given to a member's entrance into fellowship with the Church of Christ.' An order of service for the 'Recognition of New Members' was added to the Book of Offices in 1894, thus providing Wesleyans with an equivalent of confirmation, though that term was not officially commended until 1962, when there was a tendency to use too uncritically terms hardened in meaning in other communions.

The provision of a system of education went parallel with the training of new members. Sunday schools were encouraged to give definite Wesleyan teaching in 1827. Day schools on a similar doctrinal basis were encouraged from 1833. Wesleyan schools, of which there were 912 in 1873, were instructed to use the Bible, the Wesleyan Hymn Book and Catechism (itself a denominational symbol) and were to be 'avowedly and practically connected with Wesleyan Methodism as a branch of the visible church of Christ' – though Wesleyanism did not officially use the title 'church' until 1897.[76] Certainly in the Sunday schools there was a move away from the undenominational independent school to a school under stricter denominational tutelage of which the prolonged controversy over teaching writing on a Sunday was a symptom. The nineteenth century saw Wesleyanism develop the consciousness of being a 'great church'. It is not necessary to accept the whole of Bernard Semmel's thesis about the projection of English discontent into a great missionary crusade to take seriously the effect on a connexion of becoming a world-wide communion leading to a growing and expanding church consciousness.[77] John Wesley's world-parish came of age. In 1870 (a matter to be analyzed later) J. H. Rigg could typify the mood of late Victorian Methodism which had snapped the apron strings of Mother Church. 'Methodists desire,' he said, 'independence without enmity. The genius of Methodism and Anglican episcopacy are mutually repellant and exclusive . . . there can be no greater mistake than to suppose there is or ever has been, at least in the present generation, any party within Methodism, whether ministers or among the people, who have felt the slightest concern as to union with the Church of England.'[78] Behind that statement lies what we shall see as the conflict of resurgent Anglicanism in Anglo-Catholic and Evangelical alike – with Victorian Dissent of which Methodism politically if not theologically became a part. When a connexion develops into a denomination, there can be a hardening of theological arteries which prevent any blood transfusion from other traditions.

Is Methodism in the twentieth century a 'gathered church' on the pattern of the older dissent or is it a *Volkskirche* seeking to embrace all life and all people, a second parish system? In credal emphases, Methodism smacks still of the society and the connexion. A society could not set up confessional standards of documents equivalent to the Augsburg Confession, the Westminster Confession or the Thirty-Nine Articles. For long most of the latter indeed were appended to the Book of Offices. Methodism has never clearly defined her 'distinctive emphases' save as they are stated in the *Forty-Four Sermons* of John Wesley and the *Notes on the New Testament*, which, according to the Deed of Union of 1932, are 'not intended to impose a system of formal or speculative theology on Methodist preachers but to set up standards of preaching and belief which should secure loyalty to the fundamental truths of the gospel of redemption and ensure the continued witness of the church to the realities of the Christian experience of salvation.' Perhaps it was all to the good that the doctrinal standards of Methodism are a book of sermons and a commentary on the New Testament.

Methodism's constitution had pragmatic rather than dogmatic origins and by its very flexibility was a more powerful tool of evangelistic mission in the eighteenth and nineteenth centuries than the parent church. The initial impetus evaporated, however, and led to a certain ossification of tradition, particularly in the stereotyping of the class meeting, a key factor in its decline when it ceased either to be a tool of evangelism or a criterion of membership. The broader substitutes for it are a mark of widening of cultural and social concerns and at the same time a sign of lowering of spiritual temperature (some contemporaries would say standards also) and of secularization. If in the century after Wesley's conversion two great ideas had dominated Methodism, Wesley's search for Christian perfection or scriptural holiness and the Methodist people's search for a religious democracy, the latter had won the day. 'Ministers,' says Currie, 'began to emphasise fellowship and service rather than authority and control . . . when secularization eroded ethic, doctrine and ritual, the chapel, the indestructible nucleus and residuum of the movement remained.'

Some non-Methodists, perhaps romanticizing a little, avow that the weakness of modern Methodism – though there are signs of change and a revival of intense group spirituality – is the eclipse of the very feature which provided its greatest strength in the days of the society. 'The glorious failure of Methodism', wrote Bishop Wickham,[79] 'may not be entirely unrelated to the gradual neglect of (Wesley's) premises in the palmy days of the great congregations', a view underlined by John M. Todd,[80] a Roman Catholic, who wrote, 'To the outsider the disappearance of the regular class meeting as a normal part of Methodism looks almost like a fatal occurrence.' A denomination must have a society of friends – primary groups – at its heart if it is to escape the generalized, sometimes lopsided Protestantism that has often characterized modern Methodism.

But Wesleyanism was not the only Methodism that can be shown in development. Primitive Methodism illustrates much more sharply the transition from sect to denomination so beloved of modern sociologists.

If the beginnings of the first evangelical revival are now seen to be highly complex, even more is this the case with what can be called the 'second great awakening'[81] beginning in the USA about 1790, spilling over into Great Britain with the itinerancy of Lorenzo Dow, linking with the Yorkshire revival of the 1790s and marking the revival in the Potteries which came to call itself Primitive Methodism. Revivalistic evangelism of an undenominational kind was common in the 1790s. Bishops like Pretyman-Tomline of Lincoln feared a return to the days of Oliver Cromwell! Primitive Methodism is a classic case of development from what Wilson calls 'conversionist sect' to 'denomination'. This is much more so than the evolution of Wesleyanism which carried far more Anglican churchly corpuscles in its bloodstream and was never a classic sect. The growth of the normal equipment of a denomination took a generation or so – chapels with consequent debts, central bureaucracy, trained minis-ters replacing 'raw lads' – and lasses – with extraordinary figures like Sir William Hartley[82] – fuelling an educational programme giving Primitive Methodism a college second to none in England, with Arthur S. Peake combining the warm piety of his fathers with a new style of liberal evangelicalism which typifies the acceptance of status in society. This was very different from the 'Christ against culture' of the days of Clowes and Bourne, though there was always a Puritan-like thirst for knowledge in an autodidact like Bourne who was converted through books.[83] Bourne, for all his Wesleyanism, clearly belonged to the revivalist ethos, as did William Clowes, converted dancer, revivalist potter, whose story is a miracle of grace.[84] When Clowes follows Bourne, expelled from Wesleyanism for not attending 'class' which clearly meant attending or 'setting up other forms of worship' and in Bourne's case taking out a preacher's licence without permission – the group of Camp Meeting Methodists led by Bourne and the 'Clowesites' combined in what the eccentric James Crawfoot, in 1812, called Primitive Methodism.

The Second Revival found a ready soil in the Cheshire Plain and the Potteries where the parish system was weak. Here were pockets of undenominational revivalism which crystallized in the Quaker or Independent Methodists of Warrington and Macclesfield, the Band Room Methodists of Manchester, the revivalists of Leeds under Sigston, who emerge again in the 1820s when the Brunswick Chapel trustees installed their organ. Then there were the 'Magic Methodists' of Delamere Forest who specialised in trance-like states led by James Crawfoot, the 'old man of the forest'. Revivalism shades off into all kinds of pre-millenial groups like the followers of Joanna Southcott, which J. F. C. Harrison has recently analysed in *The Second Coming*. The links here are with Quakerism and left wing relics of Puritanism, much of which was picked up by the Primitive Methodists when their revival moved swiftly down the Trent Valley in the Great Midlands revival after the end of the Napoleonic Wars – one of the most successful revivals in British church history. Here surely were the heartlands of Lollardy and radical Puritanism. Weavers and outworkers were leaders of radicalism and revival for centuries. Primitive Methodism is in some ways a revivalistic form of Quakerism.[85] Not for nothing were they nicknamed with the seventeenth-century term 'ranter'. We can see in this an attempt to recall revivalist roots in contrast to the staid, more urban, increasingly bourgeois style of Wesleyanism which repelled them.

Their camp meetings beginning at Mow Cop on 31 May 1807 were sober and tame – religious wakes – compared with the religious 'pop festivals' of America lasting for days out on 'the frontier'. The Wesleyan Conference of 1807 dissociated itself from camp meetings in England. The bugbear was clearly Lorenzo Dow. In Ireland he had been accused of Republicanism. Thomas Coke threatened to report him to Chief Secretary Castlereagh if he did not cease his activities.[86] That was in 1799. Now he was in England again. This was the period of the Napoleonic Wars – invasion scares and fears of Jacobinism were still rife. Governmental action might be taken against the Methodists. Toleration had only survived 'by a whisker' in 1800.[87] Indeed in 1811 Lord Sidmouth, the Home Secretary, with apparent support from Thomas Coke and Adam Clarke – who clearly disliked Dow – sought to pilot his notorious Bill through the Lords. Magistrate Sparrow of Stafford had written to Sidmouth stating that fifteen potters had asked for licences as Methodist preachers – Bourne

certainly had a licence to go ahead with the Mow Cop meetings.
Sidmouth disliked what he called 'blacksmiths, cobblers, tailors,
pedlars, chimney sweeps and what not' being granted licences.
The Bill to demand that preachers must have settled congregations
which would have poleaxed local preaching in Wesleyanism, as well
as in revivalism, failed.[88] But Wesleyan fears were not without cause
– the Kilhamite schism was not long previous and it was prone to
revivalism which sent shivers down the spines of young ministers
like Jabez Bunting who had quickly forgotten his own radical origins.
The whole matter is the perennial tension between order and ardour.
Ironically, within a very short time, some of the revivalists were
complaining of what they called 'the Tunstall non-mission law', a
demand for a time of consolidation and discipline before the revival
spread again. More than once Bourne had to apply the axe to those
who appeared to him to be what he had seemed to his superiors.

The early Primitive Methodist style was of cottage meetings, camp
meetings and class groups – a kind of exuberant Quakerism with no
trace of clericalism and as yet small-scale and local. At the first
Assembly (a Quaker term) or Conference of 1820 there were 7,842
members, 8 circuits and 48 'travelling' preachers. The heroic days
of Primitive Methodism were those of the great Midlands revival of
1814–25 when the preachers – men and women for this sect would,
like the Quakers, tolerate no barriers of sex – moved down the Valley
of the Trent with Clowes, later, moving into the East Riding and the
North West. Villages – especially the industrial villages – could be
missioned by zealous preachers with an exuberant, almost Franciscan optimism – preaching, praying, singing with equal fervour
offering a gospel of forgiveness which could reach men and women
whom their more sober Anglican and Wesleyan contemporaries
could not reach.

It is tempting to seek economic and social roots and causes for the
success of revival and indeed there is no doubt that Primitive
Methodism was particularly sensitive to cyclical fluctuations and
periods of unemployment. Earlier historians, such as H. B. Kendall,
explained fluctuations in membership figures primarily in economic
terms. It is interesting that the first fall in Wesleyan numbers
coincided with the Midlands revival in Primitive Methodism which
was clearly appealing to a different and lower stratum of the
population. The year of the so-called 'Peterloo Massacre' in Manchester in 1819 marked a great increase – have we here what E. P.
Thompson called 'the chiliasm of the despairing and the defeated'?[89]
The years of economic depression and great unemployment from
1824 to 1825, were years of crisis for the Primitives when Bourne and
Clowes tried to prune the ranks of the 'travelling preachers' of

undesirable time-servers, men perhaps seeking employment as preachers rather than semi-starvation on the parish. Certainly E. J. Hobsbawm is right to point to the way in which Primitive Methodism could quickly establish societies in village or semi-village areas of relatively underdeveloped industry[90] – a pattern of living which tended to disappear as the modern pattern of urbanization and factory industry began. W. R. Ward, too, has pointed to the effects of enclosures, battles over tithes, the unpopularity of the clergy, especially those on 'the Bench'.[91] Labourers seeking an end to dependency could easily become followers of Ned Ludd or later, in 1830, Captain Swing – smashing power-looms and threshing-machines, or sucked into revivalist groups, or both at the same time. Hugh Bourne in 1821 in a chapel of which he was the legal owner, ordered out a man he called a 'speeching radical'.[92]

Country villages with social homogoneity were a Primitive Methodist seedbed as was the 'miserable zone of petty and archaic industries in the West Midlands'. Wiltshire, Hampshire and Berkshire witnessed much persecution by squire and parson who equated ranters with rickburners. But by the Conference of 1842, membership had risen to 85,575 – swifter increases, even allowing for booming population, than the primary growth of Wesley's connexion. It is, however, sociologically significant, that even William Clowes could not achieve much in London. The rural and industrial village was the typical centre of a Primitive Methodist society.

The sect soon showed signs of what Max Weber called the 'routinization of charisma', though for long local areas had very considerable autonomy, especially after the creation of districts in 1824. Lincolnshire can be used as a typical example. This was a time when farm labourers were degraded into helpless and abject helots, forelock pulling charity receivers.[93] Into the villages came the 'ranters' preaching their three Rs – ruin, repentance and redemption. Very quickly the new sect developed its own 'feasts and fasts', in open opposition to the church calendar, a matter on which Durkheim and social anthropologists like Mary Douglas have thrown much light. Preaching services, prayer meetings, 'protracted meetings' lasting, on and off, several evenings, love feasts which were always more common than sacraments and later, in the era of consolidation after 1840, the Sunday school anniversary and procession, begging for villagers' pence rather than their souls, and the chapel anniversary when the poor tried manfully to pay off chapel debts. The congregations were largely composed of labourers with the leading lay man often enough a shopkeeper. At Ebenezer Chapel, Halifax, none of the trustees could vote after 1832. A trustees' minute book from Metcombe, a Dorsetshire village, shows that as late as 1892 five trustees were labourers, two farmers, two blacksmiths and there was the village grocer, who not surprisingly was the treasurer.[94]

The chapel gave people a sense of belonging at a time of social tension, a high proportion of members holding some office. Women and the poor had scope. While a 'no politics' rule might restrain pulpit radicals, there was no bar on participation in unions. The skill in speech and organization learned in chapel could spill over into local and union politics. In Oxfordshire Pamela Horn has shown that all the chief officers of the Oxford branch of the Agricultural Union were Methodists, mainly Primitives.[95] Joseph Arch, champion hedge-cutter and Primitive Methodist preacher, founded the Agricultural Workers Union in 1872. Early in life the class distinctions which made his mother subservient to the squire's lady at Holy Communion alienated him from the parish church, though he returned to it later in life. Antagonism between 'church' and 'chapel' in this period had social as well as theological roots.

In 1872 the Bishop of Oxford – J. F. Mackarness – devoted his first charge to attacking Nonconformity. He denied to its ministers and preachers the validity of their call and went on to accuse them of filching promising sons from the church. He taunted the ministers with 'desiring a social equality with the parish clergy which nothing, not even a revolution, could give them'. If we move later into Norfolk we find the unions copying Primitive Methodist techniques – camp meetings and love feasts – which further heightened the tension between 'church' and 'chapel'. Clearly within the counties of Lincolnshire, Norfolk and Suffolk, Primitive Methodism played an important role in the origin and development of the Revolt of the Field between 1870 and 1900.[96] Men like Sir George Edwards, whose pilgrimage took him from crow-scaring to parliament, was typical of those who combined their theology with radical politics, even if not many actually prayed for the death of blacklegs in a strike as happened in the 1840s at Seaton Delaval.[97] Sectarian involvement in mining unions in Derbyshire and Nottinghamshire and in Chartism parallels the slightly later agricultural struggle.[98] In the last analysis Primitive Methodism produced the sober, hard-working, thrifty 'labour aristocrat' who would fight indeed for his place in the sun but who would tend to be a conciliator rather than a revolutionary and who would later be as opposed to the working class scapegrace as to the hard-line Marxist. So the sect developing into a denomination can act as an analgesic against the pains of labour and help to produce a viable class society.[99]

Primitive Methodism created a religious 'counter culture' which offered an alternative to the established church to village culture and working-class culture alike. As James Obelkevich put it, 'It appeared at a critical moment as the traditional culture was passing but before the subsequent working class culture had developed to replace it.'[100] The sect became a denomination, however, since it was never to rally in opposition to the society in which it was cradled. Worship became less spontaneous and charismatic, service books were produced and sometimes used, especially for the rites of passage. New hymn books in 1853 and 1886 replaced the revivalist books. The first call for a ministerial training college came from Sunderland in 1844 and the later colleges there and at Manchester were its fruits – not without protest from those who feared that the edge of revivalism would be blunted. The denomination had its bookroom, its magazines, its two small public schools, its theological college and in the end a centralized Conference taking over much of the power of the districts.[101]

A growing church consciousness marked the Primitive Methodism of the late Victorian period. The Thanksgiving Fund of 1900 enabled new building schemes to be carried out in areas where 'leakage' of membership was feared. The title 'church' rather than 'connexion' appeared on class tickets in 1902. In 1912 the Hymnal of 1886 was given a supplement, a collection which catches the somewhat exuberant and romantic atmosphere of Edwardian Methodism. Primitive Methodism had its Forward Movement, though on a smaller scale than that of Wesleyanism. A fitting headquarters for the denomination was acquired in Holborn Hall in 1912.

The year 1907 saw the centenary of the 'days praying on Mow Hill'. The denomination which began with the Potteries revival could boast of an increase of 4,638 members in 1905, the largest since 1833 which may be a spin-off of the Welsh Revival, but a slow decline in numbers relative to population marked the last generation of Primitive Methodism. This earthy little communion is a fine laboratory in which to test church development from sect to denomination. In the process there was a shift from a close-knit sectarian style to a more broadly based church life. Here lies an important paradox. Hugh McLeod, working recently on several London regions,[102] shows what David Clark has also shown in a Sheffield mining village/ suburb that working-class people both within and outside the church are more prone to be locals, more prone both to parochialism and sectarianism. Primitive Methodism retained a localist outlook because of its class structure rather longer than Wesleyanism, where there was more spatial and cognitive mobility through education, work and marriage. I suspect that the effect of the work of A. S. Peake and his friends, in a remarkable late burst of scholarship in the last generation of Primitive Methodism, was to enable ministers to express a greater breadth of thought and culture within local congregations than had previously been the case.

The drive towards a union with other Methodists coincided with the breakdown of a sectarian outlook. Primitive Methodism approached union with an awareness that 'leakage' of members due to migration south was greater than that in Wesleyanism, though there was an increase in the number of churches in London, the South East, the Thames Valley and the South Midlands. Labour aristocracy was becoming middle class.

When churches unite they bring together not so much doctrines and liturgy but people. Primitive Methodism brought into the union of Methodists in 1932 men and women who combined a simple, almost Quakerly style, a deep concern for social justice brought out of the struggles for workers' rights in mining and in the agricultural struggles.[103] Certainly a deep fissure had developed between religion and labour politics which has widened since. Primitive Methodism, even if seen as an interim faith, played a role as a midwife in the painful birth of modern English socialism out of all proportion to its numerical size. In the next generation, I would hazard the guess that the 'black' churches in Britain will perform a parallel social function. The sect group enables a part of an alienated sub-culture of society to find meaning and purpose. As it develops into a denomination, it can act as a bridge between that sub-group and others higher in the social scale, producing conciliation.

6

Methodists, Evangelicals and High Churchmen

It is possible to trace fairly clearly the ancestry of Methodism in Wesley's rooting in Puritanism, upbringing in Anglicanism, in the impact of Jeremy Taylor, Thomas à Kempis, William Law and non-juring thought on him with a good deal of influence from later Counter Reformation spirituality. The blending of these influences with Moravian theology issued in that 'evangelical Arminianism' which George Croft called 'an original and unique synthesis of the protestant ethic of grace with the catholic ethic of holiness'.[1] The origins of the Evangelical Party in the Church of England are less easy to determine. In 1943 Charles Smyth stated that there were three questions of paramount importance connected with Anglican evangelicalism which still need careful investigation.[2] The questions were 1) What is the ancestry of the Evangelical Movement in the Church of England? 2) How did this movement organize itself? 3) What became of it after 1833? We would add a fourth and shall be especially concerned with it. What was its relationship to Wesleyanism?

To the first question various answers have been given. Denominational bias appears to obscure the issue. Anglicans have tended to stress the differences between the Evangelicals and the Methodists, while Methodists have tended to stress the similarities. Opponents, like Sydney Smith, lumped them all together as equally ridiculous 'not troubling ourselves to point out the finer shades and nicer discriminations of lunacy'.[3] Abbey and Overton maintained that the line of demarcation between the Evangelicals and the Methodists is 'really very distinct',[4] while A. W. Harrison stressed the similarities – 'The Evangelical was a Methodist who preserved his respectability by remaining in the church.'[5] The question is obscured by the often misleading use of party terminology such as 'low-churchman', Calvinist, Evangelical and Methodist, without giving the words any precise meaning.

More recent studies such as those of J. D. Walsh, G. C. B. Davies,

M. Hennell, J. S. Reynolds and A. S. Wood have suggested that in many ways the Methodists and Evangelicals were parallel and complementary with close similarities but not necessarily the same origins.[6] No longer can it be said that 'the Evangelical Movement in the Church of England was one of the offshoots of the great Methodist Revival of the eighteenth century'[7] but rather that the evangelical movement was parallel to the Methodist and not derived from it.[8] This is now almost a piece of received orthodoxy! The revival in Wales, pioneered by Griffith Jones and Howell Harris, was under way some time before Wesley's 'evangelical conversion'. The evangelical movement in Cornwall seems to have owed little or nothing to the Wesleys – though the parallel influence of the religious societies can be noted.[9] The early Anglican evangelicals were probably more profoundly influenced by Puritan writers of the sixteenth and seventeenth centuries than were the Wesleys, a matter which was to become clear in the 'Calvinist controversy' which drove a deep wedge between Methodists and some Evangelicals for a time later in the eighteenth century.[10]

Some degree of clarity in party terminology is necessary before we look more closely at relationships. It needs to be made clear that the term 'low-churchman' as used in the eighteenth and early nineteenth centuries implies the latitudinarianism which was dominant throughout the period. The low-churchman, usually Whig in politics and often sitting loosely to doctrinal niceties, was in turn opposed to Methodists, Evangelicals and Tractarians. It was not until the middle years of the next century that some kind of alliance was made between Evangelical and low-churchman against the principles of the Tractarians, though Peter Toon has recently shown the complexity of that statement,[11] rendering inaccurate the strictures of Charles Smyth: 'It is not the habit of church parties to steer straight courses but the passage of the low church party from Whig latitudinarianism by way of the Feathers' Tavern Petition, Canon Sydney Smith, the Church Association and John Kensit to a squalid negative fundamentalism has a fascination all its own.'[12] Indeed it has, but we shall need to avoid muddling the mainline Evangelicals with the 'Recordites' and Orangeman and there is now, and always has been, much more to the low-churchman than negatives. The great Victorian broad-churchmen like Stanley Arnold and Tait were much more residuary legatees of latitudinarianism than were the 'Recordites' who abhorred them.

The word 'Methodist' was often used as an all-embracing term including Wesleyans, Calvinistic Methodists and Anglican evangelicals, particularly by the opponents of all three groups. 'Methodist' was certainly a term of derision applied to the members of the Holy

Club in Oxford. It was appropriated by Wesley and his followers as an honourable name as in the term 'people called Methodists'. The term spilled over, however, into general evangelicalism to apply 'to all persons, whether clergy or laity, who preach or profess the doctrines of the Reformation, as expressed in the articles of liturgy of our church'.[13] Like Thomas Scott, Alexander Knox, who stands aloof from the scene, and had so much in common with high-churchmen, numbered himself among the Methodists, defining it as 'that spiritual view of religion which implies an habitual devotedness for God'.[14] The broad definition was disliked by many Evangelicals typified in William Richardson in 1809, referring to Joseph Milner's *Essay on Methodism*. 'Though we ought patiently to bear the stigma of Methodism, we ought not to legitimate the term when applied to us or embody ourselves who act in an orderly way with the proper Methodists. What was termed Methodism is now termed Evangelical religion.'[15] We shall follow Richardson and limit 'Methodism' to the followers of John Wesley, 'Evangelical' to refer to a party allegiance which was becoming fashionable by 1770 when A. M. Toplady refers to Wesley's complaint that the 'Evangelical clergy are leaving no stone unturned to raise John Calvin's ghost'.[16] We shall use the term to refer to those Anglicans who, while fully in sympathy with the renewal of preaching based on the doctrine of justification by faith through grace, remained loyal to the Establishment and the parish system.

> An Evangelical Anglican has a strong attachment to the Prot-estantism of the national church with its Articles of Religion and Prayer Book. He believes that the Bible is authoritative in matters of faith and conduct and is to be read individually and in the house as well as in the church. He emphasises the doctrine of justification by faith but with good works and a specific (holy) lifestyle as the proof of true faith. He claims to enjoy a personal relationship with God through Christ, the origins of which are usually traced not to sacramental grace but to a conversion experience. And he sees the primary task of the church in terms of evangelism and mission and so emphasises preaching at home and abroad.[17]

It has often been assumed that the division between Methodist and Evangelical in the eighteenth century was basically doctrinal. 'The Calvinistic controversy' was perhaps more than anything else the cause which led to the parting of the ways between the Wesleyan Methodists and the Evangelicals proper.'[18] This particular contro-versy conducted often with great bitterness and vituperation, and of which the only good gifts to posterity have been the hymns of Charles Wesley and Augustus Montague Toplady, certainly was a divisive factor, though its effect can be exaggerated. In 1740 Wesley and Whitefield, though at one in itinerant preaching, were seen on different sides of this particular fence, and after 1770 the Countess of Huntingdon and some of her followers repeatedly accused the Methodists of teaching salvation by works to be rebutted by the counter charge of antinomianism. Into the intricacies of the arguments we need not go. The main bones of contention were Wesley's teaching on Christian perfection and the doctrine of double predestination which the Wesleyans denied, though Wesley admitted that the 'true gospel touches the very edge of Calvinism'. Walker of Truro, who rejected Wesley's doctrine of perfection, accused the Methodists also of thinking that believing was merely 'feeling', a charge repeated by Henry Venn who wrote in 1763: 'It is much to be lamented that our Christian brethren the Methodists make the ground of their assurance an inward feeling instead of the faithfulness of Jehovah, the sensation of a fluctuating heart instead of the unchangeable premises of God.'[19] Enthusiasm was the bugbear, refuted by implication by Fletcher of Madeley who could assert 'I build my faith not on my experience, though this increases it, but upon the revealed truth of God'.[20]

The preaching by Evangelical clergymen of the doctrines of double predestination and final perseverance presented Wesley with a problem of deciding what advice to give to the Methodist people – should they attend on such preachers or not? Wesley's advice in 1782 was that 'it was highly expedient all the Methodists (so-called) who had been bred therein should attend the service of the church as often as possible but that secondly if the minister began either to preach the absolute decrees or to rail at and ridicule Christian perfection, they should quickly and silently go out of the church, yet attend it again at the next opportunity'.[21] In 1786 he was still troubled with the problem. 'Eight or ten preachers, it is probable (but I have not met with one yet) will say something about leaving the church before the Conference ends. It is not unlikely many will be driven out of it where there are Calvinist ministers. The last time I was at Scarborough I earnestly exhorted our people to go to church and I went myself. But the wretched minister preached such a sermon that I could not in conscience advise them to hear him any more.'[22] Yet in 1787 Wesley could speak of 'every year more and more of the clergy being convinced of the truth and growing well-affected towards us'[23] but nevertheless the great majority of those clergy of the established church (Adam of Wintringham was a notable exemption) who had been affected by the Evangelical Revival had adopted its Calvinist not its Arminian form.[24] The breach between Wesley and the Countess of Huntingdon was clearly due to doctrinal disagreement typified by the termination of the concern of John Fletcher and Joseph Benson (1749–1821) with the College at Trevecca for the training of the ministry, the history of which is an interesting exercise in ecumenism of an evangelical kind.

Yet we must note that both Calvinist and Arminian evangelical shared a common Augustinianism. Many Evangelicals – particularly of the second generation – were mild in their presentation of Calvinism. Like Charles Simeon they realized that the gulf between them and the Methodists was not as great as had earlier been made out.[25] When Wesley and Simeon met on 30 October 1787 Simeon discovered that there was far more agreement among them than differences – they both agreed that salvation was by Christ from first to last. 'Then, Sir, with your leave I will put up my dagger again for this is all my Calvinism – this is my salvation, my justification, my final perseverance. It is in substance all that I hold and as I hold it and therefore if you please, instead of searching out terms and phrases to be the grounds of contention, we will cordially unite in those things wherein we agree.'[26] Maybe as Ronald Knox put it, they were trying to make a 'molehill out of a mountain'.[27] The breach had already been made and Calvinistic and Wesleyan evangelicals pursued separate paths, yet it is not possible to account for the rise of the missionary movement without noting the way in which moderate Calvinist and Arminian were producing a style of evangelicalism where agreements were more important than disagreements. Rigid predestination was hard to square with the missionary impulse of the revival. The second generation of Anglican evangelicals were 'sublapsarian'. Similar styles of Calvinism began to prevail among some of the Baptists in what can be called 'Fullerism'[28] which lay behind the evangelicalism of William Carey. Calvinism was not the greatest barrier between the Wesleyans and the Evangelicals. The organization which Wesley built was in itself the divisive force. The Evangelicals never had the close knit organization of the Methodists. Wesley's comment in 1769 that 'the ministers of our church who believe and preach salvation by faith . . . are a rope of sand and such they will continue' was not entirely wide of the mark.[29] Whitefield lacked Wesley's organizing ability and 'apart from the influence of the Countess of Huntingdon in providing a centre and nucleus round which the Calvinist tradition might group its adherents, it remained by comparison with Wesley's societies inchoate and amorphous', until the days of the Clerical Associations, and even they were not really connexional.[30]

Charles Smyth has said that the 'history of the Evangelical Revival is essentially a history of personalities rather than opinions'.[31] The leading personalities of evangelical thought were a very diverse group and it is not easy to make generalizations about their relationship with Methodism. Samuel Walker (1714–1761) of Truro, Thomas Adam (1701–1784) of Wintringham and William Grimshaw (1708–1763) of Haworth provide links between Wesley and the second generation of Evangelicals. Grimshaw was for a time, in effect, one of Wesley's clerical assistants, making his vicarage a Methodist headquarters, but, as we have seen, though he had no objection to working in other men's parishes, he gave up close connexions with Wesley when preachers began to be licensed as dissenters. Walker and Adam broke more fundamentally with Wesley over the problem of church order, in particular the problem of connexionalism versus the parish systems.[32] We have already quoted from the Wesley-Walker correspondence and need not repeat the debate. Walker's main objection to Wesley's methods concerned lay preaching and the itinerancy, also the control of the Methodist societies by sympathetic Anglican clergy. Walker was quite clear that his duty was to remain within the parish boundaries ordering his society on strictly Anglican lines. Wesley was just as insistent on itinerancy. The same problem arose at Huddersfield when Henry Venn (1725–1797) was vicar. He wished the Methodist Society to be under his care, though the members of it wished to have their own preachers. 'These eagerly desire them to preach there still; not in opposition to Mr Venn (whom they love, esteem and constantly attend) but to supply what they do not find in his preaching. It is a tender point. Where there is a gospel ministry already, we do not desire to preach, but whether we can leave off preaching because such a one comes after is another question . . .'[33] A compromise was reached on 7 August 1761 when it was arranged that the preachers should come monthly. Later the preachers were withdrawn altogether for a time, though John Pawson asserted that they returned without Wesley's knowledge, provoking Venn's curate to entreat people from house to house not to hear them. In 1764 the twelve clergymen present at Conference requested withdrawal of Methodist preachers from parishes with an evangelical incumbent.[34] Charles Wesley supported this request but John would not give up his societies. Occasionally an evangelical incumbent moved in the opposite direction. Joseph Easterbook at the Temple Church, Bristol apparently attached his converts to Methodist classes.[35]

   Wesley's problem was one which beset Methodist and Evangelical alike. What guarantee was there of a continuity of an evangelical presentation of Christianity in a particular parish? One solution was the provision of 'proprietory' or private chapels such as those of Lady Huntingdon, the Lock Hospital and Bedford Chapel, but neither proprietory chapels nor 'lectureships' was a lasting guarantee of evangelicalism. In Halifax the proprietory chapel belonging to the Akroyd family was a failure and was sold at an auction in an inn to the Wesleyans, becoming the ancestor of the present circuit church in that town.[36] The problem at its most acute and ironic can be seen at Truro, Huddersfield and Reading.[37] Walker at Truro organized his own parish society forbidding real links with the Methodists. When he died, his successor, Charles Pye, is reported to have said 'My pulpit stinks of Calvinism that not a century will purge it'. The ultimate consequence was the Congregationalist Church founded in 1770. Walker had so impressed on his converts that they must not become Methodists that they became Independent! In 1766 Wesley had written 'at noon, I preached in Truro. I was in hopes when Mr Walker died the enmity in those who were called his people would have died also. But it is not so; they still look upon us as rank heretics and will have no fellowship with us.'[38]

In Huddersfield the problem had the same ironic consequences. When Henry Venn decided to resign the cure, he wrote at once to Lady Huntingdon imploring her to press for the nomination of his successor. He pressed the claim of his curate Riland. The patron, however, bestowed the living on Harcar Crook, a clergyman of different churchmanship, whose first act was to suspend the Thursday evening 'lecture'. The congregation dispersed, despite the curate reminding them that they had the gospel in the prayers and could pray for the conversion of the vicar! The same process occurred in Reading after the death of the Hon. W. B. Cadogan in 1807 and at Wallingford when Thomas Pentycross died in 1808. Evangelical congregations were always liable to fissiparism at this time. The ultimate solution of the problem was the creation of the Simeon Trust in 1817 for the purchase of advowsons followed by the Church Pastoral Aid Society (1836) and the high-church Additional Curates Society (1837) which had the effect of hardening party lines and which has bedevilled the parish system making Anglicanism in practice Congregationalist with party theological colleges backing up the system.

The Evangelicals had to decide what their attitude to church order was to be. This naturally influenced their atitude to the Methodists. John Berridge (1716–1793) serves as an illustration of what we can call the 'irregular' or 'half-regular' solution of the problem, Charles Simeon (1759–1836) as the supreme example of the 'regular' solution.[39] Berridge had no scruples about breaking the normal rule of church order 'and sure there is a cause where souls are perishing for lack of knowledge. Must salvation give place to a fanciful decency and sinners go flocking to hell through our dread of irregularity!' He was an Anglican but quite prepared to sit loose to the niceties of canon law. 'In birth and education I am both a churchman and a dissenter – I love both and could be either and wish real gospel ministers of every denomination could embrace one another ... establishments are commonly of an intolerant spirit and draw in shoals of hirelings by their loaves and fishes; yet I am very thankful for an establishment which affords me a preaching place and an eating house without clapping a padlock on my lips or fetters on my feet.'[40] For Berridge there was but one canon: 'Go preach the gospel to every creature' and if the parish priests would not do it, then he must. This type of thinking introduces a new division of churchman which cuts across the old distinction of low and high Anglican and dissenter. Division into evangelical and formal could lead to the kind of Donatism we have already seen in Methodism. Human beings came to be divided into two classes – the converted, the 'vital' Christians; and the unconverted, themselves either infidels or 'formal' Christians. On this basis the 'awakened' in church and dissent could and did work together, encouraged by Newton at Olney and by Berridge at Everton.

Ultimately, however, the churchmen could not stomach 'the clergymen beating the bush and the dissenters catching the game'.[41] The regular party was to win the day led by Simeon who sought to solve the problem of church order by 'steering the Evangelicals between the Scylla of an academic latitudinarianism and the Charybdis of that pastoral enthusiasm which walks disorderly in its indiscriminate and unthinking zeal'.[42] Simeon, though always friendly with Berridge, was greatly influenced by Henry Venn, whom he met at Yelling and though wont, at times, to be irregular, 'himself conditioned the younger man to avoid excess of irregularity'. Simeon, whom Macaulay reckoned to have more sway than any prelate, marks the real beginning of what can be called an Evangelical 'party' in the Church of England with a definite ethos and definite principles – principles which governed its relationship with Methodism during this period. 'It was Simeon more than even the greatest of his predecessors who taught and exemplified the fact that the warmest Evangelical without any real sacrifice of interdenominational paternity in Christ can and should be watchfully loyal to the order and organization of the English church in the normal exercise of its energies.'

Simeon who was Vicar of Holy Trinity Cambridge from 1783 to 1836, organized his parish on a society basis but, like Walker at Truro, on strictly Anglican lines. He made sure his flock were not dissipated by the dissenters. 'Were the bishops acquainted with the ministers who are called Evangelicals, they would soon see the importance, yes, and the absolute necessity of such meetings, not merely for the edification of the people but chiefly for the preservation of the Established church . . . where nothing of that kind is established, the members of any church are only as a rope and may easily be scattered with every wind of doctrine or drawn aside by any proselytizing society.'[43] Simeon made no doubt of his preference for Anglicanism over Dissent with its lack of formal liturgy and its tyranny of people over pastor (a familiar Wesleyan complaint at the time also). He was always prepared to co-operate with Dissent but would not preach in dissenting meeting houses. John Venn adopted a similar policy. He warned Edward of Kings Lynn about admitting Dr Thomas Coke to his pulpit: 'They would esteem you a Methodist preacher in your heart who was restrained only by the love of emolument in the church, from openly connecting yourself with them.'[44] Simeon's conduct led some to say that he was more of a 'church-man than a gospel-man' but such phrases beg more questions than they answer. Simeon represents, as we shall see, an Anglican style prepared to co-operate within certain limits with Methodism and Dissent, while pointing out what he felt to be the deficiencies of Dissent yet never 'unchurching' dissenting Christians or denying that they were part of the Church of Christ. This has remained by and large the evangelical stance.

Thus the fundamental divergence between Evangelicals and Methodists was over the problem of church order or rather how the spreading of scriptural holiness could be contained in parish boundaries, though later this was eclipsed by differences over Establishment with episcopal pressure falling on any irregularity, with toleration itself in danger.[45] 'The Church of England was by far the most important of the national institutions about which the Evangelicals in the period under discussion had to make up their minds . . . It seemed that England could become as righteous a nation as the degeneracy of the times allowed, if only the Evangelicals could capture the national church.' By 1800 the separation on the former issue is fairly clear. The French Revolution tended to harden divisions – no longer could an Evangelical feel free as John Newton had done to go to a dissenting meeting house. Wilberforce and Hannah More were willing, it seems, to deny that they had visited dissenting meetings, though in Wilberforce's case his Anglo-Catholic sons were at pains to defend their father from having agreed to unite with dissenters, admitting that he and his friends were 'hardly to be blamed for their "holy daring" ', which the torpor of the church had made necessary.[46] Henry Martyn typifies the new attitude when he notes in his *Journal* for 2 September 1804: 'Mr Andrews, a Methodist, begged me to preach at their chapel, which I refused, of course.'[47]

The refusal was an example of the Simeonite view of church order which had prevailed over that of Berridge and the semi-irregulars.

The divergences between Methodists and Evangelicals may be summarized as varied concepts of church order, differences in theology concerned mainly with election and perfection, the stress (which increased in the post-French Revolutionary tensions) on the need for Establishment for purposes of social cohesion and ecclesiastical discipline, which rather dwarf the church order issue. Finally there was a distinct sociological difference.[48] The Evangelicals – Lady Huntingdon took an early lead here – were able to reach the upper classes in a way which Methodism never did. Methodism might boast a few squires such as Robert Carr Brackenbury (1752–1818) and 'a few rich ones over whom the gospel sways' but no one who 'wears a coronet and prays'.[49] There was a greater degree of respectability in the Establishment than in Methodism. Walker, as early as the 1750s, feared that 'meekness of wisdom' is not among them (that is the Methodists). 'If it were, they would know their place better and be subject. It has been a great fault all along, to have made the low people of your council.' 'The Evangelical Party,' claims Angus Buchanan with some exaggeration, 'was decisively an upper class party. When Evangelicals ministered to the "lower orders" as they did, to their great credit, in many industrial parishes and through the devoted labours of lay people such as Hannah More, their methods were rigidly paternalistic. The recipients of their philanthropy were given no opportunity to assume leadership themselves.' Halévy[50] is probably right in revealing a sociological ladder up which richer members of Wesleyan societies might climb.[51]

Yet despite these divisions there was a basic unity between Evangelicals and Methodists which showed itself in active co-operation in the anti-slavery movement, to some extent on the mission field, in the British and Foreign Bible Society and the general drift of theology, where the agreements (as Simeon clearly saw) were far greater than the disagreements. The anti-slavery movement was one of the leading concerns of the Evangelical Revival.[52] John Wesley himself was one of the pioneers with his *Thoughts on Slavery* of 1774.[53] The last letter he wrote was to Wilberforce.[54] 'Unless the Divine power has raised you up to be an Athanasius *contra mundum* I see not how you can go through your glorious enterprise in opposing that execrable villainy which is the scandal of England and of human nature . . . Go on in the name of God and in the power of His might till even American slavery (the vilest that ever saw the sun) shall vanish away before it.' In the agitation of 1792 twenty-one nonconforming bodies including Roman Catholics sent in petitions securing a total of 132,978 signatures. The Methodists, however, sent petitions with 229,426 names.[55] Conference gave its heartiest support to the anti-slavery movement. By a rare incursion into party politics Wilberforce was given active and open support in the election at York in 1806 and 'it is no exaggeration to say that a major reason why Wilberforce retained his seat was the untiring endeavours of Methodists in York to secure his election'.[56] In the fight against slavery there were strange alliances – Jeremy Bentham and William Wilberforce were agreed here if in nothing else! Bentham even said 'If to be a "saint" is to be against slavery – then I am a "saint" – saintship for me'.[57] The 'saints' – as the Evangelicals of Clapham were called, were the motive power behind the movement. They formed a group 'whose brains and brilliancy could not be denied even by those who sneered at their religion'.[58] The Clapham group taught a method of agitation and a strategy of organization and propaganda quite new in English history. There was much common ground here with the thinkers of the Enlightenment, however much they differed on other issues.[59] Liberty, benevolence and happiness were key watchwords. The evangelical mind accepted much of the moral philosophy of the day – notably the belief in liberty as a cardinal virtue, in benevolence as the duty of men and in happiness as a proper goal. The first the Evangelical saw in terms of the freedom of the sons of God and set forth a style of 'liberation theology' which links the liberation of soul and body, the second he saw as ineffective without a Christian imperative. The third he believed to be vain if sought as an object in itself. 'Their ability to transpose, to supercharge these values stemmed from a desolating conviction of their own sin, the assurance that sin is forgiven and could be overcome by the grace of God and by the consequential assurance that they could overcome the effect of sin in other men by the same grace.' It has been shown in the notable study of the late Roger Anstey that in the 1806–7 abolition of the slave trade, unpredictable and fortuitous politico-economic elements combined with the limited but noteworthy operation of moral ideals.

In the later stages of the agitation Methodists were prominent. Joseph Butterworth (1770–1826) and Thomas Thompson (1754–1828), both of whom were Methodist members of parliament, Butterworth sitting between 1812 and 1818 and again from 1820 to 1826, were in constant touch with the Clapham Evangelicals. Co-operation here was on a personal rather than an organized basis. Adam Clarke, Thomas Coke and later Jabez Bunting and Richard Watson (1791–1833) were prominent in the anti-slavery movement. In 1817 Watson attracted the attention of Macaulay who wrote to Hannah More, 'Our great meetings this year have certainly been better conducted than I have ever known them – Watson, the

Wesleyan Methodist, spoke with singular delicacy and feeling and with a degree of good taste that would have done credit to even such a man as Reginald Heber. He is certainly both an able and honest man.'[60] Bunting and Watson were fervent in their support of the Anti-Slavery Society (1823) which is not surprising when it is realized that of 32,000 Methodist members in the West Indies in 1823, 23,000 were slaves and often persecuted for their faith.[61] In 1825 and 1830 Conference pronounced on the slavery issue, in 1825 denouncing it as 'one of the most heinous of our public offences' and in 1830 urging Methodists to use the general election in the cause of the abolition of slavery.[62] In the former year Conference also thanked Thomas Fowell Buxton and Joseph Butterworth for their efforts in the Commons on behalf of the Revd W. J. Shrewsbury (1795–1886), one of the several Wesleyan missionaries who had been molested in Barbados and elsewhere.[63] In cases like that of Shrewsbury and the Revd John Smith in Demarara, Evangelical and dissenter were always in close co-operation.

It is significant that in 1832 – the year of the great Reform Bill – when Michael Sadler (1780–1835), the factory reformer, who had once had Methodist connexions, and Thomas Babington Macaulay contested the constituency of Leeds, Watson urged Methodists not to hesitate between the two but to vote for Macaulay because of his record in the struggle. Macaulay was elected. This could be ammunition for the view propounded by Bernard Semmel that the Wesleyans, spearheaded by Bunting and Watson, syphoned off energy, including the pennies of the poor, into a great missionary crusade against the Kingdom of Satan in tune with other Evangelicals and that British imperialism, which picked up the 'England land of destiny' theme from the seventeenth century. Perhaps indeed 'heathens who bowed down to wood and stone were rather more exciting than local lapsed Christians who were often dirty, drunken and dangerous'.[64] Not so much should be read into the Macaulay election. Jabez Bunting supported at the same time a Tory as against a radical, Thornley, an abolitionist, at Liverpool.[65] James Stephen, future colonial secretary, saw Methodism as the church's ally in overseas mission. 'It is enough to know that wherever I find a colony the most peaceful and the most orderly, and in which the views of the British Parliament are most fully carried into effect, there I find a colony where Wesleyan Missionaries have been most laborious and successful.'[66]

The struggle against negro slavery made Protestants aware of their responsibilities in taking the gospel to other races. The years from 1792 to 1818 saw the first explosion of the modern missionary movement which was to lay the foundation of the world communions and indeed of the ecumenical movement as well as the now rather undervalued principle of trusteeship, even if from the beginning there was the inevitable link with economic and later nationalistic imperialism. Forces inherent in Calvinism at its best and in Methodism prepared the way for the upsurge of missionary enterprise in the last decade of the eighteenth century.[67] William Carey was instrumental in founding the Baptist Missionary Society in October 1792, to be followed in 1795 by the London Missionary Society – supported largely by Independents, Presbyterians and a few Anglicans like Dr Thomas Haweis, Rector of Aldwinkle and Pentycross, Vicar of Wallingford. The society was to be a missionary society upon a large and liberal plan for sending ministers of Christ to preach the gospel among the heathen. The meeting of directors stated its aims on 9 May 1796:

> It is declared to be a fundamental principle of the Missionary Society that our design is not to send Presbyterianism, Independency, Episcopacy or any other form of church order and government (about which there may be differences among serious persons) but the glorious gospel of the Blessed God to the heathen; and that it shall be left (as it ever ought to be left) to the minds of the persons whom God will cast into the fellowship of His Son from among them to assume for themselves such form of church government as to them shall appear most agreeable to the word of God.[68]

This was a symptom of what we can call the ecumenical movement of the 1790s. It was to be short lived. The LMS was a challenge to Evangelicals. Should they support it or be content with the SPG or found a society of their own? To a man of Charles Simeon's principles there was but one answer. He could not apply the interdenominational principle on the mission field. 'We cannot join the (London) Missionary Society, yet I bless God for they have stood forth . . . Directly not a moment to be lost.'[69] He lent his arm to the foundation in 1799 of a missionary society in direct connexion with and under the sanction of the Church of England – the Society for Missions to Africa and the East, which ripened into the Church Missionary Society. The missionary thinking of the Eclectic Society of Simeon and Venn had reached fruition when at the Castle and Falcon in Aldersgate Street on 12 April 1799 the new society came into being with Venn as Chairman, Thornton as Treasurer and Wilberforce and Grant as Vice-Presidents.[70] Venn had laid down the dictum that the society was to be founded 'on the church principle but not the High Church principle'[71] – thus distinguishing it from both the SPG and the LMS. There was no overt element of rivalry with other societies – 'a friendly intercourse shall be maintained with other Protestant societies engaged in the same benevolent design of propagating the gospel of Jesus Christ.'[72] Methodism's response was also in the end denominational, a point not entirely made clear by Semmel.

For some time Wesleyan money was going to the LMS, provoking 'godly jealousy' in Methodist leaders such as Coke and later Jabez Bunting. Coke writes in October 1812, 'The LMS are forming committees of two or three of our friends to raise annual subscriptions among our societies for the support of *their* missions. He sees no reason why we should throw "thousands into their laps" when we are so pressed with debt, and if we are to employ hundreds of thousands of pounds in Asia, shall we employ them in establishing Calvinism in that vast country instead of Methodism?' Coke's enthusiasm, the aggressiveness of the LMS in fund raising, the support of Bunting, Watson and others, the foundation of local missionary societies like that in the Leeds district in 1813 culminated in the Wesleyan Methodist Missionary Society of 1818 which came under the direct control of the Wesleyan Conference with every member automatically a member of the society.

Thus the various societies developed under the auspices of the separated denominations spreading their own concepts of church order in the lands to which their missionaries were sent. Co-operation between Methodist and Evangelical was of a purely personal character, though cordial. William Fox who had spent ten years in the Gambia said in 1851 respecting the CMS and WMMS: 'Between the Church and Wesleyan missionaries the utmost cordiality appears at all times to have existed: nor does the history of the mission furnish a single example to the contrary.'[73]

If the missionary societies had to work on parallel lines, there were other ways in which Evangelicals and Methodists did co-operate directly, notably in the distribution of Christian literature. The Religious Tract Society of 1799 was interdenominational from the start. It did a great deal to spread evangelical thought in the form of cheap tracts designed often to counteract the radical tracts and papers of the kind sponsored by Richard Carlile and William Cobbett.[74] Hugh Richmond's *The Dairyman's Daughter* and *The Sinner's Friend* sold enormous numbers. In this age of societies and pressure groups which now appear appallingly patronizing to the poor, one group could quickly sponsor another. Such was the case with the British and Foreign Bible Society in which again the Clapham sect took the leading part.[75]

In the provision of scriptures, however, a Methodist sponsored organization must take precedence in time. The founding of the Navy and Army Bible Society was due largely to the efforts of John Davies and George Cussons, two Methodist laymen.[76] The society developed from a chance conversation between these two on 10 September 1779 and with the financial aid of John Thornton of Clapham, through William Romaine, many bibles were distributed during the following months to regular troops and militiamen. The movement was ultimately advocated by two bishops and later by the Archbishop of Canterbury and the Duke of York.

There was again happy co-operation in the BFBS on whose committee there were three secretaries – an Anglican, a foreign Protestant and a dissenter. The primary object of the Society was to distribute the scriptures 'without note or comment', a fact which led many Anglicans to feel that it smacked too much of biblicism, Chillingworthian sentiments about 'the Bible and the Bible alone being the religion of protestants'. Bishop Marsh of Peterborough, avowed enemy of Calvinism, Charles Daubeny and others opposed the Society for not including the Book of Common Prayer with the Bible. The status of the Apocrypha furnished much material for argument as did the status of Unitarians in the Society upon which Rowland Hill made the apt comment, 'It is preposterous to refuse to let Socinians distribute the only antidote to their errors – maybe he would accept the Bible from the Devil himself, only he could take it with a pair of tongs.' Despite difficulties – it is claimed that no public prayer was offered at meetings of the Society until 1857 because of wrangles over styles of liturgy or lack of it[77] and bishops' charges critical of the Society – Evangelical and Methodist were able to serve here together. For some years Dr Adam Clarke, Methodism's leading scholar, was loaned by the Wesleyan Conference to the Society, a foreshadowing of the happy relationships that had for so long existed between Anglican, Methodist and dissenter in the field of biblical scholarship which was a prime factor in ushering in modern ecumenism.[78]

The catalogue of societies could be continued – all the criticism that could be made of their patronizing tone has been made by Ford K. Brown with the devastating criticism that 'Wilberforce adopted the impossible task of seeking to reform the morals and manners of a society, while disturbing no element of its socially immoral structure'.[79] Evangelical discipline and responsibility before the great taskmaster's eye could so easily be secularized as respectability. It was certainly the cardinal factor in what Harold Perkin has called the 'battle for the heart' which was turning the fleshy, earthy, plain-speaking England of Fielding and Johnson (but also the England of Gin Lane and Beer Street) into the conventionally respectable, carefully-worded England of Dickens and Matthew Arnold –

inhibited, polite, orderly, tender-minded and sometimes hypocritical which could link with utilitarianism in its stress on talent, industry and merit, propagating the great Victorian myth of the self-made man.[80] But co-operation was not always manifest in the evangelical sub-culture. In 1810 the SPCK – for long almost dormant – had begun the distribution of cheap tracts on parallel lines to the Religious Tract Society, though with a much more strictly Anglican bias. For instance, on the SPCK list of pamphlets from 1803 to 1829 was a *Dialogue between a minister of the church and his Parishioner concerning those who are called Evangelical Ministers* by Thomas Sikes, Vicar of Guilsborough. In the dialogue the vicar remonstrates with one of his parishioners for going to a neighbouring village to attend the ministrations of an evangelical clergyman. 'The dissenting teacher stands upon his ground with honour but the Evangelical plays the hypocrite in a most shocking manner. He receives the bishop's ordination which puts him into the church and then directly in opposition to it.' There was little hope of dissenters working with Anglicans here, but there was more of it in societies such as the London Society for Promoting Christianity Among the Jews (1809), though later dissenters withdrew from this, and the various societies which had as their aim the correction and education of public morals and overt social control. In 1787 Wilberforce had stated that 'God Almighty has set before me two objects – the suppression of the slave trade and the reformation of manners'. The second object used the methods and tools of the groups who sought to suppress vice at the end of the seventeenth century by the use of informers. The Proclamation Society was set up in 1787 to implement the Royal Proclamation against vice and immorality issued in June 1787. In 1802 the Society for the Suppression of Vice was created which is now best known for Sydney Smith's gibe in the *Edinburgh Review* for 1808 that it was 'the Society for the Suppression of the Vices of those with under £500 a year'. This society was limited in membership to Anglicans but its aims had the overt support of Methodism.[81]

Co-operation, then, was widespread in the anti-slavery movement, in overseas missions and in the societies for the dissemination of Christian literature and for the spread of the *mores* of the evangelical world. There *were* barriers of church order, but these barriers were never totally inhibiting. There was no unchurching. In Wilberforce's words from the highly influential *Practical View* of 1798, 'Let them cultivate a catholic spirit (echoes of John Wesley's sermon) of universal goodwill, and of amiable friendship towards all those, of whatever sect or denomination, who differing from them in non-essentials, agree with them in the grand fundamentals of religion.'[82] Despite the differences, there was agreement in the 'grand fundamentals' in both ethical conduct and general theological outlook. The *Methodist Magazine*, the *Evangelical Magazine*, the *Christian Observer* and the *Eclectic Review* with minor differences sought to spread the same kind of strict code of conduct and social control in which Sunday observance played a growing part and in which theatres, romantic novels, balls and card playing were equally frowned upon. It was John Pawson, President of the Wesleyan Conference, who burned a copy of Shakespeare's plays with John Wesley's marginal notes as 'worthless lumber'. Another Methodist, John Styles, wrote on Shakespeare, 'Barefaced obscenities, low vulgarity and nauseous vice so permanently figure in and pollute his pages that we cannot but lament the luckless hour in which he became a writer for the stage.'[83] Perhaps the Methodists were less obsessed with some of this. Their lower social scale would make other temptations more obvious. Pre-millenarianism, also, was much more typical of the Anglican than of the Methodist evangelical.

In theology, as in morals, there was a measure of broad agreement between Evangelical and Methodist particularly after the 'Calvinist controversy' had settled into a disagreement on the doctrines of justification and sanctification. Basic to evangelical and Methodist theology was the belief in the depravity of man and original sin, doctrines taught in Collect, Prayer Book and Articles. Samuel Bradburn, the Methodist, in 1792 said that the universal corruption of human nature generally termed original sin is the leading principle of Christianity,[84] even though John Wesley always began with universal love and original righteousness. It was sentiments such as those of Bradburn which caused F. D. Maurice to remark that 'immensely valuable as I hold the Methodist preaching of the last age to have been, with the Evangelical movement in the church and among the Dissenters which was the result of it – utterly dead as I conceive the faith of the English nation would have become without the rekindling of it – I cannot but perceive that it made sinful man and not the God of all grace the foundation of Christian theology.'[85] Man's sin needs atonement.

The other great prop of evangelical theology was the death of Christ conceived as a substitutionary atonement for the sin of mankind. The stress lay on soteriology rather than Christology, atonement rather than incarnation, *Christus redemptor* rather than *Christus consummator*.[86] Justification by faith with the subjective experience of conversion were alike stressed with correspondingly less stress on baptism, which Charles Simeon saw as a change of *state* but not a change of *nature*, a foreshadowing of battles to come, as in the Gorham case.[87] The eucharist, which as we have seen was certainly not neglected by Wesley, even if his followers pushed it to a less central place, was always revered by Evangelicals as a means of grace and it is clear that a revival of eucharistic faith and practice (not least weekly communion) is as much to be attributed to Evangelicals as to Tractarians.[88] Indeed it is possible to see Wesley's eucharistic thinking as a link, through cross-bench figures like Alexander Knox, with the neo-Anglicanism of the Oxford Movement.[89] Evangelicalism concealed the seeds of a church renewal of a far more comprehensive kind than that which was carried out by the Methodist bodies or by the Evangelicals in the Church of England. Wesley's legacy was never fully used up by his direct successors and largely ignored by the Tractarians. It is difficult to find Brilioth's view that 'it was in some measure his spirit which was to fertilize the organism of High Churchmanship that it once more could bear offspring' other than somewhat romantic.[90] The rediscovery by Anglicans of John Wesley – sacramentalist – was a feature of the 1860s and 1870s but not of an earlier period.[91]

The wide diffusion of evangelical moral codes gave rise to the frequently asserted notion that the Evangelical Party was dominant in the English church at the beginning of the nineteenth century. Lecky in 1878 wrote of the Evangelical Movement becoming dominant 'before the close of the eighteenth century' continuing in that position until the rise of the Tractarians.[92] Much more accurate was W. J. Conybeare's article of 1853 and Gladstone's statement of July 1879 that one twentieth of the clergy were evangelical before 1820.[93] 'But as a party, whatever else it may have been, it was the very reverse of dominant. It was active, useful, respected, healthy and thriving but it was repressed and struggling and in some sense rebellious.' Even Gladstone's estimate may have been exaggerated. Recent research by Michael Hennell and Peter Toon bears this out.[94] At the beginning of the nineteenth century, evangelical clergy were caught up in what has been called a move from 'status' professionalism to 'occupational' professionalism in which a man's skill and expertise became more important than his social status.[95] The demand in evangelical circles was for a new style of parish clergyman – upright, zealous, a capable preacher and organizer with a multiplicity of religious meetings and societies in the parish.[96]

Typical of the new breed in the large towns were Hugh McNeile in Liverpool, Hugh Stowell at Manchester, Daniel Wilson at Islington, W. W. Champneys at Whitechapel and J. C. Miller, Rector of Birmingham from 1846 to 1866.[97] McNeile and Stowell shade off into Orange politics and the so-called 'Protestant Crusade' in Ireland; Miller was much more the mainstream Evangelical. Whilst there was cordiality between Miller and dissenters like John Angell James in Birmingham,[98] there was a barrier of social caste between Evangelical and Methodist. Aggressive Anglicanism was meeting Dissent, which, through its grip on the middle classes, was developing political muscle. Methodism was not yet fully part of the dissenting political scene. Typical of Methodist sentiment was a letter to Jabez Bunting from the Superintendent of the Sheffield circuit in 1829 who remarked that though his society was making converts among the poor, the rich were flocking to the Anglican churches. 'Two new ones have been opened and a third is nearly finished, all supplied by what are called evangelical clergymen, chiefly young, active and zealous men who strive to equal us in good work and then they are of the Establishment.'[99] The reference to Evangelicals is interesting here, for I find no evidence that they were favourable to Methodism at this time. Later in the century, in the sparse parishes of the diocese of York which had spawned hundreds of chapels, the Archbishop, Thomson, a leading Evangelical, countered Dissent and secularism with the by then familiar recipe of money, men, churches and parsonages.[100] Evangelical and Methodist had co-operated in societies in the age of Wilberforce and were to do so still in the Evangelical Alliance (1846) of which for a time W. M. Bunting was, like his father before him, an honorary secretary,[101] but the Evangelicals could scorn the Wesleyans in their parishes because the chapel was not necessary any more. They began to solve the problem also of the 'eloquent convert' who could easily turn Methodist if not given scope.[102] Evangelicals, too, tended to support the Establishment while the Tractarians above all were concerned with spiritual autonomy, hence their stress on apostolic succession and tradition, matters which were secondary adiaphora or dangerous by-ways to many Evangelicals.

Methodism never quite equalled the fervent anti-Romanism of *The Record* (founded 1828) and its supporters, though Wesleyanism had at times a distinctly Orange tint, especially, as we shall see later, over the grants to Maynooth Seminary and in the early days of the Alliance, though 'the alliance could not turn the great agitation against the papal aggression to any permanent advantage'. The astute Wesleyan theologian William Arthur's (1819–1901) lengthy *The Pope, the Kings and the People* (1877) is an eccentric riposte to the First Vatican Council full of the world-wide Jesuit conspiracy. It is reasonably sane in comparison with some evangelical outbursts, nor did Methodism espouse the intense pre-millenarianism of some Evangelicals. The somewhat harsh Calvinism of the 'Recordites' and Orangemen produced a style of evangelicalism which linked up with a fear of the end of Establishment in England, as well as its inevitable doom in Ireland. The 'ecumenism' which was represented by the Evangelical Alliance was a grouping of those who had a dogged belief in the plenary inspiration of the Bible, a stress on imputed righteousness and an antipathy to what John Angell James, of Birmingham, in 1842 called the three Ps – 'Popery, Puseyism and Plymouth Brethrenism'. Some of the political implications of this we will indicate later. There was a subtle but perceptible difference of ethos between the quietism of Keswick and the holiness traditions of Methodism, which were firmly Arminian.[103] It has often (up to today) been the case that the hardline Anglican evangelical has not unchurched his Methodist neighbour because of lack of valid ministry but because of what he deems unsound and modernistic theology. The consequence was a theological isolationism and an aloofness and lack of genuine reciprocity unless one used the required theological code.

It has often been stated that Methodists and Evangelicals were essentially individualistic with a very loosely formulated doctrine of the church. The matter is relevant to the history of ecumenism, since it raises the question of episcopacy, intercommunion and the vexed question of confirmation which was a bone of contention in the Anglicanism of the last generation and still raises its head, when a Methodist of good standing is episcopally confirmed on joining an Anglican church, as if the life and the rites of the other church were neither valid nor regular. Norman Sykes (anticipated long before by Edward Bickersteth in 1844) showed, conclusively, in his outline of the Anglican attitude to episcopacy since the Elizabethan Settlement, that the exclusive episcopalian position taken up by the Tractarians and their successor had not been the norm.[104] 'It was one of the characteristic *differentiae* of the Anglican theological position in an age, when its opponents alike presbyterian and papist advanced exclusive claims for their particular form of ecclesiastical polity, to combine the defence of the primitive and apostolic nature of episcopacy with the allowance of other forms of church government. The Anglican attitude was to marshal the evidence both spiritual and patristic for episcopacy without asserting exclusive validity for an episcopal ministry or unchurching non-episcopal churches.' If the extreme Anglo-Catholic or Puritan pushed an exclusive view, the *via media* has been generally upheld by most representative Anglican theologians. Certainly this was the case in the eighteenth century. The so-called 'branch' theory of the church which allowed a special validity to the episcopal communions, even if they existed in parallel rivalry, was not normal Anglican thinking, though it must be made clear that the apologists sometimes drew a distinction between foreign Protestants and 'our separatists here at home', as Wake called them, who had, as far as Anglicans were concerned, transgressed the *cuius regio, eius religio* (whose is the rule, his religion prevails) concept, thus weakening the Protestant front against Rome by dissenting from the Establishment on secondary grounds.[105]

We have already noted the controversial practice of 'occasional conformity' whereby dissenters showed 'charity towards the church', connived at by some Anglicans, violently disliked by the more Tory clergy and by the stricter dissenters like Daniel Defoe who saw it as 'playing "bo-peep" with God Almighty'.[106] The rubric of the Prayer Book of 1662 stating that 'none shall be admitted to the Holy Communion until such time as they be confirmed or be ready and desirous to be confirmed' was rarely quoted in the eighteenth century. Confirmation in any case was often a most perfunctory business. Many folk were probably confirmed more than once. Archbishop Vernon-Harcourt of York may not have been typical, but it was his custom to say the words of confirmation once while extending his hands over the congregation! In 1722 at Wolverhampton the bishop found there had been no confirmation for twenty-seven years – 'Certainly it ill becomes the critics of the railroad and motor car ages to disparage the endeavours of bishops of previous centuries, even the eighteenth, until before casting their stones they have made trial of the task under like conditions.' This may be so, but presbyteral confirmation would have solved it speedily!

Many Methodists clearly were confirmed and would not come under the negative of the rubric. Strange anomalies of practice have been recorded. Thus Adam Clarke relates that after having been commissioned to preach by John Wesley he was later confirmed in 1782 when at Kingswood. As a boy he had been prepared for communion by the parson with the aid of the catechism but no mention of confirmation.[107] Confirmation, in the theology of the period, was not considered the main rite of Christian initiation but rather the confirming of baptismal vows. In Jeremy Taylor's words 'Confirmation is the consummation and perfection, the corroboration and strength of Baptism and baptismal grace for in Baptism we undertake to do our duty but in confirmation we receive strength to do it . . . In Baptism we give up our names to Christ, but in confirmation we put our seal to the profession and God puts his seal to the promise.' Daniel Waterland gave four signs of necessary preparation of which confirmation was not one. They were baptism, competent knowledge, sound faith and true repentance.[108] Confirmation besides is 'highly expedient' but baptism is strictly necessary. This was clearly John Wesley's view. He left confirmation out of the *Sunday Service* which was not only intended for America. In fact in Wesleyanism, membership of a society became the normal perquisite of admission to communion. After controversy in 1889 the Wesleyan Conference declared, 'That the Table of the Lord should be open to all comers is surely a great discredit and a serious peril to any church.'[109] In certain respects the Wesleyans were stricter in matters of rubric than Anglicans, though the 'Open Table' clearly became the practice, whatever rubrics might say.

If episcopal confirmation were not given the place later accorded to it by the Oxford Movement and better transport systems, what of an episcopally ordained ministry? Here again Anglican practice does not conform to the norm that the Tractarians later desired. Latitudinarians like Bishop Warburton saw church order as being variable; Bishop Sir George Pretyman-Tomline, an old opponent of Wesley, readily acknowledged that there is no precept in the New Testament which commands that every church should be governed by bishops.[110] Thinking like that of Warburton and Pretyman is reflected in practice where the employment by even the SPCK of foreign ministers in Lutheran orders during the first century of its history was generally unchallenged. Lutheran ordination was clearly believed to be valid if irregular. As Norman Sykes commented, 'The patronage and employment by the SPCK of the German-Lutheran ministers, though a recognition de facto of the validity (as distinct from the regularity) of their orders, did not imply an acceptance of them *de jure* . . . Nevertheless it is difficult to explain the society's policy in sending out ministers ordained as Mr Spetschneider has testified to have been ordained (in 1818) save on the basis of the recognition that Lutheran ordination was valid, though irregular.' When Reginald Heber was on the continent in 1806 he communicated with the Lutherans, the normal Anglican practice before the 'old Catholics' appeared on the European scene.[111] By 1825 the use of foreign ministers by CMS and SPCK had largely ceased, as much due to evangelical zeal in securing a bishopric in India as anything else. Episcopally ordained ministers became the norm on the mission field.

It is against this background that Wesley's churchmanship and that of the Evangelicals must be judged, not that of the Tracts. Wesley and Charles Simeon alike derived their churchmanship from the wide diversity of opinion of the Hanoverian age. Simeon clearly was in the tradition of post-Reformation Anglican churchmanship, acting in typical pre-Tractarian manner when visiting Scotland. 'As an episcopalian, therefore, I preached in episcopal chapels, and as a member of the Established church, I preached in the presbyterian churches – after all, where the King attended, there a clergyman may preach.'[112]

There was, however, another group of Anglicans who impinged upon Methodist and Evangelical, opposing both as compromising church order. These were the high-churchmen or perhaps better the 'orthodox'. These were those who ascribed to the church a divine origin and an existence independent of the secular society. Generally speaking in religion and in theology these men were the successors of Caroline Anglicanism. The 'orthodox' could trace their pedigree through the Caroline Divines, the Non-Jurors and William Law who were also all among the spiritual ancestors of Wesley. These were those who came among the Tractarians to be thought of as the *fortes ante Agamemnone*, that thin red line linking the seventeenth century with Keble and Pusey.[113]

The thinking of this group is seen at its sharpest in Archdeacon Daubeny whose *Guide to the Church* was published in 1798, a year after Wilberforce's *Practical View*. Daubeny criticizes Wilberforce for making the church one of the 'non-essentials of the faith. Is it a matter of indifference whether Christians belong as members of the Church of Christ or members of a schismatic congregation which is a "synagogue of the devil"?'[114] The guarantee of the church for Daubeny is episcopacy, the apostolic ministry. It is unquestionably of the *esse* of the church. Dissenting ministers and sacraments are outside the church. Bishop van Mildert of Durham stated a similar view in his Bampton lectures of 1814 and like Bishop Herbert Marsh and Bishop Samuel Horsley was opposed to Methodists and Evangelicals alike. Horsley complained of 'disorderly zeal' in the Methodists and saw them as the unwilling tools of the Jacobins. He defined his orthodoxy as true high-churchmanship. 'He who thinks of God's ministers as the mere servants of the state is out of the church, severed by a kind of self excommunication.' Thomas Sikes, the Rector of Guilsborough, who later made the famous prophecy, reported by Pusey, that, whereas the church is hardly mentioned now, 'we shall soon hear about nothing else',[115] was a parochial representative of the same style of thinking. 'He who would look for Christianity without bishops, may as well look for it without sacraments.' For that 'saucy itinerant', Wesley, he has no room. 'No clergyman has the liberty of officiating where he pleases and to whom he pleases; he cannot do this in this kingdom without intrusion on the cure of other ministers.'[116] This is true 'whether he practise the more generous means of openly dissenting from the church, or the insidious mode of assuming the form of a "true" churchman.' Sikes likewise objects to 'occasional conformity' – just as occasional whoredom destroys chastity, so occasional schism destroys communion. It is 'disgraceful and indefensible'.

The group of high-churchmen, who came to be known as the Clapton Sect (Clapton was the home of Joshua Watson) or the Hackney Phalanx (from H. H. Norris, rector of Hackney), men like Daubeny, Sikes, Watson, Norris, Hugh James Rose and Christopher

Wordsworth, form, with Bishop Jebb and Alexander Knox, a link between the old high-church Anglican tradition and the Oxford Movement. Knox shared many of the presuppositions of the high-churchmen, but inherited with his high-churchmanship a good deal of the thinking of the Wesleys. He hoped, indeed, 'that the time will yet come, and that it is not at any very great distance (though I confess as yet I see no sign of its approach) when the providential deposit which distinguishes the Church of England will be rightly appreciated; and Mr Wesley's designation as the precursive announcer of its hitherto undeveloped excellences will be fully understood and adequately recognized.'[117]

Knox stands as a remote and eirenical figure in the strife of ideas that has been described. He sought to be both Catholic and Protestant at the same time and saw in Wesley the unison of Greek and Latin, Augustine and Chrysostom. Like Wesley he revered the liturgy and the ancient church and realized more than his fellow high-churchmen that in attacking Methodism and Evangelicalism they were attacking the notions that could give their own doctrines that power they lacked. 'No church on earth has more intrinsic excellence; yet no church probably has less practical influence.' Knox is a strange cross-bencher, rare in any age, who saw the essential catholicity of Wesley's thought in a way hidden from the Tractarians.[118]

The tragedy of nineteenth-century English religion is that Methodist, Evangelical and high-churchmen (whether orthodox or Tractarian) never realized how much goodly heritage they had in common, splitting into warring factions, two inside and one outside the Church of England. The two souls that seemed to live at ease in the breast of Alexander Knox could not dwell together in the English church. Evangelical and Tractarian saw themselves as opposites rather than complements. Methodism, separate from evangelicalism, save for the ways of co-operation that we have discussed, and High Church alike drifted into a theological isolation and narrowness that for long frustrated the impact it might have had on the English church and nation.

7

The Rise of the Nonconformist Platform.
Dissent, Methodism, the State and Politics 1791–1852

The problem of the relationship between church and state raises issues which go to the roots of political philosophy and indeed the problem of the true nature of civil society with its 'associations' between the individual and the state, which can be defined as 'an association which, acting through law as promulgated by a government endowed to this end with coercive power, maintains within a comunity territorially demarcated the universal external conditions of social order'. In England two great questions were raised in the nineteenth century. If a nation's constitution is democratic, should not all religions be equal before the law? Is Establishment, i.e. a state religion, as distinct from bodies tolerated and legally recognized, compatible with equality before the law and with democracy? The relationship of church and state was changed fundamentally in the years 1828–9 by the repeal of the Test and Corporation Acts and Roman Catholic emancipation. England as a society acknowledged the reality of religious plurality. Richard Hooker's dream of 'one commonwealth and one church' was dead, despite Thomas Arnold's desire to perpetuate it by a comprehension of dissenters in a church, the breadth of which *The Times* dismissed as 'an ecclesiastical Noah's Ark'.[1] It is significant that it was in 1829 that La Mennais in France published *Of the Progress of Revolution and the War against the Church* in which he demanded freedom for the church from state dominance and from the pressures of liberalism, a parallel reaction to that of Newman, Keble and Pusey which triggered off the Oxford Movement in 1833. In Scotland, too, the Disruption of 1843 led by Thomas Chalmers over state patronage (not in this case Establishment as such) which created the Free Kirk, like the Oxford Movement, asserted the autonomy of the church in relation to the state.[2]

The events of 1828–9 have a long pre-history which we can trace back to the 'atomic fall out' of ideas from the American and French Revolutions which profoundly affected the subsequent history of Dissent (including Methodism) and the Established Church. Indeed no Establishment could feel secure after the events of 1789 and its consequences, which became the symbol of an international conspiracy against all law and all government and even religion which made Dissent more suspect. 'To write of Nonconformity and Dissenters,' wrote Edmund Calamy, 'is in the esteem of some to write of schismatics and rebels – to commend them is little better than to write in praise of Nero.'[3] Throughout the eighteenth century dissenters still lived under the stigma of revolution and regicide. Although there were frequent compensatory Indemnity Acts, the Test and Corporation Acts remained in force officially inhibiting dissenters from holding office in the state. Many dissenters, no doubt, would have wished to be free of the entail of the past but were not allowed to forget, nor were they forgiven whatever their mercantile enterprise might do for the nation. In 1790 Gilbert Wakefield's *Constitutional Layman* described them, ironically, as a 'set of puritanical, republican rebels – sworn enemies to our King, our Bishops, our clergy and the whole church'.[4] They were victims of a kind of political original sin, retaining because of it the mentality of revolt, embodying what Edmund Burke in another connexion called 'the dissidence of Dissent and the Protestanism of the protestant religion'. Eighteenth-century Dissent still retained a great interest in politics. If there was a creed common to much of the Nonconformity of the period it was a religio-political one, a rejection of hierarchical authority, the natural rights of determination according to conscience, power residing in the congregation.

The consequences of the American Declaration of Independence in 1776 were, in America, a new pattern of relationships between the state and the churches with independent Anglican and Methodist churches in 1784. Article Six of the Constitution prohibited religious tests for federal office, the first Amendment providing that 'Congress shall make no laws regarding an establishment of religion or prohibiting the exercise thereof'. Religious intolerance was incompatible with a philosophy of natural rights, 'life, liberty and the pursuit of happiness'. There was in the case of America mutual recognition by the state of the churches and by the churches of the state. Church property was to have charitable status, state money could be granted to chaplains. The consequence was a growing acceptance of denominationalism, the growth of the voluntary principle in church matters and the steady advance of a patriotic piety which could be secularized as the divine mission of the American people. From this period, too, stems the 'frontier' tradition of revival which, as we have seen, was to spill over into England, beginning but not ending with Lorenzo Dow. The American War of Independence and the Wilkes agitation produced among many dissenters an estrangement from the House of Hanover which deepened during the years after. The beginning of the French Revolution brought this to the fore.[5]

The historiography of the relationship of Dissent to the French Revolution has often been vitiated by an overemphasis on the 'rational Dissenters',[6] led by men of the calibre of Richard Price (1723–1791) and Joseph Priestley (1733–1804), products of the most liberal of the dissenting academies, forming a cultural élite of radical thought within the dissenting community. The opinions of Price and Priestley were well enough known. Like the young Wordsworth, they hailed the revolution as a great harbinger of liberation.

> Bliss was it in that dawn to be alive
> But to be young was very heaven.[7]

Richard Price, who died before the Terror began, had said in the sermon 'On the love of our country' which so provoked Burke, 'I could almost say "Lord now lettest Thou thy servant depart in peace, for mine eyes have seen Thy Salvation." I have lived to see thirty millions of people, indignant and resolute, spurning at slavery and demanding liberty with an irresistible voice, their King led in triumph and an arbitrary monarch surrendering himself to his subjects.' Robert Hall, the Baptist, somewhat later spoke of the revolution as the 'most splendid event recorded in the annals of history'. It would not be difficult to produce a long catena of quotations from dissenter and Whig politician to this effect. Charles James Fox and Romilly hailed it as the happiest event in history. Horace Walpole was heard to congratulate Hannah More on the fall of the Bastille! It might be noted that ardour was somewhat cooled when the revolution devoured its children. 'One might as well,' said Romilly, 'think of establishing a republic of tigers in some forest of Africa as of maintaining a free government among such monsters.'[8] When in 1798 a Baptist pastor, John Martin, declared in a sermon that 'should the French land, some, yea many, of those different and differing people [Dissenters] would unite to encourage the French', there was a considerable furore. After a hasty enquiry Martin was expelled from his denomination.[9]

Halévy was on safe ground when he said that the advocates of revolution were the exception among the Baptists and the Independents and that 'all contemporary evidence agrees that if the old Nonconformist denominations remained faithful to Whiggism the vast majority of their members belonged to the right wing of the party'.[10] Bernard Manning endorses this view:

The accident that one of the greatest writers of English chose that sermon [The love of our country] as the text for his *Reflections on the French Revolution* has perhaps given undue prominence to one side of Dissent in the late eighteenth century. Some persons – more ingenious than the textbooks, have attempted to draw a firm line of distinction between the sluggish, conventional patriotism of the 'orthodox dissenters' and the clear-eyed prophetic revolutionary doctrine of the Unitarians. Such a distinction cannot bear examination, for at the very time when the Deputies spoke for the whole body of Protestant Dissenters (on 22 April 1789) with such perfervid affection for the King and the constitution, they were probably more under Unitarian than any other influence.[11]

However true these observations may be, the reaction of 'rational dissent' to the French Revolution affected government policy towards all dissenters, not least Methodists. The outbreak of the revolution effectively put an end to any hope of an immediate repeal of the Test and Corporation Acts or of a repeal of the so-called Clarendon Code. Henry Beaufoy attempted to obtain repeal of the Test Acts in 1787 and 1789, repeating the familiar arguments about the reduction of Holy Communion to what William Cowper called an 'office key, a picklock to a place'. 'The Saviour of the world instituted the Eucharist in commemoration of his death – an event so tremendous that nature, afflicted, hid herself in darkness – that the British legislature has made it a qualification for gauging beer barrels and soap-boilers' tubs, for writing custom house dockets and debentures and for seizing smuggled tea.'[12]

Such arguments would carry little weight with Pitt, who felt that the Test Act kept out of office all those who thought so ill of the church that they refused to communicate with it. Beaufoy was defeated by 178 votes to 100 in 1787 and in 1789 by 122 votes to 102. Fox spoke in favour in 1790 but the French Revolution had altered the whole complexion of events. Pitt was now openly hostile. Burke could raise the spectre of Priestley whose views on Establishment were predictable: 'When I see the fungus of an establishment upon the noble plant of Christianity, drawing its best juices, when I see this sloth upon its stately branches, gnawing it and stripping it bare ... must it not without delay extirpate the fungus, destroy the sloth?'[13] Fox was defeated by 294 votes to 105. A similar fate was meted out to a comprehensive Toleration Bill of Lord Stanhope in the Lords in 1789, the bishops being on the side of the opponents. The defeat inflicted on Fox's motion of 2 March 1790 for the repeal of the Test Act was decisive enough to 'bludgeon the question out of politics for many a long year'.[14]

What happened in Parliament was paralleled on a more violent scale in the country. On 13 July 1791 and for five days afterwards[15] what a contemporary described as the 'bunting, beggarly, brass making, brazen faced . . . bustling, booby Birmingham mob'[16] was raising almost for the last time the old cry, 'the church in danger, the King in danger'. The country gentlemen were calling out an urban mob to draw the dissenting teeth of the Birmingham bourgeoisie. Priestley's house and chapel were wrecked. He was virtually chased out of England. The populace showed an anti-foreign bias and were not likely to idolize radicals and free thinkers as they had idolized Wilkes. There were disturbances at Manchester. In Leeds Paine's effigy was paraded and burnt, as it was in Durham, as a 'guy' on 5 November. If the Gordon Riots had demonstrated that John Bull would not stomach concessions to popery, these Birmingham and London rabblings were a sign that they would not tolerate Protestant dissenters or even Whig gentry dallying with the dangerous doctrine of a foreign revolution. The liberalism of Pitt was a thing of the past. The remainder of his ministry witnessed a kind of repression through fear of Jacobinism that was unparalleled in the eighteenth century. The grim figure of the Jacobin brooded over every debate.

Methodist Conference opinion was not unsympathetic to repressive measures. The Christian conservatism of Burke was more to the taste of many Methodists than the rationalism and doctrinaire acceptance of Jeffersonian ideals of liberty, equality and conscience. Wesley's political opinions were still dominant. His 'Christian Toryism' was long to influence Methodist thought, even if it never meant blind allegiance to any one faction. The 'no-politics' rule was not necessarily an invitation to support the *status quo*, though it often appeared so and more radical opinion always disliked it.[17] Any idea that the people were the source of power was abhorrent to Wesley: rulers were given their power by God alone as an accommodation to human sinfulness.[18] Wesley's system of government fitted in with his political theory. This was an area where he simply followed fashion. Any totally representative theory of government was rejected on moral, practical and theological grounds; the people were not fit or qualified to govern. Power, in any case, came from above – from God – and not from below. Any idea of a social contract would have seemed quite immoral to Wesley whose view in this particular matter was closer to Burke than to Locke or the philosophical radicals. Rights are only to be seen in a context of duties. 'The state is a partnership in all science, a partnership in all art; a partnership in every virtue and in all perfection. As the end of such a partnership cannot be obtained in many generations, it becomes a partnership not only between those who are living but between those who are living, those who are dead and those who are about to be born.' The poor and oppressed might think otherwise! But from this hierocratic style of thinking could stem a flexibility to the future and a horror of the doctrinaire schemes of rational democracy. Only those who cannot conceive that some Christians may not be left wingers can fail to see some mobility in the tradition of 'Christian Conservatism'.

Gordon Rupp's warning has, however, to be heeded. 'Great are the temptations which come when Satan appears as an angel of light; but the most sinister of all temptations to the church is that which comes, as it came to the Wesleyans and the Roman Catholics in the nineteenth century, when the angel of light is disguised as Satan, and when the call of divine truth, divine compassion and divine justice is unheard and unheeded because it is embedded in an ideology atheistic, unchristian, anti-clerical and profane.'[19]

Official Methodism professed loyalty to church and king in a series of monotonous statements. So in 1792 Conference stated 'None of us shall either in writing or in conversation speak lightly or irreverently of the government under which he lives. We are to observe that the oracles of God command us to be subject to the higher powers and that honour to the King is there connected with the fear of God.' To the Irish Conference of 1797 the customary letter of greeting added 'We shall lose all the turbulent disturbers of our Zion – all who have embraced the sentiments of Paine and place a great part of their religion in contending for (what they call) liberty.' However; by 1811, as we shall see, Conference could sing another tune and it can be said, too, that 'Methodism gave a new interpretation to the church combining a voluntary principle with authoritarian government an individualist and Puritan basis of salvation with a universal application of the doctrine'.[20]

The 1797 Conference statement refers to the Kilhamite agitation that disturbed and divided Methodism between 1795 and 1798. It is an illustration of the impact of dissenting and radical ideas. Kilham considered himself an out and out dissenter, alienated from and opposed to the church and Establishment.[21] His reforming pamphlets *Martin Luther, Aquila and Priscilla, Paul and Silas, Trueman and Freeman* and *The Progress of Liberty among the People called Methodists* are an interesting mixture of ideas derived from Scotland, America and France – they used the clichés of the age just as Marxist clichés tend to be used by the 'theologians of liberation' today. In Kilham's constitution power comes 'from below'. This was, as yet, unacceptable, though by an irony not uncommon in ecclesiastical politics, most of his proposals were later taken on board the Wesleyan system. E. R. Taylor's comment is apt. Kilham wanted to follow the logic of what he thought was a democratic system. 'He overlooked the essentially autocratic character of Methodist organization and saw only the semblance of democratic institutions.' His view was 'unhistorical but prophetic'.[22] It is true that the Wesleyans refused to countenance the vital item of Kilham's programme – the representation of the people in all stages of connexional government, but it can be argued, as by Semmel, that there was an inherent liberalism in the Methodist system that was bound ultimately to make itself felt.[23] Kilham was perhaps more than prophetic. The ordinary people had no part in shaping, organizing or managing the social or economic affairs of the nation, they had no vote and no voice in fixing wages or terms of labour. Methodism gave men and women responsibilities that they had not known before. From privilege and responsibility in the religious community would stem a natural desire for such privileges and rights in the state. The 'natural rights' theories, even if they were really incompatible with the Methodist doctrine of human depravity and were condemned by Jeremy Bentham as 'nonsense on stilts', could not go long unheard. The Kilhamite controversy reveals that lay Wesleyanism was spawning a more democratic and more dissenting doctrine of church polity than that of the more conservative itinerant preachers and the more affluent members, who were later to float Jabez Bunting as their leader. Even if the New Connexion did not draw off many members, it was a portent of strains within the connexional system – and the expulsion of Kilham a sad price for loyalty to the Establishment.[24]

Radical views in one section of Wesleyanism served to increase ecclesiastical and governmental fears of subversive and Jacobinical opinion within Dissent. Neither bishops nor the government were likely to differentiate between the various denominations of dissenters and Methodists, especially when itinerant preachers swarmed over the land. In 1800 the Bishop of Rochester, Samuel Horsley, who was a notable leader of clerical opinion, feared that 'the Jacobins of this country are making a tool of Methodism just as the *illuminés* made a tool of Freemasonry, while the real Methodist, like the real Freemason, is kept in ignorance of the wicked enterprise the counterfeit has in mind'.[25] Sunday schools came likewise under episcopal threat. Such conspiracy theories were common. Many pamphlets of the period make similar charges, suggesting that a body of Anglican opinion not only linked Methodism with Dissent but linked it with the comparison being made between contemporary Dissent and the Puritanism of the Great Rebellion. Thus religious hatreds became bound up again with political hatreds, with the ever present fear of revolution stemming either from a militant radical Dissent or a militant proletariat.

Between 1799 and 1811 there were signs of a definite hardening of the Anglican attitude to Methodism going alongside a rather self-conscious profession of loyalty on the part of the Wesleyans which may have masked more radical views. The supporters of the Establishment began to turn to the Toleration Act, noticing that its provisions did not include the innumerable preachers and teachers that Methodism was raising up. Fear of rural 'ranterism' was increasing. Pitt, at the instigation of Pretyman-Tomline, Bishop of Lincoln, even contemplated introducing a Bill in 1799 more closely defining toleration. Wilberforce strongly opposed this measure and in 1800 prevented interference with itinerant preachers. Point was, however, given to the fears of the government by the *Report of the Clergy of Lincoln* of the previous year which discussed Methodism. The Methodists were neatly divided into those who still attended church and their own chapels, those who attended chapel only, and a third group vaguely but ominously described as 'commonly ignorant men with gross, opposing views'. The *Report* notes the fact that the Methodists generally did not consider themselves to be dissenters.[26] The clergy recommended 'explanations and amendment of the Toleration Act', a fact which links with the contemplated Bill in the Commons. Joseph Benson answered the charges contained in this document against Methodism, for fear that the *Report* would prejudice the government against it. Governmental fears of revolution had two conflicting effects on Wesleyanism – it made it fearful of anything suggesting real Dissent, hardening its core of conservatism, and at the same time precipitated a slide into the dissenting camp through the political action it was now necessary to take to combat growing governmental intolerance. The Committee of Privileges was ready for political action.[27]

The rumblings of suspicion were first heard in the matter of the exemption from the militia of licensed preachers.[28] The large number of Methodist preachers now licensed and the widespread itinerancy of the minor connexions created the problem which had not arisen with the fixed pastorates of the older dissenting bodies. *The Sketch of the History of the Protestant Dissenting Deputies*, published in 1813, analyses the returns made at the request of Lord Sidmouth, revealing that the number of persons taking the oath under the Toleration Act of 1689 was 80 from 1760 to 1766, but 1,318 from 1795 to 1801, and 1,068 from 1802 to 1808, with that year showing the highest figure. The number of registered or recorded buildings was 671 from 1760 to 1766 compared with 3,680 from 1802 to 1808.[29] Clearly the conditions were very different from those of 1689 when a status almost as clearly defined as that of the incumbent of the parish was contemplated. An official enquiry revealed that the number of churches and dissenting chapels in parishes of over 1,000 inhabitants was 2,533 Anglican places of worship as against 3,438 meeting houses.[30] Lord Harrowby, speaking in the Lords, prophesied a day when the majority of the nation would be Nonconformist. Sidmouth stated on 2 June 1809 that he had reason to believe that licences were taken out to avoid the militia.[31] This matter was a concern of Conference in 1803 and again in 1809, the first date coinciding with the setting up by the Wesleyan Conference of the Committee of Privileges, distinctly parallel to the Protestant Dissenting Deputies. The Committee had been set up following investigations of the matter of Sunday drilling of the militia in Jersey, which provoked correspondence between Thomas Coke and Lord Liverpool, leading to the refusal of the Royal Assent to an Act of 1798 of the States in Jersey banishing those who would not bear arms on a Sunday.[32]

The politics of these matters is complex. During the first ten years of the nineteenth century there were several difficulties of this kind. On the whole the government showed itself willing to listen to sober dissenting opinion. The Whigs needed Nonconformist support to obtain majorities in the boroughs, the Tories were beginning to consider the possibility of securing the backing of evangelical noncon-formity.[33] Freedom of worship in the army was granted in 1802, though W. H. Rule was to fight many battles with officialdom on this matter well into the Victorian age.[34] In local affairs the situation was by no means so tolerant. Parson and squire continued the petty persecution that has done so much to sour relationships between 'church' and 'chapel'. 'Nothing,' says Bernard Manning,

> but the exact perusal of the ... Minutes (of the Protestant Dissenting Deputies) will suffice to show the vast extent, the meanness, the venom, the relentlessness of the persecution which went on, sometimes within the law, sometimes outside it. No matter was too paltry, no grief too poignant, no place too sacred, no rite too solemn, no violence too scandalous, no unchivalry too despicable. It is a squalid but a necessary enquiry. So much has been heard of the dissidence of Dissent and the unreasonable readiness of Dissenters to take offence that it is important to examine the soil which has produced the unlucky side of Nonconformity.[35]

Manning was a doughty and sometimes partial champion of orthodox Dissent but his words are applicable to this period.

Myles quotes several examples of local persecution and of other actions in which the Magistracy and the Court of King's Bench gave verdicts in favour of the Methodists. The opposition of squire and parson was paralleled by what amounts to a press campaign against

Methodism in which such diverse characters as Sydney Smith, Leigh Hunt, Robert Southey and William Cobbett played a part. T. E. Owen in *Methodism Unmasked* (1802) rails at the Methodists for refusing to bear arms on Sunday.[36] Itinerancy should be suppressed. Cobbett's *Weekly Register* makes the same point: 'The drilling on Sunday is, it appears, contrary to the dictates of certain Methodistical Conferences. I cannot but spurn at the thought of making all the people of England bend to the humours of a perverse, insolent and factious sect of wretches who have generally speaking been guilty of the most base and detestable crimes.' The *Examiner* in 1809 carried a series of articles by the editor under the title of *An Attempt to show the Folly and Danger of Methodism*. Leigh Hunt claimed that the watch night and love feasts are the occasion of eroticism. At the same time he calls the Methodists melancholy and miserable – people who gave thanks to God when Sadlers Wells was burned down! Ridicule was the best weapon against such people. Sydney Smith could supply plenty of that! His biting and yet lovable scorn was poured for years on the 'nasty and numerous vermin of Methodism' until he turned to the 'pragmatical, perpendicular, Puseyite prigs'. January 1808 saw an article in the *Edinburgh Review*, a note 'On the Increase of Methodism and Dissension' by R. A. Ingram. 'To the learning, the moderation and the rational piety of the Establishment we must earnestly wish a victory over the nonsense, the melancholy and the madness of the Tabernacle.' The *Quarterly Review* joined in with an article in November 1810 from the pen of Southey. Admitting the role of Methodism – 'industry and sobriety, quiet and orderly habits and the comfort that results from them will be found its fruits, yet the preachers,' he says, 'have unpleasant faces. They have already attained as distinct a physiognomy as the Jews or the Gipsies – coarse, hard and dismal visages as if some spirit of darkness had got into them and was looking out at them.' Methodism, he feared, was already a distinct people in the state. Certainly much of this is perverse but Wesleyanism was a fairly tight self-contained group. Attacks of this nature produced again attempts at self-justification and measures of self-defence which pushed them further into Dissent. The first is typified by the attempts to suppress camp meetings in 1807, which led locally to the expulsion of Hugh Bourne and William Clowes and the subsequent establishment of Primitive Methodism.[37]

The other side of the picture is seen in the constitutional battle with Lord Sidmouth from 1810 to 1812 out of which the political forces of Dissent emerged victorious and in which the Wesleyan Connexion made its first real incursion into the field of ecclesiastical and national politics.[38] On 2 June 1809 Lord Sidmouth (1757–1844), an inveterate Tory, formerly Prime Minister Addington and a loyal

Anglican (who as Prime Minister had abolished income tax), stated in the House of Lords that 'he had reason to believe many persons took out licences as dissenting ministers under the Toleration Act, for no other purpose than that of obtaining an exemption from parish service under the militia'. Sidmouth had received information from Justices of the Peace like Mr Sparrow of Stafford who had written to say that fifteen men, of whom nine were journeymen potters, had presented themselves to take the oath as Methodist preachers. Ten of them had declared that they had no particular congregation. This is a reflection of the Potteries and Cheshire revival which fuelled Primitive Methodism. On 18 June 1810 Sidmouth declared his intention to bring in a Bill to prevent any person taking out a certificate as preacher or teacher unless he had attained the age of twenty-two, was appointed to a congregation and could produce testimonials of his fitness for office. On 29 April 1811 Sidmouth gave notice that his Bill would be introduced on 9 May. The debate began that day with Sidmouth claiming that 'at most of the Quarter Sessions where the oaths were taken and the declaration made, it was now understood that any person whatsoever, however ignorant and illiterate, whether descending from a chimney or a pillory, if he appeared before the Quarter Sessions . . . taking oaths – could demand a certificate.' Among the list he had noted from two archdeaconries there were men who had been 'blacksmiths, cobblers, tailors, pedlars, chimney sweepers and what not'. Sidmouth wished each preacher to be guaranteed by six substantial householders. At the end of the speech he made clear that he regarded the Church of England as the great preservative of the principles and morals of the people – unfortunately we were in danger of having 'an Established church and a sectarian people'. Opponents of the Bill on its first reading included leaders of Whig thought such as Lord Holland and the Earl of Stanhope who thought it a breach of the principles of toleration.[39]

The *Methodist Magazine* gives some indication of the tremendous stir that the publication of the Bill made throughout Methodism for it became clear that the Bill was aimed at Methodism and would, if passed, put in jeopardy every local preacher, if not every itinerant. Adam Clarke and Thomas Coke sought an interview with Sidmouth. He appears to have allayed their fears,[40] but not those of the Committee of Privileges which was quickly convened. Coke seems to have thought that Wilberforce was behind Sidmouth, but was disabused of his misunderstanding throwing himself behind the connexional solicitor, Thomas Allan (whose place in Methodist politics has recently been established), Joseph Butterworth MP (1770–1826) and Thomas Thompson MP (1754–1828). The

Committee sought through a delegation to 'kill' the Bill by securing its withdrawal, but failed. The point was made about the particular nature of Methodist preachers and stress was laid on their work for 'the instruction of the ignorant and the relief of the miserable' and the fact that the connexion was not antagonistic to the Church of England – points which were germane and pertinent at the time when the young Jabez Bunting was confronting the Luddites in Halifax and when pious versions of what has become the 'Halévy thesis', that Methodism produced stability, were expedient and had some credence.

The second reading of the Bill was fixed for 17 May, which gave the dissenters little time to mobilize public opinion. Yet 700 petitions were presented by 'the Deputies' and 30,000 signatures by the Wesleyans.[41] Sidmouth refused to withdraw the Bill at Lord Liverpool's behest. In the debate the Archbishop of Canterbury (Charles Manners-Sutton), though acknowledging the Bill 'to be of the utmost utility to the community', deemed it unwise to proceed. Lord Stanhope noted that the petitions proved the strength of public opinion. 'He hated,' he said, 'the name of Toleration; it was a beggarly, narrow, worthless word. It did not go far enough; he hated toleration because he loved liberty.' This was the Whiggish sentiment of a *politique* which can be contrasted with the Tory establishment thinking of laymen like Sidmouth and bishops like van Mildert who in 1821 could say, 'We concede toleration freely and fully. We claim only to be equally unmolested in our privileges, and thus to preserve the relations of peace and amity. What more does Christian charity require?' Dissenters were not any longer prepared to accept that kind of argument. The affair of Sidmouth's Bill revealed the first stirrings of the Nonconformist conscience or 'platform', for except for Thomas Belsham, the eminent Unitarian, and some of his élitist friends, the full weight of Dissent was thrown again at the Bill. This included the Wesleyans who were taking a crucial step into the dissenting camp. When it became clear that the Bill would not pass through the House of Lords, it was dropped, never to appear again. 'The defeat was an important turning point. A Tory attempt at religious restriction had failed, not least because Tory ministers were unwilling to court opposition. This was a sign that Anglican exclusiveness could expect little effective sympathy even from ultra Tories when they had to meet the pressures of office in a plural society.'[42]

Conference in 1811 and the dissenting Deputies alike capitalized on their success. The creation of the Protestant Society for the Protection of Religious Liberty of 1811 was a sign that certain elements in Dissent were prepared to battle at once for the abolition of 'every penal law which prevented the complete enjoyment of religious liberty'.[43] For a time the battle shifted to the localities where magistrates interpreted the Toleration Act harshly. The Justice of the Peace could almost be said to rule the countryside during the reign of the first three Georges. In Petty or Quarter Sessions they combined judicial and administrative functions covering practically every facet of life – law and order, prisons, Poor Law, the labour code, highways, bridges, weights and measures, production and distribution, 'rates, recognizances, records, perjury, piracy and play houses, dissenters, dogs and drains'. According to the Webbs, by 1832 there were 1,354 clerical magistrates, a quarter of the whole bench. 'Never before or since has England seen so much clerical government as in the half century before the Reform Act', with the preserving of social cohesion high on the agenda.[44] Typical of what could happen was in Swansea where two ministers had their appeal against the militia ballot refused as they were not ministers of a separate congregation.[45] Likewise at Leeds in February 1812 several preachers were refused licences on the same grounds.[46] Not all cases, however, went against the preachers. In one riot against a Methodist congregation at Pershore, the defendants were reminded by the judge that the parties assembled were not a private meeting to hear an 'enthusiast' but to hear a licensed preacher in a licensed meeting house. Another case, this time in Berkshire, was tried before a magistrate who imposed a penalty of £20 on a Methodist preacher for 'unlawful preaching' and then again before the Quarter Sessions, where the conviction was quashed.[47]

This local uncertainty led both the Deputies and the Wesleyan Committee of Privileges to strike while the iron was still hot. Early in 1812 the Deputies' Chairman, William Smith, had a meeting with Prime Minister Spencer Perceval producing a Bill embodying the views of Dissent against the 'Five Mile' and 'Conventicle Acts'. The assassination of Perceval did not delay the matter. The Bill (which, clearly, has the skilled hand of Thomas Allan upon it as well as the omnipresent Smith) received the Royal Assent on 29 July 1812.[48] This Act marks the end of the penal legislation which had so plagued John Wesley. The political point was that the state could no longer be guaranteed to come to the aid of the church. Plurality was now well over the horizon.

Conference in 1812 duly rendered thanks to the Committee of Privileges while exhorting its members 'to fear the Lord and the King and meddle not with them that are given to change'. 'Murmuring and discontent' did not help the poor.[49] This was the time when Jabez Bunting, in Halifax, refused to conduct the burial of a Luddite, though he attended his funeral and his friend Thomas Jackson was battling for law and order down the hill in Sowerby Bridge. Adam

Clarke and Joseph Butterworth appended a letter to superintendent ministers making clear the provisions of the new Bill, especially pointing out that Methodists need not renounce their Anglicanism to gain protection under the Toleration Act. Thanks are added to a notable cross section of English political life including the Archbishop of Canterbury, Liverpool, Castlereagh, Stanhope, Holland, Wilberforce, Stephen and Babington. This Act marks the beginning of the end of the epoch which began in 1689. Credit must go to a coordination of Wesleyan and dissenting sentiment, a sign as yet no bigger than a man's hand of the great Free Church Alliance of the late Victorian age. Government realized the strength of the unity of Dissent. It would, too, as Halévy pointed out, have been folly to antagonize Dissent, when the supporters of Catholic emancipation were stronger than they had ever been.[50] Adam Clarke and the old guard of Wesleyans might still proclaim themselves 'thorough members of the Church of England'. 'I believe I am a Methodist of the old school,' he wrote in 1821 to Alexander Knox.[51] 'I can say to you that the attachment of the Methodist body to the Established Church is now greater than I ever knew it. Whether right or wrong, dissenterism in all its principles is wholly alien to my Creed and feeling.' There is no reason to doubt Clarke's sincerity in this matter and there is little reason to doubt either that many Methodists would concur, but the pressure of events was pushing the Wesleyans into the dissenting camp. Clarke's sentiment neatly expresses the tension among the Methodists between a Church of England that had forsaken them and a Dissent which they disliked, but in whose image they grew year by year.

Wesley's conservatism which so deeply influenced Methodism remained as a backcloth to Wesleyan thought well into the nineteenth century. Adam Clarke – though I suspect he could think dangerous radical thoughts at times! – uttered sentiments on the constitution worthy of the Duke of Wellington.[52] The 'no politics' rule was not so much a sign of a rigid adherence to a *status quo* (even if it had that effect at times) but a statement of the view that Wesleyanism was basically a religious not a political society. Moral issues were part of Christian sentiment – slavery was chief among them, an example of the crusading fervour which so often serves as 'politics' for many dissenters, who attribute greater weight to Conference votes and resolutions than they usually warrant. It needs to be remembered, too, that something like the 'no politics' rule prevailed also in the Church of England and that 'politics' in an age before great party manifestos and the power of the omnicompetent state often meant 'faction' rather than party politics in a modern sense. 'It was much easier for churchmen to decide what was a party or political matter and what was a constitutional issue affecting the interests of the church or a moral question affecting religion when legislation was little concerned with social and economic relationships.'[53] The Toryism (much more accurately conservatism and quietism) of Wesleyanism can be exaggerated, but clearly in the 1820s there was opposition to radicalism of all kinds, a political quietism which may have masked a fear of repression not far below the surface.

With the internal battles within Methodism we are not concerned here save to note that John Kent and David Gowland have shown that the old stereotypes of 'dominant Toryism' and 'underlying liberalism' are too simplistic a summary with which to typify Methodism, though it is clear that the low Methodism of the Protestant Reformers and the Warrenites were normally more liberal or radical than the high Methodism of Jabez Bunting and his lay and ministerial allies who would be thought conservative by those who approved their policies and dangerous innovators by those who thought them destructive of true Methodism.[54]

In the 1820s Wesleyanism, pulling itself together financially, and beset by tensions caused by revivalism, social radicalism, by the Sunday schools and the post-war fall in prices reaching painful breaking point in inner-city areas like Leeds, was largely politically quiescent.[55] There was support for the repeal of the Test and Corporation Acts in 1828 which in the end was supported even by van Mildert who paid tribute in the House of Lords 'to the obligations we owe to them in literature, in arts and sciences, in religion, in biblical criticism and even in government itself', a phrase like later Lambeth Conferences in generous mood.[56] On the emancipation of the Roman Catholics there was division. G. I. T. Machin speaks of Methodists forming a 'solid corps in the anti-Catholic resistance'.[57] The Irish Catholic Relief Acts of 1791 and 1793 had removed most of the remaining serious restrictions on the worship of the Catholic community together with disabilities concerning property, but the struggle for full emancipation was hampered by anti-papist prejudice fostered by Evangelical and Methodist alike. Some Wesleyan chapels seem to have been prominent in organizing 'no popery' petitions. The *Leeds Mercury* for 10 January 1829 reports that the Wesleyan minister at Cadishead invited his congregation to sign a petition against concessions to the Catholics (a moral not a political issue no doubt!) but the congregation walked out.[58] This may have been exceptional – the *Mercury* could be depended on for a liberal view! Wesleyanism was thus divided, with the powerful figure of the President, Jabez Bunting, then approaching the peak of his power and influence, crucially on the side of emancipation in contrast with many Wesleyans and many high-churchmen, including Newman, who had not yet looked in the mirror and seen the Donatist or Monophysite face.

Into the complexities of the passing of the Roman Catholic Emancipation Act we need not go. The recent research of David Hempton reveals a consistent anti-Catholic stream in Wesleyanism,[59] which was to emerge in full spate over the increased grant to the College of Maynooth in 1845 when Jabez Bunting found himself, not for the first time, opposed to Peel.[60] To typecast Wesleyan leaders as supporters of Toryism is far too simplistic.[61] Jabez Bunting, it can be argued, was more old Whig than old Tory, but old Whig in the last analysis implies an alignment with the dissenting side, even if he wished to stand 'stock still' on the middle ground between the Establishment and Dissent, friendlier to Establishment than to Dissent, whose pseudo-democratic procedures stuck in his gullet. In 1834 Bunting, writing to James Kendall, a high-church Wesleyan, then a minister at Arbroath, expressed the views espoused by many Wesleyans in the 1820s and 1830s.

> I believe that a great majority of the most thoughtful and influential persons in our connexion, both ministers and laymen, are friendly to the principle of an establishment, when connected with that of perfect religious liberty and protection to all other denominations . . . I do not think it probable that we can even *formally* unite with the Church of England so as to be amalgamated in one body. The present discipline of that church must exclude, in a sense, all separatists. But I think we are bound by every principle of expediency and duty to maintain the most friendly feelings towards the church, and to discountenance as far as we can without making ourselves *partisans* that bitter and unchristian hostility towards our two venerable National Establishments which is now too much in fashion . . .[62]

The last sentence is very much the Wesleyan sentiment of the year when Joseph Rayner Stephens (1805–79) was compelled to resign the connexion on the issue of church and state, being secretary of an anti-state church society in Ashton. Having laid the foundations for a thesis that Wesleyanism was nevertheless moving towards active Dissent by 1820, we now briefly analyse the continuing of the movement by looking at the relationship of Wesleyanism to Establishment in the 1830s, the curious love-hate relationship to the Peelite administration in the 1840s and the creation of a Wesleyan education policy which made a very important contribution to the 'dual' system of English education.

'In England and Scotland . . . the development of a self-conscious middle class in the early nineteenth century led to a widespread attack on the power and privilege of the Established Church . . . the characteristic form of this revolt was religious Nonconformity.' The Reform Bill of 1832 drew Nonconformist support (and more episcopal opposition than support)[63] and no doubt gave some dissenters the franchise with the Wesleyans tending to vote Whig-Liberal[64] but more vital was the Municipal Corporation Act of 1835 which gave power in the towns and cities to the assertive middle-class element which provided the older Dissent and especially Methodism with its constituency.[65] Not for nothing was Salem Methodist New Connexion Chapel at Halifax called the 'Mares' Nest'[66] as, of course, was the more prestigious Unitarian Church of the Messiah in Birmingham, where Joseph Chamberlain worshipped. It was often enough in the towns that Dissent could equal (or outface) Anglicanism in numbers, in power and in purpose as in Leeds where in the time of Hook and Baines, the battlefield of politics was the battlefield of 'church' and 'chapel'.[67] 'It is Methodism that all the pious among the churchmen unconsciously talk,' said Hook. Dissent had now the right to office; its disabilities, it was thought, might soon be put into limbo, but the struggle for equality was contested every inch of the way by a resurgent Anglicanism, a matter which still rankles deep in the bosom of nonconformity, even if there is more to be said on the Anglican side than appears the case in Nonconformist historiography.[68]

There were five areas of disability. The most important was the Church Rate which provided many occasions of bitterness with dissenters elected as 'vestrymen' with the express purpose of keeping the rates down. In this matter more than a generation of sour struggle in vestry meetings, in the courts, in the Commons and the Lords, poisoned church relations. The Church Rate represented the traditional duty of all the parishioners to maintain the fabric of the church. Dissenters objected to maintaining their own chapel and contributing to the parish church. The bitterness was not ended until 1868, one factor in which was Wesleyan refusal to toe the dissenting hard line.[69] Anglicans could say that all could take advantage of parish facilities and that dissenters were guilty of humbug when they wished to bury their dead in the parish churchyard for which they no longer paid upkeep.[70] Wesleyans consistently put the brake on strident dissent at this point.

Leeds provided a flashpoint. When Hook became vicar in 1837 he found the parish largely controlled by dissenting church wardens elected not only to keep down the rates but to oppose changes in worship. Hook's parish contained, of course, many Methodists led by a local alderman who opposed the Rate, being encouraged by the wealthy liberal itinerant Thomas Galland (d. 1843). Hook asserted that a Wesleyan Methodist who supported legislation for the abolition of church rates was disloyal to the principles of Wesleyanism. Galland opposed this view in a letter to the *Leeds Mercury* which was sharply criticized by Jabez Bunting.

> I think the letter unwise and indiscreet. There are principles we are pledged to maintain; they are our property; they are Wesleyan. We do not insist on your agreeing with our holding principles; but we must act upon our Wesleyan principles. Ours is the Wesleyan principle acknowledged. We will think no worse of you, we will give you a hearty shake of the hand and will not go to extremes. We will treat you with forbearance, and will not wound your feelings . . . Ours is and must be to all eternity, Wesleyanism . . .[71]

Little did Bunting foresee that most Methodist homes would be adorned by a portrait of Mr Gladstone before the end of the century and that, although precursors of the Liberation Society (1853) led by Edward Miall,[72] like the Religious Freedom Society (1839) and the Society for the Abolition of Church Rates (1838), had little overt official Wesleyan support, at local level support was growing fuelled often enough by abhorrence of 'Puseyite' tendencies, not least in Leeds.

The case of Joseph Rayner Stephens in 1834 is the best illustration of Wesleyan hesitancy. Stephens, son of doughty old Conservative John Stephens, and himself really a romantic Tory, when stationed as a minister in Ashton, supported openly a society for the separation of the church from the state, acting as secretary and publicly associating himself and Wesleyanism with the cause of disestablishment despite his superintendent minister's protest. If Stephens got support, offence was also caused to many Wesleyans. He was hauled before District Meeting which 'required him to abstain in the future from public agitation of the question'. Stephens refused, claiming that he had acted in his private capacity and not as a Wesleyan Methodist Minister, stating that the separation of church and state was not an anti-Wesleyan notion. The case was brought before Conference. Debate there ended with Stephens' withdrawal from the connexion and the beginning of his career as a Chartist.

As debate illustrated the tensions at the heart of Wesleyanism,[73] Jabez Bunting was in his most characteristic mood for this decade.

> Our question is not whether at the beginning it was best to unite church and state, nor whether if the house had to be constructed now it should be just as it is; our point is, must Wesleyan ministers arm themselves with pickaxes and pull down the house in which our father was born and in which he thought he died . . . Remember

when we gave our people the sacrament in our own chapels we publicly guarded against its being taken as a sign of separation. For the Conference to join in the agitation against church and state would require a new constitution; and we have no right to alter the constitution without calling a convention – and what would be gained by so doing?

Bunting claimed that Wesley would have dismissed any preacher who agitated against the Establishment. 'Mr Wesley dissented by employing lay-ministers but he maintained a friendliness to the church. He was nearer the church than to Dissent . . . Our principle is Dissent when we must but be on friendly terms when we can.' Bunting made clear his own antipathy to Dissent. 'If I went from the Methodists I would go to the church rather than Dissent. One of its first principles is – Every man shall choose his own minister. Can we be friendly to that?'

Bunting's view met with opposition from a growing liberal group led by Joseph Beaumont (1794–1855) and Thomas Galland. They were not altogether opposed to the silencing of Stephens but felt that Bunting also had transgressed politically by overt support of the Tory candidate at Finsbury. 'My difficulty,' remarked Dr Beaumont, 'is with the brethren who, while gagging others, say and do what they please' and he was joined by Dr Samuel Warren (himself a stormy petrel of Conference on the brink of defection over the Theological Institution) who said, 'But I think if one brother lets off a squib [J. R. Stephens we may suppose] and you extinguish him for so doing, you ought to extinguish a brother who lets off a rocket on the other side of the street.' Many rockets were to be released before the divisions revealed in the case of J. R. Stephens were to end in further Methodist schism. On the scale of national politics it could be argued that Wesleyan neutrality saved the Establishment from undue pressure in the period of Melbourne's ministry. John Vincent ironically points to the fact that, as usual, Wesleyanism gained nothing from loyalty to an Establishment which increasingly unchurched them. 'They were not usually of the right social class to obtain parliamentary seats or magistracies, or even to reach the dizzy heights of local Tory society which in Rochdale, for example, revolved around the parish church, the Flying Horse Inn, the grammar school and the local militia.'[74]

Some concessions were wrung by dissenters out of the Melbourne administration in the 1830s. From 1753 to 1836 dissenting marriages were neither legal nor tolerated. Harwicke's Act of 1753 had been intended to stop clandestine marriages, such as those occurring at the Fleet Prison, but it had imposed grave disabilities on dissenters, for they normally had to be married at the parish church by the parish minister with the rite of the Book of Common Prayer. In 1834 and 1835 Bills were produced to satisfy dissenters in this matter, but it was not until 1836 that a general civil registration of births, deaths and marriages was secured by Lord John Russell's two Acts, the effect of which was the appointing of civil registrars and the ending of legal necessity for the Prayer Book office.[75] This Act broke the Anglican monopoly, though for years dissenters could grumble that notices of application for dissenting marriages had to be read before the Guardians of the Poor, a matter rectified in 1856. Not until 1898 could an 'authorized person' act in lieu of the Registrar. Wesleyans were slow to take advantage of the 1836 provisions – in 1838 there were 5,654 marriages in Roman Catholic or Protestant chapels, of which only 175 were Methodist. Indeed in 1837 Jabez Bunting denounced the Bill in Conference: 'I am glad the people have had the discretion to wait. I wish the Conference to come to no decision. It is not a matter of conscience.' W. M. Bunting, son of Jabez, though no sycophant, made a statement echoing Puritan sentiment from the time of the Westminster Assembly – 'Marriage is no part of the ministerial function. The apostles did not marry people. The distinction must be kept up between the sacraments and marriage . . . we did not seek the Bill. I have no objection to it in perpetuity . . . I should like to go to church to be married to my wife once a quarter.'[76] Beaumont wanted the ceremony in Wesleyan chapels – 'So long as we refuse to marry our own people, we shall be said to admit that we are not full ministers' – a telling point. Conference sanctioned the practice of registration officially in 1845 but of 7,669 dissenting marriages in 1846 only 394 were Methodist.[77] For a long time many Methodists, including prominent Wesleyans like Henry Hartley Fowler, the first Lord Wolverhampton, preferred to be married in the parish church, even though later in the century the Wesleyans took the lead in dissenting pressure for equality in this matter.

Joseph Beaumont in the Conference debate on the Marriage Act also referred to other dissenting grievances. 'If reference be made to the church, it should be coupled with condemnation of the cruelty, bigotry etc. of clergymen who refuse to bury children not baptized by themselves.'

Dissenting burials and dissenters' baptisms caused many minor and petty struggles between 'church' and 'chapel' in the nineteenth century. Methodists were often deeply involved. The legal position in 1800 was that any baptized person living within a parish could be buried in the parish churchyard, the religious ceremony at the graveyard being conducted by the parish minister or another clergyman. This, at once, raised the question of what constituted a valid baptism since the unbaptized can be refused burial, a matter of grave concern to those who do not practise infant baptism.[78] In 1808–9 a Test Case was fought on the issue involving the Revd John Wight Wickes, Rector of Belton in Rutland, who had refused to bury the infant child of a man whom he considered a 'deluded, infatuated and ignorant disciple of the lowest description of Methodists'. Wickes was suspended for six months, legal opinion being that so long as the person had been baptized (by Anglican, Roman or dissenter) Canon 68 compelled the incumbent to inter any corpse brought to the churchyard. A similar distressing case was fought in 1840–1.[79] In 1841 the Revd T. S. Escott, Vicar of Gedney, not only refused to bury a child baptized by a Wesleyan minister but described the itinerant preachers as 'beings who pretend to be ministers of the gospel and really are ministers of hell and dissenting mountebanks'. An appeal was made by the Wesleyan Committee of Privileges to the Bishop of Lincoln – John Kaye – and the case was fought in the Court of Arches, which ruled that baptism by Wesleyan Methodists was valid by canon law and civil law. Escott appealed to the Privy Council who confirmed the judgment of the inferior court. The decision was of crucial importance. Without it the administration of the sacrament of baptism by Wesleyan Methodists must have ceased. Certainly the decision in favour of the Wesleyans had the effect of increasing the church consciousness of Wesleyanism.

A later rather ridiculous case, paralleling the more notorious Akenham Burial Case,[80] was the affair of the Owston Ferry churchyard. In May 1874, the Vicar of Owston Ferry, G. E. Smith, declined to allow the title 'the Reverend' to appear on the tombstone of the daughter of H. Keet, a Wesleyan minister. The Arcbishop of Canterbury, A. C. Tait, in a letter to *The Times* (11 August 1874) agreed with the Wesleyan claim to use the title but the Bishop of Lincoln, Christopher Wordsworth, upheld Mr Smith's actions on the grounds that Wesleyan ministers not being in holy orders, had no right to the title 'Reverend' and that, in any case, this was contrary both to the wishes of John Wesley and to the Conference resolutions of 1793. The previous year the bishop had issued a Pastoral to the Wesleyans inviting them to return to the mother church on the principles of their founder somewhat similar to Bishop Phillpott's similar appeal of 1833.[81] Vehement controversy followed both these actions. The Wesleyan Conference of 1874 showed considerable anti-Anglican feeling. Mr Smith's decision regarding the tombstone was upheld in the Court of Arches but overruled in the Privy Council. Wesleyanism now took the initiative in the whole matter of practical disabilities with the Committee of Privileges, soon backed by its secretary Robert Perks, eclipsing the Liberation Society in political

activity. Dr Wordsworth bitterly opposed Osborne Morgan's Burial
Law Amendment Bill in 1880, a bill which 'may imperil the existence
of the Church of England, not indeed as a spiritual society but as a
national institution'[82] – a throwback to a confessional view which
was now impossible. The Bill, which owed not a little to the advocacy
of Henry Hartley Fowler (1830–1911)[83] became law, enabling
dissenting ministers to hold their own services in the churchyard
after due notice had been given to the incumbent. P. T. Marsh calls
this act the 'last major political victory of militant Dissent in
England'.[84] Several necessary clarifications, after it was clear that
some incumbents like the rector of Tarporley in Cheshire in 1886
were not prepared to accept the spirit of the Act, culminated in the
Burials Act of 1900 ending grievances over consecrated ground and
fees. So there ended what B. L. Manning called 'the dreariest and
most unedifying in all the campaigns' in church-chapel strife[85] of
which the final legacy are the hideous rival chapels in public
cemeteries (one of which in these ecumenical days is often a sexton's
toolshed!) and decaying dissenting burial grounds in Yorkshire. In
these skirmishes Wesleyans found themselves in sheer self defence
drawn more and more into the dissenting camp with Perks prepared
to make the maximum political capital out of it.

Another great disability felt by dissenters was their exclusion from
the ancient English universities – not a few Free Church scholars got
their degrees from Scotland, including Wesleyan theologians like
W. B. Pope. Only in 1871 was the door completely open except for
divinity chairs and degrees, the battle for equality still maundering
on with Cuthbert Turner fighting a rearguard action of singular
futility as late as 1919.[86] Wesleyans, though quickly making use of
the newly-formed University of London, were not as closely involved
in the campaign to open the older universities as other dissenters.
Like F. D. Maurice, some of them might find 'subscription no
bondage' and not a few would have been episcopally confirmed. The
attempts to secure admission in the 1830s were a failure as were the
early attempts to abolish church rates. The 1830s saw both dissenting
disappointment at their Whig allies and the increasing self-
confidence of the Church of England which had begun to recover
from the unpopularity of the Reform Bill period. 'At the moment of
its greatest unpopularity, the church began slowly to move its great
bulk along the road to recovery, aided by the work of Peel and Bishop
Blomfield who were the secular saviours of the church and made
possible a continuing confessional national church.'[87]

The education issue showed that this was not to be uncontested.
Wesleyanism here again plays an ambiguous role. We have already
seen two aspects of this in a parallel study with Catholicism and a

glance at the role of education in the growth of denominational maturity. We look now at rival ideas of education itself and of the state, for strife here caused Sir James Graham to write in a celebrated letter to Brougham that 'religion, the keystone of education, is in this country the bar to its progress'[88] – a typical attempt to smear Dissent.

Early conflicts occurred in the Sunday schools, especially those of an independent and undenominational character whose sturdy reluctance to submit to ministerial dominance was a painful thorn in the flesh to Jabez Bunting. They were 'attached to their chapels rather as the white dominions were to the mother country'. W. R. Ward contrasts church and chapel here a little too starkly. 'The public which the church met in Baptism, Methodism met in Sunday school and its old informal relations with the schools became as uneasy as the Anglicans' attempts to fit their inherited doctrine and discipline of baptism to new circumstances.'[89]

The Sunday School Movement owed much to Methodist support and was at first a means of co-operation with Anglicans. Many of the early schools were taken to worship at the parish church like the Sunday school in Drury Lane attached to West Street Chapel which worshipped at St Mary le Strand, and that at Great Bridgewater Chapel, Manchester, which attended St Peter's.[90] Parallels can be drawn with the charity-schools at the beginning of the century, though in the latter movement the element of bourgeois social control can be exaggerated and they were often subject to what W. R. Ward called 'gusts of popular radicalism'.[91] In Stockport there was for a time a period of close co-operation and from 1784 in Manchester a committee to co-ordinate the work.[92] By 1800 the co-operation of denominations was beginning to wane. 'In the Charity School Movement at the beginning of the century, Dissent had parted company with Anglicanism because of the supposed taint of Jacobitism. Now it was the Anglicans who parted company with Dissent, because it was supposed to be tainted with the subversive doctrines of the French Revolution on the one hand and Methodism on the other.' On 5 May 1800 in Stockport the schools were divided between the Anglicans and the dissenters, and as the dissenters, especially the Methodists, were rapidly building chapels, the Anglicans feared that the Methodists were seeking to 'make proselytes of the children and by every artifice to draw them from the church into the conventicle'. Hannah More, in Somerset, would have little to do with the Methodists. She had employed a Mrs Easterbrook as a mistress in one of her schools but admitted, 'I am afraid she is a Methodist', and when one of her schoolmasters was accused of being a Methodist he was forbidden to teach in the village.[93]

Gradually Sunday schools became more denominational in

character and more closely attached to either church or chapel. Not until 1820 did Conference declare that weekly meetings for children should be established in each town. In 1827 a set of rules for management was issued, seeking to bring schools into direct affiliation with local societies.

> Schools designed for the religious education of poor children ought to be conducted in direct and avowed connexion with some particular branch of the visible church of Christ . . . The children of members and those even of constant hearers in the congregation are, in an important sense, the children of the church . . . Many of them have been by holy baptism solemnly recognized as among the objects of pastoral charge and as entitled to the care and spiritual assistance of Christian people.

When schools were set up, the superintendent minister was to be responsible. The Sunday school hymnal and Wesleyan catechism were to be used. These regulations, affirmed again in 1837, were not only factors in denominational self-confidence, but evidence of a total independence from the Church of England and the early 'ecumenical movement' of non-denominational popular religion.[94]

The Sunday school may be cosidered in many ways the root out of which day schools appeared. Here again there was division between church and Dissent – between the National Society for Promoting the Education of the Poor in the Principles of the Established Church (1811), using Bell's monitorial system and catechetical in style with a firm base in the link between church and state in social control, and the British and Foreign Schools Society (1808, 1814), using the system of the Quaker, Joseph Lancaster, and teaching a simple non-denominational bible-based faith. These two societies achieved a fair measure of success and were rewarded by grants from the government in 1833, one-twentieth of the grants given in Prussia but a foreshadowing of state financed education. The National Society, backed by the more affluent Anglican constituency, outpaced the British Society, claiming £70,000 out of £100,000 in five years and receiving £125,000 in 1848. At their peak the voluntary schools numbered 14,479 in 1890.[95]

Orthodox Dissent was divided throughout the century on the role of the state in the field of education.[96] Voluntaryism implied a very limited view of the state, which was a mere machine not a living organism. Joseph Priestley stated that, 'Education is a branch of civil liberty which ought by no means to be surrendered into the hands of the magistrate; and that the best interests of society require that the right of conducting it should be inviolably preserved by individuals.' In 1843 Edward Baines, the leading voluntaryist, declared that, 'I am compelled to declare my opinion that it is *not* the province of a government to educate the people . . . The proper province of government is to make and administer the laws to protect person and property and to conduct the external relations of a country but it is *not* its province to train the mind and morals of the people, any more than it is to supply them with food or govern their families.'[97] Even in 1843 this was inadequate – the period of 'legislative quiescence and old Toryism', as A. V. Dicey called it, was giving way to more interventionist views typified by Chadwick's work for public health. Soon Professor Robert Vaughan, a leading Congregationalist, though he later became more voluntaryist, began to campaign for secular schools. 'If Nonconformity persisted in resisting all government educational grants, then in practice they were saying it is better the people should be wholly without education than that they should not receive a religious education', which latches on to the views of men like Sir James Kay-Shuttleworth (secretary to the Committee of Council on Education) who worked ceaselessly for a national system because one child in fourteen only was in school. 'Here,' he said, 'in a country where the aristocracy is richer and more powerful than that of any other country in the world, the poor are more pauperized, more numerous in comparison to other classes, more irreligious and very much worse educated than any other European country solely excepting Russia, Turkey, Southern Italy, Portugal and Spain.'[98]

Dissenters in the 1860s began to swing to the view that the state must intervene. By 1870 R. W. Dale of Birmingham and the Education League, founded in 1809, were demanding compulsory, free, rate-supported, non-denominational education, or even secular education with the churches supplying the religious education, which was symbolic of Nonconformist optimism about the role of the churches still in national life. This was a mild English version of the French slogan – *l'obligation, la gratuité, la laïcité* with which Gambetta lambasted the Catholics – *le cléricalisme voilà l'énnemi*. Nonconformity provided a cushion against complete secularism.[99]

Anglicans could counter all this by saying that religion was so much part of life that it could not be taught like algebra. It is a life, a community, a tradition, hence the stress still remaining on a confessional state which had a duty to educate in the religion of the community. Undenominational religious education or simple bible education seemed to be really the religion of Dissent and thereby inadequate. Bishop Kirk was saying the same about agreed syllabuses two generations later. The century ended, as Halévy put it, with 'state schools supported by the Free Churches, free schools favoured by the state church',[100] but this is to anticipate.

Strife on this issue began when Brougham's proposals of 1820 for the maintenance of schools from the parish rate was rejected with dissenting approval. Dissenters would not tolerate any suggestion of the parson having power in state education, an attitude which led Brougham to talk in 1843 of 'worthy and conscientious men who hate the Established Church more than they love education'.[104] Wesleyanism, at first, largely supported the voluntary system beginning in 1833 in a very modest way the setting up of Wesleyan day schools on strictly Wesleyan principles. In 1837, two years before the Committee of the Privy Council for Education was set up by the government, a Wesleyan Education Committee was appointed which presented in 1841 (modified later by John Scott) a draft plan for Wesleyan education. Under this plan Wesleyan schools were to use the Authorized Version and Wesleyan hymn book and catechism and were to be 'avowedly and practically connected as to their government and denomination with Wesleyan Methodism as a branch of the visible church of Christ, while avoiding sectarian exclusiveness'.[102]

The first major clash with the government came in 1838–9 over Lord John Russell's proposals for a state Normal College for the training of teachers and a much more liberal grants system which appeared to subsidize other denominations besides the Establishment. Dissent on the whole was satisfied, Anglicans from Bishop Phillpotts to Bishop Blomfield and Lord Ashley were furious.[103] Ashley wrote to Bunting for support against the Bill. Anglicans disliked inspection of schools, Wesleyans still suspected Anglican monopoly, but were fearful of the subsidization of popery, not least by the use of the Douai version of the Bible by Roman Catholics. Bunting made clear his views, declaring that he was against schools being established by the state. The *Leeds Mercury* accused him of inconsistency, demanding for Wesleyans rights he would not concede to Catholics. The *Watchman* re-iterated the sentiments of Bunting – 'From all that we can see, we deprecate the influence of government with the education of the people and are of the opinion that each Christian society should educate for itself and for its God as large a proportion as it can of the children of the poor.'[104] There was an Orange tint to the whole matter with Daniel O'Connor accusing Wesleyans of being no friends to religious liberty.

The Committee of Privileges acted in the matter. There were 2,872 petitions against the measure. The proposals' failure was due in no small measure to the Wesleyan reaction. Methodist opinion could no longer be ignored on any public issue, a fact which Lord Stanley and others acknowledged. 'Which,' he asked, 'next to the Established Church was the most important, the most numerous and which was the most jealous, the most active in the cause of education of all those sects into which the other protestant portion of all the community was divided? – the country would answer him – beyond comparison the Wesleyans.' 'The Wesleyans . . . we never counted on the Wesleyans,' said Tadpole in Disraeli's *Coningsby*. The Wesleyans, urged on by John Scott in 1843, multiplied the building of their own day schools of which there were 700 by 1870.[105]

The voluntary system was again upheld in the failure of Sir James Graham's Bill of 1843[106] which sought as part of a factory act to establish compulsory education for children in certain industries under the clear auspices of the established church. Dissenting rhetoric called this Bill 'a severer blow at religious liberty than has been aimed at it since the rejection of Lord Sidmouth's Bill in 1811'. In short it was the greatest legislative evil that 'inherited intolerance could have devised or clerical tyranny in dark and barbarous ages might have gloried to impose'. Dissenters felt doubly assaulted for the state appeared to interfere both in industry and in education. Debate could centre on the stage at which necessary state aid turned into improper state control and state church control to boot. Dissenters were not prepared to accept any form of education and the gibes of Ashley that the 'really suffering parties were the bodies of neglected children . . . now consigned to an eternity of ignorance' were not entirely fair to them. The Wesleyan Committee of Privileges discussed the matter with Bunting in the dilemma of having to admit he was opposed to the church. 'We are not churchmen. I for one cannot be a churchman or at least a church minister . . . In a sense we are Dissenters, yet there is a sense in which we are not, but only Nonconformists.' This was now mere semantics. He wanted Christian training as an essential part of national education but 'each section of the church should instruct its own children and as many others as choose to put their children under its instruction'. Wesleyans must dig their hands into their pockets – and must protest against Puseyism.

Here was the rub. The *Minutes* of the Conference of 1843 underline Bunting's opinion. Graham's Bill is called 'most objectionable and alarming . . . and likely to inflict the greatest injury to the numerous Sunday and week day schools already supported by the voluntary zeal and liberality of the Wesleyan body . . . We are friendly to the Establishment but not those grievous errors which are now tolerated within her pale.' Reaction to the Bill seemed to have committed Wesleyans to the voluntary principle. The Bill itself was a gross miscalculation on the part of Peel and his Home Secretary, Graham, for it brought the wrath of Dissent against the government including Bunting and the Wesleyans who now clearly feared Puseyism in the parishes and the schools. The Bill was withdrawn. It was, says Norman Gash, a victory for Dissent over what seemed a threatened invasion of Anglican dominated state education in the industrial areas and a victory for public opinion over the executive and the politicians.[107] Lord Ashley's comment was apt. He blamed 'the perilous pranks of Dr Pusey and his disciples . . . The Wesleyan Methodists, hitherto friendly to the church as they showed in 1839, are actuated by a deep and conscientious fear of Popery in the Church of England.' A national system of education was delayed by decades until 1870 and the nuisance value of Protestant Nonconformity had been more than demonstrated.[108]

The Dissenters' Chapels Bill of the next year – allowing Unitarians much greater flexibility over trust law – aroused Bunting's ire further – 'this vile Bill', he called it.[109] The third occasion on which the 'old Whig' Bunting opposed Peel was over the proposed increase of grant from £9,000 to £27,000 with £30,000 for capital expenditure to St Patrick's College, Maynooth, the Roman Catholic seminary in Ireland, in 1845.[110] It is paradoxical, and wholly Irish, that an English government could subsidize a Roman College, when it dare not appear to subsidize a college of either established church! W. M. Bunting (who was more liberal in Conference than his father, more Tory outside) was heard to state that having played a part in securing the election of Peel's government, he would have now to work to get it out. Ireland provides a *Leitmotiv* of Wesleyan sensitivity for the rest of the century. William Arthur (despite the 'no politics' rule) campaigned against Home Rule in 1886. 'Wesleyanism formed the backbone of Nonconformist unionism. There were marked electoral effects where Wesleyans were numerous.' If Bunting had attacked the Tories in the 1840s, there were Wesleyans prepared to desert the Gladstonian ship over Home Rule later in the century. Ireland always made it difficult to typecast Wesleyan political alignments.[111]

The views of the Buntings in the 1840s were widely held in Wesleyanism if the *Watchman* newspaper is an accurate barometer.[112] It swung to a position not unlike that of Thomas Chalmers in the Church of Scotland, who spearheaded the Disruption of 1843, the impact of which on Wesleyanism has never been made clear.

Jabez Bunting, who had close dealings with Chalmers, began to see the Scottish evangelicals before the Disruption as playing a role in Scotland, parallel to that of Methodism in England. 'I once hoped that such a thing was possible as an Established Church without state interference but I now see that it is impossible. I wish two thousand clergymen would leave the English Church in the same way.'[113] Minor matters like the use of the term 'Free Church' instead of Dissent or Nonconformist and 'manse' for the minister's house were signs of an increasing Scots influence on English dissent after the Disruption. A clear comparison was made between Moderator Chalmers presiding over the Free Kirk Assembly and President Hannah in 1842 presiding over Conference – the comparison was not frivolous. Was Wesleyanism now the Free Kirk of England?[114]

For Wesleyanism, the Peel administration revealed a resurgent Anglicanism which had to be resisted. The mood had begun in 1839 with opposition to the Whig proposals, though here an alliance was possible with Anglicans. Now Puseyism, perhaps sometimes a cloak for fear of greater power, produced a consistent anti-government stance and a new alliance with nonconformity. Graham's Bill was certainly 'killed' by it. For the Church of England there was the stark realization that no longer would the Tory Party support them through thick or thin. 'On the education front the defeat of Graham's Factory Education Bill destroyed whatever hopes the Establishment had retained of being the sole vehicle for the education of the people.'[115] If the Church of England had ever been the Tory Party at prayer, it ceased to be such during the ministry of Peel. If Wesleyanism had appeared Tory in the 1820s and 1830s it was now still somewhat conservative socially but not to be relied on by Tory governments. This was true of Jabez Bunting himself.[116] The year of the Graham Act was the year of the foundation of the Evangelical Alliance which can be seen as an anti-Roman style of Protestant undenominationalism with which Wesleyanism had powerful links, though they were not permanent. In this group the Buntings played, for a time, leading roles. Maynooth only added fuel to the growing fire.

For the Church of England it was the moment of truth – it was one denomination among others. It had now to find its own autonomy if necessary against the state. It did so with the use of money, power and influence especially in education in an increasingly pluralist but not secular state.

The opinions of William Ewart Gladstone on church matters from his book *The State in its Relationship with the Church* (1838) have a fascination all of their own.[117] His view was fundamentally Tractarian – a strong confessional church, aided but not controlled by the state, and as a logical conclusion positive freedom for Nonconformity, indeed total freedom if dissent had become a majority as in Ireland – this was the lesson of Maynooth – but a continuing of the link if it did not positively grate on a majority as in England. Strident Liberation Society claims were never conceded.[118] From 'the rising hope of those stern unbending Tories' as Macaulay put it, he became the Liberal leader whom Methodists could follow because they shared a common moralism, a common concern for personal and corporate holiness. Politically the emergence of two great political parties, rooted in the religious and constitutional issues thrown up by the events of the 1830s and 1840s, was becoming clear. If the Church of England became again the 'Tory Party at prayer' it was after 1868 and centred around the defence of its schools from what was seen as the twin enemies of undenominational dissent and secularism, a defence which brought together high churchmen and low in another of those strange alliances which distinguish modern Anglican history.[119]

But the position was complicated, as might be expected, by the Wesleyans. Having opposed Peel on the Education Bill of 1843, the Chapels Bill of 1844 and Maynooth, official Wesleyanism changed tack in 1847, a *volte face* which seemed a betrayal of Dissent and voluntaryism to many northern laymen and was a cause of the schism to come after 1849.[120] The Wesleyans – urged on by Ashley who seems an *eminence grise* on these occasions – not only accepted voluntaryism and pushed on with their own school and college building programme (Westminster College opened in 1851) but were also prepared to accept direct subsidies from the state and later to accept the necessity and desirability of a full state system of elementary and secondary education which enabled them to accept the 1870 Education Act with an equanimity denied to the rest of Dissent.[121]

Wesleyanism from 1847 onwards had a foot in both camps. It is possible to see a continuity of policy from John Scott (1792–1868), first Principal of Westminster College, James H. Rigg (1821–1909) whose abilities were noted by Gladstone and John Scott Lidgett (1854–1953), Scott's grandson,[122] who was involved in educational matters all his ministry, not least drawing some of the sting of dissenting attitudes on the Balfour Act of 1902 which abolished school boards and created the LEAs but retained grants to church schools, and finally negotiating on behalf of Methodism with A. W. Harrison in the talks which led to the Education Act of 1944, of which R. A. Butler was the final architect.[123] The stance of these men was fundamentally what became the compromise of the 'dual' system so that Wesleyans, though desirous of bringing every child within reach of non-sectarian religious teaching resisted both secularism and the excluding of church schools including their own.[124] It must be admitted that common policy was not easily achieved. William Arthur, from his Irish experience, was a notable exponent of a purely state system, a stance parallel to that of R. W. Dale. Might it be argued that Wesleyan opinion, cushioning the more strident cries of secularists and anti-Anglicans, inhibited a full confrontation between clerical and anti-clerical as in France where *laïcité* meant frank secularism, or in Germany, where Bismarck confronted Catholicism in the *Kulturkampf*?[125] B. L. Manning's fears that the 'self opinionated Gallios of the Board of Education' supported by 'Whitehall agnostics' would enable Roman Catholicism to get dominating purchase on the education system has proved to be exaggerated.[126] 'The Roman Church once firmly entrenched in the dual system will make the descendents of the Forsters and the Webbs see that it does matter whether religious justice is given or not. The privileged position of the denomination schools is introducing a clerical and non-clerical struggle compared with which the old antagonism of church and chapel will seem like child's play.' Manning, now, would be more likely to raise his other ghost of the omnicompetent state for 'Leviathan is a foe more dangerous than the scarlet woman or the man of sin'. Manning's position (and that of Dissent generally) has been criticized from within his own tradition by John Huxtable who saw far more validity in the Anglican position that religious values are an integral part of education and also by Norman Sykes, who nevertheless was sensitive to the dangers of totalitarianism, what J. N. Figgis was to call 'that passion for state absolutism which is the child of the Renaissance and Reform and the grandchild of the pagan state'. England has retained a plural system, though the constantly threatened suppression of the private sector in the interests of egalitarianism raises the issues again in a sharp form – with Methodism fully involved as it retains a strong stake in independent secondary education.

The cry for disestablishment now comes from some Anglicans who are no longer prepared even to accept the utility arguments for Establishment which flow from Warburton through Gladstone and Mandell Creighton[127] who asserted that 'a national church means a national recognition of the law of God. Without a national church there cannot be that . . . That an ancient nation like England should deliberately repudiate any organic connexion between the basis of its national life and the profession of the Christian faith seems to me a calamity which could never be repaired.' In the harmless suggestions of the Chadwick Report of 1970, the role of genuine dissenter was played by Miss Valerie Pitt who urged disestablishment.[128] 'Christianity is not a folk or tribal religion, it is a gospel, a revealed religion, demanding an active and personal aspect. To be a Christian a man must answer "Jesus is Lord" – writing C of E on a form is not enough . . . A church's national character is a matter of how it understands its churchly calling and does not depend for the reality on the status which the national community gives it.' Miss Pitt's points could hardly have been made better by B. L. Manning who in his evidence to the 1935 Commission pointed out that it is asking very much of our non-Christian and anti-Christian population to have any sort of established church. Manning follows up with a characteristic assertion that 'the establishment of one, even the largest section of the fragments into which the Latin church is divided in this country, has inevitably, as a matter of history, caused political and ecclesiastical injustice to the other fragments'. Nevertheless Manning shrunk from full disestablishment for he contemplated with horror the thought of the Church of England as a 'disestablished self-governing episcopal sect' – Free churchmen indeed now defend Establishment sometimes rather as Bunting did in the 1830s! Is a modern state in any way responsible for the religious and moral thinking of its citizens? Is it or ought it to be totally neutral in such matters? D. L. Munby in 1963 traced his idea of a secular society which was pluralist, tolerant, pragmatic, with no ruling ideology or world view. Establishments were simply 'vestigial survivals of the past of little practical value'. This liberal style of state is now being rejected in an increasingly totalitarian world![129]

To summarize a complex tale and point to consequences is not easy. From 1811 Wesleyanism was pushed into the dissenting camp but always uneasily and never finally. The Wesleyan version of the Nonconformist conscience was always tinged with that evangelical pietism and moralism which was its characteristic stance and was typified in the crusades against slavery, popery in any form and later Bulgarian Horrors and American Massacres[130] (the Turk became a convenient symbol for all that was evil), the massive crusade for total abstinence and prohibition[131] and in our day the opposition to the heresy of apartheid in South Africa. There is a consistency here below the surface. This is the implicit right to raise moral issues which lies behind the phrase, 'what is morally wrong can never be politically right',[132] which Hugh Price Hughes used about C. S. Parnell's adultery in 1890 but which echoes through Victorian Nonconformist politics. The inherent danger is of self righteousness, what Kitson Clark called the 'old Puritan vice of imputing base motives to the other side and dividing the world sharply and inaccurately into the godly and the ungodly, a habit which even at this day has descended on several who would not recognize its ancestry and have abandoned the creed which originated it'.[133]

Along with this goes the tendency to oversimplify complex moral issues in the area between international and personal ethics which has tended to bedevil what little Methodist moral theology there has been – though the writings of S. E. Keeble, W. F. Lofthouse and Edward Rogers have been notable exceptions. It may well be that the crusading style of politics only achieves anything (abolition of slavery, 1811 and 1843 are good examples) when other power groups in English society align themselves with nonconformity. On its own

Methodism has never had the political 'clout' to do much. It has often enough underlined E. R. Norman's interesting but controversial thesis that clerical (and lay?) élites tend to follow intellectual fashion.[134] Thus Hugh Price Hughes espoused both collectivism of a moderate kind and imperialism at the same time, curiously parallel to Bishop Westcott of Durham who like Hughes supported the Boer War.[135] 'We have to show that we are still worthy to hold both by might and counsel, the Empire which has been entrusted to us, to protect those who rightly look to us for help and bear patiently the thankless burden of the white man and train uncivilized races to a nobler life . . . Imperialism is the practical advocacy of a fellowship with a view to the completeness of their separate development.' To this sentiment Hughes and his lay allies would have said 'amen' and he would have seen his vision of Methodism as a superior religion with in such a 'fellowship'.

What may be said for the Nonconformist conscience may be noted elsewhere, balancing somewhat the salutary and stern critiques of Henry Rack and John Kent.[136] By 1914 the Nonconformist platform, as we have traced it from Sidmouth's Bill to the education controversy was as dead as the dodo. The great alliance with Whigs and Liberals was no more. More Methodists than ever voted Conservative and have continued to do so, while many others (especially among the groups closest to the intellegentsia) have tended to a mild, conciliatory socialism[137] of which Arthur Henderson, George Thomas (Lord Tonypandy) and Lord Soper – though he touches the fringe of a pacifist element which was more Quaker than Methodist – are superb examples. Most Methodists were mediators in social conflict[138] as they tended to be in the great church-chapel struggles of early Victorian England which we have summarized.[139]

8

Methodism and the Oxford Movement – Aggressive Anglicanism and Militant Dissent

In 1868 there appeared in *Punch*[1] a cartoon showing Dr Edward Bouverie Pusey, dressed in cassock, gown and bands, inviting a demure and obviously Wesleyan lady to accompany him to church. She politely declines. Above her is a portrait of John Wesley clad in similar fashion to Dr Pusey! The cartoon reflected Pusey's disillusioment about the possibility of union with Rome, the cool reception of his *Eirenicons* and his letter of that year to the Wesleyan Conference. The President of Conference (S. H. Hall) remarked in his address that the '*via media* between Anglicanism and Dissent was their proper designation . . . Whilst we hold this midway position, we are still prepared to regard . . . with respect and affection the state church, so long as she remains faithful to her calling.' Elements in Conference moved further than these eminently Buntingite sentiments by adapting a popular song:

> You offer one hand to the Papal band
> And the other to us extend.
> Can you really hope that we and the Pope
> Can acknowledge a mutual friend?
> You tell us our bark is not an ark,
> We don't believe that's true.
> We'd trust a raft before your craft,
> Just paddle your own canoe.

How did these two traditions beginning in clerical circles in Oxford, both stressing holiness and aspiration in Christian living, appear as polarities rather than complements on the ecclesiastical scene? A comparison between Newman's sermon on the text 'Holiness without which no man may see the Lord' and John Wesley's 1733 university sermon preached from the same pulpit on the 'Circumcision of the Heart' shows striking similarities.[2] Was it the

Oxford Movement, primarily, which pushed Wesleyanism into the Free Church Alliance? Previous chapters have, I hope, indicated the complexities of the question. What have the Oxford Movement and its aftermath in common with Methodism and where are the dissimilarities? These are not easy questions to answer and have not ever been adequately explored – the historiography of the whole subject is astonishingly thin.[3]

The Oxford Movement (as indeed Methodism also) must be seen in a European setting. It is part of what has loosely been called Romanticism.[4] In its cultural manifestations – in music, art, poetry, the novel – the heart, the feelings, the imagination came to the forefront rather than the cool light of the rationalist intellect.[5] Could it be said that both John Wesley and Jean-Jacques Rousseau, in their quite different ways, were protesting passionately against excessive intellectualism, external social conformity and religious indifference? In Chateaubriand (1768–1848), especially in *Le Génie du Christianisme*, we find moonlight and forests, Gothic ruins, distant church bells and all the rest. For him the proof of Christianity's appeal lay in its evocation of beauty, an argument which appealed to a generation starved by years of dreary rationalism.[6] It is not difficult to see the parallels between the Christians of the Oxford Movement with their love of the past and a romanticized view of the Church of the Fathers with the authoritarian views of Joseph de Maistre (1752–1821) and the early La Mennais (1782–1854)[7] in the aftermath of Napoleon, as well as contemporary high-churchmen in Lutheranism.

The Evangelicals first, then the Romantics taught men like Keble and Newman not to be afraid of their feelings – this can be said despite the reticence and the modest approach to feeling typified by Isaac Williams' tract *On Reserve in Communicating Religious Knowledge*. The poetry, for instance, of *The Christian Year* (1827) is the outward sign of a new style of high-churchman.

> Son of my soul, Thou Saviour dear
> It is not night when Thou art near.
> . . . If some poor wandering child of Thine
> Have spurned today the voice divine,
> Now Lord the gracious work begin,
> Let me no more lie down in sin.

John Wesley might have found *that* a trifle sentimental, had it been written by his brother! Here was a concern for the evocative and the reverent, a sense of the whispering beauty and truth of divinity as its presence surrounded the soul.[8] There are subtle links between evangelical, catholic and romantic even if Newman, in the end, turned against the evangelical emphases of his youth, and Keble never really understood them.[9] In England William Blake can be taken as the supreme example of romantic revolt. 'All the destruction in Christian Europe has arisen from Deism which is natural religion,' thunders Blake. The same sentiments are expressed in the mysterious and tumultuous Preface to Milton culminating in the now hackneyed 'Jerusalem'.

'Romance,' says C. S. Lewis, 'includes among other things a spirit of adventure, a subjective emphasis, a cult of the marvellous and the titanic, a revolt against artificiality, a naturalism and a longing for a mysterious object.' The collision between the disciplined practicality of the eighteenth century and this kind of vision is what gives a clue to the nineteenth century. Newman stands on that bridge. 'Deductions have no power of persuasion. The heart is commonly reached not through reason but through the imagination, by means of direct impressions, by the testimony of facts and events, by history, by description. Persons influence us, voices melt us, looks subdue us, deeds inflame us. Many a man will live and die upon a dogma; no man will be a martyr for a conclusion.'[10] Add to this the earlier *Sturm und Drang* in Germany, the Lake poets, the pervasive influence of Coleridge[11] and we have the cultural setting of Tractarianism. Likewise popular romanticism[12] with its innumerable lesser poets, hymn writers, novelists – often mawkish to modern taste – assumes its importance. Catholic revivals in France go on alongside the great intellectual battles in Oxford and had their later influence when the second generation of Tractarians took the battle to the parishes in an evangelical Catholicism.[13]

Despite all the assertions to the contrary, 'there was a sense in which the Oxford Movement was not so much a protest against a totally arid religious terrain as itself a manifestation of an existing religious renaissance.'[14] It was certainly the most decisive movement in nineteenth-century English church history, especially if it is seen in the context of the church reforms which made its ideals a practical possibility. In part the Oxford Movement and its aftermath was a revival of the historical sense so lacking in latitudinarianism, a return to the pre-Reformation innocence of the Middle Ages, a bringing back of old ritual, a return to the austere example of the saints, at its heart a ceaseless search for holiness and communion with God. But the 'trigger' of the movement was not religion but politics. There was revolution in France again in 1830, the emancipation of the Roman Catholics in 1829 following the repeal of the Test and Corporation Acts of 1828, the Reform Bill of 1832 were all pointers to a new plurality or to stark secularism. Parliament was no longer the lay voice of the Church of England, if it ever had been. A hot-blooded Tory radical like Hurrell Fronde saw the Reform Bill as pouring into the House of Commons 'the turbid waters of sheer mammonry, democracy and republicanism'.[15] The liberalism of the Whigs saw sheer commonsense, the greatest happiness of the greatest number of Irishmen in the financially advantageous diminishing of the number of Irish bishoprics from twenty-two to twelve. This move further gave the impression that the pagans, the Protestants and the papists were storming the gates. The radical Tory MP Joseph Hume advised young men that it was useless their being ordained. He expressed a hope that these foolish ordinations would cease. If, however, he warned them, they persisted in anything so absurd, they could expect no compensation when the Church of England falls as it undoubtedly would, a sentiment echoed by Jeremy Bentham who believed 'the Church of England ripe for dissolution'.[16] The cry, 'the Church in Danger', was no empty clarion. The consequence for the Oxford Reformers was a new search for authority, for the real sovereignty of the church which could no longer lie in the Erastian state. Harold Laski, in his first book, *Studies in the Problem of Sovereignty*, spotted this common feature of the Oxford Movement and the Scottish Disruption a decade later. 'It is not a little curious that more attention should not have been paid to the remarkable analogy between the Oxford Movement and the Disruption of 1843 in the established Church of Scotland. Each was essentially an anti-Erastian movement. It was against an all-absorptive state that each group of men was contending . . . In each case, as was well enough admitted by contemporaries, the attempt was made . . . to work out a doctrine of the church which, neglecting the state, gave the church the general organization of a perfect society' or, as Brilioth put it, 'The great discovery of the Oxford Movement was that the church was a living organism.'[17]

It was the search for a sovereignty above any state which led Keble to assert the danger of 'national apostacy'[18] and led Newman and Pusey in the *Tracts for the Times* to assert the church's apostolicity through an apostolic ministry. That doctrine of succession, with its ecclesial concomitant the 'branch' theory of the church, became a *Leitmotiv* in Anglo-Catholic apologetic. The movement is, however, distorted, if it is not seen as fundamentally a quest for authority, the authority of true corporate holiness and devotion. Without the realization that the movement was concerned at the deepest level with holiness, it will be misunderstood and was almost wilfully misunderstood by Wesleyans who saw only a threat to themselves. The tragedy was that the Tractarians were fundamentally Arminian as were the Wesleyans, deriving much of their aspiring spirituality from many of the same sources from which the Wesleys drank so freely.[19] The 'thin red line' of high-churchmen[20] continuing the traditions of the Caroline Divines and the Non-Jurors, men like William Jones of Nayland, Charles Daubeny, John Keble's father, and Thomas Sikes of Guilsborough who uttered the famous prophecy about the doctrine of the church, now suppressed, but when revived leading 'to one great outcry of Popery from one end of the land to the other' were as isolated from Wesley as much as from the Evangelicals, scorning his disobedience as an act of schism.[21] They would have agreed with Alexander Knox (though he was friendly to Wesley) that the Church of England is 'not Protestant but a reformed part of the church Catholic'.[22]

Another pointer to a resurgence of Anglicanism, which will assume greater importance later, was that small group of high-churchmen which cohered around the parish church of Hackney, often known as the 'Hackney Phalanx' – as if to mimic the Clapham Sect – men like Joshua Watson (1771–1853), a London wine merchant,[23] and his brother, the rector, and H. H. Norris, rector of North Hackney. This group had a passion for education, pioneering not only the National Society for the Education of the Poor According to the Principles of the Established Church (1811) but also the Church Building Society (1817) created to provide churches for a rapidly growing population and to counter Dissent. In 1818 £1,000,000 was obtained from the government as a thank offering for Waterloo, followed by another £500,000 in 1824 with the Society itself raising over £6,000,000 between 1818 and 1833 with parallel moves to recruit and train new staff for them. The model for the whole enterprise was clearly the rural parish with the hope that the model might yet be used to christianize the towns, despite Disraeli's famous riposte to Archbishop Longley's lament 'The church has lost the towns' – 'Your grace, the church has never had the towns.'[24]

If the Oxford Movement produced spiritual renewal and 'strengthened the Church of England in its soul',[25] it can be argued that the reforms begun under Peel's brief administration of 1834 gave the church the means, by astute if slow distribution of wealth, to make the renewal possible – 'without them it is difficult to conceive how the ideals of pastoral work, propagated by the Oxford Movement, could have been put into practice'.[26] Together with the church building movement, the reforms, with the renewal of the parish system, mark a resurgence of Anglicanism which could begin to compete with and beat Dissent at its own expansionist game.[27] The Oxford Movement was to provide some of the men who could staff the new churches, men trained in an orderly life of devotion and morality by sacramental devotion, fasting and other forms of devotion and including, for some, a rule of celibacy and the practice of auricular confession. This was in contrast with what Hurrell Fronde came to scorn as 'that transcendental idea of the English gentleman which forms the basis of Toryism'.[28] It was soon to have its impact in parishes in town and country alike, but more especially in rural areas where churchly apostolic zeal met Methodist zeal head on.

We need not tell again the story of the years from 1833 to 1845[29] but we shall briefly analyse the impact of the Oxford Movement on the Church of England and then on Methodism. Three theological *Leitmotivs* quickly emerge.

Firstly the stress on apostolicity and apostolic ministry, stemming from the problem of determining the source of authority. This seems almost an obsession from the time of Tract 1 when Newman asserted, 'We must necessarily consider none to be really ordained who have not been thus ordained.' This doctrine alone, which has an oddly un-Anglican ring about it, especially if Hooker is taken as normative[30] (and this despite Keble's superb work on Hooker), drove a wedge between the Church of England and Protestant churches at home and abroad. The Reformation was the Oxford Movement's blind spot. Too easily Hurrell Fronde could see it as a 'limb wrongly set'.[31] Neither Luther nor Calvin were ever adequately explored by Anglicans of the Catholic tradition, a matter still the case as late as the pamphlet *Catholicity* of 1947, when the 'liberal Protestantism' of the post-Enlightenment era was seen as the yardstick with which Protestantism could be judged and found wanting in Catholicity.[32] In fairness, the doctrine of apostolic succession should never be separated from the priority of the corporate holiness of the church. The danger was that of isolating ministry from church and utterly unchurching other groups and thus thinking of their means of grace as mere uncovenanted mercies which was clearly the position of Charles Gore at the turn of the century.[33] Newman was more subtle. 'It is often said of us by way of reproach, that we leave Dissenters to the "uncovenanted mercies of God"; nay, in a sense, we leave ourselves; there is not one of us but has exceeded by transgressions the revealed Ritual and finds himself in consequence thrown upon those infinite resources of Divine Love which are stored in Christ but have not been drawn out into form in the appointment of the gospel.'[34] Newman's subtleties were lost on the Wesleyans who, at the time of their own crisis of identity, found themselves repudiated.

The second *Leitmotiv* was the re-assertion of a passion for holiness. There is certainly a parallel here with Wesley, though it was never adequately explored. Newman and Pusey came at the matter from a different angle. They and their friends stressed holiness as moral effort as well as the gift of the Holy Spirit, the absolute prerequisite and condition of any title to expect divine assistance, even though (as with Wesley) the idea of merit disappeared. To be justified 'is to receive the Divine Presence within us and to be made a Temple of the Holy Ghost'.[35] The Tractarians believed that the Evangelicals with their stress on *imputed* righteousness dodged the issues of moral theology and stopped short at the atonement, ignoring the taking of the manhood of Christ into God which made full atonement and reconciliation possible by the gradual hallowing of human lives through the actual presence of the divine life therein. They refused to isolate atonement from incarnation. Their vision of incarnation was one involving an actual objective entry of the divine life into humanity which is mediated in the case of individual men and women through the sacrament of baptism.[36] This issues in the gradual conforming of the individual believer to the image of Christ in which the Eucharist plays a vital role as a means of infused grace. Stress is thus on Christ in us (*in nobis*) as well as for us (*pro nobis*). 'Whether we say we are justified by faith or by works or by sacraments, all these but mean this one doctrine that we are justified by grace which is given through sacrament, impetrated (i.e. besought) by faith, manifested in works.'[37] Pusey and Keble were always fearful of an imputed righteousness which could, they believed, lead to that antinomianism which Catholics have always tended to accuse Protestants of espousing,[38] without realizing that imputed righteousness could be the doorway to sanctification, from being 'declared' righteous to bring 'made' righteous. In Max Beerbohm's modern story (based on *Beauty and the Beast* or *The Frog Prince*?) *The Happy Hypocrite*, a wicked man, Lord George Hell, falls in love with a good and beautiful girl. He dare not go to her as he is, so he buys a wax mask, puts it on and so disguised woos and weds her. Then someone denounces him and says: 'Strip off that mask and you will find the evil face of Lord George Hell.' But he has become like the mask. Her love and his love – inadequate though it is – have made him what he only seemed to be. This may be more like Zinzendorf than Wesley.

> Jesu Thy blood and righteousness
> My beauty are, my glorious dress,
> Midst flaming worlds, in these arrayed
> With joy shall I lift up my head. (MHB 370).

Wesley, like Pusey, though with a different *initial* definition of justification, safeguarded himself against the threat of antinomianism with a doctrine of sanctification which can be seen as 'faith working through love'. Would not Wesley have said 'amen' to Pusey when he said, 'If we would see Him in His sacraments, we must see Him also wherever He has declared Himself and especially in His poor . . . real love to Christ must issue in love to all who are Christ's and real love to Christ's poor must issue in self denying love towards them.'[39] If Wesley could agree with that, so could Luther who saw justified man as being 'Christ to his neighbour.' But Pusey explored neither Luther nor Wesley.

The third *Leitmotiv* is the doctrine of reserve in communicating religious knowledge. Isaac Williams' two Tracts are only part of a whole approach to spirituality. The Tractarians were confronted by a phase of evangelicalism which appeared to make feeling, which is subjective and only imperfectly under the control of the will, the test of justification. They wearied of the over familiarity with religious things of some of their contemporaries. They stressed the need for awe, reserve, mystical awareness[40] – Pusey, it must be added, made the preaching of the cross quite central. It was, he said, through evangelicalism that 'a vivid and energetic, however partial, preaching of the corruption of human nature and of the cross ... by the Providence of God broke in upon an age of torpor and smooth easy ways in religion'. But he deplored Wesleyanism which 'threatens to be one of the most dreadful scourges with which the church was ever afflicted, the great antagonist of penitence'. It was mere naked gospel denuded of the sacramental robe of the apostolic order which protects and graces the soul.[41] Pusey, however, was not guilty of purely *ex opera operato* doctrines of the sacraments. He certainly did not deny (in controversy with William Goode, the leading evangelical theologian) the need for conversion. 'If Mr Goode means by this that an adult is not necessarily in a state of grace and so may require a solid and entire conversion notwithstanding the gift of God in baptism, no Christian instructed in the first principles of the faith would contend with him.' He might have been quoting Wesley! Pusey's preaching of the cross, evoking awe and adoration, was combined with strict observance of the routine means of grace. There is a tragedy of polarization here. The Wesleyan stress on holiness (at least in the mainstream of the tradition) and the sheer wonder at God's grace that lies deep in Charles Wesley's hymns – 'the wonder why such love for me' could not be hidden in the heart – but had to be expressed outwardly and 'with a trumpet voice'. This might have given an evangelistic edge to the rather academic and even sombre approach of the early Tractarians, and produced an evangelical Catholicism in an earlier generation than was actually the case. N. F. S. Grundtvig, the Danish religious leader, made the precise point when visiting Oxford. 'Could these two movements find each other and coalesce, could they, at the same time, have their eyes opened for the importance of the word of faith in the Christian congregation, then the conditions of a rich church life would be in existence in England.' But the cultural divide was simply too great.[42]

What were the consequences of the Oxford Movement? Firstly

new styles of church life, worship and architecture began to appear and the changes were pervasive.[43] If we went back to the year 1830 in many a parish we would find worship rather bare even for an Irish evangelical of the strictest sort today. Choirs were rare, the musicians' bench was dying out. The service was often a mere dialogue between parson and clerk, the parson donning a Geneva gown to preach. Neither Pusey nor Newman were interested in ceremonial. For Pusey the simplicity of English usage was appropriate for the penitential state of divided Christendom. Yet Pusey paved the way for change by making the eucharist the focus of religious life. The ceremonial (or popularly 'ritualistic') phase stems from men like John Mason Neale (1818–1866), the translator of medieval hymns, and the Cambridge Camden Society of 1839.[43] Neale began from a quite different position from that of the original Tractarians. Newman and Pusey began with the problem of authority and then asked how to apply their theological position. Neale said, '*Lex orandi* is *lex credendi*', how should man worship? The early Tractarians were concerned for truth, then for the practical issues in worship. They were not innovators in worship, but clearly pointed the way to it. The innovators in worship looked back from present custom to past styles and later to contemporary Roman Catholic practice, then rather romantic and florid, typified in the thinking and building of Pugin.

At Exeter the redoubtable Bishop Phillpotts sought to restore the surplice – there were riots! It became a party badge as it had been in the Vestiarian Controversy in Elizabethan times, masking as always weightier matters! The 'ornaments rubric' of the Book of Common Prayer, laying down that the practice of the second year of King Edward VI's reign was normative became again a bone of contention. Evangelicals disputed the position that alb, cope and chasuble were allowable! W. J. E. Bennett at St. Paul's Knightsbridge in 1840 began to introduce lighted candles, intoning of services and a surpliced choir. He began to preach in a surplice and adopted the 'eastward' position in the great prayer of the eucharist. A high value was put on adoration, all the resources of music, art, colour should be used. Bennett and A. H. Mackonochie, at St. Alban's Holborn, began to copy the exuberance of contemporary continental and English Roman models from Pugin downwards, bringing down on themselves the old cry of 'no popery'.

There followed the sad story of pettiness on the one hand – though some Evangelicals really did fear an undermining of Reformation principles and theology and it was not a baseless fear – and on the other hand disobedience to episcopal authority on the part of some 'ritualists' which made their espousal of apostolic succession seem ambivalent. Sydney Smith's mordant line, 'He's only for the Bishop when the Bishop is for him', was not far from the target! The English Church Union of 1859 was an umbrella organization for support and protection. Certainly great changes were afoot – more frequent communion, greater orderliness of worship, things in church were much less dull, for ornate ceremonial often accompanied fiery preaching with French models of parish mission adopted. By 1890 the average evangelical church was carrying out the ideals of the early Tractarians.

On Methodism and Dissent the effects were ambivalent. Clearly the widespread use of the Gothic style of architecture was a spin-off of romanticism beginning with the Unitarians.[44] 'It was high time,' says Horton Davies, 'to turn away from Renaissance architecture, whether neo-Roman, Georgian or neo-Grecian Victorian which was so strongly anthoprocentric in its celebration of man's dignity, to a more theocentric architecture. This was the Gothic, first produced by the men of faith in an age of faith.'[45] This sentiment has a whiff of the romantic about it, for Gothic architecture was not ideal for the average act of Methodist worship even that of, for example, Trinity Chapel, Wolverhampton, where Henry Hartley Fowler ruled the roost and which could turn on a liturgical service equal to any parish church in the town. Nonconformist spires (or 'spirelets' in John Betjeman's verse) went up to rival Tractarian ones. Thus in Halifax, Crossley's 'Square Church' shot up a spire (now an illuminated shell) to match Giles Scott's All Souls', built by the rival Anglican mill-owner Akroyd. There was an element of Nonconformist triumphalism about all this as in the description of the church in Grantham, where Mrs Margaret Thatcher was baptized.

> Magnificent indeed it is
> And stately it doth stand.
> It stands in Finkin Street
> The centre of the town.
> The Philosophic Institute
> Is rather lower down.[46]

There were, however, those who saw in Grecian and Gothic rather more than the apeing of the Establishment and expression of social power in the high street and the council. P. T. Forsyth saw Gothic as evocative of the transcendent, so often lacking in dissenting worship then and now.[47] Forsyth was by no means a lone voice, though in worship styles the chapel with dominant organ was more typical of the Nonconformist style of popular romanticism with preacher larger than life flanked by great choirs singing *Messiah* and *Elijah* and a weekly anthem and canticle in the larger places. Richness was certainly added to some services, banality to many. Wesleyan

Gothic certainly has links with the later Tractarians – as early as 1850 F. J. Jobson defended Gothic as *Christian* architecture.[48] Gladstone noticed that Nonconformists were using crosses on the outside of chapels, organs within them, painted architecture, that flagrant piece of symbolism the steeple, windows filled with subjects in stained glass, elaborate chanting and so forth. But probably more typical was Sir Isaac Holden (1807–97), business tycoon, who abhorred both 'Gothic' and 'liturgy', seeing them as an imitation of the Establishment and a hindrance to mission to the masses.

There was a more purely theological side to all this. The case of G. C. Gorham illustrated the sharp debate in Anglicanism over the meaning of baptism.[49] No overt liturgical changes in the Prayer Book were forthcoming in the Church of England, rather a new strictness in interpreting rubrics and the coincidence of railways and the proper parochial celebration of confirmation. In Wesleyanism it was a different story.[50] Even before 1850 we can detect subtle changes in Methodist statements on baptism, the eucharist, the church and in the general pattern of Methodist worship and churchmanship, though for some time phrases were used which would have sounded too 'Anglican' for the next generation. In 1837 we have already noted that Methodists were urged to 'consecrate your children under the bond of the Covenant in his visible church by Baptism. By baptism you place your children within the pale of the visible church . . . they are grafted into the body of Christ's disciples.' In 1840 it was directed that 'the sacrament shall always be administered according to the liturgy of the Church of England or according to the abridgment of that liturgy by Mr. Wesley'. In 1842 Conference urged Methodists to regard the sacrament of the Lord's Supper as a 'divinely appointed channel, through which the Spirit may convey to your penitent and believing hearts – pardoning, strengthening or sanctifying grace as your circumstances may require – remembering that the gospel way of faith is as remote from a Socinian disregard of things external as it is free from popish superstition'.

There is evidence of what W. F. Swift called 'the chaotic liturgical situation' in Wesleyanism. By 1874 the mood of Conference was changing. A committee (deriving from the acceptance of a 'memorial' from the Islington circuit) was set up to revise 'the Liturgy and Book of Offices especially with a view to the removal of all expressions which are susceptible of a sense contrary to the principles of our evangelical Protestantism'. Any trace of phrases suggesting baptismal regeneration were expunged from the office for Holy Baptism and even the simple 'manual acts' in the eucharistic prayer disappeared in the Communion rite of the revised *Book of Public Prayers and Services* of 1882 which remained the norm (save for those chapels which used the Book of Common Prayer) until 1936 – this despite the espousal of baptismal regeneration and high Calvinistic sacramentalism in William Burt Pope's *Compendium of Christian Theology*.[50] The liturgical changes illustrate an 'overgrown fear of Popery' in Wesleyan circles at the time of the ritual persecutions and the Public Worship Regulation Act of 1874.

Secondly, a new style of parish clergyman became the norm. Parson Woodforde, living the comfortable life of a small squire – taking the necessary services on a Sunday, visiting where there was illness or death, playing cards and dining with his neighbours, probably serving as a JP – began to develop into a much more professional character. Certainly the 'new parson' was still gentry rather than lower middle class but much more priestly. In urban areas the new model was typified by Walter Farquhar Hook (1798–1875) who became vicar of Leeds in 1837. He found the town a hotbed of Dissent, not least Methodism. For twenty years he sought by worship, teaching, visiting, caring and organizing to build up the parish. 'I do not oppose dissenters by disputations and wrangling but I seek to exhibit to the world, the church in her beauty. Let the services of the church be properly performed and right minded people will soon learn to love her.'[51] Beneath Hook's eirenic temper lay a latent triumphalism and the beginning of a battle to take on Dissent in its heartlands which increased as the century wore on and was by means confined to the Tractarians. Here is the parson as the 'organization man', the professional priest prepared to go to tough places like Leeds or the East End of London and slog it out for years on end.[52] In large urban parishes a fleet of curates, as later at the famous St Mary's Portsea, would be made available. Here was a 'different kind of gentleman' to the parson on his glebe and the change keyed in with the rise of the professions – law, medicine, teaching, the civil service. The arrival of the new style priest combined with the Peelite reforms to produce a new Anglicanism ready for the shock revealed by the Religious Census of 1851.

Thirdly, the Tractarian revival ended the old High Church-Tory alliance. The Tractarians were not afraid to criticize any government opposing what they felt to be the church's interests. They weakened the church in popular esteem by making laymen suspicious of innovating clergymen. They weakened the Church of England in politics and perhaps popular esteem – they strengthened its soul.[53] The second generation of Tractarians began to develop a theology of the incarnation which, when combined with some of the insights of F. D. Maurice, took the social life of man seriously and began to espouse radicalism in politics. No-one was to exemplify this more than Charles Gore who abhorred *laissez-faire* individualism – 'Each man for himself and God for us all as the elephant said when he danced among the chickens.' The vials of wrath of the more socialistic wing of the high-churchmen were poured out on dissenters as allies of mammon and cruel individualism.[54] The paradox here is that it is *this* generation of high-churchmen whose style of preaching and evangelism more nearly resembled that of the Methodists. The earlier Anglo-Catholics clearly took up French Catholic styles of mission – John Kent is, I think, right here against Dieter Voll,[55] but later a type of evangelical Catholicism can be detected which makes Voll's point of value.

John Neville Figgis (1866–1919) is an outstanding figure of this circle.[56] In upbringing Figgis was an Evangelical – his father J. B. Figgis was a leading member of the Countess of Huntingdon's connexion. Neville Figgis became an agnostic in the proper sense of the word. He underwent a crisis of his unbelief and a conversion back to Christianity, this time in its Anglo-Catholic form, though he called himself 'evangelical Catholic' and always combined with his sacramentalism a personal sense of commitment to him whom he again and again called 'the strange man on the cross'. 'I think we can say that as far as creed goes a man is a Christian or a non-Christian as far as he can enter into the spirit of the hymn, "When I survey the wondrous cross".' For Figgis only a full-blooded orthodox Christology with a stress on the atonement could meet the real needs of mankind. Figgis sought always to secure personalism in his presentation of the faith. Like any evangelical, Figgis asserted that 'faith is personal trust in a person'. The human burden of sin can only be rolled off at the foot of the cross. Like G. A. Studdert-Kennedy, he could talk of making 'the great gamble with Christ'. Yet while he stressed conversion greatly, he did not make it the criterion of being a Christian. 'This is élitism, the danger of Puritanism in any age.' Within what he called the 'democracy of the Catholic church' there must be room for all temperaments, not just for those whom William James called the 'twice born' of whom Figgis himself was clearly one. The faith is personal but never individualistic. This is underlined by the place of the eucharist in Christian devotion and its utter centrality in the life of the priest. There is an almost rapturous sense in Figgis of the dignity and glory of being a member of a church in which St Athanasius, St Augustine, St Catharine, St Francis, John Wesley and John Henry Newman are our contemporaries. Figgis was one of the most powerful preachers of his day though, like P. T. Forsyth, one suspects his appeal was more particularly to the idealism of students. How many contemporary preachers would end a university sermon – 'Someone said, a highway robber asks your money or your life but Christ asks both. May God grant you to give both'?[57] Perhaps Gore might have said that, or Bishop King who gloried to be the bishop of the poor in John Wesley's diocese and whose preaching was often called Methodist in style.[58] Evangelical Catholics were nearer to the spirit of Wesley than the formal Wesleyanism of J. H. Rigg. The paradox is given another twist when one recalls that these men had to ally with Toryism to safeguard church schools, so that the High Church-Tory alliance reappears at the turn of the century in a strange way.[59]

Fourthly, the Oxford Movement exacerbated relationships between the Church of England and both continental Protestantism and English dissenters by the insistence on episcopacy and an apostolic ministry as the very essence of the church. An example of this was the furore over the Jerusalem Bishopric of 1841 when Newman denounced Lutheranism and Catholicism as 'heresies repugnant to scripture and anathematized by East as well as West'.[60] This brought episcopacy to the fore as the *sine qua non* of all re-union discussions. This is indisputable, even if the Tractarians were mistaken in their view that they were defending traditional Anglicanism. Their viewpoint was certainly selective if not innovatory and clearly threatening to any closer relations with the Wesleyans. In the 1820s and 1830s private attempts at reconciliation were not uncommon. Mark Robinson of Beverely in 1824 offered and initiated a scheme which was answered by Richard Watson and the doctor-theologian Humphrey Sandwith (1792–1874).[61] In 1836 a Wesleyan minister James Kendall (1799–1859) wrote bitterly against what he called 'Methodist dissent' offering a scheme of union.[62] 'Methodist dissenters are not Wesleyan Methodists. Primitive Methodism! Pitiful delusion! The Primitive Methodists were pious members of the Church of England united together in a religious society.' His scheme (not altogether unlike that of Samuel Bradburn in 1792) included the suggestion that the bishops should ordain all eligible and willing itinerant preachers, that suitable chapels should be consecrated, that accredited local preachers should be employed as at present but not employed to preach at consecrated chapels. A bishop was to be invited to be present at Conference.

Kendall wrote as an outspoken and rather unhappy Wesleyan longing for re-union, though it is to be noted that he also wrote a pamphlet against the Tractarian doctrine of 'apostolic succession'. His scheme was no more likely to commend itself than were the propositions of 1836 of Richard Polwhele, an Anglican clergyman.[63] Polwhele, who earlier had been an opponent of the Methodists – he had edited Lavington's *Enthusiasm of Methodists and Papists compar'd* – stated that there were three chief parties among the Methodists – those friendly to the church, those who hold their own services and those who attack the church. 'It were useless,' he says, 'to attempt a coalition with these people by any plan requiring the extinction of the present system. They are too well persuaded of its merits to suffer it to be destroyed. And Methodism feels less desire to be incorporated with the church than the church to be incorporated within Methodism.' Polwhele's scheme was little short of the incorporation of Wesleyanism into the Establishment and was decades too late! The day of what J. H. Rigg called 'independence without enmity' had arrived[64] and was soon to turn into a time when he could say that 'the genius of Methodism as now fully organized into a church and that of Anglican Episcopacy are mutually repellent and exclusive'. Attempts to bridge the gulf petered out under pressure of what came quickly to be called 'Puseyism' so easily lined up with 'popery'. The consequences were firstly suspicion among Wesleyans, then a full scale attempt at a refutation of the Tracts and the setting forth of a rival ecclesiology, which could counter the rebellions within and the snarling foes outside the camp.

The suspicion of Puseyism was fully aroused by 1842. In April of that year, John Hannah (1792–1867) of the Wesleyan Theological Institute, shortly to be President of the Conference, wrote to the London ministers:

> I am informed, at the meeting of the London Preachers on Tuesday last (at which meeting I was not present) it was alleged or at least strongly insinuated that certain commendations which I was supposed to have bestowed on the 'Oxford Divines' had given the unhappy young men who had recently left the institution a predisposition in favour of the views which they now profess to entertain. May I request that if you have any reason to suspect me as guilty of so mischievous a piece of conduct, you will have the goodness to place it before me in direct manner and a definite form. I hope you will excuse me if I press the request, for the matter may be of more serious consequence to me in relation to my future movements than you are perhaps aware.[65]

The undertones of the letter are clear enough and the last point may not be unconnected with the fact that Hannah's brilliant son had become an Anglican priest (as did the sons of John Farrar and James Dixon). The earlier points illustrate the suspicion between high-churchmen and Wesleyans opening up three years before Newman became a Roman Catholic.

A good sounding board here is the rough diamond scholar Thomas Jackson (1785–1873) who was Connexional Editor from 1824–42 and theological tutor at Richmond from 1842–61.[66] Jackson's stance was that of a typical Methodist of the earlier years of the century who retained a wistful love of Anglicanism. In 1834 (the year after the Assize Sermon), Jackson addressed Conference on *The Church and the Methodists*, one of the last Wesleyan apologies before the impact of Tractarianism. He states that

> No attacks on the church as a National Establishment have ever been countenanced by 'the Body' [this was the year of J. R. Stephen's enforced resignation], the principles of strict Dissent have never been professed or assumed . . . Let the voluntary principle be carried as far as it possibly can, in the advancement of Christian instruction – yet after all the country cannot do without an Establishment either in resisting Popery, Socinianism and infidelity or in the maintenance of Christian godliness and public virtue.

The same tone is maintained in 1837 in another pamphlet.[67] 'The Church of England he has long been taught to venerate and he cherishes a growing conviction that her preservation in all her integrity is essential to the well-being of these realms.' Jackson maintains that schism is within the church and that the Methodists in the present day were 'in the church' in any just sense and therefore have not separated from it.

> The fact is that the population of the country has immensely outgrown the means of the Establishment and there are hundreds of thousands of people for whose spiritual necessities she makes no adequate provision whatever . . . these people, it is said, are separated from the church and by attending the Methodist chapel are involved in the sin of schism. If they belonged to the church, why did not the church instruct and save them? They are separated from nothing but ignorance and sin.

Jackson gives an interesting sidelight on the Methodist worship of the time when he says that he would give the churchman to whom he writes a 'ticket of admittance' to the Lord's Supper and that 'You shall attend any of the chapels where our regular ministers officiate on the forenoon of the Lord's Day as you please, and if you do not find the liturgy or the lessons read, I will forfeit five pounds.' By 1842 the Tractarian Movement was influencing Anglicanism at parish level. Methodists began to fear that the Establishment could no longer protect England from the bogey of 'popery'. Anglo-Catholicism was first mentioned at the Conference of 1842. In that year a series of *Wesleyan Tracts for the Times* was published to counterbalance the Oxford tracts. We need not repeat the analysis of the tracts given by John Bowmer[68] save to point out that the argument about schism being 'within the church' appears again and another familiar

Wesleyan argument is again put forward. 'The Methodists . . . have never yet as a body renounced all connexion with the Establishment; they have never disowned her fundamental doctrines nor prohibited attendance on her services, nor made it binding upon the people to forsake her communion in order to belong to them.'

It is illuminating to compare the topics and style of these *Wesleyan Tracts* with the replies of Anglican evangelicals to the Tracts. The same topics are raised, though Peter Toon's researches reveal the Anglicans operating on a slightly wider front – the Bible and tradition, the doctrine of justification and its relation to baptism and sanctification, the relation of regeneration to the sacrament of baptism, the nature of the church, the validity of non-episcopal ordination to the presbyterate, the presence of Christ in the eucharist.[69] 'The Evangelicals, while seeking to preserve intimate relationship between justification and baptism, differed from the Tractarians in that they insisted that justifying faith in adults is always preliminary to the sacrament and, though increased and enriched by the sacrament, is not the fruit of it, as Tractarians taught.'[70] On justification all agreed on its meritorious cause – the atonement wrought by Christ, the differences (as Newman well knew!) were over the formal cause – imputed or imparted – and the instrumental cause, baptism or saving faith. We have already noted the Wesleyan position here which is rather nearer to Newman than to the Evangelicals at some points. Justification, says Newman, 'comes through the sacraments, is received by faith, consists in God's inward presence and lives in obedience'.[71]

In the same year as the *Wesleyan Tracts*, Jackson published his *Answer to the Question, Why are You a Wesleyan Methodist?* Attacks on Methodists by Anglo-Catholics provoked this pamphlet, though Jackson proclaims again his friendship for the church. 'For the Church of England as a whole and as a *Protestant* Establishment I have long entertained what I conceive to be a just and sincere respect; nor shall anything absolutely alienate me from her ordinances. Some of the best hours of my life have been spent in the use of her truly sublime and evangelical liturgy. The sanctified scholarship of her sons has produced the richest theological literature in the world.'[72]

Jackson's tune, however, had changed in a reply he made that same year to the attacks on Methodism contained in E. B. Pusey's *Letter to the Archbishop of Canterbury*.[73] In the first edition of the letter Pusey had written of the Evangelicals:

> In contrast with the period in which the consciousness of the great truths of the gospel had become obscure and dim, they seized on, as Your Grace knows familiarly, one or two fundamental truths, or

rather they condensed the whole gospel into the two fundamental truths of nature and grace, that by nature we are corrupt, by grace we are saved. Our corruption by nature, our justification by faith were not a summary only, but in this meagre form the whole substance of their teaching. Faith alone was made the act of the mind – believing and appropriating to itself the merits of our Blessed Lord, the rest of the Christian system or God's gifts – the church, the sacraments, good works, holiness, self-discipline, repentance were looked upon but as introductory or subsidiary; or to follow as a matter of course upon these, but if thought of any value in themselves, pernicious.

This is parallel to much of Newman's polemic.

Wesleyanism is referred to in the third edition. Pusey points to what he calls the Wesleyan heresy of making justification by faith practically a 'justification by feelings'. 'Believe (not in Christ) that you will be saved and you will be saved' was early a Wesleyan doctrine, but its character was being held in check partly by the church-system in which those who adopted it had been educated, partly by the continued use of the sacraments of the church. 'In the section of the Wesleyan body which is becoming more alienated from the church and ceases to communicate with it, the original error has been fatally developing itself . . . the mind is worked up until it loses its fear and gains what it thinks an assurance of salvation . . . the "means of grace" are with him not the sacraments but the "class meeting", "bands", "love-feasts" . . . the state of their feelings not God's commandments are the standards, whereby they judge themselves.' Pusey's basic point had been made as early as 1742 in Dean Tucker's critique of Methodism. There seems little doubt that in the Wesleyanism of Pusey's time there was sometimes a substitution of 'feelings' for Wesley's doctrine of assurance so often misunderstood. Anglican writers have noted a cleavage between Methodist and Anglican thought at this point. In 1871 in his Bampton Lectures G. Curteis maintained that the real point at issue between the Establishment and Wesleyanism were the doctrines of instantaneous conversion and Christian perfection. From what to what did Wesley move on 24 May 1738? 'In the answer to that question lies the whole doctrinal difference between modern Wesleyanism and the Church of England. I am not aware of any other cause of severance.' Curteis was not writing from a Tractarian standpoint, but several of his points were similar to those of Pusey.[74]

Jackson's long reply containing catenas of quotation from the Bible, seeks to refute Pusey at this point. Scripture, the Homilies, Wesley's sermons are all used to show that Pusey had quite mistaken

Methodist thinking on present salvation, assurance and repentance. Jackson pits the very best Methodist thinking against Pusey, who had taken as his norm not John Wesley or Jabez Bunting but average Wesleyanism and contemporary revivalism. The controversy which abruptly ended – for Pusey made no reply to Jackson – showed the deepening alienation on fundamental matters of personal and corporate piety between Wesleyanism and the growing Anglo-Catholicism. As an incidental, Jackson's reply reveals that the practice of 'occasional conformity' was not dead in 1842. 'I have known a body of Wesleyans who were accustomed to hard labour during the week and to whom the rest of the Sabbath was indeed a relief and a blessing – cheerfully walk six or eight miles on that day to receive the Lord's Supper at the hands of a pious clergyman.' The letter ends with an attack on the Oxford Movement in general and on Tract 90 in particular. What Brilioth calls 'that melancholy document'[75] calls forth from Jackson phrases like 'flagrant dishonesty' and 'Jesuitical morality'.

Fear of and attacks ·by the Tractarians could easily lead to the narrowing of theological horizons in Methodism. The sacramental inheritance of the Wesleys both in theology and practice was largely lost – though William Burt Pope as theologian maintained the depth of that tradition of scriptural Catholic orthodoxy. The process of alienation was well under way by 1850 and by then any hope of theological synthesis between Tractarian and Wesleyan had vanished. Methodist attitudes towards Anglicanism changed from the friendliness and profound respect of Adam Clarke, Richard Watson and Jabez Bunting to the aloofness and coldness of James Rigg in the 1860s and 1870s, though he mellowed into a much warmer cultural approximation in his mature years, when he was in turn alienated from aggressive Dissent over education. Rigg could say in 1868 (the year of Pusey's letter to Conference);

> No real Methodist could ever find himself content and at home in the stately but cold cloisters of the Anglican church. Methodists much prefer their own sanctuary which, though it be less and lowlier, has in it much of the life and joy and fellowship which befits the communion of saints . . . There can be no greater mistake than to suppose there is or ever has been, at least in the present generation, any party within Methodism, whether ministers or among the people, who have felt the slightest concern as to union with the Church of England.[76]

The Oxford Movement was certainly a factor in a growing ecclesial self-consciousness in Wesleyanism, though this is complicated by the tension between high and low Methodism. High Methodism fuelled this by *apologiae* for the Wesleyan system like those of John Beecham, Alfred Barrett and later James H. Rigg who saw Methodism as fulfilling all the scriptural criteria of church order with a form of presbyteral succession and superintendent ministers who were tantamount to an episcopate in their authority.[77] Perhaps Wesleyanism would now have to be the great breakwater against the swelling tide of popery, formerly the role of the Establishment. A Free Kirk of England! Jabez Bunting, who had in the 1830s propounded his 'stock still' policy, now stated 'unless the Church of England will protest against Puseyism in some intelligent form, it will be the duty of the Methodists to protest against the Church of England'.[78] We have already seen the political consequences of this in a shift away from the Toryism of Peel. Within Methodism there was a deep hurt at being unchurched by the Tractarians which led to an assertion of churchliness, typified at a minor point by ministers wearing clerical robes. One of these men, S. D. Waddy (1804–76), later Governor of Wesley College, Sheffield, saw this as one of several organic changes 'which must take place in the churchly character of the Connexion'.[79] Bunting defused this particular controversy at Conference,[80] but it was a straw in the wind. The high Wesleyans were moving into a position of positive Free Churchmanship. Low Wesleyans were already there though their churchmanship was more revivalist, local and non-ministerial in style as well as more prone to voluntaryism in political affairs, especially education. These two incompatible models of church and ministry split Wesleyanism apart, leading to the secessions of 1827, 1835, 1849 and the coalition of the United Methodist Free Churches of 1857.

A fifth consequence of the Oxford Movement was the revival within the Church of England of the celibate and monastic life for both men and women, characterized by the work of Miss Priscilla Sellon, the Society of St John the Evangelist (the Cowley Fathers), the Society of the Sacred Mission (1891 – Kelham) and the Community of the Resurrection founded by Charles Gore in 1892.[81] Deep suspicions were aroused with the fear of a reversion to the worst of mediaevalism, yet in Methodism, Thomas Bowman Stephenson and Hugh Price Hughes were willing, while avoiding permanent vows of celibacy or poverty, to explore new models of Christian commitment – Anglo-Catholic, Roman Catholic, Lutheran or Salvation Army. Their thinking resulted in the National Children's Home (with its Sister-hood of nurses and teachers), the Wesley Deaconess Order (and its equivalent in United Methodism) and Hughes' Sisterhood at the West London Mission. There is a confluence of streams here which is part of a wider emancipation of women. Samuel Chadwick's churchmanship was somewhat different from that of Hughes, but when Principal of Cliff College, he said that if he could come on earth again he would choose to be an abbot. He read deeply in Catholic spiritual literature, in his early ministry regularly fasted, received the eucharist frequently, ruled Cliff College with almost monastic asceticism and saw his evangelists as preaching friars. While at Oxford Place Mission in Leeds he introduced Lenten devotions which seemed popish to some Methodists. This was a striving after a deeper spirituality than that found in contemporary evangelicalism.[82]

Sixthly, the Oxford Movement frightened the more moderately churchly Evangelicals into making common cause with the more right wing Evangelical churchmen who worked with dissenters and who made little of the value of the historic episcopate, shading off into supporters of Orange politics in Ireland and 'no popery everywhere else'. It made insistence on the sacrament suspected as savouring of popery. 'The Evangelicalism of the ritual persecutions was a negative product of the Oxford Movement.'[83] Methodism to some extent shared in this – Rigg had read his Walsh[84] and earlier, prompted by a rash of Anglo-Catholic polemics which claimed Wesley for themselves,[85] propagated two specious legends based on misleading evidence which J. E. Rattenbury called the 'Myth of the conversion' and the 'Myth of the rags of popery'.[86] Wesley was said to have changed his basic stance on the sacraments after his evangelical awakening or 'second journey' of 1738 (Rigg even speaks of his 'after life') and to have gradually shaken off the 'graveclothes of superstition' to make him the neat Victorian evangelical Methodist whose image Rigg wished to foster. Rattenbury perhaps over-reacted to Rigg for there was some change in Wesley's stance: he may even be said to have 'reverted to type' but not in the way Rigg thought. We have already noted the effect on liturgy.

In churchmanship there followed a more positive era than that dominated by Rigg with the renewed Catholic churchmanship of Hugh Price Hughes and Scott Lidgett (influenced deeply by W. B. Pope) who burst out of a narrow Wesleyan world into a Free Churchmanship which, with all its perilous triumphalism, had a vision of a united church. This was an indirect but very positive result of the Oxford Movement and led to a renewed sense of churchmanship in orthodox dissent likewise and was, as we shall see, a most important factor in the ecumenical movement.[87]

Eighthly, and vital to our argument, leaders like Samuel Wilberforce (1805–73) managed to bring together primitive Tractarianism and the evangelical heritage into a new and living synthesis.[88] This new type of churchmanship is decidedly indebted both to the Oxford Movement and to evangelicalism. Wilberforce (following Blomfield), like Jabez Bunting in Wesleyanism, expressed a style of church leadership which combined bureaucracy with spiritual oversight and which was not really viable until new modes of communication, especially the railway, made speedy travel possible for bishops and popular preachers alike. I would argue that while clearly the Oxford Movement was one important factor in pushing Wesleyanism into the Free Church camp, it was this change of Anglican style which was just as crucial, leading to a threatened but resurgent Anglicanism (spurred on by the goad of the 1851 census figures)[89] which clashed politically and socially with a Methodism past the peak of its growth in relationship to population by 1840.[90] The deep antagonism of the middle and later years of the Victorian Age has many causes, some of which we now analyse.

Firstly, the Church of England woke up to its responsibility to new urban populations, areas where Methodism had moved in to fill the gaps in the parish system. Typical was the district around Halifax in West Yorkshire where the largest parish in the country divided into three parochial chapelries with its chapels of ease and the odd proprietory chapel catered for almost the whole of Calderdale. Now reforming forces found men, the new professional clergy, evangelical and catholic, to whom we have already referred, new churches which, like railway systems, were to become an encumbrance to the next generation but one. Mission was doubtless still seen in rural and simplistic terms – plant a man, build a church and the parish system would do the trick, a view not unlike that of Thomas Chalmers in his Glasgow days – parallels in the kirk are worth exploring.

Hook in Leeds can again be the classic example.[91] In 1841 he was faced with a parish of 125,000 people, comprising eleven townships and including among its twenty-one Anglican chapels, eighteen curacies without cure of souls. By 1851 the old parish had been divided into seventeen parishes, all of them endowed with their own incumbents, while the clergy had increased from twenty-five to sixty. Dissent was met on its own terms in its heartlands. While Methodism had been strong during the superintendency of Fowler in the 1830s, it had a period of conflict and doldrum during Hook's reign which did so much to set the tone (as did J. C. Miller, the Evangelical in Birmingham) of the large town church with S. S. Wesley (who had opened Brunswick's notorious organ!) as his director of music.

Rural examples sharpen the picture. Samuel Wilberforce, when Bishop of Oxford, increased the livings of his diocese from 356 to 630 with enormous fund-raising schemes.[92] John Kaye (1781–1853) had 200 parsonages in the diocese of Lincoln built or rendered habitable.[93] The number of resident clergy increased again in the heartlands of rural Wesleyanism and Primitive Methodism. This was the backcloth to the uneasy episcopate of Christopher Wordsworth, whose clumsy attempts at rapprochement so annoyed the Wesleyans and that of the saintly Bishop King who, while personally friendly to Methodists and often called 'nowt but an old Methody', sought to win dissenters back to the fold.[94] In England between 1801 and 1831, 331 churches were built; between 1831 and 1861, 3,061 – church expansion equalling chapel growth.[95] In the 1840s (when the Oxford Movement really made its impact on Dissent) the number of clergy in England and Wales increased from 14,613 to 17,631.[96] Anglicanism was resurgent and prone to look askance at what the clerical patron of the Queen's College, Birmingham called at the time 'the subtle designs of the Jesuits and the insidious intrusion of malignant Dissenters'.[97]

In area after area the same tale could be told. Before Victoria came to the throne, Professor Gash[98] was right to call the Wesleyan Methodists 'the best organized and for certain purposes the most efficient religious body in England. Bunting, in his prime, was the head of the most powerful vehicle for protest, petition and publicity in English society.' He goes on to observe that the years 1815 to 1832 marked the period of greatest weakness of the Church of England relative to the other Protestant churches since the Commonwealth. There may be some exaggeration there but the scene changed rapidly after 1830. In 1836, to give one example, Joseph Sutcliffe complained to Jabez Bunting from Bayswater,[99] 'Methodism has now to work its own way with a Socinian and a Calvinistic clergy on the one hand, who steal the rich from us; and with an overflowing swarm of ranters on the other, who gather up the poor. Our trustees also offend by pewing out the chapels and leaving but a *crib* for the poor, and even the crib is in many instances occupied by classes of Sunday scholars in the morning, who perfume the house of God with school effluvia . . .' We note the blanket reference to clergy – evangelical as well as broad. Later in the century in the sparse parishes of the diocese of York which had spawned hundreds of chapels, the Archbishop – Thomson – a leading Evangelical, countered Dissent and secularism with the now familiar recipe.[100]

The bishops, made mobile by the railways, were on the attack! We have already quoted Mackarness' charge to the Oxford clergy in the 1870s taunting dissenters with a desire for equality which 'not even a revolution could give them'.[101] This aggressiveness was by no means unique. The 'revolt of the field' revealed the unpopularity of the clergy. Disputes over tithe and rates became mixed up with rick-burning and ranterism. The early agricultural unions – which we have encountered in analysing Primitive Methodism – revealed a latent dislike of the pretensions of parsons and their patronizing ladies. If Joseph Arch left the church because his mother was 'blacklisted' for insubordination to the squire's lady, so did Joseph Ashby of Tysoe, who became a Wesleyan.[102] Even so broad-church a bishop as J. C. Ellicott of Gloucester,[103] friend of W. F. Moulton, was highly critical, to put it at its best, of rural unionists which alienated him from radical dissenter and Methodist alike. Evangelical and Methodist had co-operated in the age of Wilberforce, especially in the anti-slavery movement, but the Evangelicals could scorn the Wesleyans or Primitives in their parish especially when they had begun to solve the problem of the 'eloquent convert' who would, in an earlier generation, have turned Methodist if not given scope.[104] Evangelicals, too, tended to support the Establishment while the Tractarians, above all, were concerned with spiritual autonomy, hence their stress on apostolicity, succession and toleration and, while desperately concerned about Catholicity, held dissenters in general contempt. Free Church Alliance was the consequence of this phase of Anglican aggression.

The parallels between Tractarianism and continental romanticism and ultramontanism, outlined clearly by Bishop E. A. Knox among others[105] are clearly important, though as C. C. J. Webb pointed out, the cultural isolation of English thought from continental thought meant that they were largely only parallel with mission as a link rather than thought, though Webb, I think, is less convincing than Knox at this point. Indeed one of the most trenchant critiques made of the Oxford Movement was by that veteran evangelical leader, who had not disdained high-church support over church schools! He argued that Tractarianism was a phase in a more general revival of religion in Europe in the second quarter of the nineteenth century; it was a tragically mistaken phase, because the Tractarians, especially Newman and Fronde, impressed by the 'encircling gloom' of the 1830s, found 'the root of all evil in the rebellion against the Divine authority of the church, the great and romantic church of the Middle Ages, and thought that if this authority could be restored all would be well' – whereas Knox said the true danger to Christianity lay in the liberal theology of Strauss and his successors. The Tractarians may have found favour with the clergy and the 'cultured despisers of the Evangelical bourgeoisie' but missed the real point. 'Oxford prepared for the storm by study of Caroline and Patristic theology. Cambridge by study of scripture, in which Thirlwall, Alford, Lightfoot, Westcott and Hort led the way.'[106]

This was a harsh judgment on Newman who had said that 'we cannot if we would move ourselves back into the time of the Fathers; we must in spite of ourselves be churchmen of our own time not of any other were it only for the reason that we are born in the nineteenth century not the fourth'.[107] Robert Isaac Wilberforce can be shown to

be very unromantic also in his attitude at this precise point.[108] Knox
agrees rightly that the real danger to Christianity (if that is how we
are to view it!) lay in the new theologies of Germany. In Pusey the
Tractarians had a leader who was quite aware of the issues but
had laid them on one side. But the Evangelicals were even more
obscurantist at this point – and Knox, indeed, in his autobiography
comments on the Pusey-Evangelical alliance as 'a common opposition to what we called "Neologianism", that is to the teaching of
Strauss and Renan, to the philosophy of Comte and John Stuart
Mill, to Colenso's attack on the Pentateuch and to the conclusions
drawn from Darwinism gave us a common ground with Pusey and
his followers'.[109]

The Wesleyans were in like case, although William Arthur in
Religion without God (1887) and *God without religion* (1887) showed
himself well aware of where the shoe pinched.[110] Like Pusey, Methodism's greatest systematic theologian W. B. Pope (1822–1903) was
well aware of German theology, translating some of the more
conservative Christological material. Like Pusey, he seemed
unwilling to tackle what now seem the crucial issues, though premature retirement due to depression may have been one reason. Scott
Lidgett always avowed that his own breadth of theological awareness
came from Pope as much as from F. D. Maurice[111] and acknowledges
a common debt to Newman. The massive contribution of Pope to
Wesleyanism clearly owed not a little to the resurgence of Catholicism. A comparison of Pope and Newman (Pope's brother,
Thomas, was Newman's lieutenant at the Oratory, another brother
was headmaster of the Oratory School, though I have not found any
trace of direct contact between Newman and W. B. Pope) on the
doctrine of holiness reveals not a few common features, not least the
stress on sanctification as loving, moral concern which divides both
from Evangelicals of the Calvinist variety.[112]

Knox's 'apostolic blows and knocks' clearly had some point though
it is heavily dependent on earlier argument by Mark Pattison and J.
A. Froude. 'It was ludicrous, had it not been so inexpressibly sad,
that against the deluge of Strauss' *Life of Jesus* the great and brilliant
Newman provided no better refuge for his followers than the *Lives of
the Saints.*' It was A. P. Stanley who had remarked 'How different the
fortunes of the Church of England might have been if Newman had
been able to read German . . . All the grand development of human
reason from Aristotle down to Hegel was a sealed book to him.' J. A.
Froude withdrew from the lives of the saints project. 'St Patrick I
found once lighted a fire with icicles, changed a Welsh marauder
into a wolf, and floated to Ireland upon an altar stone. I thought it

nonsense . . . I had to retreat out of my occupation, and let the series go on without me.'

At this point Knox conveniently forgot not only the *Library of the Fathers* and the *Library of Anglo-Catholic Theology*, but also the contribution to the life of devotion and worship and the creative thinking stemming from the doctrine of development. 'Oxford had not even sympathy to offer to the orthodox Germans whom W G. Ward in his rashness had pronounced worse than atheists.' Oxford had no 'rational defence against a deliberate onslaught on the foundations of the Holy Catholic Church'. Knox, too, says that the Anglo-Catholics failed at a crucial point – they did not succeed in increasing the authority of the clergy over the laity who persisted in what he called the national refusal to be governed by the clergy even in things spiritual.[113] The same tension divided high and low Methodists. Knox's arguments have weight, for not until Charles Gore did the Tractarians produce a leader capable of tackling modern issues and he did not really begin his writing career until the publication of *Lux Mundi*.

The influence of the Oxford Movement, as we have seen, was subtle and pervasive, often mixed up with a wider romanticism. Pugin was almost as influential in Nonconformity as in Catholicism. More elaborate worship, even if purged of unevangelical sentiments, characterized Nonconformity as much as Anglicanism. The parallels which R. N. Flew and C. C. J. Webb noticed – the quest for holiness, disciplined devotion through confessional or class meeting and sacramental devotion were overlaid by acrimony and disagreement. Trevor Dearing's suggestive *Wesleyan and Tractarian Worship* reveals so much in common between Wesley and the Tractarians but it must be admitted that the *context* of the nineteenth-century traumas we have outlined make the parallels largely academic. The two traditions have not been able even late in the twentieth century to share their treasures, except marginally, in hymnody.

The claim so often made that it was the Oxford Movement which pushed Methodism into the Free Church camp needs, as we have seen, to be put in the context of the sociological complexities of the Victorian church-chapel conflict. Clearly it was – and is – a major factor in keeping the two traditions of Anglicanism and Methodism institutionally apart. By 1890 Wesleyanism was firmly in the Free Church camp, if somewhat uneasily massed under the Liberal banner. The Free Church phase of Methodist history was both anti-ecumenical – Hugh Price Hughes, at the opening of the Oxford Place Mission in Leeds could afford to waste energy lambasting the Roman Catholics in the morning and the Anglicans at night[114] – with near its heart a fear of Rome and what was thought to be the pseudo-

Rome of the Anglo-Catholics, yet also ecumenical in that this period saw the renaissance of thinking about the nature of the church in the Free Churches which, led by P. T. Forsyth, Scott Lidgett, Charles Berry, J. H. Shakespeare and A. S. Peake, was to issue not only in a call for Free Church Federation but a new approach to Anglicanism and the wider church. To that part of the story we now turn.

9

From Lunn to Flew –
Methodism and the Wider Ecumenism
1890–1955

We have seen the crucial importance of the struggle between a resurgent Anglicanism and a militant Dissent fuelled by the urban middle class demanding their place in the sun. In rural areas the 'revolt of the field' saw the emergence of a strong rural working class prepared to be patronized no longer by parson, squire or their ladies. Sir Ernest Baker's generalization was still true of the Victorian age. 'Apart from any question of their relative numerical strength, it may be said that the general relations, the general balance and the general interaction of Anglicanism and Nonconformity have been a cardinal factor in English life and developments for three centuries.'[1] The Oxford Movement 'at once an opposition to Nonconformity and an expression of Nonconformity' had the effect of raising barriers between Anglicanism and Dissent, including Methodism, which have proved so far intractable. It is possible to exaggerate the theological strength of the Tractarian Movement.[2] Free Churchmen and Anglicans alike have a habit of underestimating evangelical theology but if Catholics hold on to an outmoded view of apostolic succession long after its apparent explosion by critical scholarship, Evangelicals and some broad-churchmen have hung on to the virtues of Establishment, which at its best is securing 'the greatest holiness of the greatest number', at its worst a clinging on to power. The Oxford Movement also indirectly produced what can only be called a recovery of a more 'Catholic doctrine of the church among the mainstream of dissenting groups, which found its practical expression in the movement for Free Church unity and its theological expression in the ecclesiology of William Burt Pope and later Peter Taylor Forsyth (though *his* mentor was F. D. Maurice) and the Catholic free churchmanship of Hugh Price Hughes and John Scott Lidgett, even if they are not always typical of Free Church opinion.[3]

We shall look briefly at changes within the Free Churches and then at the movement stemming from Anglican initiatives. At a time when, sociologically, the Free Churches were losing their cohesion – it was quite possible after the Irish Home Rule split for a dissenter to be a unionist or Liberal unionist following in the wake of Joseph Chamberlain,[4] the churches began to draw closer together. Even the Congregational Union in 1885 claimed that the 'time was gone when any order of churches can flourish simply by its polity'.[5] This Union held a joint congress with the Baptists in 1886. Two years later, following several ineffective Anglican feelers towards what came to be called 'Home Reunion', the Lambeth Conference of 1888 set out the so-called 'Lambeth Quadrilateral', to which we shall later return. In 1892, the first Free Church Congress was held in Manchester.[6] Wesleyan leaders like Hughes and Lidgett were involved from the beginning in the Free Church unity movement and contributed greatly to it. Local Free Church councils sprang up after 1892, notably in Birmingham, despite the grave and prophetic warnings of R. W. Dale[7] who feared alignment with Liberalism in an exclusive manner. Dale gloried in the contribution of individuals (including himself) to the civic gospel. 'The men who took part in the Movement had learned the principles on which they acted, and caught the spirit by which they were inspired, very largely in the Nonconformist Churches of Birmingham' but he said, 'I do not want to see a Nonconformist party in Birmingham . . . I have the greatest fears of what will come from the present passion of some excellent persons to capture Christian churches and to change them into political and municipal caucuses . . . I have no objection to political caucuses; they are necessary but God forbid that any church of which I may even be minister or member should be a caucus.' The fully organized National Council of Evangelical Free Churches, elected on a representative basis, met for the first time in 1896, with Hughes as President. Hughes (and in this he followed Charles Berry, the Congregationalist of Wolverhampton) was quite clear that Free Church unity meant something organic; it was churchmanship not individualism.[8] 'The unit of this movement is not the individual Christian but the church. Therein it differs *toto caelo* from the Evangelical Alliance, which is merely a fortuitous concourse of Evangelical individuals who meet together occasionally to say that they love one another.' Hughes surely knew that the Evangelical Alliance could be more than that, when there was anti-Romanism afoot! We are, he claimed, 'Catholic high-churchmen' – hence the refusal to admit either the Salvation Army, on the grounds of their lack of sacraments and the Unitarians, for lack of sound doctrine, on to the Federal Council. His expression of high-churchmanship was, however, firmly opposed both to the church of Rome and to

Anglo-Catholicism, which he saw as infecting and infesting the Church of England. 'We are not one in the Pope, we are not one in the Crown but we are one in Christ. The Roman Catholic stands for the supremacy of the Pope, the Anglican Catholic for the supremacy of the Crown [Keble would turn in his grave at that!], and the Scriptural Catholic for the supremacy of Christ.' The curious triumphalism of the latter phrase must have escaped him! This rhetorical stance spilled over into Liberal imperialism and the notion that Free Churchmanship represented the majority view in the Empire which had prescriptive rights, it seemed, over benighted nations, a view fuelled by the missionary thinking of the time which simply followed secular fashion.[9] Hughes did not espouse an anti-Anglican stance except on the knotty issues of Establishment and ritualism, which he saw as a revival of 'extreme mediaeval clericalism'. He made it clear that the Free Churches must see that England, 'the land of civil and religious freedom, the land of Gospel light, shall never sink to the degraded level of Spain'. The Free Church movement on its positive side sought a deepening of spiritual life and evangelism of the vast unchurched masses. This policy was set out in the Free Church Catechism of 1899 which paradoxically was approved of at key points by Charles Gore and criticized by the veteran Conservative Wesleyan, Marshall Randles (who sought for a time to prevent Scott Lidgett delivering his Fernley Lecture on the Atonement and was remembered by students for his assertion that the Devil used asbestos in Hell.)[10] and practised in the Simultaneous Mission to London of January 1901, followed soon after by missions in the provinces in which the Wesleyan Gipsy Smith played a leading part.[11]

Revival and social agitation coincided in this period. The social agitation coincided both with increasing co-operation between the Free Churches and the last great head on 'church-chapel' clash over the Balfour Education Act of 1902 which, as we have seen, enabled a majority of Free Churchmen to find a common politico-religious cause. While Anglo-Catholics were involved in this battle and the fears and bogies of sacerdotalism were raised by Free Churchmen, it was doughty Evangelicals like Bishop E. A. Knox who defended Anglican schools and the Establishment against what was seen as a secular attack, which indeed it was in the hands of John Clifford, as J. N. Figgis made clear.[12] The typical British compromise of the dual system, state and Church schools in symbiosis, the latter heavily subsidized by central or local government, was not stable before World War One. The Free Church case was based on difficulties in single school areas where, even if there was conscience clause, Free Church parents felt inhibited in using it and petty dominance by parson and squire and school mistress was not uncommon. It is significant that of the Methodist groups, it was the Primitive Methodists who were the most affected and the most vehement in their protests, a reflection of their rural strength.[13] Some Free Churchmen preferred distraint of goods or prison to what John Clifford had called 'Rome on the Rates'. It is a paradox that it was Anglicans like Figgis who pleaded for the autonomy of the church (rather than the Free Churches), taking over the very vocabulary of the Free Kirk protest on the issue of spiritual freedom. Wesleyan opinion was always divided on this issue, as it had been since the days when J. H. Rigg and William Arthur argued the case for and against denominational education.[14] Scott Lidgett emerged as the supreme diplomat, instrumental in preventing the total identification of the Free Church Council with political party cries. Indeed, the Wesleyans were often on the horns of a dilemma. Sociologically they were Free Churchmen, theologically the links with Anglicanism were still strong. This ambivalence was clearly evident in the deep traumas in Wesleyanism over Methodist Union which leaders like J. E. Rattenbury could not divorce from a longing for reunion with Anglicanism.

During the First World War, when co-operation between all the churches grew very greatly, not least in chaplaincies, the Free Churches grew closer together, though Wesleyans held themselves somewhat aloof. The Baptist, J. H. Shakespeare (1857–1928), began to adumbrate a united Free Church of England as a first stage to full corporate re-union with the Church of England, including the acceptance of the historic episcopate. 'Denominationalism is a decaying idea – it certainly does not commend itself to a nation in a socialistic age nor to the very people upon whom its success depends.'[15] The first step for Shakespeare was some kind of federation, an approach which had the support of two leading Free Church thinkers, P. T. Forsyth and J. H. Moulton.[16] Federation has been criticized by Bishop Lesslie Newbigin[17] as 'reunion without repentance' but the subsequent history of re-union schemes in England bears out the realism of Forsyth and Shakespeare. Scott Lidgett, who always saw corporate union as his ultimate goal and was even prepared for re-ordination to achieve it, a view not shared, I suspect, by many, stood further to the right than J. H. Moulton, who saw federation as an interim and perhaps penultimate goal, what Forsyth called the 'united states of the Church'. Lidgett shared Shakespeare's final goal but was realistic enough to say, 'Where there are no differences our watchword must be union; where they are comparatively slight, federation; where they are more serious, yet not destructive of the fundamental agreement of Christianity, co-operation in order to defend and promote the supreme interests and applications of our common Christian life.'[18]

Shakespeare's dream was not to be fulfilled. The Wesleyans were lukewarm on the whole issue despite the advocacy of Scott Lidgett, J. S. Banks, Sir Robert Perks and Arthur Henderson. In July 1918 the Wesleyan Conference decided to defer the proposals for a year,[19] Sir Robert Perks reneging on his previous support. The Federal Council of the Evangelical Free Churches was inaugurated in October, 1919 without benefit of Wesleyans, though they took their place in 1920, providing a moderator in 1923 – in the person of the ubiquitous and inevitable Scott Lidgett. Henceforward two Free Church bodies ran on parallel lines before the amalgamation which produced the Free Church Council in 1940. Free Church Federation – never quite the system Forsyth, let alone Shakespeare wanted – did little to bring the Free Churches into formal union and perpetrated the curious myth of the Free Church existing alongside the Catholic Community and the Church of England, but which is too nebulous to be effective and is now a pale shadow, with most of its work taken over by the British Council of Churches, which itself tends to be a radical tail wagging a conservative dog. Not until 1972 did the most obvious union (seen as desirable by B. L. Manning[20] in 1933, a generation before) become a fact with the creation of the United Reformed Church, a union between the Presbyterian Church of England and a majority of the Congregational Church (formerly Union).

Nevertheless the Free Church Council provided a valuable clearing house in negotiations with the Church of England. If the late nineteenth century saw the Free Churches growing together, the gulf between dissenter and Anglican was greater than ever, exacerbated by political conflict and the alignment of the Free Churches behind the Liberal Party. J. H. Rigg (1821)–1909) was representative of much Wesleyan opinion and by no means anti-ecumenical. Indeed, his stance on education was condemned by some Wesleyans as too pro-Anglican when he sat on the Royal Commission on Education along with Cardinal Manning and R. W. Dale.[21] For Rigg 'it is just as likely that Methodism should absorb Anglican Episcopacy as that Anglican Episcopacy should absorb Methodism . . . as a world power Methodism is the more potent in its operation and influence'.[22] He maintained that 'there was then no party within Methodism who had felt the slightest concern as to union with the Church of England'. Benjamin Hellier, a little later, stated why, in his view, union was not possible.

As to what high-churchmen tell us about our departure from

Wesley's principles . . . our answer is plain. We know that we have departed from them and should have been very foolish if we had not. We greatly reverence Wesley's memory: but we never held him infallible and on this matter we know that he was mistaken. Wesley said, 'If the Methodists ever leave the Church of England, God will leave them'. We have left the church but God has not left us. He is with us as surely as he ever was with our fathers. And this is to us demonstration that on this point Wesley was in error. As to the idle dream of the re-union of Methodism with the Church of England, there is one short but sufficient objection; new wine must not be put into old bottles.

Hellier listed five reasons why the union of Methodism with the Church of England was impracticable. In the first instance, the Church of England was a house divided against itself. The two Convocations and the high-church party would never reach a common mind. Second, the Methodist Conference would likewise never reach a common mind on re-union. Third, the minds of both churches would not arrive at a common policy, even if they could agree among themselves. Fourth, if the Convocations and the Conference did reach a common mind, their suggestions would prove unacceptable to the Methodist people as a whole. Finally, even if the first four points were met, Hellier believed that the sanction of Parliament would be withheld.

These things considered and without saying what may or may not be possible one hundred years hence when you and I shall no longer be dwelling upon this earth, we may say that the question of organic union between the Methodists and the Church of England is one which belongs to the region of pure speculation and as a question on which practical men can take action, it has not yet come within the field of vision.

The irony of what *did* happen a century after Hellier, need not be laboured.[23] Rigg and Hellier were reacting[24] against the style of approach to the Wesleyans typified by Bishop Christopher Wordsworth's Pastoral of 1873 to the Wesleyans of his Lincoln diocese,[25] clumsy in its patronizing tone. 'Olive branches launched from a catapult' is J. A. Newton's description.[26] He recalls the marvellous riposte of William Arthur when asked if he would not like to preach in the Cathedral – after re-ordination. Indeed, 'but I would also be glad to preach in a wheelbarrow'.[27]

There were signs in the nineteenth century of a more realistic approach from the Church of England.[28] In 1834, A. P. Stanley desired the admittance of dissenters to the universities, a matter at that time opposed by F. D. Maurice. When Dean of Westminster, he was a noted early ecumenist, personally friendly to Wesleyans like J. H. Rigg.[29] In 1857, the Archbishop of Canterbury (J. B. Sumner, an Evangelical) invited leading Nonconformists to Lambeth Palace – indeed William M. Bunting[30] (son of Jabez), then honorary secretary of the Evangelical Alliance, led prayers. For his pains, Summer was accused of introducing 'Spurgeonism' into the Church. In 1856, John Lonsdale, Bishop of Lichfield, brought before Convocation a petition signed by a number of clergy and laity 'laying to heart the great dangers we are in by our unhappy divisions and earnestly desiring a closer union among Christians' and asked, 'What impeded Wesleyans from returning to the Church of England?' The redoutable Phillpots of Exeter made clear that only repentance for a state of schism would suffice. The Church Congress at Wolverhampton in 1867, devoted one of its sessions to the 'best means of bringing non-conformists into union with the Church'. The motion was introduced by Lord Lyttelton, who was, among his many accomplishments, Principal of the Queen's College at Birmingham. He suggested various cosmetic changes in the Articles and the formation of a Committee of Association of laity and clergy, for the promotion of re-union of Christians at home. Convocation had its Committee for Home Reunion of the Divided Members of Christ's Body (an interesting title in itself), which presented a report also in 1867. Much of it reads now like pompous nonsense – certain Methodist ministers were to be admitted to the diaconate and priesthood, chapels were to be licensed for Holy Communion, some ministers were to be consecrated bishop 'so long as they did not perpetuate the succession'. More positive was the Home Reunion Society, chaired by the evangelically minded and eirenic Lord Nelson. But these were mere flurries.

Cultural isolation of long duration, as well as Anglican militancy spearheaded by the demand for freedom for Church schools, must not be overlooked either. 'Generally speaking', said the gentle J. H. Moulton,[31] 'our church stood nearer to the Church of England than it did to other Methodist communities, not to speak of other dissenting communities. The Oxford Movement changed all that.' As we have shown, the story is more complex but biographies[32] reveal that in many parishes churchmen and Methodists simply did not meet. The battles of Dissent for equality, contested at every ditch by the Establishment, with corresponding truculence, added fuel to the fires of bitterness. This was clearly not just the aftermath of the Oxford Movement but a resurgence of a triumphalist attitude which was to be found also among Evangelicals, especially over matters like the 'revolt of the field' which appeared to threaten social cohesion.

While in the Victorian period it had been the broad-churchmen like Dean Stanley, who had shown the warmest approach to the Wesleyans – an echo of Thomas Arnold's idea of preserving Establishment by widening it, allowing both 'the morning song of the lark' and the evening 'song of the nightingale',[33] now it was 'liberal Catholics' like H. H. Kelly and T. A. Lacey[34] who were opening up, before the First World War and during it, new possibilities of mutual recognition. The roots, however, of twentieth-century ecumenism ran deeply back into the nineteenth century. However intransigent they may appear, the Tractarians desired union, if clumsily. There was the pervasive influence of the YMCA,[35] which moulded men like J. R. Mott,[36] the American Methodist layman, and the contribution, much undervalued by historians[37] of Dwight L. Moody, whose appeal to J. R. Mott and to acute theological minds like George Adam Smith, R. W. Dale, Nathan Söderblom and James Hope Moulton[38] has never been properly explored. Moulton's personal testimony is interesting. 'The student movement shows the way. It owed its birth, if we may select any single cause beyond others, to Moody and Sankey's memorable mission in Cambridge thirty years ago when I was a freshman. We who remember that wonderful week can understand best how it would effect the ecclesiastical views of the straightest sectarian.' Thus revivalism is strangely blended with the 'ecumenical movement of scholarship' and the World Christian Student Movement. The key example of the links in scholarship was the close co-operation between biblical scholars in producing a Revised Version of the Scriptures. In this enterprise, W. F. Moulton, the Wesleyan headmaster of the Leys School, Cambridge and J. D. Geden, the Methodist Hebrew scholar, played a notable part.[39] The meetings of the revisers were not without bitter controversy, involving A. C. Tait, because of the invitation by Dean Stanley to all the participants (including a Unitarian, Vance Smith) to a Communion service in Henry VII's chapel.[40] F. J. A. Hort regarded it as 'the beginning of a new period in church history'.[41] W. F. Moulton's work to widen the unity felt so deeply between himself and the Cambridge triumvirate of Westcott, Lightfoot and Hort, underlined the distance still to be travelled. Moulton could get no bishop to participate in the centenary of John Wesley's death, which fell when he was president of the Wesleyan Conference.[42] Yet a kind of ecumenical movement was growing in scholarly circles which moved right across the barriers of denomination as in the Oxford school of theology in the days of the underrated Edwin Hatch (whose writing drew upon him the wrath of Anglo-Catholics and the critical comment of Charles Gore), William Sanday, A. M. Fairbairn, J. V. Bartlet (these mark the arrival of Dissent in Oxford) and the eccentric T. K. Cheyne.

Free Churchmen were not guilty of mere cultural aggression when they moved colleges like Mansfield or Manchester to Oxford and when the Methodists founded the Leys School and later Wesley House at Cambridge. There was a recognition of new freedoms (with the dangers we have hinted at in Chapter 3) both of theological scholarship and of theological sharing. The days of denominational exclusiveness were over. The Wesleyan James Hope Moulton at King's College, Cambridge and Manchester and the Primitive Methodist Arthur S. Peake, firstly at Merton College, Oxford and then again at Manchester, were scholars known and respected far beyond their denominations, at a time when clergy and ministers were beginning to imbibe critical studies from writers in confessions other than their own.

A particular Methodist contribution was the initiatives of the somewhat eccentric character, Sir Henry S. Lunn (1859–1939).[43] Ordained in 1886 as a Wesleyan minister, he was for a short spell a medical missionary in India. He was then deeply involved with Hugh Price Hughes, his mentor, in the 'Missionary Controversy' which brought no great credit to official Methodism. Resigning from the ministry, he was offered ordination to the Anglican priesthood with indecent haste by Frederick Temple but became for a few years a minister of the Methodist Episcopal Church (Swiss Conference). Later, in 1910, while remaining a Wesleyan layman, he was confirmed by the Bishop of London. He typified a style of high-church Wesleyan who longed for union with the Church of England and never considered himself a dissenter but 'at most a noncon-forming member of the Church of England'.[44]

Percy Bunting (grandson of Jabez Bunting) was associated with him in the publication of the eclectic and ecumenical *Review of the Churches* (1891–1896; 1924–1930) with its team of formidable, diverse editors (F. W. Farrar, Percy Bunting, Donald Fraser, Alexander Mackennel and John Clifford) and used his expertise and money as a travel consultant in pioneering the fruitful and creative Grindelwald Conferences from 1893 to 1896, which brought together Christians of all kinds who were able to meet, talk and pray in delightful surroundings. Dr. Perowne, the Bishop of Worcester, administered Communion at one of the first Conferences according to 'a form prescribed in the Prayer Book to leading ministers and other represen-tatives of the Scottish Presbyterian and English Nonconformist Churches, all of them devoutly kneeling'.[45] The consequence in high-church circles paralleled Stanley's 'Revisers Communion' and later events at Kikuyu in 1913. At the 1893 Conferences the discussion centred on a definition of the Church. Hugh Price Hughes made clear his commitment. 'I wish to say that the distinctive object of this Reunion Conference is not to promote the fellowship of individual Christians, not even to promote the return of individual Christians to particular communities of Christians but the organized reunion of Christian communities'. Absorption of the Wordsworthian type was dismissed as 'just the sort of scheme likely to be propounded by a good honest soul who lives up in a balloon, far, far away from all the facts of life'. In a characteristic mixture of prophecy and bombast, Hughes stated:

> It has been pointed out to me that if the Church gave way on the point of re-ordination, they would be abandoning all hope of reunion either with the Roman or Greek Church. But I would ask them – is there any hope of any reunion of the kind? Rome despises and renounces your orders, and attacks you in every land. What chance have you of reunion with Rome? Not the least. Moreover, the future of the world belongs, not to Rome, but to the great Protestant communities. Even today, we dominate the earth . . . to the vain hope of reunion with Rome many Anglicans are sacrificing real, inestimable and world-wide blessing.[46]

Lunn was able to bring together the unlike-minded and although no apparent notice was taken of missionary enterprise or the World Christian Student Federation consummated in 1895, which was such a pregnant source of later ecumenical leadership, 'it may fairly be claimed that the *Review of the Churches* and the Grindelwald Conferences began a new phase in the growth of the ecumenical idea'.[47]

These foreshadowings all anticipated the Edinburgh Missionary Conference of 1910, which has often been seen as the real beginning of the modern ecumenical moment. Methodist participation was wholehearted as in all subsequent conferences, with J. R. Mott assuming a leadership role of crucial significance.[48]

After the First World War, the mood of idealism and the new Christian brotherhood forged in the trenches, was caught up in the Lambeth Conference of 1920. Here again there were harbingers. Out of liberal Anglicanism, if that term is allowable, there emerged the attempt by F. J. A. Hort, J. B. Lightfoot and Edwin Hatch to set out the development of Christian ministry and institutions. Lightfoot, while firmly episcopalian, showed that in the New Testament 'bishop' and 'presbyter' represented office and function. Hatch clearly elaborated an episcopacy 'from below' rather than an 'essential ministry' ordained by Christ. T. M. Lindsay was a Scottish pioneer in the same area, as had been the Wesleyan, Benjamin Gregory, somewhat earlier.[49] Too easily this approach was swamped by the Anglo-Catholic approach of Charles Gore and Cuthbert

Turner, who readily found holes in Hatch's arguments.[50] Hatch's mantle, however, fell on A. M. Fairbairn and William Sanday, whose protégés (including Turner) play an interesting role at a crucial stage of ecumenism. Arthur Cayley Headlam, A. S. Peake and Vernon Bartlet[51] were leading figures in the events which surrounded the Lambeth appeal to all Christian peoples of 1920 with its clarion call for a 'Church genuinely catholic, loyal to all truth and gathering into its fellowship all who profess and call themselves Christians', which Scott Lidgett, the Wesleyan, with what seems now like slight exaggeration, hailed 'as the most important ecclesiastical event since the Reformation',[52] since it could have marked a great breakthrough in church relations but for what, with trenchant scorn, Dean Inge of St Paul's, echoed by H. H. Henson, called the 'almost superstitious glorification of the episcopal office'.[53] The liberal Catholic approaches of H. H. Kelly and T. A. Lacey and a flurry of conference material emanating from groups meeting at Mansfield College, Oxford, Cambridge and Swanwick between 1916 and 1920[54] must be balanced by the other side of the medal in the response of Bishop Frank Weston[55] to the Kikuyu Conference proposals for East African Federation and the united Communion service associated with it. This episode revealed the ability of Anglo-Catholics to show an intransigence on any actual scheme not involving overt 'ordination' of the non-episcopally ordained which has torpedoed several subsequent schemes in England and soured relationships between the Church of England and the Church of South India after 1947.

The key theological figure in the 1920 approach was Sanday's pupil and coadjutor, A. C. Headlam, whose *Doctrine of the Church and Christian Reunion* (1920) came out a month or so before Lambeth. Headlam went beyond turning St Augustine's arguments on validity and efficaciousness on its head, refusing at any point to isolate ministry from church. He could then see schism *within* the church not between 'the church' (in all its various 'branches') and what Anglicans usually call 'other Christian bodies'. *Both* sides are schismatic. This viewpoint was later developed by O. C. Quick and S. L. Greenslade.[56] Headlam's way through the log jam is mutual recognition of each others ministries followed by invariable episcopal ordination for the future. Headlam's arguments are well within an Anglican framework and ethos as a comparison with P. T. Forsyth's *The Church and the Sacraments* (1917)[57] would show, with its stress on the apostolic succession of gospel grace 'in its creative self-organising and self-recuperative power . . . The prolongation of the apostolate and the legatee of its unique authority . . . is the New Testament . . . the Apostolic Succession was at first a succession of truth'. Only the

Gospel regularizes the ministry. Forsyth was sharpening what he had previously stated in *Positive Preaching and Modern Mind* (1907).

> The first apostles were neither priests nor bishops. They were preachers, missionaries, heralds of the Cross and agents of the Gospel. The Apostolic succession is the evangelical. It is with the preachers of the Word and not with the priestly operators of the work or with its episcopal organisers . . . the great apostolate is one, not in the heredity of a historic line but in the solidarity of a historic Gospel, not in a continuous stream but in an organic Word.

Even if Forsyth's Teutonic 'either . . . ors' spoil his case somewhat, it is a pity that at this point the Free Churches did not develop and offer their own theology instead of allowing themselves always to be drawn into Anglican arguments. Dialogue might have been more free, for while Headlam argued for removing the log jam and mutual recognition, Charles Gore consistently argued that Christ instituted in his church by succession from the apostles a permanent ministry of truth and grace 'of the word and sacraments' as an indispensable part of her organization and corporate life. For him the bishop is the source of the power to perpetuate the ministry. Gore did not hesitate to draw the conclusion that Newman had drawn, 'that we must necessarily consider none to be *really* ordained who have not *thus* been ordained'. Between Headlam and Gore, the Lambeth Fathers had to tread a risky path.[58]

If Headlam's argument holds water, common ground for recognition can be found in the four sides of that Quadrilateral which originated not with Lambeth Fathers but with the American William Reed Huntington (1838–1918)[59] who himself had been deeply influenced by F. D. Maurice's six points or marks of the church.[60] Huntington's scheme was incorporated into a declaration concerning union adopted by the House of Bishops at Chicago in 1886. Huntington wanted to find the bedrock of Anglicanism, not in a 'flutter of surplices, a vision of village spires and cathedral towers, a somewhat still and stately company of deans, prebendaries and cloisters'. What began as a minimum of *doctrine* became a minimum of *negotiation* for union. In its original Chicago form the Quadrilateral was stated to be consistent with principles 'incapable of compromise or surrender'. The four sides were:

1. The Holy Scriptures of the Old and New Testament as the revealed Word of God.
2. The Nicene Creed as the sufficient statement of the Christian Faith.
3. The two sacraments – Baptism and the Supper of the Lord –

ministered with unfailing use of Christ's words of institution and the elements ordained by Him.

4. The Historic Episcopate, locally adapted in the methods of its administration to the varying needs of the nations and peoples called of God into the unity of His Church.

This Chicago Quadrilateral was, with some changes, accepted by the 1888 Lambeth Conference Committee on Home Reunion as supplying 'a basis on which approach may be, under God's blessing, made towards Home Reunion'. The Committee changed the form of the first three points to read:[61]

1. The Holy Scriptures of the Old and New Testaments as 'containing all things necessary to salvation' and as being the rule and ultimate standard of faith.

2. The Apostles' Creed as the Baptismal symbol; and the Nicene Creed as the sufficient statement of the Christian Faith.

3. The two Sacraments instituted by Christ Himself – Baptism and the Supper of the Lord – etc.

The fourth point remained – the hinge on which the door swung open or remained shut. The controversy within Anglicanism has been, as Brandreth made clear, whether the Quadrilateral was a *terminus a quo* from which there could be no dispensation or a *terminus ad quem*, that is to say, a sufficient basis for reunion rather than as originally intended, a basis for discussion with a view to reunion.[62] The Quadrilateral (which had received cool treatment from Wesleyanism when first propounded) appeared in a modified but fundamentally similar form in 1920. Headlam saw the acceptance by all of the episcopate not so much as merely the *bene esse*, an 'apostolic institution, I think it is dangerous to be without' or the *esse* (Gore and Weston's view) which would be quite unacceptable to Free Churchman or any Evangelical with sinew in his theology, but as the fullness, the completion or *plene esse*. Headlam did not use this precise terminology, which only became fashionable later, but it is not an unfair gloss.

The Lambeth Fathers accepted the spiritual validity of Free Church ministries.[63] 'It is not that we call in question for a moment the spiritual reality of those communions which do not possess the Episcopate. On the contrary, we thankfully acknowledge that these ministries have been manifestly blessed and used by the Holy Spirit as effective means of Grace.' Another phrase, 'within their several spheres', was later inserted into a key memorandum in 1923, apparently by Bishop Talbot,[64] which appeared hamfistedly to take away with one hand what had been given by another. The mutuality was by no means as complete as Headlam could wish and seemed in the last analysis to imply a limited jurisdiction with, as a logical rider, the need for the re-ordination of Free Church ministers which (unless I misunderstand his argument) Scott Lidgett, in 1920, would have accepted.[65] The Commission set up by the Free Churches and the Church of England, headed by Archbishop Lang, produced fruitful debates, not least the beginning of a theological undergirding to what became the Church of South India of 1947, the scheme which originated in 1919 before the Lambeth Appeal was issued.

The Appeal was clearly a reversal of the classical Augustinian position. It seemed as if they were actually saying '*ubi Christus, ibi ecclesia*', 'where Christ is, there is the church'. Anglican bishops would willingly accept wider commissioning from fellow Christians but, 'It is our hope that the same motive would lead ministers who have not received it to accept a commission through episcopal ordination, so obtaining for them a ministry throughout the whole fellowship. In so doing no one of us could possibly be taken to repudiate his past ministry.' This was a vain hope, displaying almost incredible theological clumsiness, despite the grace of the appeal in general. The Free Church Council responded to the Appeal in September, 1920,[66] issuing a full statement in May, 1921, by which time the Presbyterian P. Carnegie Simpson emerged as the Free Church spokesman, whom Headlam characteristically called 'truculent'. He was rarely outpointed as befitted a pupil and biographer of Principal Rainy. Three main issues were set out:
1. Recognition of churches
2. Episcopal ordination
3. Scriptural freedom.

The blunt question is asked: are non-episcopal communions part of the church of Christ and their ministries ministries of Christ's word and sacrament? Concerning episcopacy it is made clear that re-ordination is quite unacceptable. Any recommissioning must be clear in intention. 'To begin to build a union in the Church of Christ on a conscious ambiguity is not, it seems to us, to build in God's name and in God's way' – a matter of debate which recurred in the Anglican-Methodist scheme of 1963. The Free Churches made their individual responses.[67] The Wesleyan response of July 1922 was the longest reply. It clearly accepted three sides of the Quadrilateral but on church government made the point sharply 'the proposal to make episcopal ordination an essential part of the scheme of union, if it be interpreted as implying re-ordination, could not be accepted by those who believe themselves to be already ministers in the Church of God' nor could any fellowship be abrogated with non-episcopal groups.

Methodists on the Free Church committee set up in response to the appeal were W. T. Davison, H. Maldwyn Hughes, Scott Lidgett, Walter H. Armstrong, A. S. Peake and T. Nightingale. On the joint

Anglican-Free Church committee set up at Archbishop Davidson's initiative, Scott Lidgett and Peake clearly played a substantial role. The Anglicans attempted to clarify statements about the ministry in the Memorandum of 6 July 1923.[68] Words like 'valid' or 'invalid', referring to ministries ought not to be used; it is said that Anglicans regard these ministries as '*being within their several spheres* (this is Talbot's phrase) real ministries in the universal church . . . yet ministries, even when so regarded, may be in varying degrees irregular or defective'. Certainly episcopal ordination was required in Anglican eucharists. The Free Churches, in September, 1923,[69] made plain that for them this took away in practice what had been granted in theory and rightly pointed to Anglican practice before 1662 in this matter. The nub of the negotiations lay here and a second Anglican Memorandum in June 1925[70] made clear that 'spiritual efficacy' does not necessarily imply due authority. Granting of 'authority' by a bishop or ordination *sub conditione* is put forward as a way out of this impasse. This position was clearly unacceptable to most Free Churchmen owing to its blatant ambiguity and slur on previous ordination.[71]

The literature of the decade was varied.[72] On the Free Church side Carnegie Simpson and Anderson Scott stated the classic Presbyterian position. Methodist contributions to this somewhat disappointing series of Conferences and resolutions were notable for the statesman-like approach of Scott Lidgett, who looked beyond minutiae to the great vision of the church in Ephesians. His willingness to be re-ordained disappeared! But perhaps the finest Methodist writing on the matter in this period was by A. S. Peake in his presidential address to the Free Church Council of 1928, 'Pray for the peace of Jerusalem'.[73] He gave it as his opinion that reciprocal authorization of ministries would be necessary for a united ministry but rejected re-ordination. Episcopacy he accepted as the probable norm of ministry in a united church. 'To an episcopacy which would be constitutional and not prelatical, there would be no objection, provided that no theory of episcopacy as of the essence of the Church is demanded.' To the Free Churches Peake gave a warning, 'Free Churchmen may make the mistake of the Bourbons, if forgetting that all life involves development, adjustment to environment, they insist as a matter of principle on retaining their organisation in its traditional form.'

Peake was noticeably eirenic in acknowledging that if the Church of England

insists on conditions that we find distasteful, it is not from any spirit of arrogance but largely because surrender might cause

insuperable difficulties for re-union with the Eastern Orthodox
Churches and with Rome. The problem, it must be remembered,
is not simply one of Home Reunion . . . it is recognized on the
Anglican side that the ministry of the regularly constituted Free
Churches is a true ministry within the Church of Christ. But from
the Anglican point of view episcopacy must be retained in the
United Church because its abandonment would not only be the
surrender of something which all value highly and very many
regard as essential but it would snap one of the chief links with the
Eastern and Roman Communions.

This condition is, however, qualified by the proviso that it must be
'constitutional' and not 'prelatical' and it should be combined with
elements of congregational and presbyteral order. The sovereignty
of the Pope was undermined by a passage of brilliant irony, which
made it clear that Peake had not bowed down in the House of
Rimmon. He added, 'The ministry has nothing which the whole
body does not possess, though functions which belong to the Church
as a whole may be fitly exercised by a special order. But should the
body be totally deprived of its ministry it can replace it out of its own
resources.' Sacerdotalism, though not the priestly character of the
church, is likewise rejected: 'As Protestants we stand for the priesthood of all believers, for the right of private judgement [here speaks
the liberal], for the unrestricted use of scripture, for the freedom of
the Christian man, for the direct access of the soul to God.' – all
matters, no doubt, which for Peake were the principles of the
Protestant Reformation.

The original Free Church replies to the Lambeth Appeal made
clear difficulties over Establishment and over the safeguarding of
Reformation principles – though these were not defined, as was also
the case with the Methodist Deed of Union of 1932, though Scott
Lidgett was as clear as Peake about his personal definition of what
they are. The former issue was highlighted by the Prayer Book
controversies of 1927–8 and the subsequent policy by which bishops
exercised their *ius liturgicum* to enable the technically illegal Prayer
Book of 1928 to be used. Carnegie Simpson,[74] in a famous phrase,
thought the solution at the least 'hardly cricket' and most Free
Churchman would have endorsed the remark of Bernard Lord
Manning[75] about the Church of England receiving the benefit of
Establishment but objecting only when the shoe pinches, as over the
Prayer Book. 'The situation was not new, the relation of Parliament
to the Established Church had always been indefensible; but it was
denounced as wicked only when it became unpleasant.' The Prayer
Book controversy may lie behind the failure of the Lambeth Confer-

ence of 1930 to push forward the initiatives of 1920, a matter of deep regret to leaders like William Temple[76] and Headlam, who grumbled about negative Nonconformist response. At that Conference, Carnegie Simpson told the bishops, by implication, that if he had to take episcopacy into his system, would it not be safer to take the Roman rather than the Anglican form of it, since Anglicanism practised a minority form of it.[77] The bishops did not take the joke, if joke it was, for Simpson was a master of irony. The point still stands, unless *Apostolicae Curae*, declaring Anglican orders totally null and utterly void, is revoked in some way by the Pope.

The practical consequence of the Lambeth conversations was the possibility of exchanges of preachers and occasional acts of communion by Free Church or Presbyterian members cut off from their own worship, which was encouraged by Convocation in 1932 as well as limited intercommunion in schools and colleges where no Free Church services were held, though this was severely limited and could hinge on the opinion of bishop or chaplain. Anglo-Catholics would not normally encourage or participate in such limited openings of what were usually called 'Anglican altars'. In the 1940s, Bishop Kirk of Oxford, incurred William Temple's wrath by forbidding Dr R. N. Flew,[78] chairman of the World Faith and Order Commission on the Church and principal of Wesley House, from preaching at the country wedding of another Methodist minister, then working for the BBC, who was marrying a vicar's daughter. Such pettiness is remembered long after its occurrence. Kirk could defend his case with trenchant and transparent honesty of argument[79] – after all, Anglican congregations do not come to church to be 'afflicted with Free Church preaching'! As late as 1952 the writer was barred from the altar of his college at Cambridge, though a regular chapel attender and on the best of terms with the chaplains, who held the then fashionable 'Mason-Dix' line on confirmation.[80]

The debates of the 1920s, at least, laid down the lines of future approaches, not least the protracted but successful negotiations in South India which very much followed the lines suggested by Headlam, which we have called a standing on the head of Augustine, though the ecclesiologies of both Augustine and Cyprian were still alive and well. The Church of England was also concerned in probes towards both the Roman Catholics (as in the abortive Malines conversations) and the Orthodox. There were also deep disagreements within the Church of England, represented theologically by A. C. Headlam and O. C. Quick on the one hand, Charles Gore, Frank Weston and the formidable lay professor, Cuthbert Turner, on the other, though Turner[81] moved far towards Headlam's position when (referring to the joint committee at Bangalore in June, 1928) he accepted totally liberty of interpretation concerning episcopacy: 'Since Anglicans themselves have complete liberty of interpretation in this matter, it is obvious that the same liberty of interpretation cannot be denied to those who unite with us.' Turner, in his notable review of Headlam's book, concedes entirely Headlam's point about succession being not from consecrator to consecrator but from predecessor to successor and concedes the danger of a magical conception if an undue emphasis is placed on the episcopal conse-crator, yet he does not want to deny the view which stresses continuity of order. 'Nevertheless no one doubted and no one doubts that by whatever channel the bestowal of the Spirit was mediated to man, the source of the gift was in God and in God alone.' Crude 'pipe-line' theories were as clearly rejected by Turner as much as by Headlam. In the Free Churches there was sharp division between Lidgett, Peake and Simpson and the redoutable Baptist classicist, T. R. Glover, who deplored studied ambiguity.[82] 'If union depends upon artificial fog, I for one, am for daylight, for straight thinking and straight speech' – a stance not without relevance for the breakdown of the later Anglican-Methodist conversations in the 1970s, when both C. K. Barrett and Archbishop Fisher opposed the scheme from similar premises about ambiguity. As we have hinted, a unifying factor in the 1920s' discussions was the influence of some of the disciples of William Sanday – A. C. Headlam, J. V. Bartlet and A. S. Peake, Anglican, Congregationalist and Primitive Methodist, who revealed at times a notable unanimity of stance which was taken up again by the churches Unity Commission in its Report of January, 1976. Lest it be thought that it was all the dead hand of Sanday, Cuthbert Turner was equally his pupil and of rather different approach. In the end the ghosts of Weston and Gore have prevailed over the ghosts of Sanday and Headlam.

The 1920s saw a cluster of conferences illustrating the three prongs of the world-wide movement for mission and unity – the Stockholm Conference on Life and Work in 1925, the Faith and Order Confer-ence at Lausanne in 1927 and the Ecumenical Missionary Conference at Jerusalem which had developed from the setting up of the International Missionary Council of 1921. This latter conference revealed an openness to other faiths and to the contributions of the 'younger churches' which was taken up again at Tambaram in 1938, though there the voice of Karl Barth, expressed through Hendrik Kraemer, put a question mark over all religion.[83] The 1924 Confer-ence on Christian Politics, Economics and Citizenship,[84] meeting at Birmingham, with its aim of establishing a 'norm of Christian thought and action for the further working out of Christian order', foreshadowed a good deal of the thinking which formulated the welfare state of the post-1945 era and had a notable contribution to it from Methodists like W. R. Maltby, Henry Carter, Benson Perkins, Ryder Smith, S. E. Keeble and the formidable figure of W. F. Lofthouse, principal of Handsworth College, who appears as a Methodist spokesman of weight at nearly all the ecumenical conferences in the 1920s and 1930s with his trenchantly Protestant and yet deeply sympathetic approach to the breadth of Christian tradition.[85] Lofthouse pioneered the teaching of sociology to ordinands and was a leading protagonist of social change. His liberal, yet never unchurchly, Methodist position emerged at the Lausanne Conference in 1927, in the Wesleyan statement on theological issues.[86] After the conference both the Primitive Methodist and the United Methodist Conferences issued statements, quickly forgotten, I suppose, in the countdown to Methodist union, which can clearly be interpreted as accepting the possibility of a modified episcopacy following some kind of mutual acceptance, a prophetic stance from such a quarter. 'We could hope', said the United Methodists,

> that in any approach to union it would be found possible to conserve for the United Church what is best in the episcopal, the presbyteral and congregational systems of church government. If a United Church is possible only on a basis of episcopacy, in the judgement of this Conference the acceptance of episcopacy would not be held to imply any particular interpretation of episcopacy as e.g. that it is of the *esse* rather than the *bene esse* of the Church, that it depends for its authority upon Apostolic Succession in the commonly understood sense of that term, or that it is sacerdotal in its character and its functions. Nor should the acceptance of episcopacy in the interests of union imply any adverse judgement upon the validity of those forms of ministry which have hitherto 'been used and blessed by the Spirit of God' in the non-episcopal communions.[87]

The Methodist Church, in 1934 (two years after its own union), accepted the prototype of the South India scheme with its mutual acceptance of ministries and consequent episcopal system, due partly to the outstanding and unexpected advocacy by Lofthouse,[88] though not without rearguard action from Henry Bett, the Church historian who taught at the same college as Lofthouse! Bett took the line of Bernard Manning that the history of the episcopal system was so besmirched that the Free Churches were better without it.[89] Bett's position was brilliantly expressed in the evocative *Spirit of Methodism* (1937) and though unfashionable, is not without its force. Certainly Bernard Manning's point, expressed as early as 1919 in his first book

The People's Faith in the Time of Wyclif that continuity must not only be sought in terms of ministry is still of vital importance when the status and function of the ordained ministry too much dominates re-union discussions.[90] There can be, and is, continuity in faith when continuity of ministerial succession is broken.

The 1930s saw slow progress in Britain following the disappointing Lambeth Conference of 1930. Religious broadcasting (an underrated ecumenical element) began to break down denominational exclusive-ness, The Friends of Re-union, including Lofthouse and Flew, brought together many church leaders who wanted unity desperately despite the snags. Two documents suggesting prototypes of the future from different angles were rather quickly overtaken by the outbreak of world war in 1939. In 1936 there appeared *A Sketch of a United Church*[91] with a foreword by Archbishop Lang. It was the result of a commission of thirty-eight, equally divided between Anglican and Free Churchmen. Episcopacy was accepted as the norm, though such acceptance 'would not imply the acceptance of any theory as to its origin or character'. Congregational and Presbyterian elements should be included alongside the episcopal – though it is not always spelt out precisely what this may mean in practice. *The Sketch* also made clear two theories of episcopal origins, that from 'above' and that from 'below' – baldly that of Gore and of Lightfoot and his followers. This particular dichotomy was soon overtaken by the debate engendered by the Anglo-Catholic presentation by Kenneth Kirk and his team in the *Apostolic Ministry* (1946)[92] and the equally trenchant rebuttal of the *shaliach* theory of apostolic succession by the Presbyterian scholar, T. W. Manson, in *The Church's Ministry* (1948). W. F. Lofthouse[93] was quick to point out that the *Sketch* had many of the features of the South India scheme but 'it does not go so far in the evangelical direction', which presumably meant that it was not so trenchant on the regularity of Free Church ministries as Lofthouse would have wished. *The Sketch* was followed by an *Outline of a Reunion Scheme for the Church of England and the Free Churches in England* (1938).[94] As in *The Sketch*, episcopacy, but not any theory of it, was to be the norm but with a general assembly of diocesan synods and local Congregational councils. Free Church opinion made Lofthouse's point again about the 'principles of evangelical freedom' raising again the question whether the Church of England really accepted the Free Churches as 'churches' in the full sense. The touchy matter of lay people being permitted to preside at the eucharist was also raised by Congregationalists. The Free Churches, too, were unable to contemplate any union which would divide them from churches with whom they were at present in communion. The somewhat negative Free Church reply is dated 1941. The matter thus stood until after the Second World War when the initiative was seized by Archbishop Geoffrey Fisher in his Cambridge sermon of November, 1946.[95]

The Methodist Conference produced in 1937 a statement on the *Nature of the Christian Church according to the Teaching of the Methodists*, which set out a Methodist and Protestant case which was open to further development.[96] Clearly this document owed much to the mind and pen of Robert Newton Flew, who was becoming the key spokesman of Methodism in ecclesiological matters. It could be said, without disrespect to either, that he operated on a somewhat narrower base than Lofthouse, who was inclined to write and review on everything under the sun. His writings are marked by the clarity of a preacher and lecturer.[97] The approach was along the lines of the 'comparative ecclesiology' encouraged by the world Faith and Order Movement and a rationale of the Methodist Church of 1932 which 'claims and cherishes its place in the Holy Catholic Church which is the Body of Christ'.[98] Flew's own *Jesus and His Church* (1938) is a classic statement of Protestant scholarship, representing the Methodist tradition of New Testament critical study at its ripest, just as the work of the young Anglican scholar, Arthur Michael Ramsey. *The Gospel and the Catholic Church* (1936) represented the standpoint of that liberal Catholicism which dominated ecumenical discussion for four or five decades and undergirded the future Anglican-Methodist 'Conversations'. Flew, who later is said to have stated that Kingsley Barrett, of his old pupils, best represented his views on church order and on relationships with the Church of England, became the dominant Methodist figure (along with Howard Watkin-Jones and, as an emerging personality, Harold Roberts) in that period of 'Faith and Order' when comparative ecclesiology was the vogue, culminating in the volume *The Nature of the Church*, prepared for the Conference at Lund in 1951 in which, Flew as chairman, wrote the chapter on the Church of Rome at a time when Roman Catholics before the Second Vatican Council were not permitted to contribute. The chapter is a superb ecumenical *tour de force*. This era which had seen the creation of the British Council of Churches in 1942 and the World Council of Churches in 1948 reached its apogee, at least in the rarified world of theological conferences, at Lund in 1951 when younger scholars like Thomas Torrance showed impatience with comparative ecclesiology. They wished to press back to a common Christology and when spurred on by a communication from C. H. Dodd, began to consider the conditioning or even determining influence of what were then called 'non-theological' factors like class structure or nationalism on schemes for re-union.[100] This blast of secular air was long overdue.

10

'The Walk to the Paradise Garden'

A. The Anglican-Methodist Unity Scheme 1955–1972. A Methodist Viewpoint

So long as Christians of one Communion part company with Christians of another Communion at the Table of the Lord, it is improbable that the world will believe that they hold the secret of a fellowship which overlaps religious, cultural, economic and racial differences. The quest of Christian unity assumes an urgency which cannot be exaggerated when the disabling consequences of our divisions are seen against the background of a generation which so often either repudiates Christian values or dissociates them from the Christian faith.

So said an official Methodist statement in 1952.[1] It is a theological commonplace in ecumenical documents, though little sociological evidence is ever furnished for it. It was with sentiments like that in mind that Geoffrey Fisher, Archbishop of Canterbury, in his famous Cambridge University Sermon on 3 November 1946, *A Step Forward in Church Relations*,[2] invited the Free Churches to consider whether they might take some form of the 'historic episcopate' into their systems, in order to facilitate the promotion of full intercommunion, which would imply a 'ministry mutually acknowledged by all, possessing not only the inward call of the spirit but also the authority which each church in conscience requires'. Fisher was preaching from a clear Anglican viewpoint, seeking to safeguard the position of the Church of England, not only in the Anglican Communion but as an established church.

It is one thing for four dioceses in India to go out of the Anglican Communion into a province with a constitution of its own and a position in the Catholic Church still to win. But for the Church of England to go out of the Anglican Communion would disrupt that Communion by depriving it of its nodal point . . . the time may come when in the service of the unity of the Church, the Anglican Churches can cease to exist as a distinct group. But that time is not yet in sight for us and the Free Churches might well say the same for their own groups.

Positive responses were made to Fisher's initiative, the resulting conversations, chaired by A. E. J. Rawlinson (Bishop of Derby) and Nathaniel Micklem, producing the report *Church Relations in England* in the name of the Church of England and the Evangelical Free Churches. The first meeting of the joint committee was in May 1947, the report being presented in 1950. Methodist signatories of this report were Newton Flew, H. T. Wigley, Harold Roberts and Howard Watkin-Jones. It took into its system much of the thinking consequent on the Lambeth Appeal and looked to Free Churches with what could be parallel episcopates to that of the Church of England as a pointer to Church unity. Post-war Methodism was faced by four alternative choices. There was the possibility of a world Methodist Church. This would have been a largely Anglo-Saxon white Church dominated by the USA, which at that time would have been unpopular in Asia and Africa. English Methodism would be united with those whom they never saw, divided from folk in the same street. Another choice was Free Church Union, a possibility since the days of Hugh Price Hughes. But the Baptist Union had clearly said 'No' to any form of organic union, Congregationalists and Presbyterians were entering the last stage of the negotiations which led to the United Reformed Church of 1972. This possibility has always had its Methodist supporters. The third choice was to remain an independent church. Rupert Davies, risking prophecy, said,

> In this case, it will improve its worship, its organization, its techniques of evangelism, its ways of raising money, its training of its ministry. It will continue to take part in co-operative enterprise with other Churches and learn much from them. But it will probably dwindle in size to a certain point and then remain constant, protected from further erosion by the compactness of its organization and the corporateness of its spirit and its effects on the world outside its walls will probably become less and less.[3]

Ironically, as we shall see, Methodism has had to pursue this option whether it wished to or not. The fourth option was, in the light of *Church Relations in England*, to explore the possibility of some sort of *rapprochement* with the Church of England.

The Methodist Conference in 1952 received a positive report from its own Faith and Order Committee and in 1953, alone of the Free Churches, approved a suggestion that exploratory conversations should be held with the Church of England provided that:

(a) the Church of England acknowledges that our divisions are within the Christian Body which is throughout in a state of schism.

(b) that the same liberty of interpretation of the nature of episcopacy and of priesthood would be accorded to the Methodist Church as prevails in the Church of England.

(c) that the Methodist Church would be free to preserve the relations of intercommunion and fellowship with other non-episcopal Churches which it now enjoys.

The Convocations of the Church of England in 1955 consented to discussions, agreeing to regard all discussions between the Methodist Church and the Church of England as taking place 'within the Body of Christ'. But matters of Anglican 'essential order and discipline would need to be safeguarded' as would 'the office and function of a priest in the Church of God'. There was a lack of precision here which seems like an attempt to paper over the cracks of theological divergence. With hindsight, it would have been wise for Methodism to have pursued this matter further.[4] The Committee was set up in 1955 to explore means of bringing the churches into closer relationship through intercommunion, though its conversations were to be 'unrestricted in scope' and the Committee felt impelled to make clear 'that in seeking for closer relations between our churches, nothing less than the visible unity of the whole body of Christ is our goal'.[5] Intercommunion itself as the experiences of the Free Churches indicate does not bring fuller union nearer. 'In the course of our discussion we are led with impressive unanimity to the conviction that nothing short of organic unity, whatever form it may take, should be our final goal.'[6] That, then, was the goal, very different from that of Archbishop Fisher who made the point, in season and out, from then onwards long after his retirement.[7]

The immediate terms of reference were concerned with intercommunion with churches, existing as 'parallel entities . . . something less than complete unity but more than a relation of partial intercommunion between separate churches'.[8] The statement was an interim one, but key suggestions were thrown up by the powerful team led by George Bell, Bishop of Chichester, and Dr Harold Roberts.[9] The Methodist team was broadly based – H. Roberts, E. W. Baker, L. Davison, T. E. Jessop, W. W. Lee, P. H. Race, E. G. Rupp, W. E. Sangster, C. D. Monahan, N. H. Snaith, L. D. Weatherhead and one woman, Dr Dorothy Farrar, of Ilkley and Halifax. On the Anglican side there was a strange lack of outright evangelicals. The 'unification of ministries' was quickly seen as the key to open the door to intercommunion. Methodism clearly faced alternatives if episcopacy was to be 'taken into its system'. Firstly, as in the discussions after Lambeth 1920, re-ordination is ruled out. 'The one fatal objection to church re-union would be any requirement of the re-ordination of its ministers, which would in fact be a denial of Methodism's place in the Catholic Church.'[10] Conditional ordination, also a matter of discussion after Lambeth 1920, was seen to beg the question of the nature of ordination and might appear to be a repudiation of the heritage of the past. The consecration of some Methodist ministers as bishops by bishops in the historic succession and the laying down of a rule that in future all ordinations of Methodist ministers should be episcopal was another alternative. This bore some resemblance to the South India scheme with the same objection that it would create a dichotomy in the ministry between those who had and those who had not been episcopally ordained. This would have led to a rift in the ranks of the Methodist ministry which could be harmful. The attitude of the Lambeth Conference of 1948 to the situation in South India[11] was a warning as to the possible consequences of a step of this kind, when that scheme was hailed as of the Holy Spirit and at the same time deemed technically 'irregular' as some of the ministry of the united church would not be episcopally ordained. The fourth alternative – the position taken up in the statement – was the consecration of certain Methodist ministers as bishops in the 'historic succession'. That ploy goes back, as we have seen, to the Lambeth Conference of 1888 if not earlier. The rule would be that all future ordinations in Methodism should be episcopal and also that there should be a unification of both ministries at the start without calling upon anyone to repudiate his former ministry. The method suggested is that of the plan for church union worked out for Ceylon (Sri Lanka) and North India, though they were to be 'one stage' unions. This involves a refusal either 'to repudiate past ministries or to specify in what respect any of them may have been limited in scope and authority . . . an act of faith that in response to the prayers of the church and through the laying on of hands God will remedy any limitations which may be in his sight, in any of the several ministries'.[12]

We may note that the ministers of both communions would be involved in this – not just the Methodists. It could also be made clear that this was not ordination nor re-ordination but 're-commissioning', though clearly it was impossible to prevent some Anglo-Catholics from deeming the action to be the ordination of the Methodists for the first time. The theological principle that appears to lie behind this is that in a divided church all ministries are in some sense defective (the position of Headlam, Quick and Greenslade, who was on the Committee), each needs what the other can offer and that the 'one necessary element in the visible fellowship must be a ministry universally acknowledged'.[13] If this unification of ministries occurred, the way would be open to 'full intercommunion' and a richer relationship between the churches which would still be parallel in organization. Plans for 'concerted evangelism' might follow with a possible general assembly of the two churches – the beginning of what Gordon Rupp called 'mutual blood transfusion'.

Mutual 're-commissioning' of the ministry is the nub of the Interim Report but there are also chapters on historical factors in division (by Norman Sykes and Gordon Rupp) and on the distinctive 'gifts' which each church might bring to each other with a statement of common theological ground, an echo of Nathaniel Micklem's assertion that 'in spite of all differences of churchmanship there is not, and never has been, controversy between the Church of England and Orthodox Dissent in respect of the articles of the Christian Faith' which on the brink of the theological blizzard of the 1960s seems too complacent.[14] Immediate Methodist fears were, that in some Anglican minds, the 're-commissioning' might be thought tantamount to ordination as far as the Methodist ministers are concerned. Other Methodists might say that in no way would such a unification of ministries make clear the present status of their ministers. The point was made at the same time in Scotland where the Kirk found episcopacy an indigestible meal.[15] The statement of the General Assembly of the Church of Scotland of 1934 was relevant. 'Any agreement with regard to the orders and sacraments of the conferring churches can only be based on the recognition and equal validity of the orders and sacraments of both churches and of the equal standing of the accepted communicants and ordained ministers in each.' This was prophetic of many a battle and much heartsearching. Methodists in the Report made clear that 'Methodism could never accept either the contention that without episcopacy there is no church, nor any theory of the transmission of grace and authority which would deny her place in the Catholic Church and reduce her ministry and sacraments to spurious imitations.'[16] To the Methodists, the Anglo-Catholic argument that without a particular form of ministry there is no apostolic society, appears not far from blasphemy. The role of the laity was stressed as a Methodist characteristic. In 1958 the Dean of York had opposed the inclusion of lay people in the Convocations on the ground that this was a 'spiritual assembly'. Methodists (despite Jabez Bunting's assertion of precisely the same viewpoint in the nineteenth century) would not deem an assembly 'unspiritual' because lay persons took part in it! The principle of 'representative selection' is recognized by Methodism – the ministry is part of the priesthood of all believers. Some Methodists hold that this viewpoint rules out episcopacy which has no warrant of scripture either, others that the Deed of Union of 1932 rules out only certain views of episcopacy of an exclusive nature. Clearly some Methodists have held to a purely functional or pragmatic view of ordained ministry and need to beware of asking Anglicans to accept them in a way in which they cannot accept themselves.[17]

Links with the other Free Churches are made clear especially as two of the three participating groups in modern Methodism were dissenters from the beginning. Some modern Methodists feel closer in ethos to Anglicans than to other Freechurchmen, others by 1958 had stood for generations in the tradition of English dissent. This division between radical Dissent and historic Wesleyanism emerged clearly in the Conference debate on the Report in 1958. Those who fondly imagined that Methodism was in some way a 'bridge church' between the Church of England and Dissent were doomed to the disillusionment of all bridge dwellers. No scheme for closer relationships with Anglicans can carry the consent of Methodism if it weakens ties with the Free Churches. Closer relations with the Church of England could not be secured at the expense of relations with churches with which Methodism already enjoyed communion.

The Anglican chapter is called 'Anglican inheritance and episcopacy' and is almost solely, indeed obsessively, concerned with the 'historic episcopate'. It is claimed that this is the 'norm' of the Christian ministry and a gift which Anglicans hold in trust as their stewardship. 'In the historic episcopate the Church of England believes itself to possess a special and greatly valued link with the episcopate of the primitive church.'[18] Here is the 'orderly transmission of authority in the church from the earliest days until now'. Free Churchmen need to learn about the sense of continuity of the church down the ages, at the same time the word of God constantly reforms the church and there have been times when the Holy Spirit seems to have raised up other means to transmit 'the faith once delivered to the saints'. Methodists stress the action of God the Holy Spirit here and now in the church and find no warrant of scripture or evidence in history for any assertion that God is confined to episcopal channels. They cannot regard the succession of bishops as constituting the true and only guarantee of sacramental grace and sound doctrine. Continuity and discontinuity are very complex. One example can suffice.[19] In 1537, the Danish king Christian III annihilated the ancient independence of Norway. The last archbishop fled without an apparent concern for apostolic succession but providing himself with all the treasures he could find in Trondhjem. Exile or imprisonment or death was the lot of all the bishops save one. He trimmed his convictions to suit the conqueror. As a result Lutheran superintendents, to take the place of the lost bishops, were consecrated by a German Lutheran presbyter. Norway lost the succession. It would be impossible for any non-Anglican – or many Anglicans – to consider the Church of Norway, so nobly led by Bishop Bergrav during the Second World War, as outside the church of Christ, its sacraments mere 'uncovenanted mercies'. Anglicans need the reminder, as Leonard Hodgson put it, that 'the Church of England was episcopalian by the grace of God and also episcopalian by the accident of history'. Methodists had to ask the old question, 'Does the Church of England consider episcopacy as the *esse* of the church (the 'essential ministry' to use Gregory Dix's phrase) the *bene esse* of the church or the *plene esse* of the church in its completeness?' Methodists had to reject the first, the second is of dubious theological or historical value, the third might well be pragmatically acceptable since it looks forward to 'what episcopacy might become for us and our children'.[20]

Questions of Anglican priesthood were immediately raised. Is the ministry a sacerdotal body as in the Church of Rome or a ministry of word and sacraments as in the Reformed tradition or both? Does 'priest in the Church of God' imply *sacerdos* or presbyter? If we say, with John Milton, that 'new presbyter is but old priest writ large', then we might also say that 'old priest was still older presbyter writ larger' too! This section of the Report was in danger of isolating ministry from church. Methodism had asserted in the *Nature of the Christian Church* of 1937, that the 'true continuity of the church of past ages which we cherish is to be found in the continuity of the Christian experience, the fellowship of the gifts of the Spirit in the continuity of allegiance to our Lord, the continued proclamation of the message, the continued acceptance of the mission'.

There was, in 1958 (despite the débâcle of the 'Bishops' Report' in Scotland), a mood of some optimism though some were beginning to echo Newton Flew's warning that 'love cannot flourish at the expense of truth, that the only basis for genuine unity is an inexorable honesty'.[21] The 'ambiguous formula' must be distrusted. Conference received the Report in 1958, despite the grave misgivings expressed by, among others, Dr. C. K. Barrett about episcopacy itself and the ambiguity of 're-commissioning'. The very doctrine of grace was at stake, he observed in Conference debate.

Continuing discussions produced the 'Report of the Committee' in 1963, the crucial document. This document advocated a two stage re-union of the churches. There was to be a 'reconciliation' of both churches by means of a mutual re-commissioning of the ministry of both churches. The intention was to produce a ministry fully accredited in the eyes of the members of both churches. In the 'service of reconciliation', as it was called, the bishop would receive Methodist ministers into the fellowship of the Church of England with the laying-on of hands. 'We receive you into the fellowship of the ministry of the Church of England. Take authority to exercise *the office of priest*, to preach the Word of God and to minister the holy sacraments among us, as need shall arise and you shall be licensed to do.' By resolution of Conference (the corporate bishop) bishops and priests of the Church of England are received into the fellowship of the Methodist Church. The president lays his hand on the bishops and priests saying, 'We receive you into the fellowship of the ministry of the Methodist Church. Take authority to exercise *the office of a minister*, to preach the Word of God and to minister the holy sacraments among us – that is among the Methodists – as need shall arise and as you shall be appointed to do.'[22] There would follow the consecration of certain Methodist ministers as bishops, subsequently these bishops, with other ministers, would be the ordaining body in Methodism for all future ministers. The Methodists who signed the Report made it clear that this does not in any sense imply a slur on any past ministries or the loss of the prophetic emphasis in the Methodist concept of the ministry. 'Stage one' was designed to enable the two churches to enter into a relationship of full communion with ministers free to preach and preside at Holy Communion in either church. The two churches, at this stage, would remain parallel entities, each with its own characteristics and forms of worship, but with their representatives meeting and working actively and regularly together, the ministries and sacraments of each being acceptable and available to the other. The one change in the role of the lay person in Methodism would be that lay presidency at Holy Communion would cease as no longer necessary, since members need not be deprived any longer of frequent communion. In the hindsight of the plea expressed in the 1970s and 1980s in Anglicanism for lay persons to be occasionally permitted to preside at the eucharist, this seems now a somewhat highhanded demand. The point was not lost by the Methodist dissentients in 1963.

The interim goal of 'stage one' would be a closer co-operation of the two churches, a mutual process of learning about worship and theology, new styles of ministries to meet a changing social order, new modes of evangelism, greater use of lay people in many ways. 'Only the whole church can preach the whole Gospel to the whole world.' 'Stage two' – after a period of perhaps twenty years, though no timetable was set – would be full organic union. While left tantalizingly vague, this would clearly involve great changes in the structure of the Church *of* England to enable it to become the Church *in* England or *for* England. 'It is to be assumed that the united church will be free to settle its own forms of doctrine, worship and discipline, to appoint its own officers and to settle its disputes in its own courts with the same degree of freedom from state control as is now possessed by the Church of Scotland.'[23] This seems tantamount to some form of disestablishment which was not grasped clearly by Anglicans at the time. It was hoped that this scheme might release a log jam and that other Free Churches would opt in. What was not contemplated was the absorption of one church by the other, nor any uniformity of worship. Changes in patronage and the parson's freehold were envisaged which made the Paul Report on the *Deployment and Payment of the Clergy*, published in 1964, pale in comparison.

In the more radical quarters of both churches there was clearly a hope of an end to wasteful competition, pooling of training and educational facilities, combined education of the ordained ministry with the end of denominational seminaries, more co-operation in education, mutual learning about old and new ways of worship which were just emerging with each church's liturgical commissions going full blast, the proper use of person power with the chance of a new apostolate to secular England. But the Report, though it carried the consent of all the Anglicans – again there was no avowed evangelical on the panel, an astonishing omission – did not carry the consent of all the Methodists. A 'Dissentient View' was appended to the Report signed by four Methodists: C. K. Barrett, the New Testament scholar, Professor at Durham University; Norman Snaith, Old Testament scholar, President of the Conference in 1958; T. E. Jessop, formerly Professor of Philosophy at Hull and Thomas Meadley, Principal of Cliff College, near Sheffield, the Methodist College for lay evangelists. In origin all four were from Primitive Methodist or United Methodist stock, but that is not wholly relevant as many subsequent dissentients were from Wesleyan origins and at least two protagonists in the Conversations 'team' were not ex-Wesleyan. Their case was clearly the tip of an iceberg of dissent, some of it an emotional expression of a distaste for the whole concept of union with the Establishment, the roots of which are clearly enough shown in earlier chapters of this book. The dissentient case was firstly that episcopacy was not laid down in scripture, in which the existence of the people of God depends wholly on God's grace and man's faith. The 'service of reconciliation' presented grave difficulties. Anglo-Catholics would interpret it as the ordination for the first time of Methodist ministers. It was thus far too ambiguous. There was distaste also for the phrase 'priest in the church of God' being used of an ordained minister. We believe that the whole church is a priesthood offering Christ to men and taking the needs of the world to God. Ministers are not separate in a priestly sense. Sacrificial views of the priesthood were held by some Anglicans suggesting a need for much more clarification, as did future relationships with the Free Churches. There was the danger of dominance by the Anglo-Catholic wing of the Church of England and the possible absorption of Methodism. The dissentients implied a considerable by-passing of the evangelicals in the Church of England – Dr Barrett and Dr Snaith could not be called conservative evangelical by any stretch of the imagination and there appears, too, a lack of faith in the ability of Methodists to make their views felt. Anglicans often, in fact, fear the articulateness of a certain type of Methodist lay person. But the point was clear, tradition which they said 'represents the worldliness of the church' was eclipsing scripture by which 'bar' (the phrase originates, I think, with Daniel Jenkins)[24] Christ rules in his church. 'To move from a church committed to the evangelical faith into a heterogeneous body permitting and even encouraging unevangical doctrines and practices would be a step backward which not even the desirability of closer relations would justify.'[25] The dissentients might have reflected how Methodism happily comprehended Cliff College and Donald Soper, high church and revivalist! 'The more scriptural church would have been swallowed up by the less and the exclusiveness which bars the Lord's people from the Lord's Table would have strengthened its grip.' Difficulties over the 'closed Table' were still very real in 1963, yet it must be remembered that in all the pre-1932 Methodist churches the Table was officially 'closed' even if most presidents at the Lord's Table had come to open the Table to 'all those who love the Lord Jesus', a formula not found in any rite. There was also a complex of social issues resulting from Methodism's Victorian and post-Victorian stance on the matter of teetotalism and gambling. Methodists normally use grape juice rather than bona fide wine at Holy Communion. What would happen at 'stage two'? To many Methodists this seemed, frankly, a quibble and there is certainly no warrant of scripture for changing the matter of the eucharistic species from wine to grape juice (or bread to wafers!) but some Methodists felt this a matter of conscience, though it was not raised in the 'Dissentient View'. It was at least one of many matters for clarification.

In all the spate of documents, now so much ephemera, which rained on the churches between 1963 and 1965 when judgment had to be pronounced, it is clear that there was a strong dissentient voice in *both* churches, though honesty causes us to hazard the opinion that at local level there was much more agonizing by Methodists than by Anglicans who had nothing to lose at 'stage one'. In lay discussion what it was once fashionable to call 'non-theological' factors in church disunity loomed large.[26] Methodists disliked certain elements in Anglicanism such as its tie up with Establishment with which appeared to be pretentious power and pomposity. The sovereign's (or Parliament's) rights over the church was held to contravene the crown rights of the Redeemer, the solemn blasphemy of the *congé d'élire* or election of a bishop was an example of this. The apparent conservatism of the church, its worship, which to the dyed in the wool dissenter (unless he had the imagination of a Bernard Manning) was caricatured as dull and repetitious and cold, too much 'bowing and scraping' and too little honest to goodness preaching! The parson is irremovable, the laity passive, there is gross moral laxity on matters like drink and gambling.[27] The writer heard all this expressed many times in West Riding circuits in the debates of the 1960s. The mood was reciprocated, though it must be noted that dissenters are more prone to savour Anglicanism occasionally than the reverse. Anglicans rarely bothered to understand how a connexional system worked, the bureaucracy of central Methodism being compared to the Kremlin in one well publicized evangelical pamphlet![28] But if Methodists disliked the unconscious assumptions of superiority of Anglicans, Anglicans disliked the truculent mood which Methodists sometimes display, which we called Donatism in an earlier context. The apparent near idolatry of John Wesley stuck in Anglican throats unless they wanted to use him as a stick to beat Methodists with over matters like eucharistic poverty. There was thought to be laxity about matters of sexual conduct especially the remarriage of divorced persons on which 'Catholics' are more strict than 'Protestants', a dichotomy running back, I suspect, to the so-called 'double standard' between the 'religious' and the 'secular' Christian. Methodist worship seemed to some Anglicans sloppy 'mateyness with the Almighty' – though no strictures could be sharper than those of B. L. Manning, Wheeler Robinson and Newton Flew on dissenting inadequacies. There seemed too much noise in chapel, too little reverence and to crown it all the minister was always 'on the move' (many Anglicans *still* think Methodist ministers move every three years it seems!), always at a 'meeting', hide-bound by the rigid demands of the circuit 'plan', which made him unavailable when the vicar suddenly thought it would be rather nice if he preached at evensong next Sunday. Social differences, too, were not at all irrelevant. There was still a culture gap between 'church' and 'chapel' especially in those areas where 'chapel' was the popular establishment, as in parts of Yorkshire and Lancashire.

The dissentient case was stronger than its opponents made it out to be. Kingsley Barrett repudiated the view, expressed, for instance, by the American John Knox that second-century episcopal order was a natural development.[29]

Because it (the church) exists within the present age it inevitably takes on visible forms and the spirit works through specific gifts such as speaking with tongues, showing kindness to the needy and presiding over church meetings and these specific gifts are held on behalf of the whole body by particular persons. But the church may never identify its one form which is relative to the present age or the individuals within it who exercise gifts or even the gifts themselves with the eternal and extended purpose of God.

Ministry too easily comes to mean 'an order of spiritual bureaucrats who look after the souls of the laymen who provide their bread and butter instead of the common activity of the people of God'. This seems to be Harnack's fear of *Frühkatholizismus*, but Barrett's fear of perversion and degeneration is more realistic than Knox's smooth development theory which gets raised to an ecumenical orthodoxy in church order and liturgy alike. T. E. Jessop expressed a desire for union but not at any price. Tom Meadley espoused the way of P. T. Forsyth and asked hard questions about grace and gospel. Yet these voices were not as dominant or as strident as those who felt the emotional undertow of a century or more of cultural isolation and the effect of what Daniel Jenkins has called the 'most snobbish church in Christendom'.[30] One factor too, was overlooked by the dissentients. The assertion that Methodists would not be able to live with Anglo-Catholics overlooked the fact that some Methodists were intellectually far closer to liberal Catholicism, represented by A. M. Ramsey, for example, than to what seemed the hard neo-Puritan intellectual evangelicalism of Dr James Packer and his friends. A Methodist lay member of the Conversations team, Philip Race, expressed this in July, 1963:[31]

> What seems to me mistaken is the suggestion that Methodists would simply provide an accretion of strength to the Evangelical wing of the Church of England. I believe that Methodist churchmanship with our strong traditions of faith – with order, our discipline and our habit of singing doctrine in our hymns would find itself more in the centre, a binding and unifying force helping to strengthen the wholeness and real unity of the greater church.

Methodists only really became aware of the pressure of Anglican opinion against the Report by 1967 or even later. Quite certainly the view of Bryan Wilson[32] that the 'clergy' was likely to manipulate a re-union scheme to save their privileges in a hostile environment was belied by the facts for it was clerical pressure in the Church of England which finally ended the negotiations. In Methodism opposition was organized rather more quckly than in the Church of England. The National Liaison Committee, an umbrella organization of which the four original dissentients to the Report were members, issued a manifesto in September, 1965 after the initial acceptance of the scheme. The *Voice of Methodism* (to which the former dissentients did not subscribe) represented clearly the emotional but very deeply rooted 'gut' reaction we have been at pains to describe. It originated as a counterblast to the organization calling itself TAMU (Towards Anglican-Methodist Union) which had the aura of Establishment thinking about it.

In 1965, both churches accepted the broad outlines of the Report with desire for further clarifications. There was clearly more agony in Methodism at grass roots level than in Anglicanism and a clear possibility of schism. Attempts to amend the scheme failed. Some suggestions were not unlike the later covenant proposals or an attempt to suggest federation as a wider course. In 1967, Amos Cresswell suggested, indeed, a scheme involving other Free Churches which pointed again in that direction. It is ironic that when, out of the wreckage of the 'two stage' scheme, a covenant was devised, Dr Barrett and Mr Cresswell and others still found themselves compelled to dissent. There is more than a suspicion here of unavowed or even unconscious but very real conflict running back as far as Cavalier and Roundhead.

> On each side there are standards, ideals, habits, convictions, prejudices which together make up a distinctive mentality, largely determining our first response at least to any question that comes up. This mentality is only partly, perhaps only to a slight degree, dependent on distinctive religious convictions or traditions but it is intimately bound up with them and constantly acts upon them. We always need to ask whether our tenacity in defending certain positions may be due to something other than pure doctrinal logic. (C. H. Dodd).[33]

Steered by the sagacity of Harold Roberts, it appeared that official Methodism, which set such store by the Report, was set fair on the course of union with the Church of England. Ordination of women was deliberately held up in deference to the scheme. The title 'confirmation' was adopted for the time-honoured 'reception' or 'recognition' of new members, though Dr N. H. Snaith protested at the change, unconsciously anticipating those who now wonder what confirmation really is all about, 'a rite in search of a meaning'.[34]

A commission was set up by both churches to clarify issues still presenting difficulties. The Methodist 'team' headed by the inevitable Harold Roberts, was G. J. Ainger, E. W. Baker, H. A. G.

Belben, R. E. Davies, L. Davison, T. Lee, A. K. Lloyd, W. O. Phillipson, E. Rogers, J. C. Blake, G. T. Roberts, F. A. Rowe, P. H. Race and Miss P. Webb. The weighting of the group was hardly in the direction of academic theology! An interim statement, *Towards Reconciliation*, was produced in 1967. It was an unsigned working document to be commented upon and amended.

> The aim set before us is not the forging of an attractive and imposing ecclesiastical organization but a new obedience to the manifest will of God. We are being called with greater urgency to further the mission of the church – overseas as well as at home – by the deepening of our unity to serve our nation as one servant church, to teach the people of our nation with one Christian doctrine and with one voice to present to the world one crucified and risen Saviour.

Optimism indeed at the time of the journalistically announced death of God.[35]

On tradition and scripture, scripture is stated to be the sole authoritative source of all doctrine necessary to salvation. Tradition which is 'the living stream of the church's life' must be judged by scripture. It is acknowledged that different views of the nature of scripture are held in both churches as is the case, too, with priesthood and ministry. Both churches hold that Christ alone is Priest in his own right, that the church corporately is a holy priesthood with each Christian having a share in this. Some Anglicans hold that episcopally ordained ministers have a 'unique and indelible priestly character', they alone may preside at the Lord's Table and pronounce absolution, other Anglicans value episcopacy highly but deny any priestly character inherent in the ordained ministry save that which pertains to the priestly nature of the church. Priest to them is the same as presbyter. There is a recognized tension here, but this view is the classical Anglican view as we have seen so often. Methodists hold very diverse views, too, a fact not always appreciated by Anglicans who think Methodism to be more monochrome than it is. Methodism in accepting episcopacy was not being asked to accept a view that grace flows only through episcopal channels, 'still less that membership of an episcopally ordered church is a necessary condition of salvation, additional to faith in Christ'.[36] There is to be 'full liberty of interpretation within an invariable practice of episcopal ordination' – a matter thought restrictive consistently by Methodist dissentients. The 'service of reconciliation' is interpreted as a sharing of gifts and responsibilities but it is conceded that some may deem this to be ordination. Plurality is noted in views of the nature of the eucharist though 'any view of the Holy Communion which implies that the work of Christ was "unfinished" in the sense that we can add anything to it by anything we do or that it needs to be done again must be regarded as unscriptural'.[37] Some would say that 'remembrance' implies that we plead and re-present Christ's sacrifice before the Father. This view of the eucharist is linked with the consecration of bread and wine. Others maintain that this position has no biblical warrant. These variations of belief do not lead to a breakdown of fellowship at the Lord's Table. The controversial 'service of reconciliation' is presented in a re-written form with each participating minister affirming at the beginning that he had been ordained to the ministry of the word and sacraments. Silence would mark the laying-on of hands of the bishop with the words, 'We welcome you as fellow presbyters with us in Christ's church', but what were they before the bishop's hands touched them, asked the dissentients? The phrase, 'take authority for *the office and work of a priest*' is still there, priest being the normal word in the Book of Common Prayer as minister is the normal usage in the Methodist Book of Offices. The Report frankly states that there are some Anglicans who will interpret this as the episcopal ordination of the Methodist ministry, though most Anglicans and all Methodists would not so interpret it but see it as a re-commissioning, a widening of authority to give an ordained ministry fully accredited in the eyes of all.

There followed in 1968[38] a highly significant draft Ordinal in which the word 'presbyter' is used instead of priest or minister. This is the scriptural term *presbuteros* and has none of the offensive overtones suggesting ecclesiastical man thrust between the believer and his God which the term 'priest' has for many Protestants, a point Richard Hooker made centuries before.[39] This appeared to place the Ordinal firmly in the tradition of classical Protestantism but it was acclaimed by many Catholics also. A clear statement of a representative doctrine of ministry is found here, though little reflection of recent radical thinking about the minister's role in the secular society of the time. Other matters needing clarification were outlined in *Towards Reconciliation* – how can (not should?) Methodism's relationships with the other Free Churches be preserved? It was made clear that there would be no question of modifying these relations in any way during 'stage one'. Regarding 'stage two', it was to be born in mind that the Methodist Conference of 1964 declared that it understood the scheme as meaning that these relationships should at no stage be jeopardised – a piece of important 'kite flying' which had originated with those who had reservations about the 1963 report, including the present writer. Conscience was to be respected – understanding, charity and justice are needed.

'Certainly', says the Interim Statement, 'we do not envisage any limitations being put upon the ministry of these men during "stage one" except those which would inevitably be incurred by any conscientious inability to accept the general mind of the churches.' There is evidence that stationing of some dissentients in Methodism was not always easy at this time, it would have led to real problems later, I fear.

Two new factors were by now emerging. The first was the real entry of the Catholic community on to the ecumenical scene. Union with Rome was not on any agenda, but many Anglicans, not least Dr John Moorman, Bishop of Ripon, began to echo the almost forgotten words of the Lambeth Conference of 1908, 'There can be no fulfilment of the divine purpose in any scheme of union which does not ultimately include the great Latin church of the West.' Graham Leonard's pamphlet, *To Every Man's Conscience*, expressed a fear that the Catholic tradition in the Church of England was expendable. The ambiguities of the service of reconciliation were not removed for Dr Leonard. 'I do not see the issue whether or not Methodist ministers have been ordained but whether they have been ordained to the historic threefold ministry of the church.'[40] An alliance was beginning to form with the evangelicals, led by Dr James Packer, who wished no service of reconciliation at all and were fearful of an expendability of a particular Protestant tradition, an opening up really of the old Calvinist-Arminian divide.

The second new factor was the disillusionment of the radicals in both churches with the whole business, typified by Colin Morris'[41] outburst in *Include Me Out*. 'Our claim to offer a Gospel of reconciliation rings as shallow as the pitch of a bald-headed man selling hair restorer.' John J. Vincent's pungent remarks in his polemic *Here I Stand* were similar.[42] 'That new day can only come on the other side of the darkness of crucifixion; and we cannot be crucified, while we are still boasting about our "gifts" and "what God has done for us" . . . out of weakness, exhaustion, frustration and self sacrifice we shall find each others hands and be crucified and perhaps rise again with another "Body" altogether.' Allowing for the rhetoric, reminiscent of Hugh Price Hughes, the radicals were beginning to ask not 'Is the service of reconciliation really ordination?' but 'Will the mission of God in our day be furthered by such a scheme?'

A final report, *The Scheme*, followed in 1968. But a year or so before this, some Methodists had begun to be acutely aware of mounting pressure against the 'two stage' scheme in the Church of England. The writer, who was ecumenical secretary of a northern Methodist district, stated publicly the possibility of rejection in 1967. He proved correct in his predictions. *The Scheme* did not alter the situation.

The 1968 Report embodied much that we have already analysed.[43] A new section on Christian initiation made clear one point – it is intended that during 'stage one' Methodists who for the most part will not have been episcopally confirmed will be welcome to receive Holy Communion in Anglican churches, though confirmation will still be required of Anglicans. At 'stage one' Methodist ministers would still be able to confirm or 'receive into full membership' new members, though an effective symbol of the wider church would be the presence and ministry of the bishop. On lay ministries the negative point is again made that lay presidency at Holy Communion would disappear as no longer necessary – a matter dissentients always found objectionable as stressing a 'priestly' view of ordained ministry. On the vexed matter of the Open Table the Final Report suggests that in Methodism at 'stage one' all members, all members of other communions with which Methodism was in communion, 'and those who love the Lord Jesus and all who having been baptized, wish to show by coming to the Lord's Table their repentance and desire to be prepared for full membership or confirmation'[44] may do so. On the matter of wine at Communion, a bone of contention for Dr Leonard as well as for some Methodists, grape juice must be used but the suggestion was made that wine from which alcohol had been removed would be acceptable. For a time this appalling substance was used at the Queen's College, Birmingham, but proved acceptable to nobody, besides having a tendency to become mouldy rather rapidly. Marriage discipline was another thorny issue. Here the diversity of practice was acknowledged. The Report recommended that Anglicans marrying non-Methodists should not be married in the Methodist churches if a former partner was still living, but where a person owing allegiance to the Methodist Church – a rather loose phrase – is involved, it would not be thought a breach of the pledge to observe each other's discipline if the marriage was solemnized.[45] Here clearly was a matter for further probing during 'stage one'.

Both churches, regarded themselves as in some ways 'bridges' between Catholic and Protestant. The Methodist Conference has laid down that it must be free to preserve the relations of intercommunion with other non-episcopal churches which it now enjoys. Conference, indeed, in 1967 re-affirmed yet again the conviction that no scheme of re-union should be considered which involved any severance of full communion. There are some grave unresolved problems here as the more recent report *Intercommunion*[46] revealed but the Report states, 'We are convinced that as our two churches move forward into stage one, they should do so with the firm and declared intention that ways *shall* be found by which at stage two no relations at present maintained by either church shall be broken.' Methodist bishops need not be on the Anglican pattern, but should be elected by Conference and would include the president, ex-president, chairmen of districts etc. Dr Leonard had already asked to whom the bishops would be ultimately responsible.[47] Not a great deal of light was shed on the problem of what the Methodist bishops would actually *do* or their relationship with other bishops in the same area – the fact that a real Methodist equivalent of the bishop is not the chairman of a district but the superintendent minister of a circuit is not mentioned, an amazing omission from the Methodist side. In *The Scheme* Wales and Scotland are to be treated separately – Methodist ministers in Scotland who might wish to take part in the service of reconciliation may do so 'somewhere in England',[48] which suggests the BBC news black-out during the Second World War! The idea of a Methodist bishop in Scotland is dropped, the ghosts of John Knox and Andrew Melville were not to be raised! On matters of conscience the Anglican parson's freehold was not affected nor will the Methodist Minister's right to an appointment be effected, but the ominous phrase appears that 'the scheme must not be carried out against the wishes of a substantial minority in either church'.[49] Establishment was downplayed, there could be a 'national church' with responsibility to minister to the whole community, which sounds like an updating of Thomas Arnold. The Church of Scotland was seen as the model here, though the analogies never quite fit. Clearly 'the imposing of organisational union before the members of our churches were fully prepared for it would bring bewilderment and bitterness in plenty and cannot be the right way to proceed'.[50]

Following the Ordinal already referred to, the Report sets out the final form of the 'service of reconciliation' in the light of the criticism, both Anglican and Methodist. Here is great honesty of intention. The aim of the services – both local and national – is to bring together for unity and mission by a public liturgical action two churches whose people and ministers have long been separated. Much greater emphasis is placed in the revised services on the reconciliation of the churches – the *people* – and upon the mission to which they are called. The radical point was partly taken. Minor points are ironed out also such as the point in the original service where four priests advanced on the Methodists with arms outstretched and are never told in the rubric to put their hands down! Here is an act of commitment, intention and reconciliation. A few other points should be noted – no denial of any gift or grace already given is intended but rather an openness for the future in which God will give any further grace or commission or authority needed – this goes right back to the Lambeth 1920 conversations. At the beginning, each minister affirms that he had been ordained to the ministry of word and sacrament. There are acts of reconciliation of representative laity of both churches and reception of the presbyters of each church by the other with the laying-on of hands. The aim is a ministry wholly acceptable in each church. Here is still the crux of the whole scheme. The intention of the rite is that this is an act of mutual re-commissioning but it is frankly faced again that for some Anglicans it will be tantamount to the ordination of the Methodist ministers for the first time. A deliberate ambiguity is admitted, though dishonest subterfuge is denied – other alternatives are shown to be even more bristling with problems than the way proposed[51] – a viewpoint strangely prophetic of the débâcle of *one* alternative in 1982.

Such was the scheme on which such high hopes were placed especially in Methodism, whose leadership was apparently solidly behind it, though I suspect dissent was stronger than it appeared. Many were prepared to go a very long way to secure the realization of the very real idealism of the goal of the healing of the divisions between two churches, which had so close a symbiosis. The idealism was dashed to the ground not by Methodism which passed the scheme by majorities ranging from over 50 per cent in circuit quarterly meetings to 77.4 per cent in July 1969 in Conference and 79.4 per cent in 1970 – above the 75 per cent required in both churches, though the opposition was not negligible and included notable Methodist intellectuals of the stature of Sir Herbert Butterfield, the Cambridge historian, who feared the blunting of the edge of what he called 'insurgent Christianity'.

In Anglicanism, the opposition needs to be seen against a background of widespread apathy at local level. If, in Methodism, some of the opposition was an assertion of a local rather than a cosmopolitan style of church life, in Anglicanism the scene was more complex. Institutional persistence certainly dragged down some of the clergy. 'Little Englandism' can paralyse the English church at times when other bodies like Methodism can be said to have more of a world view. The episcopate was largely behind *The Scheme*, though there was opposition stemming from the Anglo-Catholic wing concerning the ambiguity of the service of reconciliation and the doctrine of priesthood. Lord Fisher thought *The Scheme* downright dishonest, some evangelicals saw it as unnecessary and, 'I suspect, disliked the connexionalism and plurality of thought in Methodism as well as fearing any erosion of Establishment. Dr James Packer's dissentient note to *The Scheme* confined itself to the service of reconciliation.[52] There quickly developed one of those curious alliances which bring high and low together and which have such deadly effect in Anglican history as the furore over *Essays and Reviews* in 1860 shows. In the debates in Anglican courts the bogey (so Archbishop Ramsey saw it) of a hindrance to re-union with Rome was always present. This is an illusive but important factor which was to be reckoned with in 1969 and 1972 and loomed even larger in the failure of the Covenant a decade later. The Church of England could not afford schism, its comprehensiveness prevents any union with any other body since sizeable minorities can always block any change. A resurgence of party groups now makes any breakthrough even less possible. The agony this entails for the liberal Catholic is immense.

The final figures of Anglican voting on 3 May 1972[53] reveal where the main opposition lay and also revealed the Achilles heal of synodical government, the ability of minorities to block change and the inability of Anglo-Catholics and some evangelicals to follow the lead of the bishops, whose unifying stance in matters doctrine is revealed as a somewhat hollow sham.

Bishops	74 for;	6 against;	85 per cent in favour.
Clergy	152 for;	80 against;	65.52 per cent in favour.
Laity	147 for;	87 against;	62.82 per cent in favour.

Two houses thus failed to secure the necessary 75 per cent in favour – in fact the majority was less than in 1969! Perhaps clergy and laity alike had simply not taken the scheme seriously enough.

In Methodism after 1969, there was a strange mixture of anguish and relief. The Court of Chancery heard a case brought against the Methodist Conference by certain Methodist dissentients to the scheme.[54] Mr Justice Megarry ruled that Conference is master in its own house, being the final arbiter of doctrine. *The Report of the Joint Working Group* set up by the General Synod after the second positive Methodist vote of 27 June 1970 provided what now look like interesting footnotes. It is a very Anglican document even including phrases like 'other Christian bodies' which so irritate Free Churchmen.[55] Ominous paragraphs, about the legal meaning of the service of reconciliation clarify that 'conditional ordination' was certainly one interpretation of that controversial ceremony. Canon Law would need modification to permit Methodist ministers who had gone through the service of reconciliation to preside at the eucharist in Anglican churches.[56] It could be said that this document was confirmatory to dissentients of their fears and disillusioning to those Methodists, like the writer, who had accepted the method of the service of reconciliation in deference to the consciences of those who required it. Never again could Anglo-Catholics expect such charity to their views. This was the death blow to any kind of mutual reconciliation of the style to be adopted in North India.

After the final Anglican vote of 1972, the explosion of wrath from younger radicals which some Methodists predicted did not occur. There was rather the numbness of grief. Quickly the Methodist

Constitution was restructured without benefit of bishops; women, whose ordination as late as 1970 was called an 'irritant' which must not be introduced at a crucial moment of the church's life,[57] were quickly trained and ordained. The walk to 'the Paradise Garden' had proved a cul-de-sac. Methodism had been, as D. L. Edwards put it, 'led up the garden path'[58] and now had to pursue its path alone with the consequent introversion which produces denominational self-consciousness and self-assertion, which increased in both churches in the next decade.

It is very difficult now to summarize the effect of the end of the Conversations. Clearly the North India style reconciliation of ministries was finished in England. Quite clearly a good deal of credibility was lost by ecclesiastical leadership and by the Establishment. At the time there was those who wondered whether initiative was now passing to the Church of Rome and even to Methodism which had more to contribute than some of its leaders, mesmerized by union, might seem to think. Sociologically it is very interesting that in union schemes in England it is the larger body which produces the greatest body of dissent. In the Methodist union of 1932 it was the smaller Primitive Methodist and United Methodist Churches which voted overwhelmingly in favour, while Wesleyanism took six years to get the 75 per cent majority needed with the formidable J. E. Rattenbury leading a group who feared (what an irony!) that it would jeopardize a wider union with the Establishment. In the Presbyterian-Congregationalist union, again, dissent was more evident in the larger group and this was true again with *The Scheme*.

The writer published an article a few days after the Synod's vote which called on Methodism to recover its pioneering use of manpower and buildings, to come to terms with the rebirth of the theology of experience in the charismatic movement, to find modern ways of presenting Wesley's doctrine of Christian perfection, to renew worship so that it can be a vehicle of evangelism as well as nurture. Methodism must recover, albeit in modern ways and modern terms, its passion for evangelism. Above all it must play its proper role in the great dissent of our time – a nonconformity against all that degrades people. 'World population, world poverty, pollution, the continued threat of thermo-nuclear war are the big issues.' Clearly some of this agenda was taken up in a 'recovery of nerve' in the 1970s but there arose also ominous signs of fragmentation and a growth of irrationalism which was not predictable in the 'secular sixties'. The truth of the matter could well be that Methodism was simply not strong enough for an independent mission.

B. The Churches' Unity Commission –
The Covenant

Disillusionment in some ecumenical circles when the General Synod failed to achieve the 75 per cent note necessary to accept the Anglican-Methodist Scheme was made more poignant by the formation in November 1970 of the United Church of Pakistan and the Church of North India[59] which had many characteristics of the abortive English scheme, though these were 'one stage' not 'two stage' unions. The decade of the Conversations was the period of the New Delhi World Council Assembly with its call for 'that unity which is both God's will and his gift to the church' being 'made visible as all in each place who are baptized into Christ Jesus and confess him as Lord and Saviour are brought by the Holy Spirit into one fully committed fellowship'.[60] The thinking which stemmed from New Delhi implies both 'ministry and members accepted by all' and a carrying into effect of the so-called 'Lund Principle' that churches should 'act together in all matters except those in which deep differences of conviction compel them to act separately'.[61] In England there was, alongside the agony of the Conversations, which generated bitterness as well as charity, the growth of much local co-operation manifested in Councils of Churches, The Shared Churches Act of 1969 and 325 'areas of ecumenical experiment' now called 'local ecumenical projects'. Thus local ecumenism sometimes ran ahead of what could be achieved through the General Synod and increased pressure from below for renewed attempts at *rapprochement* from above.

Was there, then, an alternative to the method of the Conversations? An alliance of dissentient voices in Anglicanism produced a scheme called *Growing into Union* which sought to reconcile evangelical and Catholic at the expense, it seemed at the time, of the connexional system of Methodism which Anglicans seem almost wilfully at times to underestimate.[62] There were, however, shafts of thinking here which were to throw some light on the problems the Churches' Unity Commission was later to combat.[63] More promising was the inauguration in October 1972 of the United Reformed Church which brought together the Presbyterian Church of England and many congregations of the Congregational Church as it had been called since 1967. The constitution of the new denomination contained an open ended intention to seek further union which indeed bore fruit in union with the majority of the congregations of the Churches of Christ with (as in North India) the possibility of a plurality of baptismal practice in one church.[64] It was from URC and Methodist initiative in May 1973 that an invitation was sent to all Christian churches in England to what came to be called 'Talks about Talks'. The spectrum was wide including Roman Catholics, Orthodox, Lutherans and members of the Congregational Federation. Anglicans were loath to appear again as the proposers of anything which might appear to be another walk up the garden path, but there was enough enthusiasm generated, fuelled by a conference at Christ Church, Oxford in January 1974 (at which the writer was present) to carry the 'Talks about Talks' into serious conversations to be instigated by the setting up of the Churches' Unity Commission on which most of the main-line churches including the Roman Catholics, the Baptist Union and the Congregational Federation were willing to be represented.[65]

Within two years the Commission had produced the *Ten Propositions* of January 1976. Behind this swift response was the fact that, despite the breakdown of union negotiations, the ecumenical climate had unfrozen centuries of ice. The Counter Reformation was over, bringing the Church of Rome into the ecumenical conversation. Christians found themselves worshipping together and working together as never before. Joint education of the ordained ministry had been instituted in Birmingham in 1970 and in federal schemes at Cambridge and Manchester. A vital link in the process which must not be overlooked was the Anglican Canon B15A which permitted Trinitarian, baptized Christians in good standing to receive the holy communion in the Church of England as guests, thus removing a stone of stumbling which had been across the path of 'occasional conformity' since 1662. This Canon makes clear that the hospitality was not permanent, the parish priest should enquire about confirmation if the member of another church communicated over a long period (which blurs the edge of the generosity in a fashion Free Churchmen are used to) but it technically cleared the way for open communion i.e. welcoming all baptized communicant members of other churches to receive communion on occasion within its fellowship. Full communion involves mutual recognition of members and ministry and this was to be the goal, or one of them, of the Churches' Unity Commission.[66]

The Commission began with a very wide constituency which was precisely what many dissentients to previous schemes had wished.

The *Ten Propositions*[67] re-affirm belief that 'the visible unity in life and mission of Christ's people is the will of God'. The means to this end should be a covenant actively to seek wider unity. This was a re-assertion of the desire to covenant for unity expressed at the British Faith and Order Conference of 1964 which had, with trepidation, suggested 1980 as a target date. Corollaries of the covenant relationship would be mutual recognition of the membership of the covenanting churches as 'true members of the Body of Christ' with mutually accepted initiation and eucharistic rites. Propositions 4–6 were crucial:

4. We agree to recognize as from an accepted date, the communicant members in good standing of the other covenanting churches as true members of the Body of Christ and welcome them to Holy Communion without condition.
5. We agree that, as from an accepted date, initiation in the covenanting churches shall be by mutually acceptable rites.
6. We agree to recognize, as from an accepted date, the ordained ministries of the other covenanting churches, as true ministries of word and sacrament in the Holy Catholic Church and we agree that all subsequent ordinations to the ministries of the covenanting churches shall be according to a common ordinal which will properly incorporate the episcopal, presbyteral and lay roles in ordination.

The rights of conscience in thought and action 'consistent with the visible unity of Christ's church' was guaranteed. The suggested date for decision on the Propositions was 1978. The Commission had appointed as its executive officer, appropriately, the United Reformed theologian, John Huxtable. Methodists on the Commission were K. G. Greet, A. J. Davies, J. E. Richardson, S. Travis and G. Wainwright.

Meanwhile in Wales in 1975, the Church in Wales, the Presbyterian Church in Wales, the Methodist Church and the United Reformed Church, entered into a covenant towards union – a solemn agreement to enter on the path of increasing co-operation and, if possible, in the end to seek organic union. Dare one say that this is a rather limited concept which may dodge the nettles which the English Covenant had to grasp[68] – though in the end the Welsh conciliar approach keeps doors open now closed in England. Paradoxically, though, in England the goal of organic union is set more remotely. Indeed the proposed covenant was not for union but for unity first (it was back to Fisher's approach of 1946). Organic union is a distant but real hope.

In October, 1977 an Anglican conference on ministry at High Leigh, took up ideas which had emanated from the French ecumenical discussions initiated by the *Groupe des Dombes*[69] – the possibility of recognizing in a non-episcopal church the reality of Catholic order without the fullness of the outward sign, such recognition being marked by a sign other than the laying-on of hands which had proved so ambiguous in the Anglican-Methodist scheme. Fr John Coventry also strongly urged this possibility. The report to the Archbishop of Canterbury in January 1978 clearly saw this as a possible way through the dilemma of securing mutual recognition. This was a notion long adumbrated (from a very different position from the *Groupe des Dombes*!) by Methodist dissentients to the service of reconciliation approach. The Anglican General Synod at York on 10 July 1978 accepted the *Ten Propositions* with the anticipated desire for clarification of the crucial Proposition 6 and with the proviso that Method A should be adopted for the taking of episcopacy into Free Church systems – that is the creation of parallel episcopates and also that recognition of ministers in the other covenanting churches will be 'effected by the action of the whole episcopate of the covenanting churches incorporating the existing ministries into the historic threefold ministry by invocation of the Spirit in a prayer which makes it clear that such incorporation is intended and conveyed by a distinctive sign for the conferring of a gift of the Spirit and the concelebration of the Holy Communion'[70] – a somewhat cumbrous liturgical request!

The Synod in November 1976 had already debated a motion that 'common statements of faith comparable with those agreed with Roman Catholic theologians on the Eucharist Ministry and Marriage be achieved with the other members of the Churches Unity Commission before the practical commitment of the Ten Propositions were undertaken'. An amended form of this motion required 'evidence of agreement on essential doctrines between the Church of England and other churches sufficient for them to enter into a covenant'. Clearly the points at issue were 'such matters as the continuity of the ministry, the proper person to ordain (and in some cases only) the proper celebrant of the eucharist'. This could hardly have been news to those who asked the question about theological agreement and somewhat late in the day to ask it! There were the seeds here of the ultimate destruction of the whole scheme.[71] The Methodists (with large majorities but little enthusiasm), the URC (not without misgivings), the Moravians (who have bishops of a non-diocesan kind) and the Churches of Christ also gave positive responses, but the Congregational Federation, the Roman Catholics and the Baptist Union (who would have difficulties over common initiation as well as over episcopacy)[72] felt obliged to proceed no further at this point while urging other still-participating churches to do so, a fact which must not be forgotten.

This element of support cleared the way for the setting up of the Churches' Council for Covenanting, chaired by Bishop Kenneth Woollcombe with the young Methodist lawyer, Philip Capper, as secretary. Other Methodist members of the Council were K. G. Greet, G. Wainwright (until May 1979), J. Job, Christina le Moignan, J. Stacey, D. Tripp and E. R. Taylor. The proposals were published in 1980,[73] receiving what could be called general approval by the General Synod of the Church of England with much more vocal support in the other churches. We have already noted the provisos which the Committee felt obliged to include owing to Anglican pressure including the crucial one 'that recognition of ministers in other covenant churches will *follow* upon the acceptance of those churches of the historic episcopate by the consecration of bishops at the inauguration of the Covenant in terms to be agreed but based on those outlined in "Method A" '. What were the aims of the Covenant, its proposals and its difficulties?

The aim was to enable the churches to recognize one another as complete Christian communities with a clear mandate to work together in mission. This was clearly not a union scheme like the Anglican-Methodist Scheme. It was to be a coming together of Christian communities, not just ordained ministries, in affirming a common faith, welcoming one another at services and sacraments, encouraging joint confirmations and joint ordinations following the covenant, accepting mutually ordained ministries with the open possibility of sharing buildings and resources. There was to be no neglect of a wider ecumenism in exclusiveness, indeed rather a commitment to non-covenanting churches. The actual proposals were complex and liturgically so finely balanced as to be far too subtle for all but the most practised eye. Whether this was the way to comprehend people was clearly more debatable but this could be merely the wisdom of hindsight.

The idea of covenant had overtones of the personal and corporate covenant of the Puritans and the Methodist service for the renewal of covenant with God[74] – not to speak of the biblical *Leitmotiv* itself from the covenant with Noah to the Lord's Supper. The act of covenant put forward here was to take place in a national and, thereby, representative act of worship lasting several hours with breaks for refreshment in the middle! Here was a gargantuan ecumenical bonanza which would demand considerable stamina! This lengthy liturgy includes a clear mutual recognition of churches. 'We shall recognize one another as Christian churches in membership and ministry' and commit ourselves to 'grow together in counsel and in action'. Confession and declaration of forgiveness leads to promises and an act of reconciliation with the shaking of hands as the ritual action. This is the first of the ritual actions in the covenant service, the other was the outstretched hand of bishops and 'other ministers who exercise comparable oversight' in the prayer invoking the Holy Spirit upon presbyteral ministries. These actions, so long requested by those who could not stomach the 'service of reconciliation' approach and in line with the approach not only of the *Groupe des Dombes* and Fr Coventry but of Headlam (in 1920), could not possibly be misunderstood by anyone as ordination. After a break, there were to follow ordinations of bishops and presbyters, the crucial blessing of episcopal, presbyteral and diaconal ministries and a renewal of baptismal promise. It is regrettable that so much of the material here was Anglican in origin, derived from the Series 3 services. The reason was sheer time budgeting but it is the kind of action which easily raises Free Church hackles. The Lord's Supper, which would follow was to use a canon created for the occasion though this was not entirely acceptable to Anglican evangelicals – a revised canon was devised but not presented to the churches before the decision on the Covenant was made. Phrases there might well have raised Methodist hackles. Why time was not permitted for a less obviously Anglican style to be devised is one of the curious anomalies of the whole matter, reflecting internal Anglican disagreement over eucharistic doctrine. Then follow regional services, again representative, including, it was hoped, ordination to the presbyterate. It may not be realized how much that would have been a departure from normal custom for Methodists, especially those stemming from the Wesleyan tradition, whose ordinations have normally been closely associated with the annual conference and are ordination to an office as distinct from ordination on the basis of a 'title' or a 'call' to a pastorate. A statement on Christian initiation is followed by an encouragement to unite for services of confirmation and reception of members with the officiant performing the role normally alloted in each church – an advance over the Anglican-Methodist Scheme, in which the bishops would confirm, downgrading the usual presbyteral role in Methodism of the local minister who had trained the candidates.

There was a dissentient statement,[75] which came before the Council late in its deliberations from three Anglicans – Bishop Leonard, Peter Boulton and O. W. H. Clarke – which finally proved the sticking point in the General Synod. These Anglicans, led by Dr Graham Leonard, Bishop of Truro, subsequently of London, offered conscientious scruples over the role of non-episcopal moderators in the United Reformed Church[76] who would continue to perform quasi-episcopal functions but would not be bishops in the historic episcopate. This

is the so-called Method C which had been a way of relieving strain
in the United Reformed Church where there was a strong dissentient
group, uneasy about the leap into episcopacy from an independent
tradition. The women ministers of the Free Churches, the precise
meaning of recognition, the right of conscience of bishops, and
ancillary matters like the cessation of what they call 'lay celebration'
of Holy Communion, an ironic thrust, in hindsight, since it is now
widely canvassed in the Church of England in an age of shortage of
priests in rural areas and eucharistic house groups[77] – these matters,
in a somewhat different form, were debated in the General Synod
which accepted the proposals provisionally. In the light of what
appeared to be an Anglican approval, the other churches involved
also gave general approval in 1980 and called for wide discussion.

The consequences of the Covenant would be that Methodism (to
use one example) would have been required to present ministers to
be consecrated as bishops. Conference would have to decide who
they might be and whether there would be a full-blown episcopal
system (the so-called Method A) or imported bishops (Method B).[78]
The Methodist episcopate need not be like the Anglican diocesan
system. There was in fact a clear desire on the part of some Methodists
that here was an opportunity[79] to show that the real *episcopos* in
Methodism is the circuit superintendent rather than the chairman
of the district, who is fundamentally an administrator, though he
has acquired recently a more pastoral role. Debate in this area would
have been very sharp had the Covenant proposals been accepted by
the Church of England. Another consequence of the Covenant would
have been members in good standing being able to play a full part
in the life of the other participating churches. Much more mutual
ministry – ordained and lay – could take place. More effective use
could be made of resources of lay and ordained persons and buildings.
Each church would preserve its autonomy but could begin to grow
together, while noting the Archbishop of Canterbury's repeated
warning about creating more bureaucracy. Much of this parallels in
another decade the hopes of 'stage one' of the Anglican-Methodist
scheme and is somewhat *déjà vu*. The whole scheme was really
Headlam *redivivus*, the débâcle was Weston and Gore *redivivus*!

The Covenant proposals received a very large positive vote in
Methodism (where debate was much less intense than over the
previous scheme) and a majority in the URC. In the General Synod
the necessary majority was not reached in the house of clergy.
Following that vote the Moravians endorsed the Covenant by a vote
of 98 per cent, an ironic conclusion to yet another ecumenical
attempt. Opposition in Methodism had been muted, though centred,
as always, on the invariability of episcopal ordinations for the future

and the fear that episcopacy would subvert the priesthood of all believers in a spirit contrary to the Deed of Union of 1932.[80] It is a strange paradox that those who talk so much of the doctrine of grace appear to wish to tie a church to its title deeds in a way reminiscent of the Wee Frees in Scotland in 1904. Underlying it is the old fear of power and prelacy and pomposity. Certainly the point could be made that we are moving into a period when paternalistic leadership seems outmoded. There was here a proper fear of appearing to restrict the grace of God at a time when new styles of church structure are struggling to be born. Also it is never clear whether Anglicans themselves are serious about bishops! Certainly Anglo-Catholics, who talk so much about them, rarely appear to accept them as leaders in doctrine or anything else. Maybe the gibe that bishops are simply a 'stud farm' for properly accredited clergy is not wide of the mark. It could be pointed out that the various Catholic episcopal systems still do not fully recognize each other. Pope may embrace 'Canterbury' but *Apostolicae Curae* still remains in the statute books, so that 'Canterbury' is still by no means recognized as a fellow bishop by the Pope. The sad element in the Methodist dissentient case appears to be lack of faith that Methodism has anything to offer Anglicans. They ought not to have been so frightened of Anglican pretentiousness, while those who thought the Covenant a way forward might have displayed less naïvety about Anglo-Catholic stubbornness. There was also far too much liturgical optimism.

There was an element of numbness and unbelief in Methodist and United Reformed circles, when the Synod vote revealed that the clergy had not obtained the necessary majority. It was almost as if the Lambeth Quadrilateral had proved impossible to *Anglicans* to accept when the others had agreed to do so! Free churchmen could well ask, what *will* satisfy some Anglican minds? The paradox is that the Anglican-Methodist scheme which gave Catholics much more was turned down also. Never again would the Catholic party have such charity shown towards their claims and consciences. The Covenant flew lower than *The Scheme* and failed also. There is an intractable element of 'little Englanderism' which is an appalling symptom of sectarianism. Dr John Habgood, the then Bishop of Durham, writing immediately after the vote,[81] spoke of the vote 'bringing to a halt a process which started with the Lambeth Conference appeal of 1920 . . . the Free Churches have every right to feel aggrieved. Their own majorities in favour of unity are unlikely to survive this rebuff. After making a huge leap in committing themselves to accept episcopacy they now find themselves rejected on grounds, which they can only regard as unreasonable. The Church of England would be foolish to expect a similar opportunity to recur.' This echoed John Huxtable, who had said in 1977:[82]

> It is impossible to exaggerate the importance of the decision taken by the Church of England; and it is greatly to be hoped that it will be able so to covenant in ways with which at least some of the Free Churches will be happy to agree. If for whatever reason it fails to do so, then the movement towards unity will be given perhaps the most serious set-back it could receive in this land; and the consequences of that failure are hard indeed to reckon. One might fear that other churches would feel too discouraged to make any further attempts to unite with it for a good many years to come.

Certain facts need analysis as contributory causes to the failure of the proposals.

Firstly the matter was rushed, with a rigid timetable. Postponement when the clear possibility of a minority report occurred would have been wise. The matter of the United Reformed moderators represented a break of a 'fundamental principle of Catholic order' to some Anglo-Catholics who seemed to have no conception of just how much the URC, heirs of Calvin, had conceded to them. Concern over women ministers was a difficulty also, clearly this was totally non-negotiable by Free Churchmen and there are also now enough Anglican women priests in the world for Catholic discomfort! The longing for re-union with Rome and the great Orthodox churches of the East emerged again, and must receive sympathy. The visit of the Pope to Britain and the report of the Anglican/Roman Catholic International Commission on *authority* may have raised Anglo-Catholic hopes too high for a speedy reconciliation between Anglicans and Roman Catholics than is likely to be the case.[83] The failure of the Covenant to secure a large enough majority could be paralleled by a future failure of an attempt at re-union with Rome. What is sauce for the Anglo-Catholic goose could be sauce for the evangelical gander. Clearly a section of the Church of England is simply not interested in any *rapprochement* with the Free Churches and must be asked what they do mean by Christian union. It would be realistic if we heard no more of the Church of England as a 'bridge church' between the Free Churches and the Church of Rome. Likewise the idea of a marvellous comprehensiveness, a great ecumenical umbrella held up by the Archbishop of Canterbury will not now claim credence. 'The term "comprehensiveness" may be used sometimes not to advertise a source of strength but to disguise and conceal deep undercurrents of profound, even passionate disagreement.'[84] The resurgence of rank party strife in the Church of England means that the Synod can now effectively scotch any movement. Clearly there can be no proper ecumenism in England without the Church of Rome, but the Church of England still holds the key to genuine re-union in England.

The effect of the breakdown of the Covenant will be that areas of ecumenical experiment (LEPs) will be under particularly hard pressure. It means, too, an isolation of Britain in world ecumenism. A French Roman Catholic scholar, Francis Frost, put it thus: 'Cet événement douloureux, a contribué à une baisse sensible de l'influence des églises britanniques non-catholiques romaines sur l'ensemble du mouvement œcuménique.'[85] There is a danger of retreat behind denominational barriers. Within Methodism the possibility of a world Methodist Church is again adumbrated, especially by Methodists in Eastern Europe and South America who feel beleaguered in the fight against unimaginable poverty or oppression. Free Churchmen could remain Protestant in isolation. The idea of a united Free Church will emerge again with high-church Methodists in the dilemma of the Anglo-Catholics. The Church of England is in danger of a retreat into sectarianism not really knowing now what a national church might be – the only justification being Gladstone's assertion that it might mean the greatest holiness of the greatest number or S. T. Coleridge's dictum about the 'Christian' (as distinct from the national church) being 'the sustaining, correcting, befriending opposite of the world; the compensating counterforce to the inherent and inevitable evils and defects of the state'.[86]

Methodism has long accepted the principle of episcopacy. It is doubtful whether it can be proceeded with now. Dissentients would no longer need to point to the historical deficiencies of such a system and those who were prepared to stomach it as a form of government for the sake of the greater good of unity would now be far more likely to join them. A possible way out of the dilemma might be presented by a closer relationship with the Moravians who once gave John Wesley a theological blood transfusion and who might be able to offer Methodism an episcopal pedigree if such were needed. 'The Moravians,' it was once claimed, 'are the only church to have accomplished the feat of retaining episcopacy without being ruled by bishops.' The pedigree of their episcopate was accepted by Potter in 1737 and in 1749 by Act of Parliament as an 'Ancient, Protestant Episcopal Church'. As the church was described as episcopal, the bishops of the Church of England met at Lambeth Palace prior to the passage of the Bill in the House of Lords and resolved not to oppose it. The later Lambeth letters to the Moravians are a curious example of what A. C. Headlam once called 'that assumption of ecclesiastical superiority which is as unseemly as it is in the Church of Rome' with patronizing reference to 'ministries ecclesiastically imperfect' and Anglicans occasionally attending presbyterian services in Scotland – like the monarch, we may presume, who had no option! The situation may be different now. Perhaps the Methodists and the United Reformed Church may learn of the reality of an alternative style of episcopacy to that of the Church of England.[87] Certainly there would be no justification for receiving the historic episcopate from the Church of England.

This is the close of a chapter of missed opportunities. For England it is the end of the Lambeth Quadrilateral as a negotiating base over the ordained ministry. The opponents of the South India scheme's successors have prevailed by blocking anything comparable in England just at the time when Free Churchmen have lost their fear of bishops because of experience of what episcopacy had become in India! The style of North India was closed off also and with the failure of the Covenant even Fisher's goal of intercommunion receded into a distant future. Both the old approach and the new have come to nothing with Anglo-Catholics rather late in the day now stating that to accept episcopacy without a theory of it is an evasion and that there is not enough doctrinal agreement either – rather odd sentiments from within the most doctrinally divided church in Christendom![88] Perhaps the whole area of what really constitutes continuity needs to be opened up again in a way that P. T. Forsyth and B. L. Manning did tentatively a generation or two ago. They seem to point to a genuine Protestant catholicity of the gospel which may yet prove to be more fruitful than the road of William Reed Huntington (and his mentor F. D. Maurice) which has proved a cul-de-sac.[89] The churches now have to come to terms with the fact that full organic union is not now the goal of many but rather some kind of conciliar fellowship which may take us not now back to the Lambeth Quadrilateral but to those all along who have advocated federation, what P. T. Forsyth called the united states of the church.

C. Antepast of Heaven. The Queen's College at Birmingham, 1970. A Personal Viewpoint

It was at the Nottingham British Faith and Order Conference of 1964[90] (which suggested 1980 as some sort of goal for corporate unity for Britain) that the idea was floated that one way to prepare for union was by the ecumenical training of the ministry. This was a decade of great theological uncertainty. Numbers of candidates for the ministry slumped as, in an age of reasonably full employment, other 'helping professions' enabled young men to find fulfilment previously found in the ministry. Acute theological uncertainty added to the difficulties. In Birmingham there were two colleges, both under pressure and keen for forward looking ventures.[91] Handsworth Methodist College, opened in 1881, which had an enviable reputation for academic excellence in the 1920s and 1930s with W. F. Lofthouse, W. F. Howard, Henry Bett and Christopher North on its staff, was ready from the Free Church side for the challenge of 1964. The Queen's College, which began with the vision of William Sands Cox in 1825 for a medical school in Birmingham and which had revived under the notable principalship of J. O. Cobham from 1934, maintained a style of liberal Catholicism. The Church of England was anxious that there should be a large well-equipped theological college, where new forms of training could be initiated in close co-operation with a university. Queen's, ideally suited for this purpose, volunteered itself. A capital grant from the Church Assembly went far towards the cost of new accommodation on the site conveniently near the University of Birmingham. The main recommendations of the Archbishops' Report, *Theological Colleges for Tomorrow* (1967), were being anticipated. Queen's, however, was not full to capacity. Bold decisions were necessary. John S. Habgood was appointed principal in 1967. He had had a distinguished career in pharmacology at King's College, Cambridge, before ordination and had been on the staff at Westcott House. Raymond Hammer, who had come to the college in 1965 from Tokyo, where he had been Professor of Theology, and Leslie Paul, the distinguished lay theologian and sociologist, author of the famous Paul Report on the *Deployment and Payment of the Clergy* and many books on the frontiers between religion, politics and sociology were joined by Rupert Hoare, now principal of Westcott House, in 1968.

Strong pressure towards ecumenism came from the Anglican-Methodist conversations. Powerful arguments were advanced to make the splendid complex at Edgbaston available to all churches which might wish to use them for the training of their ministers. Very quickly – for ecclesiastical bodies surprisingly so – negotiations were put in hand for an amalgamation of Anglican Queen's and Methodist Handsworth, which was inaugurated in October 1970 when the Archbishop of Canterbury (Dr A. M. Ramsey) and the President of the Methodist Conference (Rupert Davies) expressed the support of the British Churches. The College Council had set up an Ecumenical Negotiations Committee in 1968, whose work resulted in the owner-ship and control of Queen's being transferred to a representative ecumenical governing body which later, by Act of Parliament, enabled the college to be genuinely ecumenical in its appointments. A century before, the benefactor of the college, Dr Samuel Warneford, had warned of the 'subtle designs of the Jesuits and the insidious intrusion of malignant Dissenters' – the dissenters were now in the college, Roman Catholics on the Council and ready for theological co-operation. Warneford's portrait, ironically, still dominated the college hall.

So in October 1970 a British Ecumenical College for the training of the ordained ministry was a reality. The constituency has been largely Anglican and Methodist (about thirty-five students from each church) with a token force from the United Reformed Church. During the first ten years students included a black pastor from the Wesleyan Holiness Church, a Japanese Buddhist who wished to savour a Christian community, a Church of Scotland deaconess and steady stream of visiting students from Asia, Africa and Europe, including every two years a student from Southern Africa, sponsored by the college community. The history of the first ten years of the college marked very considerable expansion and differentiation. The West Midlands Course for Ministerial Training (sponsored by the five Midlands dioceses) opened in 1972 to train men and women for non-stipendiary training for the Church of England. More recently Methodists training for full-time ministry have joined the course, a pioneering piece of 'alternative patterns' thinking.[92] This course involves one evening a week of intensive corporate study, weekends and a fully residential week at Easter. Families, too, are involved as this style of training can be very threatening to family life. The Gilmore Course (now terminated) by which women prepared part-time for deaconess and lay service in the Church of England was also centred at Queen's. The women on this course were mature in age and experience. Their work was done at home with local tutors. They came into residence at Queen's for two periods a year, one being Holy Week. There was a whiff of the South American ideas of 'theology by extension' about the style of this course now integrated with more localized courses like the West Midlands Course. This project, together with the full-time residential training of Methodist deaconesses (now terminated) and younger Anglican women, enabled Queen's to be a laboratory for at least three distinct styles of training. For a time, too, the college concerned itself with the development of community medicine in the inner belt of Birmingham.

What are the ecumenical implications of this particular experiment? The immediate problem in 1970 was to reconcile two streams of Christian spirituality, each more diverse than meets the eye, and also two quite distinct college traditions and styles of training. There is a slight but real cultural gap between Anglican and Methodist which makes it difficult for the Anglican to notice his 'consciousness of effortless superiority' and for the Freechurchman to realize his corresponding truculence. The solution of federation, perhaps a little harshly called 'union without repentance' by Newbigin and adapted at Cambridge, was rejected. There was to be total fusion with no denominational escape hatches. All teaching (save for leavers' seminars about constitutional and legal matters) is done together so that Methodism has trusted Anglicans to teach biblical studies, while Anglicans have trusted Methodists to teach systematics and both an Orthodox layman to teach liturgics. The division of the college into working and pastoral groups enables face to face encounter, mutual sharing and support to take place. The tensions are not smoothed out however.

There is a profound theological difference between a church which practises personal *episcopē* or oversight and one which tends to operate by corporate *episcopē* from Conference to a local college oversight committee. Each generation of men and women, too, have to go through the process of learning about one another. There is no sense either in ignoring the situation of denominational continuity into which they will go to minister. This demands a staff not only of academic competence but of spiritual sensitivity, aware not only of what A. M. Allchin calls an 'ecumenism of time' but of what is happening in the world church and in the localities now.

It would be difficult to measure the early contribution here of Dr John Habgood, who was principal from 1970 until his elevation to the See of Durham in 1973. While loyal to his own Anglican tradition and exemplifying its virtues, he was always open to 'echoes' from quite diverse patterns of Christian devotions and discipleship, providing a focus of stability and creativity. Outstanding also was the pioneering work in pastoral studies of Trevor Rowe (1970–79) and in the borderlands of theology and worship that of Geoffrey Wainwright (1973–79) whose *Doxology*, a systematic theology from the standpoint of worship, epitomizes one lesson from the Queen's experiment, the paramount but not obsessive importance of worship.

The college chapel (even in the radical era of the early 1970s) became the focus of college life and sometimes tension. Any 'lowest common multiple' worship, where all cats are grey, was doomed to early failure. There had to be appreciation of traditional forms of worship in their richness and integrity with also the exploration of new forms in which risks are taken, mistakes made and openness to new patterns for the future is found, though after 1975 the appetite for constant innovation was satiated. The college alternates on Sundays between Anglican and Methodist eucharists and presidents, with an occasional Reformed rite. For the daily eucharist, a Queen's rite was developed which became widely acclaimed as admirably flexible enough for a very wide variety of styles of presentation. A daily morning office, including a proper scope for freedom in prayer with an evening daily pattern, including a weekly 'preaching service' (a blend of traditional Methodism and new insights from the Catholic revival of the 'Bible Service') completed a very rich diet of corporate worship.

Students preach and conduct worship in a wide variety of traditions and thus become familiar with many styles of Christian cultural expression including the powerful 'black' churches of Birmingham. In this context of worship, elements of one's own tradition come alive again as well as being enriched from what at first glance seems alien. Methodists often come to find the eucharist deeply satisfying as the heart of worship. Visiting Roman Catholics (even if they are not able to receive the elements of bread and wine) often remark on how much they value the integrity both liturgical and theological of a Methodist celebration – rather closer to post-Second Vatican Council Catholicism than is the somewhat fussy Anglo-Catholic style. Anglicans begin to explore preaching as an art form to be taken with the utmost professional seriousness, a matter underlined by the publication in 1973 of *Queen's Sermons* which illustrates a wide variety of styles of preaching. Queen's can indeed claim to have been in the van of a renewal of preaching. Ecumenical worship, however, does ask of any tradition, 'Is it authentic now? Does it ring true to the heart of the gospel and the great tradition?'

As a participant in this experiment from 1970 to 1981, I will chance an existential comment. There was a degree of mutual acceptance which was deeply moving even if one staff member (the Orthodox liturgist, W. J. Grisbrooke) was sadly, yet with total integrity, not able to communicate with the rest of us. So much was this the case that I became chary of any reunion scheme which did not have reciprocal acceptance at its heart, even though I once argued in favour of the 'service of reconciliation' approach with its built-in ambiguities. We passed beyond that. Anglo-Catholics of the deepest dye often came to practise intercommunion through realizing a genuine spirituality in more Protestant traditions which they had not realized existed. The Covenant scheme, which so tragically failed, incapsulated not a little of the Queen's experience.[93] The fear that people would lose hold of their own traditions has not been justified nor has there been a flurry of people crossing from one denomination to another, though this happens to a few and is not to the discredit of anyone.

In my own experience I found my own Methodist tradition of freedom in worship with a stability of structure come alive again and not least the art and craft of preaching. It was 'left-wing' Protestants at Queen's who taught me again that the psychology of a service with the sermon as a climax was not necessarily liturgically disreputable, despite my preference for a norm of preparation, word read and preached, and response. Simplicity, warmth and homeliness are not incompatible with a sensitivity to the great Catholic traditions. I came, too, to a realization of what the issues between Laudian and Puritan in seventeenth century England were about, a tension which was present earlier between Cluniac and Cistercian. Laud might say, 'Do what I say but believe what you like'; the Puritans said, 'Belief and action and outward ceremonial are inseparable.' Anglicans of a Catholic persuasion still tend to adopt a Laudian approach. I found myself Puritan in this respect and cannot and will not do what I cannot believe in, like wearing classical eucharistic vestments, bowing to the 'altar' or find 'reservation' acceptable, though one can appreciate and affirm for others the values lying behind all these matters. Let others have freedom to do what they choose, but let those who don't wish to conform, be dissenters without prejudice, which is precisely, of course, the freedom which Baxter hoped for at the Restoration of 1660 and was denied. This freedom and comprehensiveness can now be achieved in an ecumenical setting. It is far more credible than pretending (as sometimes happens in local ecumenical experiments) that an Anglican priest and a Methodist minister are exactly the same kind of animal.

There are risks in this kind of enterprise. Some feel a little cut off from their roots – an intense community life can generate an isolation or a self sufficiency which can be spiritually unhealthy. The rather humdrum life of local churches and the local community can pass one by. There were, for example, so many missionary societies which demanded our attention that there was a temptation to relate to none closely. Prayer for world mission, though not for world need, was sometimes lacking in content and contact. With all this, I became totally convinced of the need for ecumenical training of the ministry. Dare we continue any longer with denominational seminaries which ought, like Friedrich Engel's 'state', to belong in the museum with the bronze axe and the spinning wheel.

In tackling theological education, a college of this kind has constraints put on it by the external bodies who sponsor it, but Queen's has been able to develop its own style of integrating the academic and the practical. This is a partial solution of the problem of community self-containment and is very important. Each student has a placement with a secular or church agency in Birmingham. Local hospitals – general and pyschiatric – are used for clinical courses. Students need to know the world the church lives in and serves as well as the tools of Christian apologetic. This is as true for those who have worked for years in secular employment who could, at times, be curiously blinkered, as it was for those whose experience and idealism were limited to school and university – a minority now. The signs are that a certain style is becoming recognizable in men and women trained at Queen's. Not the least of its marks is its ecumenical openness which has in some places, at least, brought a new dimension into the parishes and circuits where Queen's students now serve.

Another future-oriented dimension is in co-operation with St Mary's College, Oscott. Hospital courses and practical placements are undertaken jointly. The staffs meet regularly. More demanding has been the integration of final year courses for a month each year. Residence is for a fortnight in each college with the study of the eucharist as the academic core to the course. Beyond this, for years a Roman Catholic taught introduction to the New Testament at Birmingham University attended by all Queen's students, and Reformation and Counter-Reformation studies were taught at Oscott for a decade by a Methodist, probably unique in this country, except for the teaching at Heythrop given by Marcus Ward. An enormous area of mutual learning is being opened up by this co-operation. A Methodist will not forget the look on the face of one of his Anglican colleagues who said to the assembled Oscott and Queen's students that the Church of England was like a big umbrella with room under it for all – and then realized that two thirds of his audience were dissenters, presumably preferring to stay in the rain, the 'abandoned children' of whom Newman spoke. Only in this kind of atmosphere can realization like *that* take place.

Charles Wesley called salvation the 'antepast of heaven'. An ecumenical community which is genuinely pluralistic in worship and theological style can, with all its tensions and difficulties, be a similar anticipation of what C. H. Dodd called the Divine Commonwealth,[94] which I prefer to that overworked phrase 'the coming great church' with its slight overtone of triumphalism.[95] Gordon Wakefield, the present principal of Queen's, in his inaugural lecture argued the case for theological colleges – not a closed argument by any means.

> For the world needs men and women who, with humility and meekness, yet with something of the terrible strength of the saints, will be at the disposal of their fellows; non-professionals, voluntary servants compared with the rate for the job mentality of the world, who are able to be the recipients of human woes and of the confession of sin – 'dustbins' someone has called them – while also pointing to resources of Christian experience and to the One whom we believe still lives to take away the sins of the world and bring us to the life and joy of God.

This is an argument for a separated ministry but more penetrating is that for ecumenism for a needy world with which I end this study. It helps us to face the future together. I cannot see that our different schools of churchmanship will be of primary importance in the aftermath of nuclear attack, nor that separation from one another will be the best antidote to the ills which could come upon this society before the decade is out – further economic decline, unemployment, the disarray of our humanity before the triumphs of our machines, the increased threat to those incalculably precious to God from social or psychological engineering and what they bring in their train – bureaucracy and dictatorship of right or left. We shall need each other, be the secular future light or dark. We ought therefore to train together, not only to draw on the resources of the past but to be ready for the future.

Published articles and chapters by the author bearing on this theme

'From Society to Church', *London Quarterly and Holborn Review*, April 1963, pp. 110–15.

'Bernard Lord Manning as Church Historian', *Journal of URC Historical Society* 1, No. 5, May 1975, pp. 126–38.

'J. N. Figgis – Anglican Prophet', *Theology*, October 1975, 78, pp. 538–44.

'Some Problems of Church State in England', *Epworth Review* 3, No. 1, January 1976, pp. 56–64.

'Methodist Religion 1791–1850', *A History of the Methodist Church in Great Britain* II ed. R. E. Davies, A. R. George and E. G. Rupp, Epworth Press 1978, pp. 97–112.

'John Wesley, Peoples' Theologian', *One in Christ* 14, No. 4, 1978, pp. 328–39.

'Ministry to the Whole Person – a Birmingham story 1825–1980', *Queen's Essays* ed. J. Munsey Turner, Birmingham 1980, pp. 19–39.

'Primitive Methodism' (Hartley Victoria Lecture, Manchester 1981), *Primitive Methodism from Mow Cop to Peake's Commentary*, ed. C. Dews, Leeds 1982, pp. 1–13.

'Religion and Capitalism – a Continuing Debate', *Epworth Review* 9, No. 1, January 1982, pp. 57–65.

'R. F. Wearmouth – Methodist Historian', *Wesley Historical Society* 43, Part 5, September 1982, pp. 111–16.

'Methodism in England 1900–1932', *A History of the Methodist Church in Great Britain* III ed. R. E. Davies, A. R. George and E. G. Rupp, Epworth Press 1983, pp. 309–361.

'Abandoned Children – Methodism and Catholicism' (Part of Fernley Hartley Lecture – Methodist Conference, 1982), *Epworth Review*, Vol. 10, No. 3, September 1983, pp. 42–48.

I am grateful for permission to use material from these sources.

Abbreviations in Notes

HMGB	R. E. Davies, A. R. George and E. G. Rupp (eds), *A History of the Methodist Church in Great Britain*, Epworth Press I 1965, II 1978, III 1983.
NHM	W. J. Townsend, H. B. Workman and G. Eayrs, *The New History of Methodism* (2 vols.), Hodder and Stoughton 1909.
John Wesley Oxford *Works*	Oxford Edition of the *Works* of John Wesley. 11 ed. G. R. Cragg, 1975. 25 ed. F. Baker, 1980. Letters 1. 26 ed. F. Baker, 1982. Letters 2.
Works	Standard Edition (14 vols.) ed. T. Jackson, Mason 1831ff.
Journal	*The Journal of John Wesley* (8 vols.) ed. N. Curnock, Epworth Press 1909–1916.
Sermons	*Wesley's Standard Sermons* (2 vols.) ed. E. H. Sugden, Epworth Press 1931.
Letters	*The Letters of John Wesley* (8 vols.) ed. J. Telford, Epworth Press 1931.
LQHR	The *London Quarterly and Holborn Review* 1932–1968.
WHS	The *Proceedings of the Wesley Historical Society 1899–*
Minutes	*Minutes of the Wesleyan Methodist and Methodist Conference.*
Baker, *Wesley and the Church*	Frank Baker, *John Wesley and the Church of England*, Epworth Press 1970.
Bunting 1	W. R. Ward (ed), *The Early Correspondence of Jabez Bunting 1820–1829*, Royal Historical Society 1972.
Bunting 2	W. R. Ward (ed), *Early Victorian Methodism: The Correspondence of Jabez Bunting 1830–1858*, Oxford University Press 1976.
Bunting 3	A. J. Hayes and D. A. Gowland (eds), *Scottish Methodism in the Early Victorian Period: The Scottish Correspondence of Jabez Bunting 1800–1857*, Edinburgh University Press 1981.

Notes

Introduction

1. William Temple, *The Church looks Forward*, SCM Press 1944, pp. 2–3.
2. J. D. Walsh, 'Origins of the Evangelical Revival', *Essays in Modern English Church History* ed. G. V. Bennett and J. D. Walsh, Black 1966, p. 162.
   W. R. Ward, *Religion and Society in England 1790–1850*, Batsford 1972, p. 6.
3. Robert Currie, *Methodism Divided: A study in the Sociology of Ecumenicalism*, Faber and Faber 1968, p. 14.
   R. Wilson, *Religion in Secular Society*, Watts 1966, pp. 125ff.
   Cf. David M. Thompson, 'Religious Motivation: Biographical and Sociological Problems for the Church Historian', *Studies in Church History* 15 ed. D. Baker, Cambridge University Press 1978, pp. 467–79.
4. N. Sykes, 'Ecumenical Movements in Great Britain in the Seventeenth and Eighteenth Centuries', *A History of the Ecumenical Movement 1517–1948* ed. Ruth Rouse and Stephen Neill, SPCK 1967, pp. 164–65.
5. D. Martin, 'The Denomination', *British Journal of Sociology* 13, No. 2, 1962, pp. 1–14.
   J. Wach, *The Sociology of Religion*, Routledge and Kegan Paul 1947, pp. 175–81.
   Bryan R. Wilson, *Patterns of Sectarianism*, Heinemann 1967, pp. 22–25.
6. Owen Chadwick, *The Secularization of the European Mind in the Nineteenth Century*, Cambridge University Press 1975, p. 21.
7. E.g. J. H. Moulton, *A Neglected Sacrament*, Epworth Press 1918, p. 15.
   R. E. Davies, *Methodism*, Epworth Press 2nd edn 1976, pp. 125–27.
   H. D. Rack in *HMGB* III, pp. 152–53.
8. Translated from Voltaire, *Lettres Philosophiques* (2 vols.) ed. G. Lanson, Paris 1924. Vol. I, p. 74 cited in J. Bossy, *The English Catholic Community 1570–1850*, Darton, Longman and Todd 1975, pp. 391ff.

1. Eighteenth-Century Background

1. S. Andrews, 'John Wesley and the Age of Reason', *History Today*, January 1969.
   G. Rupp, *Just Men*, Epworth Press 1977, pp. 111–31.
2. N. Sykes, *Church and State in England in the Eighteenth Century*, Cambridge University Press 1934.
   N. Sykes, *From Sheldon to Secker: Aspects of English Church History 1660–1768*, Cambridge University Press 1959.
   G. F. A. Best, *Temporal Pillars: Queen Anne's Bounty, The Ecclesiastical Commissioners and the Church of England*, Cambridge University Press 1964.

3. P. Hazard, *The European Mind 1680–1715*, Penguin Books 1964, pp. 7–13.
   Cf. P. Gay, *The Enlightenment, an Interpretation* I, *The Rise of Modern Paganism*,
   Wildwood House 1970.
   C. L. Becker, *The Heavenly City of the Eighteenth Century Philosophers*, Yale
   University Press, USA 1932.

4. H. Butterfield, *Man on his Past*, Cambridge University Press 1969 edn,
   p. 118.

5. G. R. Cragg, *From Puritanism to the Age of Reason*, Cambridge University
   Press 1950, pp. 36–60.
   H. R. McAdoo, *The Spirit of Anglicanism*, Black 1965, pp. 81ff.
   R. L. Colie, *Light and Enlightenment: A Study of the Cambridge Platonists and
   the Dutch Arminians*, Cambridge University Press 1957.

6. Yet the role of Calvin was, perhaps, crucial in 'freeing' the universe from
   apparent irrationality.
   Cf. A. G. Dickens, *Reformation and Society in Sixteenth Century Europe*, Thames
   and Hudson 1966, p. 194.
   C. Hill, *God's English Man*, Penguin Books 1972, pp. 206–207.

7. G. R. Cragg, *The Church and the Age of Reason 1648–1789*, Penguin Books
   1960, pp. 13, 80.
   A. Pope, *Poems, Epistles, Satires*, Everyman 1949, p. 122.

8. B. Willey, *The Seventeenth Century Background*, Penguin Books 1962, p. 251.
   But cf. F. A. Yates, *The Rosicrucian Enlightenment*, Paladin 1975.

9. G. Gay, op. cit., pp. 320ff.

10. Sykes, *From Sheldon to Secker*, p. 187.

11. Cited in P. E. More and F. L. Cross, *Anglicanism*, SPCK 1957, p. 12.
    Joseph Glanvill, cited in Sykes, *From Sheldon to Secker*, pp. 223–24.

12. H. Butterfield, *Christianity in European History*, Oxford University Press
    1951, p. 35.
    H. Butterfield, 'England in the Eighteenth Century', *HMGB* I, pp. 5–7.

13. Best, op. cit., p. 12.
    G. Holmes (ed), *Britain after the Glorious Revolution 1689–1714*, Macmillan
    1969, p. 164.
    E. Duffy, 'Primitive Christianity Revised: Religious Renewal in Augustine
    England', *Studies in Church History* 14 ed. D. Baker, Blackwell 1977,
    pp. 287ff.
    D. W. R. Bahlmann, *The Moral Revolution of 1688*, New Haven, USA 1957.
    G. V. Portus, *Caritas Anglicana*, Mowbray 1912.
    G. S. Wakefield, 'Religious Societies', *LQHR*, April 1963, pp. 104–110.
    W. R. Ward, 'Orthodoxy, Enlightenment and Religious Revival', *Studies
    in Church History* 17 ed. K. Robbins, Blackwell 1981, pp. 275ff.
    W. R. Ward, 'The Relations of Enlightenment and Religious Revival in
    Central Europe and in the English Speaking World', *Studies in Church
    History*, Subsidia 2 ed. D. Baker, Blackwell 1979, pp. 281ff.
    W. R. Ward, 'Power and Piety: The Origins of Religious Revival in the
    Early Eighteenth Century', *Journal of John Rylands Library*, Manchester,
    Vol. 63, Autumn 1980, pp. 231–52.

14. M. G. Jones, *The Charity School Movement*, Cambridge University Press
    1938.

15. A. Pope, *Imitations of Horace*, l. 276.

16. Hazard, op. cit., p. 295.
17. J. H. Plumb, *The Growth of Political Stability in England 1675–1725*, Penguin Books 1969, pp. 133ff.

    Holmes (ed), op. cit., especially Ch. 7, p. 174.

    G. Holmes, *The Trial of Doctor Sacheverell*, Eyre, Methuen 1973, especially Ch. 2.

    G. V. Bennett, *The Tory Crisis in Church and State 1688–1730*, Oxford University Press 1975.
18. Sykes, *From Sheldon to Secker*, p. 222.
19. G. Holmes, *Religion and Party in Late Stuart England*, Historical Association 1975, p. 30.
20. N. Sykes, *Edmund Gibson 1699–1748*, Oxford University Press 1926, p. 213.
21. Sykes, *Church and State*, p. 212.

    W. R. Ward, 'Church and Society in the First Half of the Nineteenth Century', *HMGB* II, p. 50.

    Best, op. cit., pp. 13 ff.

    J. H. Pruett, *The Parish clergy under the later Stuarts*, Chicago University Press, USA 1978, pp. 81–114, 'Leicestershire'.

    G. Holmes, *Augustan England: Professions, State and Society 1680–1730*, Allen and Unwin 1982, pp. 83–114.
22. D. McClatchey, *Oxfordshire Clergy 1771–1869*, Oxford University Press 1960, Chs. 2–5.

    HMGB II, pp. 13ff., 49–55.

    C. Hill, *Economic Problems of the Church*, Panther 1971, p. 351.
23. Sykes, *Church and State*, pp. 405–406.

    D. E. H. Mole, 'Challenge to the Church, Birmingham 1815–65', *The Vitorian City* 2 ed. H. J. Dyos and M. Wolff, Routledge and Kegan Paul 1973, p. 827.
24. Sykes, *Church and State* pp. 250–54.

    Pruett, op. cit., pp. 121–22.

    McClatchey, op. cit., p. 86.
25. B. Trinder, *The Industrial Revolution in Shropshire*, Phillimore 1973, p. 297.
26. J. D. Gay, *The Geography of Religion in England*, Duckworth 1971, pp. 69ff.

    D. Sylvester, 'The Church and the Geographer', *Liverpool Essays in Geography* ed. R. W. Steel and R. Lawton, Longman 1967.

    C. Haigh, *Reformation and Resistance in Tudor Lancashire*, Cambridge University Press 1975, Ch. 2.
27. C. Cross, *Church and People 1450–1660*, Collins 1976, p. 242.

    G. F. Nuttall, 'Methodism and the Older Dissent', *Journal of URC Historical Society* 2, 1981, pp. 259–74.

    H. Perkin, *Origin of Modern English Society 1780–1880*, Routledge and Kegan Paul 1969, pp. 33–35.
28. M. R. Watts, *The Dissenters from the Reformation to the French Revolution*. Oxford University Press 1978, pp. 267ff., 491–510.

    E. D. Bebb, *Nonconformity and Social and Economic Life 1660–1800*, Epworth Press 1935, pp. 30ff., 174–86.

    J. Bossy, *The English Catholic Community*, Darton, Longman and Todd 1975, p. 185.

    Cf. A. D. Gilbert, *Religion and Society in Industrial England: Church, Chapel and Social Change 1740–1914*, Longman 1976, p. 16.

29. G. F. Nuttall, *The Puritan Spirit*, Epworth Press 1967, pp. 67ff.

30. B. L. Manning, *Essays in Orthodox Dissent*, Independent Press 1939, pp. 171–95.
    Watts, op. cit., pp. 382ff.
    For another viewpoint: D. Davie, *A Gathered Church: The Literature of the English Dissenting Interest 1700–1930*, Routledge and Kegan Paul 1978, pp. 19–36, 111–19.

31. J. H. Colligan, *Eighteenth Century Nonconformity*, Longman 1915, pp. 90, 124.
    Cf. G. C. Bolam (ed), *The English Presbyterians*, Allen and Unwin 1968, pp. 175–218.
    Bebb, op. cit., pp. 41, 53.

32. J. D. Walsh, 'Origins of the Evangelical Revival', *Essays in Modern English Church History* ed. G. V. Bennett and J. D. Walsh, Black 1966, p. 134.

33. *HMGB* I, p. xxxvi.
    M. Schmidt, *John Wesley: A Theological Biography*, Epworth Press 1962, pp. 191–92.
    H. Bett, 'A French Marquis and the Class Meeting', *WHS* XVIII, pp. 43–45.
    F. E. Stoeffler, *German Pietism during the Eighteenth Century*, Brill 1973.

34. Bennett and Walsh, op. cit., pp. 144–48.
    J. D. Walsh, 'The Anglican Evangelicals in the Eighteenth Century' *Aspects de l'Anglicanisme* ed. M. Simon, Presses Universitaires de France Paris 1974, pp. 87–102.
    K. E. Rowe (ed), *The Place of Wesley in the Christian Tradition*, Methuchen, New Jersey, USA 1976.

35. Bennett and Walsh, op. cit., p. 157.

36. M. Hennell, *John Venn and the Clapham Sect*, Lutterworth Press 1958, pp. 16–17.

37. W. E. Gladstone, *Gleanings of Past Years* VII, John Murray 1879, pp. 205–207.
    J. D. Walsh, *Proceedings of the Royal Historical Society*, Vol. 25, 1975, pp. 1–20.

38. Perkin, op. cit., p. 35.
    Best, op. cit., pp. 137ff.

2. The Separation of Methodism from the Church of England

1. Oxford *Works* 25 1721–1739, 1980, pp. 614–17, 693.
   Cf. A. Outler, 'Do Methodists have a Doctrine of the Church', *The Doctrine of the Church* ed. D. Kirkpatrick, Epworth Press 1964, pp. 11–28.

2. George Whitefield, *Works* 1, Dilly, London 1771, p. 105, 10 November 1739.

3. *WHS* XLII, pp. 93ff.
   H. Moore, *Life of Wesley* 1, Kershaw 1824, pp. 463–65.

4. *WHS* XX, pp. 63–67; XXI, pp. 31–32.
   M. Schmidt, *John Wesley* 2, Part I, Epworth Press 1971, p. 35ff.
   Baker, *Wesley and the Church*, pp. 71, 95.
   A. R. Vidler, *Scenes from a Clerical Life*, Collins 1977, pp. 156ff. Vidler took out such a licence.

5. Schmidt, op. cit., pp. 37–38, 119.

R. W. Church, *Pascal and other Sermons*, Macmillan 1895, p. 42.

6. G. Eayrs, *Wesley: Christian Philosopher and Church Founder*, Epworth Press 1926, pp. 201ff.
   But cf. Baker, *Wesley and the Church*, p. 5.

7. J. H. Overton and H. Relton, *The English Church from George I to the end of the Eighteenth Century*, Macmillan 1906, p. 74.

8. J. Kent, *The Age of Disunity*, Epworth Press 1966, p. 182.

9. *Letters* III, p. 146, Bristol, 24 September 1755.

10. H. C. G. Moule, *Charles Simeon*, Methuen 1892, pp. 225ff.

11. L. Tyerman, *Life and Times of John Wesley* III, Hodder and Stoughton 1871, p. 636
    C. W. Williams, *John Wesley's Theology Today*, Epworth Press 1960, pp. 207–222.
    J. Kent, 'John Wesley's Churchmanship', *WHS* XXXV, pp. 10–14.

12. *Letters* III, p. 146, 24 September 1755.
    Oxford *Works* 26, pp. 592–96.
    For Walker's letter pp. 582–86, 5 September 1755.

13. *Minutes* I, p. 58.
    Tyerman, op. cit. II, p. 576.

14. *Minutes* I, 1755, p. 46.
    Works XIII, pp. 213–19.

15. *Letters* III, pp. 149ff., 31 October 1755.
    Oxford *Works* 26, pp. 609–11.
    For Adam's letter pp. 603–604.

16. G. C. B. Davies, *The Early Cornish Evangelicals*, SPCK 1951, pp. 88ff.
    Tyerman, op. cit. II, pp. 207–11, 245ff.

17. 16 August 1756.
    Tyerman, op. cit. II, p. 245.

18. To Adam, 31 October 1755.
    Letters III, p. 151.
    Oxford *Works* 26, p. 610.

19. To Walker, 3 September 1756.
    Letters III, p. 195.

20. *Letters* VIII, pp. 324, 326, 377.

21. *Letters* VIII, p. 58.

22. 11 December 1789, *Arminian Magazine*, April 1790.
    Baker, *Wesley and the Church* pp. 320–22.

23. *Letters* VII, pp. 284–85, cf. *Minutes*, 1744.
    Williams, op. cit., pp. 141ff.
    J. Wesley, *Earnest Appeal to Men of Reason and Religion*, 1743.
    Oxford *Works* 11, 1975, p. 77.

24. A. Warne, *Church and Society in Eighteenth Century Devon*, David and Charles 1969, pp. 109, 112.
    R. Polwhele (ed), *Preface* to Lavington's *Enthusiasm of Methodists and Papists Compar'd* 1820.
    Minutes I, p.35, 1747.

25. Baker, *Wesley and the Church* p. 161.
    Letters II, pp. 77–78, 184–192.
    Oxford *Works* 26, pp. 197–207.

C. Hill, 'Occasional Conformity', *Reformation, Conformity and Dissent* ed. R. B. Knox, Epworth Press 1977, pp. 199–220.

26. N. Sykes, *Edmund Gibson*, Oxford University Press 1926, pp. 301ff.
    T. Jackson (ed), *Journal of Charles Wesley* I, London 1849, p. 133.
    WHS XI, pp. 56–58, 82, 103.

27. J. S. Simon, *John Wesley and the advance of Methodism*, Epworth Press 1925, p. 58.
    But cf. Baker who stresses the use of the Huguenot Chapel (West Street) after 1743.

28. F. Baker, *The Story of Cleethorpes*, Trinity Methodist Church, Cleethorpes, 1953, pp. 24, 49.

29. Baker, *Wesley and the Church*, p. 174.

30. Tyerman, op. cit. II, pp. 383–84.
    J. S. Simon, *John Wesley: The Master Builder*, Epworth Press 1927, pp. 75ff.

31. Baker, *Wesley and the Church*, pp. 176–177.

32. *Minutes* I, p. 602, cf. p. 82, 1768.

33. 'Or Chapels' was added in 1780. Roman Catholics and Moravians used the word also.

34. T. Jackson, *Charles Wesley* II, Mason 1841, p. 219.

35. Simon, *John Wesley: The Master Builder*, p. 78.

36. *Letters* V, pp. 97–99.
    Baker, *Wesley and the Church* pp. 195–96.

37. Simon, *John Wesley: The Master Builder*, p. 116.

38. *Life of Lady Huntingdon* 2, 1838, pp. 310–14.

39. A. S. Wood, *Thomas Haweis*, SPCK 1957, pp. 149–53, 157–58, 168–69.
    A. S. Wood, *The Inextinguishable Blaze*, Paternoster Press 1960, pp. 200–204.
    A. B. Lawson, *John Wesley and the Christian Ministry*, Epworth Press 1963, p. 130.

40. *Letters* VIII, p. 92.
    Journal VIII, pp. 335ff.

41. A. W. Harrison, *Separation of Methodism from the Church of England*, Epworth Press 1945, p. 25.

42. Moore, op. cit. II, pp. 381–83.
    Tyerman, op. cit. III, pp. 512–13.
    Letters VIII, p. 231.

43. *Letters* VIII, pp. 224–25, 230–31.
    WHS XV, p. 58.

44. Baker, *Wesley and the Church* p. 115.
    Cf Kent, op. cit., pp. 182–90.

45. J. Bossy, *The English Catholic Community*, Darton, Longman and Todd 1975, p. 132.

46. G. C. B. Davies, *The Early Cornish Evangelicals*, SPCK 1951.
    Letters III, pp. 143–47.
    Tyerman, op. cit. II, pp. 199ff.
    Baker, *Wesley and the Church*, pp. 169ff.
    Oxford *Works* 26, pp. 582–86, 592–96, 606–608, 611–13.

47. *HMGB* I, pp. 242ff.
    WHS XII, pp. 81ff.
    Journal VIII, pp. 335–41.
    Baker, *Wesley and the Church*, pp. 218ff.

Cf. G. Smith, *History of Wesleyan Methodism* I, Kelly 5th edn, 1862, p. 705 for 'the Deed'.

48. Tyerman, op. cit. III, p. 418.
   J. S. Simon, *John Wesley: The Last Phase*, Epworth Press 1914, p. 215.
   A. R. George, *The Expository Times* XCI, 1980, pp. 260–64.

49. J. Whitehead, *Life of Wesley* II, London 1796, p. 404.
   Baker, *Wesley and the Church*, p. 218.

50. W. W. Sweet, *Methodism in American History*, Abingdon Press, Nashville, USA 1953, pp. 88ff.
   E. S. Bucke (ed), *History of American Methodism*, Vol. I, Abingdon Press, Nashville, USA 1964. p. 187.

51. Simon, *Last Phase*, p. 220. Cited from S. Wilberforce, *History of the Protestant Episcopal Church* (1844), pp. 182–84.

52. J. T. Addison, *The Episcopal Church in the United States 1789–1931*, Scribners, New York 1951, pp. 51–52.
   N. Sykes, *From Sheldon to Secker*, Cambridge University Press 1959, p. 210. Secker's attempt to recommend the appointment of 'Bishops in America' in 1767.
   J. E. Booty, *The Church in History*, Seabury, New York 1979, pp. 64ff.
   N. Sykes, *Edmund Gibson 1669–1748*, Oxford University Press 1926, pp. 368ff. for earlier controversies.

53. F. V. Mills, *Bishops by Ballot: The Eighteenth Century Ecclesiastical Revolution*, Oxford University Press 1978, p. 139.
   Cf. W. H. Swatos, *Into Denominationalism: The Anglican Metamorphosis*, Society for the Scientific Study of Religion, Ellington, Connecticut, USA 1979, pp. 59–72.

54. Mills, op. cit., p. 158.

55. Reprinted in 1954, CHS Austin, Texas.
   Cf. W. White, *Memoirs of the Protestant Episcopal Church Philadelphia*, Philadelphia 1820.

56. Cited in Mills, op. cit., p. 186.

57. J. Vickers, *Thomas Coke*, Epworth Press 1969, pp. 90–91, 181–91.

58. Mills, op. cit., p. 252.

59. Sweet, op. cit., pp. 94ff.
   Bucke, op. cit., p. 189.
   F. Baker, *From Wesley to Asbury*, Duke University Press, Durham, USA 1976, p. 102.
   W. R. Ward, 'The Legacy of John Wesley', *Statesmen, Scholars and Merchants* ed. A. Whiteman et al., Oxford University Press 1973, pp. 328–29.

60. *Letters* VII, pp. 30–31; VII, pp. 237–39.

61. Kent, op. cit., pp. 171ff.
   Letters II, pp. 55ff., 30 December 1745.
   Oxford *Works* 26, pp. 175–183.

62. Baker, *Wesley and the Church*, pp. 143ff.
   Cf. *Bibliography* in *HMGB* II, p. 143.

63. *Letters* III, p. 182, July 1756.

64. Lawson, op. cit., pp. 47ff.
   Letters VII, p. 21, 1780; VII, p. 284, 1785.

65. J. H. Rigg, *Relations of John Wesley and the Church of England*, London 1868, p. 41.

H. Bett, *The Spirit of Methodism*, Epworth Press 1937, pp. 79–98.
Baker, *Wesley and the Church*, pp. 159, 251.

66. J. C. Bowmer, *The Sacrament of the Lord's Supper in Early Methodism*, Black 1951, pp. 149ff.

67. *Letters* III, p. 186, 3 September 1756.

68. Rigg, op. cit., p. 26.
Moore, op. cit., II, pp. 339–40, 345.

69. Bowmer, op. cit., p. 159.
J. E. Rattenbury, *The Conversion of the Wesleys*, Epworth Press 1938, pp. 225–26.

70. R. Hooker, 'Of the Laws of Ecclesiastical Polity', *Works* ed. J. Keble etc., Oxford University Press 1881, Books III, V and VII, Vol. 1 pp. 338ff., Vol. 2 pp. 468ff., Vol. 3 pp. 140ff.
N. Sykes, *The Church of England and Non-Episcopal Churches in the Sixteenth and Seventeenth Centuries*, SPCK 1948.
N. Sykes, *Old Priest and New Presbyter*, Cambridge University Press 1956, especially Chs. 2, 6.
But cf. A. J. Mason, *Church of England and Episcopacy*, Cambridge University Press 1914, for a Tractarian viewpoint.

71. F. Baker, *From Asbury to Wesley*, p. 144.
Vickers, op. cit., p. 80.
W. R. Ward, op. cit. ed. A. Whiteman, p. 332.

72. Lawson, op. cit., p. 139.
Tyerman, op. cit. III, p. 432.
Vickers, op. cit., p. 69.

73. Whitehead, op. cit. II, p. 423.
A. R. George, 'Ordination in Methodism', *LQHR*, April 1951.
J. Nuelson, *Die Ordination in Methodismus*, Bremen 1935.

74. Vickers, op. cit., pp. 68ff.
W. R. Ward, op. cit. ed. A. Whiteman, p. 331.
J. E. Rattenbury, *Eucharistic Hymns of John and Charles Wesley*, Epworth Press 1948, p. 159.
Letters VIII, p. 90, 20 September 1788.

75. Baker, *Wesley and the Church*, p. 271. Vickers, op. cit., pp. 114ff.
Lawson, op. cit., p. 150–51.
WHS XXX, pp. 162–70.
Baker, *From Wesley to Asbury*, pp. 129–31. Asbury secured ratification by his brethren of Wesley's vicarious appointment of him as superintendent.
Bucke, op. cit., p. 205.

76. E. W. Thompson, *John Wesley: Apostolic Man*, Epworth Press 1957, especially pp. 53ff.
George, op. cit., pp. 149–51
Kent, op. cit., p. 186.

77. *Letters* VII, pp. 238–39, 262.

78. Simon, *Last Phase*, p. 229.
Whitehead, op. cit. II, p. 420.

79. Tyerman, op. cit. III, p. 439.
Baker, *Wesley and the Church*, pp. 273ff.

80. A. J. Mason, cited from G. Horne, *Works* II, p. 570.

81. A. J. Mason, *Life of Dr. Horne*, p. 158.

W. Jones, *Works* IV, p. 422.

S. Horsley, *Theological Works* III, Rivington 1845, p. 27. 1790.

Sykes, *Old Priest and New Presbyter*, pp. 173–74.

82. Baker, *From Wesley to Asbury*, pp. 103, 129.

G. Every, *The High Church Party 1688–1718*, SPCK 1956, p. 180.

83. *Letters* VII, pp. 237–39.

84. Tyerman, op. cit. III, p. 548–49.

Bett, op. cit., p. 69.

85. F. Hunter, 'Sources of Wesley's Revision of the Prayer Book', *WHS* XXIII, pp. 123–33, 173–75.

F. Hunter, 'Wesley – Separatist or Searcher for Unity?', *WHS* XXXVIII, pp. 166–69.

G. J. Cuming, *A History of Anglican Liturgy*, Macmillan 1969, p. 179.

A. E. Peaston *The Prayer Book Tradition in the Free Churches*, Clarke 1964, pp. 35ff.

J. P. Ferguson, *Samuel Clarke*, Roundwood Press 1976, pp. 162ff.

86. Baker, *Wesley and the Church*, pp. 234–55.

A. R. George, 'The Means of Grace', *HMGB* I, pp. 259–73.

87. F. Baker, 'Wesley's Ordinations', *WHS* XXIV, pp. 76ff.

H. E. Lacy, 'John Wesley's Ordinations', *WHS* XXXIII, pp. 118ff.

Tyerman, op. cit. III, pp. 549, 574.

Letters VIII, p. 105.

88. E. Hatch, *The Organization of the Early Christian Churches*, Rivington 1882, pp. 137ff.

R. A. Knox, *Enthusiasm*, Oxford University Press 1950, p. 511.

Max Warren, 'Missionary Expansion of *Ecclesia Anglicana*', *New Testament Christianity for Africa and the World* ed. M. E. Glasswell and E. W. Fashole-Luke, SPCK 1974, p. 134.

The Act is 26. George III C 84.

89. L. F. Church, *More about the Early Methodist People*, Epworth Press 1949, pp. 210–88.

HMGB I, pp. 270–3.

Minutes 1, p. 59.

Works VII, pp. 174–85.

90. M. Schmidt, *John Wesley* I, Epworth Press 1962, p. 237.

O. E. Borgen, *John Wesley on the Sacraments*, Zurich 1972.

S. Bradburn, *Are the Methodists Dissenters?* Bristol 2nd edn 1793. Cited from 1841 edition in Wesley College, Bristol.

91. Bowmer, op. cit., pp. 62ff.

92. Tyerman, op. cit. II, pp. 199ff, 380.

Baker, *Wesley and the Church*, pp. 160–179.

Joseph Benson, *Sermons* 2, London 1836, p. 342.

93. The first use was in Soho, Birmingham, by Murdock in 1803.

94. Tyerman, op. cit. III, pp. 363, 478.

Journal VII, pp. 422–23.

J. H. Overton, *The English Church in the Nineteenth Century*, Longman 1894, pp. 144–45.

Ward, op. cit., *HMGB* II, p. 53.

95. *WHS* XXXIII, pp. 118–121; XXXIV, p. 99; XXXVI, pp. 36–40, 111–114, 159; XXIV, pp. 76ff. There were 6 men ordained on 3 August 1788.

Lawson, op. cit., pp. 130ff.
96. W. Myles. *Chronological History*, London 1813, p. 175.
Baker, *Wesley and the Church*, pp. 280–81.
Smith, op. cit. II, 5th edn 1872, p. 98.
97. Baker, *Wesley and the Church*, pp. 180–96.
98. Simon, *Last Phase*, pp. 20–21, 60ff.
Baker, *Wesley and the Church*, p. 206.
Journal VIII, Appendix.
99. Baker, *Wesley and the Church*, pp. 209–12.
100. W. Myles, *Chronological History*, 1813, p. 175.
Tyerman, op. cit. III, p. 443. Letter in Methodist Church Archives, Manchester.
Baker, *Wesley and the Church*, p. 281.
101. Tyerman, op. cit. III, p. 441.
Cf. Baker, *Wesley and the Church*, p. 282.
102. S. Bradburn, op. cit.
C. A. Bradford, *Joseph Bradford*, n.d., p. 33.
Cf. Baker, *Wesley and the Church*, p. 282.

3. *Methodism, Catholicism and Patterns of Dissent*

1. W. R. Ward, *Religion and Society in England 1790–1850*, Batsford 1972, p. 35.
2. U. Henriques, *Religious Toleration in England 1787–1833*, Routledge and Kegan Paul 1961.
J. H. Plumb, *Sir Robert Walpole* I, Cresset Press 1956, pp. 266–76.
N. Hunt, *Sir Robert Walpole, Samuel Holden and the Dissenting Deputies*, Oxford University Press 1957.
R. B. Barlow, *Citizenship and Conscience*, University of Pennsylvania, Philadelphia, USA 1962, p. 74.
R. F. Wearmouth, *Methodism and the Common People of the Eighteenth Century*, Epworth Press 1945, pp. 138–64.
3. B. Greaves, 'Eighteenth Century Opposition to Methodism', *WHS* XXXI, pp. 93–98, 105–111.
D. D. Wilson, 'Hanoverian Government and Methodist Persecution', *WHS* XXXIII, pp. 94–99.
D. D. Wilson, *Many Waters cannot Quench*, Epworth Press 1969.
L. F. Church, *More about the Early Methodist People*, Epworth Press 1949, pp. 57–98.
4. J. H. Plumb, *England in the Eighteenth Century*, Penguin Books 1950, pp. 93–94.
5. A. M. Lyles, *Methodism Mocked*, Epworth Press 1960.
D. Jarrett, *England in the Age of Hogarth*, Longman 1976, pp. 181ff.
6. J. L. Waddy, *The Bitter Sacred Cup*, World Methodist Historical Society 1976. Wednesbury riots.
7. J. D. Walsh, 'Methodism and the Mob', *Studies in Church History*, Vol. 8, ed. G. J. Cuming and D. Baker, Cambridge University Press 1972, pp. 213–27.
WHS XXXIX, pp. 2–6.
8. G. F. A. Best, *Temporal Pillars*, Cambridge University Press 1964, p. 72.

D. M. McClatchey, *Oxfordshire Clergy 1771–1869*, Oxford University Press 1960, p. 179.

9. *Journal* III, p. 283.
10. E. P. Thompson, *The Making of the English Working Class*, Penguin Books 1968, pp. 66ff. for another viewpoint.
11. E. Welbourne, *The Miners' Union of Northumberland and Durham*, Cambridge University Press 1923, p. 57.
12. Bossy, op. cit., p. 254.
13. L. Festinger, *A Theory of Cognitive Dissonance*, Evanston, USA 1957.
14. Oxford *Works* 11,
    M. Schmidt, *John Wesley*, Vol. II, Part I, Epworth Press 1971, pp. 152–229.
    R. Green, *Anti-Methodist Publications*, Kelly 1902.
    Lyles, op. cit., pp. 172ff.
15. Schmidt, op. cit., p. 227.
16. Josiah Tucker, *A brief history of the Principles of Methodism etc.*, London 1742.
17. Oxford *Works* 11, pp. 16ff. The Bishop of London's Pastoral Letter 1739.
    'Observations on the Conduct and Behaviour of a certain sect usually distinguished by the name of Methodist', anon – usually attributed to Gibson. London 1744.
    Charge of the Rt Revd Father in God Edmund, Lord Bishop of London, London 1747 – no longer extant.
18. G. Horne, *Works Wrought through Faith: A Condition of our Justification. Works of George Horne*, (4 vols.), 1831, Vol. 3, Discourses LXII.
    Oxford *Works* 11.
    Wesley's reply, ibid., pp. 437ff.
    Wesley's reply to Gibson, ibid, pp. 327–31.
    Cf. 'Earnest Appeal to Men of Reason and Religion' etc., ibid., pp. 45ff.
19. Gibson, *Observations*, cited in Oxford *Works* 11, p. 13.
    Wesley's Reply, Oxford *Works* 11, pp. 335–51.
    Cf. N. Sykes, *Edmund Gibson*, Oxford University Press 1926, pp. 302–32.
20. W. Warburton, 'Doctrine of Grace', *Works* 8 ed. Hurd, Cadell and Davies 1811, pp. 318ff.
21. Wesley's Reply, Oxford *Works* 11, pp. 467–538, November 1762.
22. R. Lavington, *The Enthusiasm of Methodists and Papists Compar'd* London 1st edn 1749, 2 vol. edn 1754, ed. R. Polwhele, 1820, p. 6.
    Wesley's Reply, Oxford *Works* 11, pp. 361–436.
23. Cited by J. D. Walsh in *Aspects de l'Anglicanisme* ed. M. Simon, Paris 1974, p. 95.
24. J. Kent, *Age of Disunity*, Epworth Press 1966, p. 180.
    J. H. Overton and F. Relton, *The English Church 1714–1800*, Macmillan 1906, p. 177.
    Cf. B. Semmel, *The Methodist Revolution*, Heinemann 1974, pp. 41–55.
25. Oxford *Works* 26, pp. 153–61, 175–83, 197–207, 229–37, 244–52, 287–94.
    Letters II, pp. 77–78, 270–73.
26. *Letters* IV, pp. 376–81, (also 338–84).
    Oxford *Works* 11, pp. 111, 445ff.
    Cf. A. M. Toplady, *Historic Proof of the Doctrinal Calvinism of the Church of England* (2 vols.), London 1774.
27. John Douglas, *Criterion*, p. 179. Cited in C. J. Abbey, *The English Church and its Bishops 1700–1800* I, Longman 1887, p. 396.

28. T. Jackson, *Recollections of My Own Life and Times*, WM Conference 1873.
Cf. Warren Derry, *Dr Parr: Portrait of the Whig Dr Johnson*, Oxford University Press 1966, for a complete contrast.

29. O. Chadwick, *Victorian Miniature*, Hodder and Stoughton 1960. Mr Andrews depicted here was an Evangelical.

30. C. Field, *British Journal of Sociology* 28, July 1977, pp. 199–225.
W. J. Warner, *The Wesleyan Movement in the Industrial Revolution*, Longman 1930, pp. 248–67.
L. F. Church, *More about the Early Methodist People*, Epwroth Press 1949, pp. 1–56.
Watts, op. cit., p. 408.
R. A. Buchanan, 'Methodism and the Evangelical Revival: an Interpretation', *Anglican-Methodist Relations: Some Institutional Factors* ed. W. S. F. Pickering, Darton, Longman and Todd 1961, p. 39.

31. H. Bett, *The Early Methodist Preachers*, Epworth Press 1935, p. 33.

32. J. D. Walsh, 'Methodist and the Common People, *Peoples' History and Socialist Theory* ed. R. Samuel, Routledge and Kegan Paul 1981, pp. 354ff.
A. D. Gilbert, *Religion and Society in Industrial England*, Longman 1976, p. 83.

33. J. D. Gay, *The Geography of Religion in England*, Duckworth 1971, pp. 144–67.
D. Fraser (ed), *A History of Modern Leeds*, Manchester 1980, p. 28.
D. G. Wright and J. A. Jowitt, *Victorian Bradford*, City of Bradford 1982, p. 37–62.
M. Edwards, *After Wesley*, Epworth Press 1935, pp. 142–44, 163–71.
M. Edwards, *Methodism and England*, Epworth Press 1943, pp. 45–48.
B. Greaves, Leeds MA Thesis (1961) and Liverpool PhD (1968) on 'Methodism in Yorkshire'.

34. A. Everitt, *The Pattern of Rural Dissent in the Nineteenth Century*, Leicester University Press 1972.
R. Currie, 'A Micro-Theory of Methodist Growth', *WHS* XXXVI, 1967, pp. 65–73.
J. D. Walsh, *The Planting of Methodism in British Society*, WMHS Selly Oak Conference, 1975.
Jackson, *Recollections*, pp. 95–98, 138.
R. W. Dixon, *Life of James Dixon*, WM Conference 1874, pp. 27ff., 51ff., 133ff.
T. Jackson, *Life of Robert Newton*, Mason 1855, pp. 22ff.
Bunting 1, pp. 77–80, Hereford.

35. Gay, op. cit., p. 70–71.

36. Thompson, op. cit., pp. 385–440.
J. D. Walsh, *HMGB* I, pp. 308–315.

37. H. Perkin, *The Origins of Modern English Society 1780–1880*, Routledge and Kegan Paul 1969, pp. 196–208, 340–64.

38. G. F. Nuttall, *The Puritan Spirit*, Epworth Press 1967, pp. 67ff.
Semmel, op. cit., pp. 81–109.
HMGB I, pp. 313–14.

39. Ward, op. cit., pp. 2–53.
HMGB II, pp. 20–35.

40. A. Morey, *The Catholic Subjects of Elizabeth I*, Allen and Unwin 1978.

C. Haigh, *Reformation and Resistance in Tudor Lancashire*, Cambridge University Press 1975, pp. 247ff.

C. Haigh, 'From Monopoly to Minority: Catholicism in Early Modern England', *Transactions of the Royal Historical Society* 1981, pp. 129ff.

A. Pritchard, *Catholic Loyalism in Elizabethan England*, Scolar Press 1979, pp. 3–10, 192ff.

E. Rose, *Cases of Conscience*, Cambridge University Press 1975.

41. E. Calamy, *Historical Account of My Own Life* (2 Vols.) ed. J. T. Rutt, London 1829, Vol. I, p. 473.

C. Hill, 'Occasional Conformity', *Reformation, Conformity and Dissent: Essays in honour of Geoffrey Nuttall* ed. R. Buick Knox, Epworth Press 1977, pp. 199–220.

42. T. Shaw, *A History of Cornish Methodism*, Truro 1967, p. 31ff., 125–26.

43. E. Duffy, *Peter and Jack: Roman Catholics and Dissent in Eighteenth Century England*, Dr. Williams's Trust 1982, p. 13.

Bossy, op. cit., pp. 364ff.

44. J. Obelkevich, *Religion and Rural Society: South Lindsey 1825–1875*, Oxford University Press 1976, p. 230.

45. J. Bossy, op. cit., p. 137.

E. H. Fowler, *Life of Henry Hartley Fowler, First Viscount Wolverhampton*, Hutchinson 1912, pp. 525–70, 688.

46. B. L. Manning, *The Protestant Dissenting Deputies*, Cambridge University Press 1952, pp. 286–332.

W. G. Addison, *Religious Equality in Modern England*, SPCK 1944, pp. 117–21.

47. O. Chadwick, *The Victorian Church*, Part I, Black 1966, p. 327.

48. *NHM* I, pp. 40ff.

A. Outler (ed), *John Wesley*, Oxford University Press, 1964, p. 119.

Cf. also B. Frost and L. Pyle, *Dissent and Descent: Essays on Methodism and Roman Catholicism*, Epworth Press 1975.

49. O. Chadwick, *The Popes and European Revolution*, Oxford University Press 1981 p. 159.

W. Stark, *The Sociology of Religion* III, Routledge and Kegan Paul 1967, pp. 302ff.

J. Kent, 'Christian Theology in the Eighteenth to Twentieth Centuries', *History of Christian Doctrine* ed. H. Cunliffe-Jones with B. Drewery, T. and T. Clark 1978, p. 478.

50. Chadwick, op. cit., p. 161.

B. Trinder, *The Industrial Revolution in Shropshire*, Phillimore 1973, pp. 274ff.

51. Bossy, op. cit., Ch. 13, pp. 295ff.

52. Ibid., Ch. 14, pp. 323ff.

D. Holmes, *More Roman than Rome*, Burns and Oates 1978, pp. 101–102.

53. Bossy, op. cit., pp. 250ff, 356.

54. J. H. Ritson, *The Romance of Primitive Methodism*, Dalton 1909, Ch. XI. Did the use of the word 'manse' derive from the Free Kirk of Scotland?

55. Holmes, op. cit., p. 22.

Bossy, op. cit., pp. 298ff.

56. Bossy, op. cit., p. 298.

57. Ibid., p. 321.

58. Ibid., pp. 338ff.

59. J. Vickers, *Thomas Coke*, Epworth Press 1969, pp. 53ff.

E. B. Perkins, *Methodist Preaching Houses and the Law*, Epworth Press 1952.

60. Bossy, op. cit., p. 347.

61. *HMGB* III, pp. 279–308 148–52.

H. O. Evennett, 'Catholics and Universities 1850–1950',*The English Catholics 1850–1950* ed. G. A. Beck, Burns and Oates 1950, pp. 42–85.

H. O. Evennett, *The Catholic Schools in England and Wales*, Cambridge University Press 1944.

M. Davies (ed), *Newman and Education*, Spode House 1980,

V. A. McClelland, *Cardinal Manning*, Oxford University Press 1962, especially pp. 87ff.

V. A. McClelland, *Roman Catholics and Higher Education 1880–1903*, Oxford University Press 1973.

Holmes, op.cit., pp. 155ff., chapter on Manning.

H. F. Mathews, *Methodism and the Education of the People*, Epworth Press 1949.

J. H. Rigg, *Essays for the Times*, London 1866.

62. A. W. W. Dale, *The Life of R. W. Dale of Birmingham*, Hodder and Stoughton 1899, p. 496.

D. Price Hughes, *Life of Hugh Price Hughes*, Hodder and Stoughton 1904, p. 130.

63. D. Baker, *Partnership in Excellence: The Leys School, Cambridge, 1875–1975*, Governors of Leys School Cambridge 1975.

64. Holmes, op. cit., p. 233.

65. Beck, op. cit., pp. 291ff.

66. E. R. Wickham, *Church and People in an Industrial City*, Lutterworth Press 1957, p. 107.

67. M. Piette, *John Wesley in the Evolution of Protestantism*, Sheed and Ward 1938. *HMGB*, I, pp. 83–111.

G. Wakefield, *Methodist Devotion*, Epworth Press 1966.

68. Since this book was written, David Hempton's *Methodism and Politics in British Society 1750–1850*, Hutchinson 1984, has outlined Wesley's attitude to Catholicism – one of tolerant antagonism despite *The Letter to a Roman Catholic* of 1749. Challoner wrote in 1760 a *Caveat against the Methodists*. The parallels I have indicated do not imply agreement or friendship. This was not on the horizon at all.

Hempton, op. cit., pp. 33–49, especially 42–43.

Cf. also E. Duffy (Ed), *Challoner and His Church*, Darton, Longman and Todd 1981, pp. 90–111.

4. The Theological Legacy of John Wesley

1. D. G. Miller et al., *P. T. Forsyth, the Man, the Preachers' Theologian: Prophet for the 20th century*, Pittsburgh, USA 1981, p. 63.

2. Cf. R. Williams, *Resurrection*, Darton, Longman and Todd 1982, p. 4.

3. H. Butterfield, *The Whig Interpretation of History*, Bell 1931, pp. 9–10.

4. E.g. in T. Runyon (ed), *Sanctification and Liberation*, Nashville, USA, 1981, pp. 9–63.

Cf. R. Anstey, *The Christian*, Vol. 9, 1975, 'Lordship of Christ in History'.

5. W. Warburton, *Works*, Vol. 8, 1811, p. 380.

6. H. Bett, *The Spirit of Methodism*, Epworth Press 1937, pp. 127, 144, 165.
   H. B. Workman, 'The Place of Methodism in the life and thought of the church', *NHM* I, 1909, pp. 3–71, especially p. 27.
   G. Eayrs, *John Wesley: Christian Philosopher and Church Founder*, Epworth Press 1926, pp. 15–198.
7. K. Barth, *The Theology of Schleiermacher*, T. and T. Clark 1982. It is significant that Barth spends more time on Schleiermacher's sermons than on his systematics.
8. G. C. Cell, *The Rediscovery of John Wesley*, Henry Holt, New York 1935, p. 347.
9. The statement goes back to W. B. Fitzgerald, Secretary of the Wesley Guild, and is dated 1903. It became popular in the 1920s along with 'Wesley Day' etc.
10. J. M. Turner, *Introducing Theology*, Epworth Press 1975, pp. 78–85.
    J. M. Turner, 'John Wesley, People's Theologian', *One in Christ*, December 1978, pp. 328–39.
11. K. E. Rowe (ed), *The Place of Wesley in the Christian Tradition*, USA, 1976, pp. 15ff. Outler claims a long line of tradition stemming back to the pre-reformation tradition of English nominalism.
    G. F. Nuttall, *The Puritan Spirit*, Epworth Press 1967, pp. 67–80.
    P. M. Minus (ed), *Methodism's Destiny in an Ecumenical Age*, Abingdon, USA, 1969, pp. 56ff.
12. Four articles of the Remonstrance of 1605. H. Bettenson, *Document of the Christian Church*, Oxford University Press 1967, pp. 268–69.
13. Cited in Bett, op. cit., p. 153.
14. Cited in R. N. Flew, *The Idea of Perfection in Christian Perfection*, Oxford University Press 1934, pp. 340–41.
15. E. G. Rupp, *Methodism in Relation to Protestant Tradition*, Epworth Press 1951, p. 20.
16. G. Lawton, *Within the Rock of Ages: Life and Work of Augustus Montague Toplady*, Clarke 1983, pp. 95ff.
    Tract entitled 'An Old Fox Tarr'd and Feathered', London 1775.
    B. Semmel, *The Methodist Revolution*, Heinemann 1974, pp. 23–55.
17. *Methodist Hymn Book* no. 339, cf. nos. 49, 75, 114.
18. Nuttall, op. cit., p. 78.
19. *Letters* IV, p. 144, 1761.
    Melville Horne, *An Investigation of the Definition of Justifying Faith*, Longman 1809, pp. 1–4, 7–10, 12, 14.
    Semmel, op. cit., p. 100.
20. *Letters* IV, p. 298. To John Newton.
21. L. Newbigin, *International Review of Mission*, July 1979, pp. 301–12.
22. L. Tyerman, *Wesley's Designated Successor*, Hodder and Stoughton 1882 p. 412.
23. W. R. Davies and R. Peart, *Methodism and the Charismatic Movement*, Dent, 1973.
24. R. G. Jones and A. J. Wesson, *Towards a Radical Church*, Epworth Press 1970, pp. 65ff. A very penetrating and important chapter in an uneven book.
    For a sharper view: J. J. Vincent, *Christ and Methodism*, Epworth Press 1965.
25. *Letters* VIII, p. 238, 1790.

26. A. Outler, *John Wesley*, Oxford University Press 1964, pp. 9–10.
    J. A. Newton, 'Perfection and Spirituality in the Methodist Tradition', *Church Quarterly*, October 1970, pp. 95–103.
27. Outler, op. cit., p. 31.
    Cf. A. Outler, *Preface* to A. Whaling, *John and Charles Wesley*, SPCK 1981, p. xv.
28. W. R. Cannon, 'Perfection', *LQHR*, July 1959, p. 217.
29. *Works* 14, p. 305.
30. E. G. Rupp, 'The Plant of Salvation. Wesley's Chapel', lecture 1982.
    E. G. Rupp, *Principalities and Powers*, Epworth Press 1952, p. 82.
31. Flew, op. cit., pp. 332–36.
    F. Greeves, *The Meaning of Sin*, Epworth Press 1957, p. 167ff.
32. E. B. Pusey, *Letter to the Archbishop of Canterbury*, Oxford 3rd edn 1842.
33. P. T. Forsyth, *God the Holy Father*, Independent Press 1957 edn, pp. 102–117.
34. V. Taylor, *Forgiveness and Reconciliation*, Macmillan 1941, p. 154.
35. Especially F. D. Bruner, *A Theology of the Holy Spirit*, Hodder and Stoughton 1970.
    J. D. G. Dunn, *Baptism in the Holy Spirit*, SCM Press 1970.
    J. D. G. Dunn, *Jesus and the Spirit*, SCM Press 1975.
36. R. Watson, *Works* XII, London 1834–7, pp. 27–165.
    J. Hannah, *Introductory lectures on Theology*, Wesleyan Methodist Conference Office n.d., pp. 368ff.
    W. B. Pope, *A Compendium of Christian Theology*, Vol. 3, WM Bookroom 1880, pp. 27–100.
    A. Clarke, *Discourses*, Vol. 1, London 2nd edn 1834. *Sermons* VI, X, XI, XIII.
    W. Arthur, *The Tongue of Fire*, London 1856.
    T. Champness, *Plain Talks on Perfection*, Joyful News Bookshop 1887.
    T. Cook, *New Testament Holiness*, Kelly 1902.
    J. A. Beet, *The New Life in Christ*, Hodder and Stoughton 3rd edn 1903.
    S. Chadwick, *The Way to Pentecost*, Hodder and Stoughton 1932.
    S. Chadwick, *The Call to Christian Perfection*, Epworth 1936.
    W. Strawson, 'Methodist Theology 1850–1950', *HMGB* III, pp. 190–92, 213–15, 225–30.
37. Cf. R. Carwardine, *Transatlantic Revivalism: Popular Evangelicalism in Britain and America 1790–1865*, Greenwood 1978.
    J. Kent, *Holding the Fort: Studies in Victorian Revivalism*, Epworth Press 1978. This is highly critical of this tradition. It may not entirely reveal its lasting and profound character. Its impact was very pervasive.
38. H. Lindström, *Wesley and Sanctification*, Stockholm 1946, pp. 188ff.
    R. W. Dale, *The Evangelical Revival and other sermons*, Hodder and Stoughton 1880, pp. 1–40.
39. *NHM* I, p. 389.
40. A. H. Maslow, *Motivation and Personality*, Harper and Row, New York 1970.
    Cf. F. Wright, *Pastoral Care for lay people*, SCM Press 1982, pp. 11–22.
    M. Hill (ed), *Sociological Year Book of Religion in Britain* 5, SCM Press 1972, p. 191.
41. T. C. Oden, *The Intensive Group Experience: The New Pietism*, USA, 1967.

42. G. O'Collins, *The Second Journey*, Paulist Press 1978.

Report on the Commission of the Churches on International Affairs, World Council of Churches, 1969–70.

43. W. E. Sangster, *The Path to Perfection*, Epworth Press 1943, p. 102.

44. St Thomas Aquinas, *Summa Theologica*, Burns and Oates Vol. 30 1972, Vol. 31 1974 especially p. 125.

Cf. P. S. Watson, *Let God be God*, Epworth Press 1947, pp. 52ff.

45. H. O. Evennett, *The Spirit of the Counter Reformation*, Cambridge University Press 1968.

J. Hurstfield (ed), *The Reformation Crisis*, Edward Arnold 1965, p. 62.

K. Rowe, op. cit., pp. 25–33.

P. Schaff, *The Creeds of the Greek and Latin Churches*, New York 1877, pp. 73ff.

J. H. Newman, *Lectures on the Doctrine of Justification*, Rivington 1874, especially Chs. VI–IX.

J. H. Newman, *Parochial and Plain Sermons*, Rivington 1870, Vol. 1, No. 1, pp. 1–14.

Pope, op. cit., pp. 27–100.

W. B. Pope, *A Higher Catechism of Theology*, London 1883, pp. 196ff.

W. B. Pope, *Sermons, Addresses and Charges*, London 1878, pp. 213ff.

46. J. A. Ziesler, *The Meaning of Righteousness in Paul*, Cambridge University Press, 1972.

47. C. Wilson, *Mercantilism*, Historical Association 1958.

E. Heckscher, *Mercantilism*, Allen and Unwin, revised 1955.

F. Braudel, *The Wheels of Commerce*, Collins 1982, pp. 232ff.

48. D. Jenkins, *The British, their Identity and their Religion*, SCM Press 1975, p. 89.

49. Semmel op. cit., pp. 191–98.

R. R. Palmer, *The Age of the Democratic Revolution* I, Princeton, USA 1959, Ch. 1, pp. 1–24.

R. Niebuhr, *Christ and Culture*, Faber and Faber 1952, pp. 173ff., 218–28.

HMGB II, p. 274.

50. L. Colley, *In Defiance of Oligarchy: The Tory Party 1714–1760*, Cambridge University Press 1982.

Semmel, op. cit., pp. 56–80.

J. W. Derry, *English Politics and the American Revolution*, Dent 1976.

F. O'Gorman, *Edmund Burke and his Political Philosophy*, Allen and Unwin 1973.

F. O'Gorman, *The Emergence of the British Two Party System 1760–1832*, Edward Arnold 1982.

51. J. Walsh, 'John Wesley and the Poor', summary of lecture, West Midlands *WHS*, Spring 1980, Vol. 3, No. 5.

52. *Works* XI.

M. L. Edwards, *John Wesley and the Eighteenth Century: A Study of His Social and Political Influence*, Epworth Press 1955 edn.

W. J. Warner, *The Wesleyan Movement in the Industrial Revolution*, Longman 1930.

53. R. E. Davies (ed), *John Scott Lidgett*, Epworth Press 1957.

54. J. Kent, *The Age of Disunity*, Epworth Press 1966, Ch. 5 'Methodism and Politics in the Nineteenth Century'.

H. D. Rack, 'Wesleyan Methodism 1849–1902', *HMGB* III, pp. 142–52.

55. C. W. Williams, *John Wesley's Theology Today*, Epworth Press 1960, pp. 23–38.
    F. Hildebrandt, *Christianity According to the Wesleys*, Epworth Press 1956, p. 12.

5. From Connexion to Denomination

1. M. Weber, *The Protestant Ethic and the Spirit of Capitalism*, Allen and Unwin 1930, especially pp. 95ff.
   M. Weber, *The Sociology of Religion*, Methuen 1965 edn, p. 65f.
   E. Troeltsch, *The Social Teaching of the Christian Churches* (2 vols.), Allen and Unwin 1931, e.g. Vol. 1, pp. 331ff., Vol. 2, pp. 691ff.
2. B. R. Wilson, 'A Typology of Sects', *Sociology of Religion* ed. R. Robertson, Penguin Books 1969, pp. 361ff.
   B. R. Wilson, *Religious Sects*, Weidenfeld and Nicolson 1970.
   B. R. Wilson, *Religion in Sociological Perspective*, Oxford University Press 1982, Ch. 4 'The Sociology of Sects', pp. 89–120.
   J. M. Yinger, *Religion, Sociology and the Individual*, Macmillan, New York, 1957.
   J. M. Yinger, *The Scientific Study of Religion*, Macmillan, New York 1970.
   R. Robertson, *Sociological Interpretation of Religion*, Blackwell 1972, pp. 113ff.
   R. Niebuhr, *The Social Sources of Denominationalism*, Meridian, New York 1929.
   R. Niebuhr, *Christ and Culture*, Faber and Faber 1952.
   M. Hill, *A Sociology of Religion*, Heinemann 1973, pp. 71ff.
   E. Isichei, *Victorian Quakers*, Oxford University Press 1970.
3. L. Pope, *Millhands and Preachers*, Yale University Press, USA 1942, pp. 122ff.
4. R. Niebuhr, *Christ and Culture*, pp. 218–20.
5. H. D. Rack in *HMGB* III, pp. 156ff. An important and penetrating survey.
6. W. W. Dean, 'The Methodist Class Meeting: The Significance of its Decline', *WHS* XLIII, December 1981, pp. 41–48.
   H. D. Rack, 'The Decline of the Class Meeting and the Problem of Church Membership in Nineteenth Century Wesleyanism, *WHS* XXXIX, February 1973, pp. 12–21.
7. D. Martin, 'The Denomination', *British Journal of Sociology*, Vol. XII, No. 1, March 1962, pp. 1–14.
   Also D. Martin, *Pacifism*, Routledge and Kegan Paul 1965.
8. J. Wach, *The Sociology of Religion*, Routledge and Kegan Paul 1947, p. 175.
   Hill, op. cit., pp. 75–77.
9. C. J. Bertrand, 'Le Méthodisme – Province Méconnue de la Communion Anglicane', *Aspects de l'Anglicanisme* ed. M. Simon, Paris 1974, pp. 103–122.
10. Martin, *Pacifism*, p. 211.
    Cf. M. Hill (ed), *A Sociological Year Book of Religion in Britain* 6, SCM Press 1973, pp. 90–99, 'Methodism as a Religious Order'.
11. R. E. Davies, *Methodists and Unity*, Mowbray 1962, p. 18.
12. W. Stark, *The Sociology of Religion*, Vol. IV, Routledge and Kegan Paul 1969, p. 2.

13. E.g. E. P. Sanders (ed), *Jewish and Christian Self Definition* (2 vols.), SCM Press, 1979, 1981.

R. A. Markus, *Christianity in the Roman World*, Thames and Hudson 1974.

14. J. C. Bowmer, *Pastor and People*, Epworth Press 1975, p. 191.

15. P. Mathias, *The First Industrial Nation*, Methuen 1969, p. 186.

E. J. Hobsbawm, *Industry and Empire*, Penguin Books 1968, pp. 21, 86.

J. L. & B. Hammond, *The Town Labourer 1760–1832*, Vol. I, Guild Books 1949 edn, p. 18.

M. L. Edwards, *After Wesley 1791–1851*, Epworth Press 1935, p. 142.

16. W. R. Ward, 'The Cost of Establishment: Church Buildings in Manchester', *Studies in Church History*, Vol. III ed. G. J. Cuming, Leiden 1966, pp. 277–89.

HMGB II, p. 53. W. R. Ward.

D. A. Gowland, *Methodist Secessions*, Manchester University Press 1979, p. 1.

D. G. Wright and J. A. Jowitt (eds), *Victorian Bradford*, Bradford Metropolitan Council 1982.

D. Fraser (ed.), *A History of Modern Leeds*, Manchester University Press 1981.

17. E. R. Wickham, *Church and People in an Industrial City*, Lutterworth Press 1957, p. 80.

18. E. Halévy, *A History of the English People in 1815* 3, Penguin Books 1938, p. 21.

HMGB II, pp. 54–55, W. R. Ward.

R. F. Wearmouth, *Methodism and the Working Class in the Eighteenth Century*, Epworth Press 1945, p. 184. From Report on Act for Building Churches, 1821.

R. F. Wearmouth, *Methodism and Working Class Movements 1800–1850*, Epworth Press 1937, pp. 16–19.

J. L. and B. Hammond, op. cit., Vol. 2, pp. 94–5.

Fraser, op. cit., pp. 250ff.

Wright and Jowitt, op. cit., pp. 37–62.

19. L. F. Church, *More about the Early Methodist People*, Epworth Press 1949, pp. 255ff.

20. W. R. Ward, *Religion and Society in England 1780–1850*, Batsford 1972, p. 10.

Bowmer, op. cit., pp. 27–28.

21. G. Smith, *History of Wesleyan Methodism* 2, 5th edn, Kelly n.d., pp. 84ff., Appendix E, Appendix F.

Bowmer, op. cit., pp. 37ff.

J. Kent, *The Age of Disunity*, Epworth Press 1967, pp. 44–85.

22. Smith, op. cit., pp. 12–14, 45.

Bowmer, op. cit., pp. 20, 26, 37ff.

A. W. Harrison, *The Separation of Methodism from the Church of England*, Epworth Press 1945, p. 38.

W. J. Warner, *The Wesleyan Movement in the Industrial Revolution*, Longman 1930, pp. 198ff.

23. *WHS* VI, pp. 4–5.

24. W. Myles, *Chronological History of the People called Methodists*, London 1813, p. 209.

25. Smith, op. cit., p. 15, from letter of John Pawson 17 May 1791.

26. Smith, op. cit., p. 16.
    WHS, XXXVI, pp. 36ff., 111ff.; XXXIX, pp. 121ff.
    B. L. Semmens, *The Conference after Wesley*, National Pty Ltd, Melbourne 1971.
    J. Vickers, *Thomas Coke*, Epworth Press 1969, p. 201.
27. Wearmouth, *Common People*, p. 127. Quoted from the *Leeds Intelligencer*, May 1792.
28. *Minutes* 1792.
    Smith, op. cit., pp. 16ff.
    Myles, op. cit., pp. 218ff.
    Wesleyan Methodist Magazine, May 1845, p. 217.
29. Smith, op. cit., p. 20. Letter to Rodda, 28 March 1793, Halifax.
30. *WHS* XVII, pp. 136ff.
    A. J. Lambert, *The Chapel on the Hill*, St Stephen's Press, Bristol, 1930.
    R. Burroughs, *Ebenezer 1795–1895*, W. C. Henemans, Bristol 1895.
    Harrison, op. cit., pp. 41ff.
    Bradburn and Kilham Tracts, Hall Collection, Wesley College, Bristol.
31. S. Bradburn, *Are the Methodists Dissenters?* 1792, 2nd edn 1793.
    Bowmer, op. cit., p. 30.
32. Ward, op. cit., p. 23.
33. Ward, op. cit., p. 28.
    Bowmer, op. cit., p. 33.
34. *HMGB* I, p. 304.
35. *Minutes* 1793.
    Harrison, op. cit., pp. 42–44.
    Smith, op. cit., pp. 22ff.
    Ward, op. cit., p. 30.
    Semmens, op. cit., pp. 45ff.
36. Smith, op. cit., p. 24.
37. Harrison, op. cit., p. 44. Quoted from *Life of Kilham*, 1838, pp. 185–86.
38. Ibid., p. 42.
    WHS, XXXIX, p. 122.
39. *Minutes* 1793.
40. A. R. George, 'Ordination in Methodism', *LQHR*, April 1951, pp. 156–69.
41. *WHS* X, p. 73.
42. R. Watson, *Works* V, London 1835, p. 270.
    For another view cf. W. R. Ward, 'The Legacy of John Wesley' *Statesmen, Scholars and Merchants* ed. A. Whiteman et al., Oxford University Press 1973, pp. 323–50.
43. Smith, op. cit., pp. 96–100, Appendix G.
    Bowmer, op. cit., p. 42.
44. Smith, op. cit., p. 101.
    Myles, op. cit., pp. 225ff.
    The phrase does not occur in the *Minutes*.
45. *Minutes* 1794.
    Smith, op. cit., Appendix H.
46. Harrison, op. cit., p. 49.
47. Ward, op. cit., p. 31.
48. *WHS* XVII.
    Lambert, op. cit.

Burroughs, op. cit.

Smith, op. cit., pp.25ff., 103ff.

Harrison, op. cit., pp. 50ff.

49. Foster gives this date. In view of the date of the Trustees' Meeting, could it not have been the previous day?

Cf. J. Vickers, *Thomas Coke*, Epworth Press 1969, pp. 205–217.

50. Smith, op. cit., Appendix C.

51. Smith, op. cit., p. 27.

52. Old King Street Ebenezer was demolished in 1954.

53. Smith, op. cit., pp. 106ff.

54. Vickers, op. cit., p. 209.

The letter to J. King, 25 August 1794, is in Methodist Church Archives.

55. *Wesleyan Methodist Magazine*, 1845, p. 321.

56. In Hall Collection, Bristol.

57. Myles, op. cit., p. 229.

Ward, op. cit., pp. 34–35.

58. Myles, op. cit., p. 220.

Minutes 1795.

59. Smith, op. cit., p. 30.

Minutes 1795.

60. Myles, op. cit., p. 230.

61. *Minutes* 1795.

Smith, op. cit., Appendix D, pp. 699–700.

62. T. H. Barratt, 'The Lord's Supper in Methodism', *LQHR*, April 1923.

63. A. Whiteman et al., (eds), op. cit., pp. 239–40.

64. Vickers, op. cit., pp. 213ff.

Ward, op. cit., p. 37.

65. Bowmer, op. cit., pp. 51–61.

66. Myles, op. cit., p. 229. The New Room is now Methodist property again.

67. *WHS* XVIII, pp. 21–29.

L. F. Church, op. cit., p. 261.

68. J. Walsh, 'Methodism at the End of the Eighteenth Century', *HMGB* I, p. 288.

Cf. Wright and Jowitt, op. cit., pp. 37ff.

Cf. F. F. Bretherton, *Early Methodism in and around Chester*, Philipson and Golder, Chester 1903, pp. 152ff.

69. J. Lyth, *Glimpses of Early Methodism in York*, Sessions, York, 1885, p. 178.

E. V. Chapman, *John Wesley and Co. (Halifax)*, Halifax Printing Co. 1952, pp. 18–19, 33.

A. E. Teale, 'Methodism in Halifax and District 1780–1850', MSc Thesis, Bradford 1976.

70. *WHS* XXIX, p. 178.

G. J. Stevenson, *City Road Chapel*, London 1872, pp. 153–54.

HMGB I, p. 287.

71. John Kent, 'The Wesleyan Methodists to 1849', *HMGB* II, pp. 213–75.

J. M. Turner, 'From Society to Church', *LQHR*, April 1963, pp. 110–115.

H. D. Rack, *The Future of John Wesley's Methodism*, Lutterworth Press 1965, pp. 19ff.

Also *HMGB* III, pp. 119–66.

72. George, op. cit., *LQHR*, April 1951, pp. 156–69.
    Also *HMGB* II, pp. 143–60.
73. N. Harmon (ed), *Encyclopedia of World Methodism*, Vol. 2, Abingdon Press, Nashville, USA 1974, p. 1,835, p. 2,006. Articles by J. M. Turner.
    Bowmer, op. cit., pp. 103ff.
74. John Kent, *Jabez Bunting: The Last Wesleyan*, Epworth Press 1955.
    W. R. Ward, *Bunting* 1, pp. 4–8.
75. G. Wainwright, *Doxology*, Epworth Press 1980, p. 74.
76. J. H. Chamberlayne, 'From Sect to Church', *British Journal of Sociology* XV, 1964, pp. 139–49.
    Minutes 1827, 1833, 1837, 1846, 1878, 1894, 1897.
    F. C. Pritchard, 'Education', *HMGB* III, pp. 279–308.
    B. E. Jones, 'Society and Church in Wesleyan Methodism 1878–93', *WHS* XXXVI, Part 5, 1968, pp. 134–38.
    H. D. Rack, 'Wesleyanism and "the World" in the later Nineteenth Century', *WHS* XLII, Part 2, 1979, pp. 35–55.
77. B. Semmel, *The Methodist Revolution*, Heinemann 1973.
78. J. H. Rigg, *The Relations of John Wesley and the Wesleyan Methodists to the Church of England*, London 1868, pp. 1–15, 29, 60–61.
79. R. Currie, *Methodism Divided*, Faber and Faber 1968, pp. 80–81, 112–40.
    E. R. Wickham, *Church and People in an Industrial City*, Lutterworth Press 1957, p. 270.
80. J. M. Todd, *John Wesley and the Catholic Church*, Hodder and Stoughton 1958, p. 10.
81. J. L. Baxter, 'The Great Yorkshire Revival 1792–6', *Sociological Year Book of Religion* 7, ed. M. Hill, SCM Press 1974.
    J. Kent, *Holding the Fort*, Epworth Press 1978.
    R. Carwadine, *Transatlantic Revivalism: Popular Evangelicalism in Britain and America 1760–1865*, Greenwood 1978.
    J. F. C. Harrison, *The Second Coming. Popular Millenarianism 1780–1850*, Routledge and Kegan Paul 1979.
82. A. S. Peake, *Life of Sir William Hartley*, Hodder and Stoughton 1925.
    G. Milburn, *A School for the Prophets: Origins of Ministerial Training in the Primitive Methodist Church*, Hartley Victoria College, Manchester 1981.
83. J. T. Wilkinson, *Hugh Bourne*, Epworth Press 1952.
84. J. T. Wilkinson, *William Clowes*, Epworth Press 1951.
    William Clowes, *Journal*, reprint 1981.
85. G. F. Nuttall, *The Puritan Spirit*, Epworth Press 1967, pp. 204–213.
86. Carwardine, op. cit., p. 104.
87. Ward, op. cit., p. 52.
88. B. L. Manning, *The Protestant Dissenting Deputies*, Cambridge University Press 1952.
89. E. P. Thompson, *The Making of the English Working Classes*, Penguin Books 1968 edn, pp. 411ff.
    Bunting 1, pp. 61–63. John Stephens, Manchester.
90. E. J. Hobsbawm, *Primitive Rebels*, 1959, pp. 126–49.
91. Ward, op. cit., *HMGB* II, pp. 20–34.
92. J. T. Wilkinson, *Hugh Bourne*, p. 122.
93. J. Obelkevich, *Religion and Rural Society: South Lindsey 1825–1875*, Oxford University Press 1976, pp. 168ff.

94. M. Douglas, *Purity and Danger: An Analysis of Pollution and Tabu*, Routledge and Kegan Paul 1972.
    M. Douglas, *Natural Symbols*, Barrie and Jenkins 1973.
    Teale, op. cit., p. 208.
95. P. Horn, 'Methodism and Agricultural Trade Unionism in Oxfordshire: The 1870s', *WHS* XXXVII, Part 3, 1969, pp. 69–71.
    P. Horn, *Joseph Arch 1826–1919*, Kineton 1971.
    P. Horn, *Labouring Life in the Victorian Countryside*, Gill and Macmillan 1976, pp. 165–66.
96. N. Scotland, *Methodism and the Revolt of the Field: A Study of the Methodist Contribution to Agricultural Trade Unions in East Anglia 1872–1896*, Allan Sutton 1981.
    G. Kitson Clark, *Churchmen and the Condition of England 1832–1885*, Methuen 1973, pp. 239–66.
97. J. Kent, *Holding the Fort*, Epworth Press 1978, p. 41.
98. *WHS* XXXIX, Part 3, 1973, pp. 62–71.
    WHS XXXVII, Part 1, 1969, pp. 2–9.
    WHS XXXVII, Part 2, 1969, p. 58.
    WHS XXXVII, Part 3, 1969, p. 91.
99. H. Perkin, *Origins of Modern English Society 1780–1880*, Routledge and Kegan Paul 1969, pp. 340ff.
100. Obelkevich, op. cit., p. 258.
101. *HMGB* III, pp. 175–77, 328–33.
102. H. McLeod, *Class and Religion in the late Victorian City*, Croom Helm 1974.
     D. B. Clark, 'Aspects of Religious Activity in a Northern Suburb', *Sociological Year Book of Religion in Britain* ed. D. Martin and M. Hill, SCM Press, Vol. 3 1970, pp. 45–64, Vol. 4 1971, pp. 141–59.
103. J. M. Turner, 'Primitive Methodism', *Primitive Methodism from Mow Cop to Peake* ed. C. Dews, Yorkshire Wesleyan Historical Society 1982, pp. 1–15.
     D. Hempton's recent *Methodism and Politics 1750–1850*, Hutchinson 1984, Ch. 3 pp. 55–84 is an admirable summary of the period from 1790 to 1800.

6. *Methodists, Evangelicals and High Churchmen*

1. G. C. Cell, *The Rediscovery of John Wesley*, Henry Holt, New York 1935, p. 347.
2. C. Smyth, 'The Evangelical Movement in Perspective', *Cambridge Historical Journal*, 1943, pp. 160–74.
3. Sydney Smith, *Works*, Longman 1854 edn, pp. 86–87.
4. C. J. Abbey and J. H. Overton, *The English Church in the Eighteenth Century*, Vol. 2, Longman 1878, p. 59.
5. A. W. Harrison, *The Evangelical Revival and Christian Reunion*, Epworth Press 1942, pp.152ff.
6. J. D. Walsh, 'Origins of the Evangelical Revival', *Essays in English Church History* ed. G. V. Bennett and J. D. Walsh, SPCK 1966, pp. 132–62.
   J. D. Walsh, 'The Anglican Evangelicals in the Eighteenth Century', *Aspects de l'Anglicanisme* ed. M. Simon, Paris 1974, pp. 87–102.
   G. C. B. Davies, *The Early Cornish Evangelicals*, SPCK 1951.

M. Hennell, *John Venn and the Clapham Sect*, Lutterworth Press 1958.

J. S. Reynolds, *The Evangelicals at Oxford 1735–1871*, Blackwell 1953.

A. S. Wood, *Thomas Haweis 1731–1820*, SPCK 1957.

A. S. Wood, *The Inextinguishable Blaze*, Paternoster 1960.

Cf. John Kent, *The Age of Disunity*, Epworth Press 1966, pp. 161–67 for a critique.

7. L. E. Elliott Binns, *The Evangelical Movement in the English Church*, Methuen 1928, p. 3.

8. L. E. Elliott Binns, *The Early Evangelicals*, Lutterworth Press 1953, pp. 123, 133.

Hennell, op. cit., pp. 16–17.

9. Davies, op. cit., pp. 215ff.

G. V. Portus, *Caritas Anglicana*, Mowbray 1912.

10. Elliott Binns, *Early Evangelicals*, pp. 121, 215.

J. A. Newton, *John Wesley and the Puritans*, Dr. Williams's Trust 1964.

Cf. J. H. Pruett, *The Parish Clergy under the late Stuarts*, Chicago University Press, USA 1978, for Anglican Puritanism *after* 1662.

11. A. S. Wood, *Inextinguishable Blaze*, pp. 129ff.

P. Toon, *Evangelical Theology 1833–1856*, Marshall, Morgan and Scott 1979, pp. 5, 207ff.

E. Jay, *The Religion of the Heart: Anglican Evangelicalism and the Nineteenth Century Novel*, Oxford University Press 1979, pp. 16ff.

W. J. Conybeare, 'Church Parties', *Edinburgh Review* 2, 1853.

Y. Brilioth, *Evangelicalism and the Oxford Movement*, Oxford University Press 1934, pp. 28–30.

12. Smyth, op. cit.

13. T. Scott, *The Force of Truth* (1779), p. 13. Cited in A. S. Wood, *The Inextinguishable Blaze*, p. 129.

14. A. Knox, *Remains*, Vol. I, James Duncan 1834, pp. 70ff. *Letter* to J. Butterworth, Vol. 4, 1837, p. 105.

15. J. Milner, *Essay on Methodism*. Cited in Elliott Binns, *Early Evangelicals* p. 448.

Cf. Harrison, op. cit., p. 154.

16. A. M. Toplady, Letter to Wesley 1770. Cited in G. R. Balleine, *A History of the Evangelical Party in the Church of England*, Church Book Room Press 1951, p. 40.

17. Toon, op. cit., p. 5.

Cf. D. N. Samuel (ed), *The Evangelical Succession in the Church of England*, Clarke 1979, p. 44. A comparison of J. C. Ryle and J. Stott.

18. J. H. Overton and F. Relton, *The English Church from the Accession of George I to the end of the eighteenth century*, Macmillan 1906, p. 177.

19. Elliott Binns, *Early Evangelicals*, pp. 196ff., 215.

Davies, op. cit., pp. 158ff.

For the theology of the controversy:

cf. A. W. Harrison, *Arminianism*, Duckworth 1937, pp. 185ff.

A. S. Wood, *Inextinguishable Blaze*, pp. 176ff.

20. L. Tyerman, *Wesley's Designated Successor*, Hodder and Stoughton 1982, p. 412.

Cf. R. N. Flew and R. E. Davies (eds), *The Catholicity of Protestantism*, Lutterworth Press 1950, p. 84.

21. *Letters* VII, p. 92; VII, p. 98, 8 January 1782; VII, p. 326.
22. Baker, *Wesley and the Church*, pp. 293–94.
    Letters VII, pp. 326–27.
    Journal VI, p. 518.
23. *Letters* VII, p. 377.
24. N. Sykes, *Church and State in England in the Eighteenth Century*, Cambridge University Press 1934, p. 396.
25. Walsh, op. cit., pp. 92–94.
    Cf. A. Pollard and M. Hennell, *Charles Simeon 1759–1836*, SPCK 1964, pp. 73ff.
    H. E. Hopkins, *Charles Simeon of Cambridge*, Hodder and Stoughton 1977, pp. 173ff.
26. H. C. G. Moule, *Charles Simeon*, 1902, reprinted Inter-Varsity Fellowship 1948, p. 100.
    Journal VII, pp. 39, 337.
    Elliott Binns, *Early Evangelicals* p. 206.
27. R. A. Knox, *Enthusiasm*, Oxford University Press 1950, p. 496.
28. W. R. Ward, 'The Baptists and the Transformation of the Church', *Baptist Quarterly*, Vol. 25, No. 4, October 1973, pp. 167–84.
29. Hennell, op. cit., pp. 16–17, 268.
    Kent, op. cit., p. 167.
    L. Tyerman, *Life and Times of John Wesley* 3, Hodder and Stoughton 1871, pp. 49–50.
30. Baker, *Wesley and the Church*, Ch. XI, pp. 180–217.
    Sykes, op. cit., p. 396.
    Wood, op. cit., pp. 189ff.
31. C. Smyth, *Simeon and Church Order*, Cambridge University Press 1940, p. 6.
32. Davies, op. cit., pp. 88ff.
    Letters III, pp. 221–26.
    F. Baker, *William Grimshaw 1708–1763*, Epworth Press 1963.
    Journal IV, pp. 493–98.
33. *Letters* IV, pp. 160–61.
    Baker, *Wesley and the Church*, p. 186.
34. Tyerman, op. cit. 2, p. 511, quoted from John Pawson.
    Baker, *Wesley and the Church*, pp. 192–93.
35. Elliott Binns, *Early Evangelicals* p. 132.
36. E. V. Chapman, *Still the Light Shines: Centenary of King Cross Methodist Church, Halifax*, 1978.
37. Smyth, *Simeon and Church Order*, Chs. 5, 6, pp. 202ff.
38. Davies, op. cit., p. 212.
    Journal, V, p. 185n.
    WHS IV, pp. 191–92, 4 September 1766.
39. Smyth, *Simeon and Church Order*, Ch. 5 (Berridge), Ch. 6 (Simeon).
    Walsh, op. cit., pp. 98ff.
40. Smyth, *Simeon and Church Order*, pp. 251, 253, 256.
    Life and Times of Lady Huntingdon 2, pp. 45, 422–24.
41. W. Carus, *Memoirs of the Rev. C. Simeon*, Deighton 1847, p. 139.
42. Smyth, *Simeon and Church Order*, p. 250.
43. H. C. G. Moule, *The Evangelical School in the Church of England*, 1901, p. 12.
    Smyth, *Simeon and Church Order*, pp. xv, 289.

G. O. Trevelyan, *Life of Lord Macaulay* I, Longman 1908, p. 68.

44. Hennell, op. cit., p. 266.

H. C. G. Moule, *Charles Simeon*, p. 190.

45. W. R. Ward, *Religion and Society in England 1780–1850*, Batsford 1972, pp. 5, 40, 51–52.

G. F. A. Best, 'The Evangelicals and the Established Church in the Early Nineteenth Century', *Journal of Theological Studies* X, 1959, pp. 63–78, especially p. 78.

G. F. A. Best, 'The Protestant Constitution and its Supporters', *Transactions of the Royal Historical Society*, 5th Series, VIII, 1958.

G. F. A. Best, 'The Whigs and Church Establishment', *History* XLV, 1960, pp. 103–18.

G. F. A. Best, 'Religious Difficulties in National Education in England 1800–1870', *Cambridge Historical Journal*, Vol. XII, pp. 155–73.

46. E. M. Howse, *Saints in Politics: The Clapham Sect and the Growth of Freedom*, Routledge and Kegan Paul 1971 edn, p. 114n.

Ward, op. cit., p. 5.

Elliott Binns, *Early Evangelicals*, p. 448.

47. Henry Martyn, *Journals* etc., ed. Wilberforce, Vol. I, p. 163.

48. Elliott Binns, *Early Evangelicals*, p. 214.

L. F. Church, *More about the Early Methodist People*, Epworth Press 1949, pp. xii, 1–56.

R. A. Buchanan, 'Methodism and the Evangelical Revival: An Interpretation', *Anglican–Methodist Relations: Some Institutional Factors* ed. W. F. S. Pickering, Darton, Longman and Todd 1961, pp. 37–57.

Davies, op. cit., Chs. V, VI.

49. W. Cowper, *Poems*, Vol. 1, 1792.

50. E. Halévy, *A History of the English People in 1815*, Penguin Books 1938, p. 49.

51. W. J. Warner, *The Wesleyan Movement in the Industrial Revolution*, Longman 1930, p. 198.

52. The literature here is vast. The following are useful summaries:

R. Coupland, *William Wilberforce*, Oxford University Press 1923.

R. Coupland, *The British Anti-Slavery Movement*, Thornton Butterworth 1933.

Howse, op. cit.

R. Anstey, *The Atlantic Slave Trade and British Abolition 1760–1810*, Macmillan 1975.

53. *Works* XI, pp. 56–76.

54. *Letters* VIII, p. 265.

55. *Wesley Studies*, 1903, p. 190 cited in M. L. Edwards, *After Wesley*, Epworth Press 1935, p. 67.

56. Edwards, op. cit., pp. 68–69.

57. Howse, op. cit., pp. 131–35, 180–81.

58. Balleine, op. cit., p. 126.

59. Anstey, op. cit., pp. 157ff. A most illuminating survey.

60. Cited in E. J. Brailsford, *Richard Watson*, Culley n.d., p. 68.

61. G. G. Findlay and W. W. Holdsworth, *History of the Methodist Missionary Society 1921–4*, Vol. 2, Epworth Press 1921, pp. 93ff.

62. B. Semmel, *The Methodist Revolution*, Heinemann 1974, pp. 146–98.

J. Kent, 'The Wesleyan Methodists to 1849', *HMGB* II, pp. 274–75.

G. F. A. Best, 'Evangelicalism and the Victorians', *The Victorian Crisis of Faith* ed. A. Symondson, SPCK 1970, pp. 37–56.

Minutes 1825, 1830, 1833.

63. C. Northcott, *Slavery's Martyr: John Smith of Demerara and the Evangelical Movement 1817–1824*. Epworth Press 1976.

Coupland, *Wilberforce*, pp. 487–90.

64. Edwards, op. cit., p. 72.

Semmel, op. cit., pp. 79–80.

Ward, op. cit., pp. 128–29.

Bunting 2, pp. 17–19. Letter from Sadler to Bunting.

65. *Bunting* 2, p. 28.

Semmel, op. cit., p. 79.

66. Ibid., p. 180, for missionary enterprise in general.

Cf. M. Warren, *Social History and Christian Mission*, SCM Press 1967.

M. Warren, *The Missionary Movement from Britain in Modern History*, SCM Press 1965.

67. E. A. Payne, *The Free Church Tradition in the Life of England*, SCM Press 1944, p. 99.

G. F. Nuttall, *The Puritan Spirit*, Epworth Press 1967, pp. 67–80.

For early Methodist endeavours:

N. A. Birtwhistle, 'Methodist Missions', *HMGB* III, pp. 1–116.

68. A. S. Wood, *Thomas Haweis*, for one of the Anglican founding fathers of the LMS.

R. Lovett, *History of the LMS 1795–1895*, London 1899, pp. 5, 21, 49.

69. Cited in Smyth, op. cit., p. 294.

70. Balleine, op. cit., pp. 126ff.

71. E. Stock, *History of the CMS* 1, London 1899, p. 64.

72. Ibid., p. 71.

73. *WHS* XLII, Part 3, pp. 81–86.

Findlay and Holdsworth, op. cit. 1, pp. 37, 56ff.

Minutes 1818.

W. Fox, *History of Wesleyan Missions in West Africa*, 1850. Cited in C. P. Groves, *The Planting of Christianity in Africa* 1, Lutterworth 1948, pp. 197ff.

74. Balleine, op. cit., pp. 123, 131–32.

Stock, op. cit., p. 154.

A. Cruse, *The Englishman and his books in the early nineteenth century*, Harrap 1930, pp. 66–69.

L. James, *Fiction for the Working Man 1830–1850*, Oxford University Press 1963.

R. K. Webb, *The British Working Class Reader 1790–1848*, Allen and Unwin 1955.

75. W. Canton, *History of the British and Foreign Bible Society 1904–10* (5 vols.), London 1904.

Balleine, op. cit., pp. 132ff.

76. Church, op. cit., pp. 19ff.

77. Canton, op. cit., pp. 356ff.

Stock, op. cit., pp. 279–80.

78. J. B. B. Clarke, *Life of Adam Clarke* 2, Clarke 1833, pp. 98ff.

79. E. K. Brown, *The Fathers of the Victorians: The Age of Wilberforce*, Cambridge University Press 1961.
　　Cf. J. Kent, 'The Study of Ecclesiastical History Since 1930', *The Pelican Guide to Modern Theology*, Vol. 2 ed. J. Danielou, Penguin Books 1969, pp. 334–36.

80. M. J. Quinlan, *Victorian Prelude*, Columbia University Press, New York 1941.
　　M. Jaeger, *Before Victoria*, Chatto and Windus 1956.
　　H. Perkin, *The Origins of Modern English Society*, Routledge and Kegan Paul 1969, pp. 218ff., 271ff.
　　Best, op. cit., *The Victorian Crisis of Faith* ed. Symondson, p. 44.
　　J. M. Turner, 'Methodist Religion', *HMGB* II, pp. 97–112.

81. Baileine, op. cit., pp. 143–45.
　　Coupland, op. cit., p. 55.
　　Quinlan, op. cit., p. 204.
　　J. H. Overton, *The English Church in the Nineteenth Century 1800–1833*, Longman 1894, pp. 282–83.
　　H. Pearson, *The Smith of Smiths*, Penguin Books 1948, p. 69.

82. W. Wilberforce, *A Practical View of the Prevailing System of Professed Christians*, Ancient and Modern Library edn n.d., p. 256.

83. *NHM* I, p. 389.
　　Quinlan, op. cit., pp. 226, 235ff.

84. Hare and Bradburn Pamphlets (Hall Collection, Wesley College, Bristol), Methodism set forth and defended, 1792.

85. F. D. Maurice, *Theological Essays*, London 1853, p. xvi.
　　Cf. A. R. Vidler, *The Theology of F. D. Maurice*, SCM Press 1948, p. 37.

86. Y. Brilioth, *The Anglican Revival: Studies in the Oxford Movement*, Longman 1925, p. 41.
　　V. F. Storr, *Development of English Theology in the Nineteenth Century*, Longman 1913, pp. 63–78.
　　B. M. G. Reardon, *From Coleridge to Gore*, Longman 1971, pp. 23–31.

87. Moule, op. cit., p. 106. From the *Excellency of the Liturgy*, 1811.
　　For later Evangelical thinking:
　　cf. Toon, op. cit.
　　P. Jagger, *Clouded Witness*, T. and T. Clark 1982.

88. H. Davies, *Worship and Theology in England: From Watts and Wesley to Maurice 1690–1850*, Oxford University Press 1961, pp. 223–27.
　　M. Hennell, *Sons of the Prophets*, SPCK 1979, p. 40ff.

89. Brilioth, op. cit., pp. 45–55.
　　Yet cf. H. P. Liddon, *Life of E. B. Pusey* I, Longman 1894 edn, pp. 250–52.

90. P. Toon, 'Evangelicals and Tractarians Then and Now', *Churchman*, Vol. 93, No. 1, pp. 29–38.
　　Brilioth, op. cit., p. 30.

91. W. E. Dutton, *The Eucharistic Manuals of John and Charles Wesley*, Bull, Simmons and Co. 1871.
　　H. W. Holden, *John Wesley in Company with High Churchmen*, Church Press 1869.
　　F. Hockin, *John Wesley and Modern Methodism*, Rivington 1875, 1887.
　　R. Denny Urlin, *The Churchman's Life of Wesley*, SPCK 1886.

Cf. J. E. Rattenbury, *The Eucharistic Hymns of John and Charles Wesley*, Epworth Press 1948, pp. 86–100.

92. W. E. H. Lecky, *History of England in the Eighteenth Century* 2, Longman 1878, p. 627.

93. W. J. Conybeare, 'Church Parties', *Edinburgh Review* 98, 1853, pp. 273–342.
W. E. Gladstone, *Gleanings of Past Years* VII, London 1879, p. 215.
Howse, op. cit., pp. 172ff.
Liddon, op. cit., p. 255.
Balleine, op. cit., pp. 16–67.

94. Hennell, *Sons of the Prophets*, p. 14.
P. Toon, *Evangelical Theology 1833–1856*, Marshall, Morgan and Scott 1979, p. 2.

95. A. Russell, *The Clerical Profession*, SPCK 1980.
B. Heeney, *A Different Kind of Gentleman. Parish Clergy as Professional Men in Early and Mid Victorian England*, Archon Press, USA 1976.
D. McClatchey, *Oxfordshire Clergy 1777–1869*, Oxford University Press 1960.
P. Elliott, *The Sociology of the Professions*, Macmillan 1972.

96. Best, op. cit., *The Victorian Crisis of Faith* ed. Symondson, pp. 42–43.

97. Balleine, op. cit., pp. 148ff., 206ff., especially 220–21.
D. E. H. Mole, 'Challenge to the Church. Birmingham 1815–65', *The Victorian City* 2 ed. H. J. Dyos and M. Wolff, Routledge and Kegan Paul 1973, pp. 815–36.
D. E. H. Mole, 'J. C. Miller: A Victorian Rector of Birmingham', *Journal of Ecclesiastical History* XVII, 1966, pp. 95–103.
D. E. H. Mole, 'The Evangelical Revival in Birmingham', *West Midlands WHS*, April and December 1975, pp. 89–94, 99–106.

98. R. W. Dale, *Life and Letters of J. A. James*, Nisbet 1861.

99. *Bunting* 1, 6 June 1829, p. 208.

100. A. Kirk-Smith, *William Thomson, Archbishop of York 1819–90*, SPCK 1958, pp. 27ff.

101. Balleine, op. cit., p. 201.
Bunting 2, pp. 332–38.
E. R. Norman, *Anti-Catholicism in England*, Routledge and Kegan Paul 1968.
D. Bowen, *The Protestant Crusade in England 1800–1860*, Gill and Macmillan 1978.
G. F. A. Best, 'Popular Protestantism in Victorian Britain', *Ideas and Institutions of Victorian Britain* ed. R. Robson, Bell 1867, pp. 115ff.

102. H. D. Rack, 'Domestic Visitation. A Chapter in Nineteenth Century Evangelism', *Journal of Ecclesiastical History* 24, No. 4, October 1973, pp. 357–76.

103. Ward, op. cit., pp. 116ff., 206–35, especially p. 219.
D. N. Hempton, 'Methodism and Anti-Catholic Politics 1800–46', St Andrew's PhD Thesis, 1977.
Hennell, op. cit., pp. 47–49.
P. M. H. Bell, *Disestablishment in Ireland and Wales*, SPCK 1969.
W. H. Mackintosh, *Disestablishment and Liberation*, Epworth Press 1972.

104. N. Sykes, *Old Priest and New Presbyter: The Anglican Attitudes to Episcopacy*,

Presbyterianism and Papacy since the Reformation, Cambridge University Press 1956.

N. Sykes, *William Wake: Archbishop of Canterbury* (2 Vols.), Cambridge University Press 1957.

N. Sykes, 'Ecumenical Movements in Great Britain in the Seventeenth and Eighteenth Centuries', *A History of the Ecumenical Movement*, ed. R. Rouse and S. C. Neill, SPCK 1967, pp. 123–66.

Cf. A. J. Mason, *The Church of England and Episcopacy*, Cambridge University Press 1914.

For a more recent assessment of the Anglican Reformation:

P. Avis, *The Church in the Theology of the Reformers*, Marshall, Morgan and Scott 1981.

105. N. Sykes, *The Church of England and the Non-Episcopal Churches in the Sixteenth and Seventeenth Centuries*, SPCK 1948, pp. 12, 33ff.

Sykes, *Wake* 2, pp. 1–88.

Sykes, *Old Priest*, p. 83.

106. Cited in H. Townsend, *The Claims of the Free Churches*, Hodder and Stoughton 1949, p. 142.

107. J. W. Hunkin, *Episcopal Ordination and Confirmation in relation to Intercommunion and Reunion*, Heffer 1929, p. 105.

Clarke, op. cit. I, pp. 96, 165; III, pp. 231–33.

N. Sykes, *Church and State in England in the Eighteenth Century*, Cambridge University Press 1934, pp. 92–146, especially pp. 119–20.

108. Jeremy Taylor, *Works* 5, 1862, p. 656.

Daniel Waterland, *Works* 7 ed. by van Mildert, 1823, p. 393.

Cf. *The Theology of Christian Initiation*, Archbishops' Commission 1948.

109. For Wesley's teaching here:

cf. *WHS* XXXII, 1960, pp. 121ff., 153ff., (B. J. N. Galliers, 'Baptism in the Writings of John Wesley').

B. Holland, *Baptism in Early Methodism*, Epworth Press 1970.

O. Borgen, *John Wesley on the Sacraments*, World Methodist Church, Zürich 1972.

On admission to Holy Communion:

J. C. Bowmer, *The Sacrament of the Lord's Supper in Early Methodism*, Black 1951, pp. 103–122.

J. C. Bowmer, *The Lord's Supper in Methodism 1791–1960*, Epworth Press 1961, pp. 23–26, 42.

D. M. Baillie and J. Marsh (eds), *Intercommunion*, SCM Press 1952, p. 99.

110. Cited from Warburton and Pretyman in

Hunkin, op. cit., pp. 62–63, 71, 105.

Sykes, *Old Priest*, pp. 155ff., 164.

Rouse and Neill, op. cit., p. 161.

111. Baillie and Marsh, op. cit., pp. 93–94.

112. Smyth, op. cit., p. 301.

113. Overton, op. cit., p. 24.

Storr, op. cit., p. 79.

114. Mason, op. cit., p. 411.

115. S. Horsley, *Works* 3, 1845, pp. 27, 105.

B. Porteus, *Works* 2, 1811, p. 270.

Liddon, *Pusey* 1, pp. 257–58.

116. Mason, op. cit., pp. 425–26.
117. A. B. Webster, *Joshua Watson 1771–1855*, SPCK 1954.
118. A. Knox, *Remains* 3, 1816. *Letter* to Adam Clarke, p. 489; *Letter* to Hannah More, pp. 129ff.; 'On the Situation and Prospect of the Established Church', pp. 53ff., 130.
    Cf. J. B. Ewens, *The Three Hermits: Short studies in Christian Antiquity, Methodism and Tractarianism*, Epworth Press 1956.
    Thirty Years' Correspondence between John Jebb, Bishop of Limerick, and Alexander Knox (2 vols.), London 1836.
    Brilioth, op. cit., Appendix I, pp. 331–42.

7. *The Rise of the Nonconformist Platform*

1. R. M. McIver, *The Modern State*, Oxford University Press 1926, p. 22.
    J. N. Figgis, *Churches in the Modern State*, Longmans 1913.
    O. Chadwick, *The Victorian Church* I, Black 1966, pp. 3, 6, 45.
    T. Arnold, *Principles of Church Reform*, SPCK new edn 1962.
    For background:
    G. F. A. Best, *Temporal Pillars. Queen Anne's Bounty, the Ecclesiastical Commission, and the Church of England*, Cambridge University Press 1964, Ch. 4, 'Church, State and Society 1770–1840', pp. 137–84.
    G. Kitson Clark, *Churchmen and the Condition of England 1832–1885*, Methuen 1973, pp. 24–55.
    G. I. T. Machin, *Politics and the Churches in Great Britain 1832 to 1868*, Oxford University Press 1977, Ch. 1, pp. 1–27.
    E. R. Norman, *Church and Society in England 1770–1970*, Oxford University Press 1976, pp. 15–40.
2. A. R. Vidler, *Prophecy and Papacy: A Study of Lamennais, The Church and Revolution*, SCM Press 1959.
    Machin, op. cit., pp. 75–147.
3. Cited in F. R. Salter, 'Political Nonconformity in the 1830s', *Proceedings of the Royal Historical Society* 5th Series III, 1953.
4. Cited in A. Lincoln, *Some Political and Social Ideas of English Dissent 1767–1800* Cambridge University Press 1938, pp. 14, 20.
5. For the Revolutionary Era:
    J. D. Walsh, *New Cambridge Modern History*, Vol. 9, ed. C. W. Crawley, Cambridge University Press 1965, Ch. 6.
    J. S. McManners, *The French Revolution and the Church*, SPCK 1969.
    R. R. Palmer, *The Age of the Democratic Revolution*, Princeton University Press, USA 1959, Vol. 1, especially pp. 3–320; Vol. 2, 1964.
    R. B. Barlow, *Citizenship and Conscience: A Study in the Theory and Practice of Religious Toleration in England during the 18th century*, Pennsylvania Press, USA 1962.
    A. Goodwin, *The Friends of Liberty: The English Democratic Movement in the Age of the French Revolution*, Hutchinson 1979, Chapter on the Dissenting Interest, pp. 65–98.
    P. A. Brown, *The French Revolution in English History*, Allen and Unwin 1918.
    A. Cobban (ed), Debate on the French Revolution, Kaye 1950.
    U. Henriques, *Religious Toleration in England 1787–1833*, Routledge and Kegan Paul 1961.

6. Lincoln, op. cit., pp. 29ff.

 B. L. Manning, *The Protestant Dissenting Deputies*, Cambridge University Press 1952, pp. 53ff., 453ff.

 R. W. Davis, *Dissent in Politics 1780–1830: The Political Life of William Smith M.P.*, Epworth Press 1971, pp. 51ff.

 Goodwin, op. cit., pp. 65–98.

 J. C. Bolam et al., *The English Presbyterians*, Allen and Unwin 1968, pp. 219ff.

7. W. Wordsworth, *Prelude* XI, l. 108.

8. For citations: Brown, op. cit., pp. 38–39.

 R. Bartel, *Liberty and Terror in England: Reactions to the French Revolution*, Extracts, D. C. Heath, Boston, USA 1965.

 R. Hall, *Works*, Vol. 3, 1873 edn, p. 172.

 A. Briggs, *The Age of Improvement 1783–1867*, Longman 1959, pp. 128ff.

9. A. Halévy, *History of the English People in 1815* 3, Penguin Books 1938 edn, p. 49.

10. Halévy, op. cit. 3, p. 49.

11. Manning, op. cit., pp. 455–56, cf. Davis, op. cit., pp. 51ff. Davis is suspicious of the rhetoric of loyalty which he thinks Manning takes too literally. Manning disliked Unitarianism intensely.

12. Cited in Goodwin, op. cit., p. 80, cf. Henriques, op. cit., pp. 59–67.

 Davis, op. cit., 44–76.

 W. Cowper, *Expostulation*, lines 376–79.

13. Priestley, *Letters* to Burke, p. 84, cited in S. C. Carpenter, *Church and People 1789–1889*, SPCK 1933, p. 10.

 Cf. B. Willey, *The Eighteenth Century Background*, Penguin Books 1965 edn, Ch. 10, 'Joseph Priestley and the Socinian Moonlight'.

14. S. Maccoby, *English Radicalism 1786–1832*, Allen and Unwin 1955, p. 444.

15. R. B. Rose, *The Priestley Riots: Past and Present* 18, pp. 68–88.

16. E. P. Thompson, *The Making of the English Working Class*, Penguin Books 1968 edn p. 79.

 W. L. Mathieson, *England in Transition 1789–1832*, Longman 1920, p. 51.

17. D. M. Thompson (ed), *Nonconformity in the Nineteenth Century*, Routledge and Kegan Paul 1972, p. 99.

 J. D. Walsh, 'Methodism at the End of the Eighteenth Century', *HMGB* I, pp. 304ff.

 Norman, op. cit., pp. 75–77, for similar Anglican views.

 Cf. E. R. Taylor, *Methodism and Politics 1791–1851*, Cambridge University Press 1935, pp. 12, 114, 132–33. 'Liberals' always felt the 'rule' was stacked against them.

18. *Journal* VIII, p. 37n.

 Letters VIII, p. 196.

19. E. Burke. *Reflections on the French Revolution 1790*, Everyman edn 1950, p. 93.

 G. Rupp, *Thomas Jackson*, Epworth Press 1954, p. 39.

20. Taylor, op. cit., p. 52.

 D. M. Thompson, op. cit., p. 37.

 Minutes 1792, 1797.

 Cf. A. Cobban, *Edmund Burke and the Revolt against the Eighteenth Century*, Allen and Unwin 1929, for philosophical background.

21. G. Smith, *History of Wesleyan Methodism* 2, Kelly 1862, pp. 39, 41, 61–82.

NHM I, pp. 492ff.

HMGB II, pp. 280–94.

22. Taylor, op. cit., p. 77.

23. B. Semmel, *The Methodist Revolution*, Heinemann 1974, pp. 5ff.

24. W. J. Warner, *The Wesleyan Movement in the Industrial Revolution*, Longman 1930, p. 133.

W. R. Ward, *Religion and Society in England 1790–1850*, Batsford 1972, pp. 34–39.

25. S. Horsley, *Diocesan Charge*, 1800, p. 20.

S. Horsley, *Works* 3, Rivington 1845, p. 105.

I. Sellers, *Nineteenth Century Nonconformity*, Edward Arnold 1977, pp. 1–8.

26. Ward, op. cit., pp. 47ff.

J. H. Overton and E. Relton, *The English Church 1714–1800*, Macmillan 1906, pp. 262–64.

R. Treffry, *Memoirs of Joseph Benson*, London 1840.

R. A. Soloway, *Prelates and People: Ecclesiastical Social Thought in England 1783–1852*, Routledge and Kegan Paul 1969, pp. 50–52.

27. D. N. Hempton, 'Thomas Allan and Methodist Politics 1800–40', *History*, February 1982, pp. 13–31. The Allan Papers are in Methodist Church Archives, Manchester.

28. Halévy, op. cit. 3, p. 52.

29. Manning, op. cit., pp. 130ff.

30. Halévy, op. cit. 3, pp. 50–51.

31. Ibid., p. 50.

Manning, op. cit., p. 130.

32. W. Myles *Chronological History*, London 1813, pp. 295ff., 344.

33. Halévy, op. cit. 3, p. 51.

R. W. Davis, op. cit., p. 87.

34. W. H. Rule, *An Account of the Establishment of Wesleyan Methodism in the British Army*, Woolmer 1883.

C. H. Kelly, *Memories*, Culley 1910, pp. 110ff.

35. Manning, op. cit., p. 101.

36. T. E. Owen, *Methodism Unmasked*, London 1802, 'Hall Tracts', Wesley College, Bristol.

Cf. *Edinburgh Review* VI, 1806, pp. 341ff.

R. A. Ingram, op. cit. XIV, 1809, pp. 10ff.

Political Register, 29 May 1811. *Annual Register* 1811, London 1812, pp. 47ff.

G. S. Rowe, *WHS* VI.

Quarterly Review IV, No. 8, November 1810.

HMGB I, p. 303; II, pp. 99–100.

37. Cf. Ward, pp. 75–80 for another viewpoint. I am not entirely convinced by Ward at this point.

38. For the episode of the Sidmouth Bill:

M. Edwards, *After Wesley: Methodism 1791–1849*, Epworth Press 1935, pp. 75–82.

Manning, op. cit., pp. 130–43.

Davis, op. cit., Ch. 9, pp. 148–69.

Ward, op. cit., pp. 54–63.

E. Pellew, *Life of Lord Sidmouth* 3, London 1847, pp. 38ff.

Complete text of the Bill, *Parliamentary Debates* XIX; pp. 1,128ff.

Debates XIX, pp. 781ff.; XX, pp. 196ff.; XXII, XXIII.
Methodist Magazine, May 1811, pp. 555ff.

39. Best, op. cit., p. 173, for views of van Mildert and his like.
40. J. Vickers, *Thomas Coke, Apostle of Methodism*, Epworth Press 1969, pp. 229–30.
    Ward, op. cit., p. 55.
41. Ibid., p. 59.
42. But cf. Davis, op. cit., pp. 157, 166 for another view of Belsham.
    Manning, op. cit., p. 132.
    Ward, op. cit., p. 55.
    Machin, op. cit., p. 16.
43. H. S. Skeats and C. S. Miall, *History of the Free Churches of England 1688–1891*, Alexander and Shepheard 1891, pp. 450ff.
44. S. B. Webb, *History of English Local Government* 1, Longman 1906, Bk. 2, pp. 350–64.
    HMGB II, p. 25.
45. Manning, op. cit., p. 141.
    Ward, op. cit., p. 60.
46. Smith, op. cit., 2, p. 513.
47. Myles, op. cit., pp. 349ff.
48. Davis, op. cit., pp. 170ff.
    Ward, op. cit., pp. 62ff. The Act is 52 George III C155. It was followed in 1813 by an Act granting greater freedom to the Unitarians.
    D. M. Thompson, op. cit., pp. 29–38.
49. *Minutes* 1812, pp. 318ff. Act set out in full.
50. Halévy, op. cit. 3, p. 54.
    Edwards, op. cit., p. 81.
    K. Feiling, *The Second Tory Party 1714–1832*, Oxford University Press 1938, p. 268.
51. A. Knox, *Remains* IV, 1837, p. 51n.
    Jebb and Knox, *Correspondence* II, London 1834, p. 224.
    Letter of Jebb, 25 May 1815. Appendix to James Kendall, 'Free Strictures on Wesleyan Connexion with the Church of England', 1836, Hall Collection, Bristol.
52. A. Clarke, *Discourses on Various Subjects* III, London 1830, p. 372.
53. Norman, op. cit., p. 76.
54. J. Kent, *The Age of Disunity*, Epworth Press 1966, Ch. 5.
    D. Gowland, *Methodist Secessions*, Manchester University Press 1979.
    E. R. Taylor, 'Some Aspects of Political Alignments in Methodism after Wesley', *Epworth Review* 9, No. 2, May 1982, pp. 47–52.
    Ward, op. cit., Chs. 4, 6.
55. W. R. Ward, 'The Religion of the People and the Problem of Control 1780–1830', *Studies in Church History* 8 ed. G. J. Cuming and D. Baker, Cambridge University Press 1972, pp. 237–57.
56. Cited in Norman, op. cit., p. 78.
    D. M. Thompson, op. cit., pp. 51–61.
    For the details of the Repeal:
    Cf. Manning, op. cit., pp. 217–253.
    Davis, op. cit., pp. 212ff.

R. W. Davis, 'The Strategy of Dissent in the Repeal Campaigns 1820–8', *Journal of Modern History* 38, No. 4, 1966, pp. 374–93.

G. F. A. Best, 'The Protestant Constitution and its Supporters', *Transactions of the Royal Historical Society* 5th Series VIII, 1958, pp. 105–27.

G. F. A. Best, 'The Whigs and the Church Establishment in the Age of Grey and Peel', *History* XLV, 1960, pp. 103–118.

57. G. I. T. Machin, *The Catholic Question in English Politics 1820–1830*, Cambridge University Press 1964, p. 145.

58. Henriques, op. cit., p. 147.

59. D. Hempton, 'Methodism and Anti-Catholic Politics 1800–46', St Andrew's PhD Thesis, 1977.

D. Hempton, 'Thomas Allan and Methodist Politics 1800–40', *History*, February 1982, pp. 13–31.

Kent, op. cit., pp. 88–92.

T. Jackson, *Recollections of My Own Life and Times*, WM Conference 1873, p. 408.

60. E. R. Norman, *Anti-Catholicism in Victorian England*, Allen and Unwin 1968, Section 2 'Maynooth', pp. 23–51.

G. I. T. Machin, 'The Maynooth Grant, the Dissenters and Disestablishment 1845–7', *English Historical Review* LXXXII, 1967, pp. 61–85.

61. As, for example, Norman, *Church and Society*, p. 76.

Yet cf. *Bunting* 2, pp. 164, 203.

62. B. Gregory, *Sidelights on the Conflict of Methodism 1827–1852*, Cassell 1898. Gives many 'Buntingisms' from Fowler's *Journal* of Conference events.

Bunting 2, pp. 59–60.

63. H. McLeod, *Religion and the People of Western Europe 1789–1970*, Oxford University Press 1981, p. 106.

Soloway, op. cit., pp. 242ff.

64. J. Vincent, *Pollbooks: How Victorians Voted*, Cambridge University Press 1967.

D. Gowland shows how complex voting patterns could be.

65. F. R. Salter, *Dissenters and Public Affairs in Mid-Victorian England*, Dr Williams's Trust 1967, pp. 2–3.

66. E. V. Chapman, *John Wesley and Co. (Halifax)*, Halifax Printing Co. 1952, p. 48.

67. C. Binfield, *So Down to Prayers: Studies in English Nonconformity 1780–1920*, Dent 1977, Ch. 4 on Leeds, pp. 54–100.

68. E. R. Norman has stated an Anglican case in *Church and Society* but reflects very much the thinking of the hierarchy rather than the grass-roots.

Cf. A. D. Gilbert, *Religion and Society in Industrial England*, Longman 1976, pp. 125ff.

69. O. Anderson, 'Gladstone's Abolition of Compulsory Church Rates', *Journal of Ecclesiastical History* XXV, 1973.

Chadwick, op. cit. 1, pp. 81–95, 146–58.

Ward, *Religion and Society*, pp. 178–93 for fireworks in the North-West.

70. Norman, op. cit., p. 111.

71. Manning, op. cit., pp. 175–98. A succinct account.

Gregory, op. cit., pp. 237–41.

Bunting 2, p. 185.

C. J. Stranks, *Dean Hook*, SPCK 1954, pp. 49–52.

72. D. M. Thompson, 'The Liberation Society 1844–1868', *Pressure from Without in Early Victorian England* ed. P. Hollis, Edward Arnold 1974, pp. 210–38.

W. H. Mackintosh, *Disestablishment and Liberation: The Movement for the Separation of the Anglican Church from State Control*, Epworth Press 1972, pp. 2–43.

Binfield, op. cit., Ch. 5 'A Study of Edward Miall', pp. 101–124.

73. Thompson, *Nonconformity*, pp. 94–95.

B. Gregory, op. cit., pp. 150–67.

Smith, op. cit. 3, pp. 199ff.

Bunting 2, pp. 51, 76.

Ward, op. cit., pp. 156–59.

E. A. Rose, *Methodism in Ashton under Lyne*, J. Andrew, Ashton under Lyne.

M. S. Edwards, 'The Resignation of J. R. Stephens', *WHS* XXXVI, 1967, pp. 16–21.

74. Manning, op. cit., p. 189.

Machin, op. cit., p. 41.

J. Vincent, *The Formation of the Liberal Party 1857–1868*, Penguin Books 1972 edn, p. 147. Vincent shows the great complexity of determining party allegiance at this time. Rochdale is a good northern example. So also is Halifax.

Cf. J. A. Hargreaves, 'Political Attitudes and Activities of Methodists in the Parish of Halifax in the Age of Reform 1830–48', Huddersfield Polytechnic MA 1985.

75. Manning, op. cit., pp. 254–332. A succinct account.

W. G. Addison, *Religious Equality in Modern England 1714–1914*, SPCK 1944, pp. 62–64, 117–21.

R. T. Jones, *Congregationalism in England 1662–1962*, Independent Press 1962, pp. 205, 271.

Chadwick, op. cit. 1, p. 145.

76. Gregory, op. cit., pp. 236, 298.

Bunting 2, pp. 217–19, 319–23.

Minutes 1845.

77. Addison, op. cit., p. 63.

78. Manning, op. cit., pp. 286–332.

Best, op. cit., p. 173.

Quarterly Review VII, 1812, pp. 201–213.

For a recent summary:

Cf. P. J. Jagger, *Clouded Witness*, T. and T. Clark 1982, pp. 67ff.

79. Chadwick, op. cit. I, p. 326ff.; II, pp. 202–206.

Jones, op. cit., pp. 270–71.

See my articles in the *Encyclopedia of World Methodism* ed. N. Harmon, 1974, on the 'Gedney Case', the 'Owston Ferry Case' and ministerial titles. (They are wrongly attributed to M. Edwards.)

HMGB II, p. 240.

NHM 1, p. 403.

80. R. Fletcher, *The Akenham Burial Case*, Wildwood House 1974.

81. G. C. B. Davies, *Henry Phillpotts, Bishop of Exeter 1778–1869*, SPCK 1954, pp. 148–49.

82. *Hansard*, 3 June 1880. Cited in Norman, op. cit., p. 208.

83. E. H. Fowler, *Life of Henry Hartley Fowler, Lord Wolverhampton*, Hutchinson 1912, p. 124.

D. W. Bebbington, *The Nonconformist Conscience: Chapel and Politics 1870–1914*, Allen and Unwin 1982, pp. 30–33.

84. P. T. Marsh, *The Victorian Church in Decline*, Routledge and Kegan Paul 1969, pp. 245–63.

43 and 44 Victoria C. 41.

Norman, op. cit., pp. 208–210.

85. Manning, op. cit., p. 303.

86. C. H. Turner, *Catholic and Apostolic* ed. H. N. Bate, Mowbray 1931, p. 49.

Cf. R. F. Horton, *An Autobiography*, Allen and Unwin 1917, pp. 57–60, an earlier case.

87. N. Gash, *Reaction and Reconstruction in English Politics 1832–45*, Oxford University Press 1965, pp. 79ff.

I. Sellers, *Nineteenth Century Nonconformity*, Edward Arnold 1977, p. 69 Ch. 5 is a compressed summary of Victorian Nonconformist politics.

88. Graham to Brougham in

C. S. Parker, *Life and Letters of Sir James Graham*, Vol. 1, London 1907, p. 379.

89. Ward, op. cit., pp. 12–16, 135–41.

T. W. Laqueur, *Religion and Respectability: Sunday Schools and Working Class Culture 1780–1850*, Yale University Press, USA 1976. An important recent study.

H. F. Mathews, *Methodism and the Religion of the People 1791–1851*, Epworth Press 1949.

M. G. Jones, *The Charity School Movement*, Cambridge University Press 1938, pp. 145ff.

HMGB II, pp. 101–104.

Binfield, op. cit., p. 82.

90. Mathews, op. cit., pp. 59–60.

91. Jones, op. cit., p. 152.

Ward, op. cit., p. 136.

92. A. P. Wadsworth, *The First Manchester Sunday Schools*, John Rylands 1951.

93. Mathews, op. cit., p. 39.

94. *Minutes* 1814, 1817, 1820, 1823, 1827, 1837, 1838.

95. Chadwick, op. cit. I, pp. 338, 342; II, p. 305.

96. For the Education Controversies:

See Manning, op. cit., pp. 333–84. Manning was very fearful of Roman Catholic encroachment.

Chadwick, op. cit. I, pp. 336–46, 476–81; II, pp. 186–92, 299–308.

M. J. Cruickshank, *Church and State in English Education: 1870 to the Present Day*, Macmillan 1963.

J. Murphy, *Church, State and Schools in Great Britain 1800–1970*, Routledge and Kegan Paul 1971.

Binfield, op. cit., Chs. 4 and 5. The case for Voluntaryism.

Kitson Clark, op. cit., Ch. 4, pp. 99–140.

G. F. A. Best, 'Religious Difficulties in National Education in England', *Cambridge Historical Journal* XII, 1956, pp. 155–73.

J. T. Ward and J. H. Treble, 'Religion and Education in 1843: Reaction to the Factory Education Bill'. *Journal of Ecclesiastical History*, 1969, pp. 79ff.

D. N. Hempton, 'Wesleyan Methodism and Educational Politics in Early Nineteenth Century England', *History of Education* 8, No. 3, 1979, pp. 207–221.

F. C. Pritchard, Ch. 8 'Education', *HMGB* III pp. 279–308.

97. Cited in G. Kitson Clark, *The English Inheritance*, SCM Press 1950, pp. 119, 135.

R. W. Dale, *History of English Congregationalism*, Hodder and Stoughton 1907, p. 659. The whole chapter, pp. 646–83, is important.

98. Jones, op. cit., p. 213.

99. Norman, op. cit., pp. 193, 205, 219.

Chadwick, op. cit. II, p. 438.

For the French scene for purposes of comparison:

J. McManners, *Church and State in France 1870–1914*, SPCK 1972, especially p. 45ff.

Cf. N. Sykes, *Man as Churchman*, Cambridge University Press 1960, Ch. 4 'Church, State and Education since 1815', pp. 117–67, especially p. 131.

100. Halévy, op. cit., Epilogue, Vol. I Book 2, p. 53.

K. E. Kirk, *Beauty and Bands*, Hodder and Stoughton 1955, pp. 129ff.

101. Cited in G. M. Young, *Victorian England, Portrait of an Age*, Oxford University Press 1936, p. 51.

102. *Minutes* 1839, 1841.

103. Binfield, op. cit., p. 82.

Machin, op. cit., pp. 64–71.

Norman, op. cit., pp. 113–14.

Murphy, op. cit., pp. 19–21.

Soloway, op. cit., pp. 400–410.

104. Gregory, op. cit., p. 277.

Watchman, 3 April 1839.

Bunting 2, pp. 219–25.

Gregory, op. cit., pp. 268–78.

Ward, op. cit., pp. 244–47.

105. Mathews, op. cit., p. 133.

Minutes 1870.

106. Norman, op. cit., pp. 114–15.

Machin, op. cit., pp. 151–56.

D. M. Thompson, pp. 109–114. The Debate in Parliament.

Manning, op. cit., pp. 340–45. A trenchant polemic.

Ward, op. cit., pp. 244–54, 278.

Soloway, op. cit., pp. 411–30.

107. Gash, op. cit., p. 97.

N. Gash, *The Age of Peel*, Edward Arnold 1968, pp. 57–70. A useful summary.

108. Machin, op. cit., p. 160. Ashley to Peel, 17 June 1843.

Binfield, op. cit., p. 84.

Manning, op. cit., p. 344.

109. *Bunting* 2, p. 300.

Ward, op. cit., p. 204.

Machin, op. cit., pp. 165–66.
110. Chadwick, op. cit. I, p. 223.
E. R. Norman, *Anti-Catholicism in England*, pp. 23–51, 145–58.
Machin, op. cit., pp. 166–80.
D. H. Kerr, *Peel, Priests and Politics. Sir Robert Peel's Administration and the Roman Catholic Church in Ireland 1841–6*, Oxford University Press 1982.
111. Bebbington, op. cit., Ch. 5 'The Irish Question', pp. 84–105.
J. Kent, *The Age of Disunity*, p. 140. Cited from Anti-Maynooth Conference, 1845.
112. D. N. Hempton, 'The *Watchman* and Religious Politics in the 1830s and 1840s', *WHS* Vol. XLII Part I, May 1974, pp. 2–13. Hempton, I think, overstresses Toryism.
Watchman, 1845, pp. 103, 127, 139, 151, 163.
113. Gregory, op. cit., p. 348.
Ward, op. cit., p. 243.
114. Ward, op. cit., p. 242.
115. Ward, op. cit., p. 279.
Chadwick, op. cit. I, p. 342.
116. For an analysis of Bunting's political stance:
Kent, op. cit., pp. 137ff.
HMGB II, pp. 245ff.
117. For various interpretations of Gladstone's stance:
P. Butler, *Gladstone: Church, State and Tractarianism*, Oxford University Press 1982, p. 77ff. Change after Maynooth crucial.
Chadwick, op. cit. I, pp. 476ff. An evolving Gladstone.
Machin, op. cit., p. 84. A consistent Gladstone.
Norman, op. cit., pp. 102–104. An evolving Gladstone.
Kitson Clark, *Churchmen*, pp. 88ff. Comparison with Macaulay.
A. R. Vidler, *The Orb and the Cross: A normative study in the relations of church and state with reference to Gladstone's early writing*, SPCK 1945.
118. Chadwick op. cit. II, p. 427ff.
Norman, op. cit., pp. 196–98.
119. Norman, op. cit., pp. 187, 205.
120. F. C. Pritchard, op. cit., *HMGB* III, p. 289.
W. R. Ward, 'Church and Society in the First Half of the Nineteenth Century', *HMGB* II, pp. 63, 76.
J. Kent, 'The Wesleyan Methodists to 1849', *HMGB* II, pp. 242ff.
J. H. Rigg, *Wesleyan Methodist Reminiscences*, London 1904, Ch. 13.
Mathews, op. cit., pp. 155–57.
121. J. Telford, *Life of James Harrison Rigg*, Culley 1909, p. 181.
J. H. Rigg, *National Education in its Social Conditions and Aspects*, London 1873.
J. H. Rigg, *Essays for the Times*, London 1866.
122. F. C. Pritchard, 'The Educationalist' (Ch. 4), *John Scott Lidgett* ed. R. E. Davies, Epworth Press 1957, pp. 107–156.
123. R. A. Butler, *The Art of the Possible*, Penguin Books 1971, pp. 109–127.
124. *HMGB* III, H. D. Rack, pp. 148–52; F. C. Pritchard, p. 159.
Cruickshank, op. cit., p. 295.
125. N. Sykes, 'Religion and the Relations of Church and State', *New Cambridge Modern History*, Vol. X, Cambridge University Press, pp. 76–103.

Cf. J. S. McManners, *Lectures on European History 1789–1914*, Blackwell 1966, Ch. XIX, 'Church, State and Society', pp. 307–324.

126. Manning, op. cit., p. 367.
  Sykes, *Man as Churchman*, p. 139.
  Journal of Ecclesiastical History IV, 1953, p. 117.
  J. Huxtable, *The Preacher's Integrity*, Epworth Press 1966, pp. 155ff.
  J. N. Figgis, *Churches in the Modern State*, Longman 1913, pp. 29ff., 46ff.
  J. N. Figgis, *Anti-Christ and other Sermons*, Longman 1913, p. 266.
  D. Newsome, 'The Assault of Mammon: Charles Gore and John Neville Figgis', *Journal of Ecclesiastical History* XVII, 1966, pp. 227–41.
  Also D. R. Pugh, 'The Church and Education: Anglican Attitudes 1902', *Journal of Ecclesiastical History* XXIII, 1972, and N. J. Richards, 'The Education Bill of 1906 and the Decline of Political Nonconformity', *Journal of Ecclesiastical History* XXIII, 1972.
  D. Nicholls, *Church and State in Britain Since 1820*, Routledge and Kegan Paul 1967, pp. 119ff. John Clifford on the State.

127. Cited in W. G. Fallows, *Mandell Creighton and the English Church*, Oxford University Press 1964, p. 62.

128. *Church and State*, the Report of the Archbishop's Commission, Church Information Office 1970, especially pp. 68–79.
  The Free Churches and the State, Free Church Federal Council 1953, p. 62.
  Cf. B. L. Manning, *Essays in Orthodox Dissent*, Independent Press 1939, pp. 204–205, 209.
  E. A. Payne, *Freechurchmen, Unrepentant and Repentant*, Carey Kingsgate 1965, pp. 56–74 'The Free Churches and the State'.

129. D. L. Munby, *The Idea of a Secular Society*, Oxford University Press 1963, p. 14.
  Cf. T. S. Eliot, *The Idea of a Christian Society*, Faber and Faber 1939.

130. Cf. A. J. P. Taylor, *The Trouble Makers: Dissent over Foreign Policy 1792–1939*, Hamish Hamilton 1957, especially Ch. 4 'Gladstonian Foreign Policy: The Contradiction of Morality'.

131. B. Harrison, *Drink and the Victorians*, Faber and Faber 1971.
  HMGB III, pp. 353–56.

132. J. Kent, *Age of Disunity*, p. 139. Quotes the phrase from *Wesleyan Magazine*, May 1835.

133. G. Kitson Clark, *The English Inheritance*, Ch. 8 'Religion and Liberty: The Dissenters in the Eighteenth Century, p. 128.

134. Norman, *Church and Society*, pp. 4, 8–10. Norman's argument becomes somewhat journalistic on the modern period, but is much more penetrating on the nineteenth century.

135. Norman, op. cit., p. 185, citing B. F. Westcott, *The Obligation of Empire*, 1900, p. 6.

136. I. Bradley, *The Optimists*, Faber and Faber 1980, pp. 99–122 'The Nonconformist Conscience'.
  Bebbington, op. cit. Now the standard account
  H. D. Rack, 'The Wesleyan Methodists 1849–1902', *HMGB* III, pp. 128–48.
  J. M. Turner, 'Methodism 1900–1932', *HMGB* III, pp. 309–24, 341–61.

John Kent, 'Hugh Price Hughes and the Nonconformist Conscience', *Essays in Modern Church History* ed. G. V. Bennett and J. D. Walsh, SPCK 1966, pp. 181–205.

E. G. Rupp, 'The Influence of Victorian Nonconformity', *Listener*, 17 March 1955.

E. G. Rupp 'Evangelicalism of the Nonconformists', *Ideas and Beliefs of the Victorians*, Dutton, New York 1966, pp. 105–112.

137. R. Moore, *Pitmen, Preachers and Politics: The Effects of Methodism in a Durham Mining Community*, Cambridge University Press 1974.

138. J. M. Turner, 'R. F. Wearmouth: Methodist Historian', *WHS*, September 1982, pp. 111–16.

139. D. Hempton, *Methodism and Politics 1750–1850*, Hutchinson 1984, contains a clear analysis of some of the issues I have raised. Ch. 5 on Roman Catholic Emancipation 1790–1830 in particular breaks new ground. Ch. 6 is a good summary of the Education issue.

8. Methodism and the Oxford Movement

1. W. H. Mackintosh, *Disestablishment and Liberation: The Movement for the Separation of the Anglican Church from State Control*, Epworth Press 1972, pp. 186–87.

The *Nonconformist*, 19 August 1868, p. 814.

A. L. Drummond, *The Churches – Portrayed by Punch*, London 1947, p. 13.

H. P. Liddon, *Life of Edward B. Pusey* 4, Longmans 1897, p. 427. Liddon makes no mention of this incident in the *Life*.

J. Telford, *Life of J. H. Rigg*, Culley 1909, p. 223.

2. C. C. J. Webb, *Religious Thought in the Oxford Movement*, SPCK 1928, p. 113.

J. H. Newman, *Parochial and Plain Sermons* I, Rivington 1870, pp. 1–14.

J. Wesley, *Sermons*, pp. 266–79.

3. H. Davies, *Worship and Theology in England: From Watts and Wesley to Maurice 1690–1850*, Oxford University Press 1961, Ch. X pp. 243–82.

J. C. Bowmer, *Pastor and People*, Epworth Press 1975, Part 4, Ch. 3 'The Impact of the Oxford Movement', pp. 229–48.

E. G. Rupp, *Thomas Jackson, Methodist Patriarch*, Epworth Press 1954, pp. 22ff.

T. Dearing, *Wesleyan and Tractarian Worship*, SPCK 1966.

R. N. Flew, 'Methodism and the Catholic Tradition', *Northern Catholicism* ed. C. Harris, SPCK 1933, pp. 515–30.

H. A. Hodges and A. M. Allchin, *A Rapture of Praise*, Hodder and Stoughton 1966, pp. 9–50.

J. E. Rattenbury, *The Eucharistic Hymns of John and Charles Wesley*, Epworth Press 1948.

J. H. Rigg, *Oxford High Anglicanism and its chief leaders*, Kelly 1895.

A. M. Fairbairn, *Catholicism, Roman and Anglican*, Hodder and Stoughton 1899.

4. J. L. Talmon, *Romanticism and Revolt: Europe 1815–1848*, Thames and Hudson 1967, pp. 135ff.

M. Butler, *Romantics, Rebels and Revolutionaries*, Oxford University Press 1982.

S. Prickett, *Romanticism and Religion: The Tradition of Coleridge and Wordsworth in the Victorian Church*, Cambridge University Press 1976.

E. Routley, *English Religious Dissent*, Cambridge University Press 1960, pp. 158–62.

F. C. Gill, *The Romantic Movement and Methodism*, Epworth Press 1937.

5. Cf. M. Turnell, *The Classical Moment*, Hamish Hamilton 1947.

6. L. Bisson, *A Short History of French Literature*, Penguin Books 1943, p. 101.

7. A. R. Vidler, *Prophecy and Papacy: A Study of Lammenais, The Church and the Revolution*, SCM Press 1959.

Y. Brilioth, *Evangelicalism and the Oxford Movement*, Oxford University Press 1934.

8. O. Chadwick, *The Mind of the Oxford Movement*, Black 1960, pp. 12, 27–28.

9. D. Newsome, *The Parting of Friends*, Murray 1966, especially pp. 5ff.

E. Jay (ed), *The Evangelical and Oxford Movements*, Cambridge University Press 1983.

10. E. Routley, *English Religious Dissent*, Cambridge University Press 1960, pp. 158ff.

C. S. Lewis, '*De Descriptione Temporum*', *They asked for a Paper*, Bles 1962, pp. 9–25.

J. H. Newman, *Discussions and Arguments*, Longman 1883, p. 293.

11. B. Willey, *Samuel Taylor Coleridge*, Chatto and Windus 1972.

12. G. Kitson Clark, 'The Romantic Element 1830–1850', *Studies in English Social History* ed. J. H. Plumb, Longman 1955, pp. 211–39.

G. Kitson Clark, *The Making of Victorian England*, Methuen 1962, Ch. VI 'The Religion of the People'.

R. Chapman, *Faith and Revolt*, Weidenfeld and Nicolson 1970.

13. W. R. Ward, *Victorian Oxford*, Cass 1965.

J. Kent, *Holding the Fort*, Epworth Press 1978, pp. 236ff.

But cf.

D. Voll, *Catholic Evangelicalism: The Acceptance of Evangelical Tradition by the Oxford Movement during the second half of the nineteenth century*, Faith Press 1963.

G. Rowell, *The Vision Glorious: Themes and Personalities of the Catholic Revival in Anglicanism*, Oxford University Press 1983, pp. 137–40.

14. E. R. Norman, *Church and Society in England 1770–1970*, Oxford University Press 1976, p. 72.

15. Cited in Rowell, op. cit., p. 1.

16. O. Chadwick, *The Victorian Church* I, Black 1966, p. 47.

J. H. Overton, *The English Church in the Nineteenth Century 1800–1833*, Longman 1894, p. 12.

17. H. J. Laski, *Studies in the Problem of Sovereignty*, New Haven, USA 1917, pp. 112–13.

Y. Brilioth, *Evangelicalism*, p. 56.

Y. Brilioth, *The Anglican Revival: Studies in the Oxford Movement*, Longman 1925, p. viii, Ch. XIII, pp. 260–73.

18. For the Sermon of 14 July 1833 on 'National Apostacy' see R. P. Flindall, *The Church of England 1815–1948*, SPCK 1972, pp. 37ff. From *Sermons, Academical and Occasional*, 1848.

19. Rowell, op. cit., p. 22, on Keble's sources.

20. J. R. H. Moorman, 'Forerunners of the Oxford Movement', *Theology*, 1933.

Brilioth, *Anglican Revival*, pp. 16ff.

21. A. J. Mason, *The Church of England and Episcopacy*, Cambridge University Press 1914, pp. 411ff.

Liddon, op. cit. 1, pp. 256–62.

22. Rowell, op. cit., p. 6.

23. A. B. Webster, *Joshua Watson 1771–1855*, SPCK 1954.

24. Ibid., p. 58.

G. F. A. Best, *Temporal Pillars*, Cambridge University Press 1964, pp. 165–70.

M. H. Port, *Six Hundred New Churches*, SPCK 1961.

D. E. H. Mole, 'The Victorian Town Parish – Rural Vision and Urban Mission', *Studies in Church History* 16, ed. D. Baker, Blackwell 1980, pp. 361–71.

25. O. Chadwick, *Victorian Church* I, p. 230.

26. N. Sykes, *The English Religious Tradition*, SCM Press 1953, p. 76.

For the Reforms, cf:

O. Chadwick, *Victorian Church* I, pp. 101ff., 126ff.

Best, op. cit., pp. 239–347.

O. J. Brose, *Church and Parliament: The Reshaping of the Church of England 1828–1860*, Oxford University Press 1959.

K. A. Thompson, *Bureaucracy and Church Reform: The Organizational Response of the Church of England to Social Change 1800–1965*, Oxford University Press 1970.

27. A. D. Gilbert, *Religion and Society in Industrial England: Church Chapel and Social Change 1740–1914*, Longman 1976.

28. Cited in Best, op. cit., p. 169. From T. Mozley, *Reminiscences* 1, chiefly of Oriel College and the Oxford Movement, p. 226.

Cf. B. Heeney, *A Different Kind of Gentleman: Parish Clergy as Professional Men in Early and Mid-Victorian England*, Archon Books, USA 1976.

29. The classic account is:

R. W. Church, *The Oxford Movement: Twelve Years 1833–1845*, Macmillan 1891.

Cf. O. Chadwick, *Victorian Church* I, pp. 167ff.

D. Bowen, *The Idea of the Victorian Church*, McGill University Press, Montreal 1968.

E. Fairweather (ed), *The Oxford Movement*, Oxford University Press 1964.

Y. Brilioth, *The Anglican Revival*, for a theological account.

G. Rowell gives a lively modern interpretation though he does not dispel what John Kent calls the 'Anglican Myth'.

Cf. J. Kent, 'The Nineteenth Century in England: The Anglican Mythology', *Pelican Guide to Modern Theology*, Vol. 2, ed. J. Danielou, Penguin Books 1969, pp. 307–329.

30. N. Sykes, *Old Priest and New Presbyter*, Cambridge University Press 1956, pp. 209ff. Episcopacy and Presbyterianism since the Reformation with especial relation to the Churches of England and Scotland.

Cf. Rowell, op. cit., pp. 24–26.

31. For Froude on the Reformation, *The Remains*, Vol. 1, pp. 387, 389, 433, where the Reformers are called anti-Christ.

32. G. Dix (ed), *Catholicity: A Study in the Conflict of Christian Traditions in the West*, Dacre Press 1947, pp. 20ff.

Cf. R. N. Flew and R. E. Davies (eds), *The Catholicity of Protestantism*, Lutterworth Press 1950.

And a moderate Anglican position – *The Fullness of Christ*, SPCK 1950.

33. C. Gore, *The Church and the Ministry*, Longman 1919, revised C. H. Turner 1936, p. 305.

34. J. H. Newman, *Lectures on the Doctrine of Justification*, Rivington 1874, p. 320.

35. J. Coulson and A. M. Allchin, *The Rediscovery of Newman*, Sheed and Ward 1967, pp. 11–30, 100–122.

Rowell, op. cit., p. 14.

Cf. pp. 35ff. Keble, pp. 57ff. Newman, pp. 81ff. Pusey.

D. Newsome, 'Justification and Sanctification: Newman and the Evangelicals', *Journal of Theological Studies* New Series, Vol. 15, Part 1, 1964.

36. C. C. J. Webb, op. cit., pp. 54–55. Webb's approach to the whole matter is very penetrating, cf. Ch. IV, 'Justification', pp. 74–93.

37. J. H. Newman, *Lectures on Justification*, p. 303.

38. Cf. E. G. Rupp, *Protestant Catholicity*, Epworth Press 1960, p. 37.

E. G. Rupp, *Last Things First*, SCM Press 1963, pp. 30–31.

Cf. also C. S. Lewis, *Beyond Personality*, Bles 1944, pp. 35ff., who also refers to 'Beauty and the Beast'.

MHB 370.

G. S. Wakefield, 'A Mystical Substitute for the Glorious Gospel? A Methodist Critique of Tractarianism'. Paper given at Anglo-Catholic Congress, Oxford, July 1983.

39. Rowell, op. cit., p. 82. From E. B. Pusey, *Sermons during the season from Advent to Whitsuntide*, 1848, pp. 58–59.

40. D. Newsome, 'Newman and the Oxford Movement', *The Victorian Crisis of Faith*, ed. A. Symondson, SPCK 1970, pp. 71–90.

Rowell, op. cit., p. 33.

41. From Pusey's *Preface* to his translation of Surin's *Foundations of the Spiritual Life*, 1874, p. vif.

Davies, op. cit., p. 249.

42. Cited in Webb, op. cit., pp. 103–104. From a letter to the press of December 1849. Cf. Brilioth, *Anglican Revival*, pp. 242ff. Pusey's preaching of the cross.

Brilioth, *Evangelicalism*, p. 23.

43. Rowell, op. cit., pp. 98–115.

Chadwick, *Victorian Church* I, pp. 212–21, 491–526.

J. F. White, *The Cambridge Movement*, Cambridge University Press 1962.

J. Bentley, *Ritualism and Politics in Victorian Britain*, Oxford University Press 1978.

44. H. L. Short, 'Changing Styles in Nonconformist Architecture', the *Listener*, 17 March 1955.

G. W. Dolbey, *The Architectural Expression of Methodism 1738–1840*, Epworth Press 1964.

C. Binfield, *So Down to Prayers – Studies in English Nonconformity 1780–1920*, Dent 1977, Ch. 7 'Dissenting Gothic', pp. 145ff.

G. W. O. Addleshaw and F. Etchells, *The Architectural Setting of Anglican Worship*, SPCK 1948.

45. Davies, op. cit., p. 253.
46. E. G. Rupp, 'Some Reflections on the Origin and Development of the Methodist Tradition', *LQHR*, July 1953.
47. P. T. Forsyth, *Christ on Parnassus*, Hodder and Stoughton 1911, pp. 183ff.

    H. Davies, *Worship and Theology in England from Newman to Martineau 1850–1900*, Oxford University Press 1962, Ch. 2, 'Ecclesiastical Architecture from Grecian to Gothic'.

    N. S. Briggs, *Puritan Architecture and its Future*, Lutterworth Press 1946.

    John Betjeman, *Collected Poems*, John Murray 1970.

    Routley, op. cit., pp. 168ff.
48. Davies, *Newman to Martineau*, pp. 58f., quoting F. J. Jobson's *Wesleyan Defence of Gothic*, 1850.

    For Holden, E. Jennings, 'Sir Isaac Holden Bart – His Place in the Wesleyan Connexion', *WHS* XLIII, pp. 111–26, 150–58.

    W. E. Gladstone, *The Church of England and Ritualism*, London 1875, p. 24.
49. Chadwick, *Victorian Church* I, pp. 250ff.

    J. C. Nias, *Gorham and the Bishop of Exeter*, SPCK 1951.

    P. Jagger, *Clouded Witness: Initiation in the Church of England in the Mid-Victorian Period 1850–1875*, T. and T. Clark 1982.
50. *Minutes* 1837, 1840, 1842, 1874, 1882.

    HMGB II, p. 123ff.

    W. F. Swift, 'The Sunday Service of the Methodists', *WHS* XXXI, pp. 112–18, 133–43.

    W. B. Pope, *Compendium* 3, WM Bookroom 1880, pp. 299ff.

    J. C. Bowmer, *The Lord's Supper in Methodism 1791–1960*, Epworth Press 1961, pp. 18–33.
51. C. J. Stranks, *Dean Hook*, Mowbray 1954, pp. 42ff.

    Cf. D. E. H. Mole, 'Challenge to the Church. Birmingham 1815–1865', *The Victorian City* 2 ed. H. J. Dyos and M. Wolff, Routledge and Kegan Paul 1973, pp. 815–36.

    D. E. H. Mole, 'J. C. Miller: A Victorian Rector of Birmingham', *Journal of Ecclesiastical History* XVII, 1966, pp. 95–103.

    For the later period:

    J. Kent, *The Role of Religion in the Cultural Structure of the Late Victorian City*, Royal Historical Society 1973, pp. 153–73.
52. Cf. Heeney, op. cit.

    P. C. Hammond, *The Parson and the Victorian Parish*, Hodder and Stoughton 1977.

    A. Russell, *The Clerical Profession*, SPCK 1980.

    D. McClatchey, *Oxfordshire Clergy 1777–1869*, Oxford University Press 1960.

    C. K. F. Brown, *A History of the English Clergy 1800–1900*, Faith Press 1953.
53. Chadwick, *Victorian Church* I, pp. 222–31.
54. G. Prestige, *The Life of Charles Gore*, Heinemann 1935, p. 97.

    M. B. Reckitt (ed), *For Christ and the People*, SPCK 1968, p. 74.

    D. Newsome, 'The Assault of Mammon: Gore and Figgis', *Journal of Ecclesiastical History* XVII, 1966, pp. 227–41.
55. Kent, op. cit., pp. 236ff.

    Cf. R. Jeffery's article on 'Richard Twigg', *New Fire*, Vol. 6, No. 42, Spring 1980.

M. Smith (ed), *Benson of Cowley*, Oxford University Press 1980.

56. J. M. Turner, 'J. N. Figgis: Anglican Prophet', *Theology* 78, October 1975, pp. 538–44.

    M. G. Tucker, *John Neville Figgis*, SPCK 1950.

57. J. N. Figgis, *The Gospel and Human Needs*, Longman 1908, pp. 35, 73, 78, 103, 108, 110.

    J. N. Figgis, *Anti-Christ and other Sermons*, Longman 1911, pp. 6, 22, 81, 115, 150, 287ff.

    J. N. Figgis, *Civilization at the Cross Roads*, Longman 1912, pp. 122, 127, 161, 231.

    J. N. Figgis, *The Fellowship of the Mystery*, Longman 1914, pp. ix, 149, 157ff.

    J. N. Figgis, *Hopes for English Religion*, Longman 1919, pp. 23, 32, 201–2.

58. J. A. Newton, *Search for a Saint: Edward King*, Epworth Press 1977, pp. 71, 80–91.

    J. A. Newton, 'Bishop King and Nonconformity', *Theology* 74, August 1971, pp. 339ff.

59. D. R. Pugh, 'The Church and Education: Anglican Attitudes – 1902', *Journal of Ecclesiastical History*, Vol. 23, No. 3, July 1972, pp. 219–32.

    N. J. Richards, 'The Education Bill of 1906 and the Decline of Political Nonconformity', *Journal of Ecclesiastical History*, Vol. 23, No. 1, January 1972, pp. 49–63.

60. Chadwick, *Victorian Church* I, pp. 189ff.

61. W. R. Ward, *Religion and Society in England 1790–1850*, Batsford 1972, pp. 153–55.

    Bunting 1, pp. 98ff.

62. J. Kendall, 'Miscellaneous and Free Strictures on the Practical Position of the Wesleyan Connexion Towards the Church of England with other Correlative Observations', 1836, Hall Pamphlets, Wesley College, Bristol.

63. Polemical Tracts – Anti-Methodist, Vol. 11, Hall Collection.

    R. Polwhele, *Letter* to the Bishop of Exeter proposing a scheme of coalition between Wesleyans and the Church of England, Truro 1836.

64. J. H. Rigg, *The Churchmanship of John Wesley etc.*, WM Bookroom 1886, p. 114.

    J. H. Rigg, *Relations of John Wesley and the Church of England*, WM Bookroom 1868, pp. 29, 60–61.

    J. H. Rigg, 'Wesley and the Church of England', *Wesley Memorial Volume* ed. J. O. A. Clarke, USA 1880.

    J. H. Rigg, *John Wesley, the Church of England and Wesleyan Methodism*, WM Bookroom 1883.

65. Letter in Archives of Wesley College, Bristol.

66. E. G. Rupp, *Thomas Jackson, Methodist Patriarch*, Epworth Press 1954.

    T. Jackson, *Recollections of My Own Life and Times* ed. B. Frankland, WM Conference 1878.

67. T. Jackson, *The Church and the Methodists*, London 1834.

    T. Jackson, *The Wesleyans Vindicated . . . in a Dialogue between a Churchman and a Methodist*, London 1837.

68. Bowmer, op. cit., pp. 229ff.

    HMGB II, p. 219.

69. P. Toon, 'Evangelicals and Tractarians! Then and Now', *Churchman* 93, No. 1, pp. 29–38.

P. Toon, *Evangelical Theology 1833–1856: A Response to Tractarianism,* Marshall, Morgan and Scott 1979.

Brilioth, op. cit., pp. 274ff., 'The Doctrine of Justification'.

70. Toon, *Evangelical Theology,* p. 164.

71. Newman, *Doctrine of Justification,* p. 278.

72. T. Jackson, *An Answer,* 1860 edn, p. 8.

73. E. B. Pusey, *Letter to the Archbishop of Canterbury,* Oxford 3rd edn 1842, pp. 159–63.

T. Jackson, *Letter* to the Revd Edward B. Pusey DD, 1842.

74. G. Curteis, *Dissent in its Relation to the Church of England,* Macmillan 1871, 1899 edn, p. 360.

75. Brilioth, op. cit., p. 155.

76. J. H. Rigg, *Churchmanship of John Wesley,* p. 14.

77. J. Beecham, *An Essay on the Constitution of Wesleyan Methodism,* London 1829.

A. Barrett, *An Essay on the Pastoral Office,* London 1839.

A. Barrett, *Catholic and Evangelical Principles,* London 1843.

A. Barrett, *The Ministry and Polity of the Christian Church,* London 1854.

J. H. Rigg, *The Principles of Wesleyan Methodism,* London 1850.

J. H. Rigg, *Congregational Independency and Wesleyan Connexionalism Contrasted,* London 1851.

J. H. Rigg, *A Comparative View of Church Organizations,* London 1887.

78. B. Gregory, *Sidelights on the Conflicts of Methodism 1827–1852,* Cassell 1898, p. 317.

Bowmer, op. cit., p. 234.

79. Ward, op. cit., p. 254.

Bunting 2, pp. 253, 256ff.

80. Gregory, op. cit., pp. 303ff.

81. Rowell, op. cit., Ch. V, pp. 98ff.

A. M. Allchin, *The Silent Rebellion,* SCM Press 1958.

P. Anson, *The Call of the Cloister,* SPCK 1964.

M. Hill, *The Religious Order: A study of virtuoso religion and its legitimisation in the nineteenth century Church of England,* Heinemann 1973.

W. Bradfield, *Life of Thomas Bowman Stephenson,* Kelly 1913.

D. Price Hughes, *Life of Hugh Price Hughes,* Hodder and Stoughton 1904, pp. 201ff.

82. D. Howarth, *How Great a Flame: Samuel Chadwick 50 years on,* Cliff College 1982, pp. 17, 22–23, 34–35.

83. Toon, op. cit., p. 209. This corrects earlier misleading comments by Brilioth and Smyth.

E.g. Y. Brilioth, *Evangelicalism and the Oxford Movement,* p. 30.

84. The second edition (1899) of *Oxford High Churchmanship* shows traces of the influence of the notorious *Secret History of the Oxford Movement* by William Walsh of 1897.

85. E.g. R. Denny Urlin, *The Churchman's Life of Wesley,* SPCK 3rd edn 1886.

H. W. Holden (an old Methodist), *John Wesley in Company with High Churchmen,* Church Press 1869.

W. E. Dutton, *The Eucharistic Memorials of John and Charles Wesley,* Bull, Simmons and Co. 1871.

F. Hockin, *John Wesley and Modern Methodism*, Rivington 1887.

86. J. E. Rattenbury, *The Eucharistic Hymns of John and Charles Wesley*, Epworth Press 1948, pp. 86–100.

J. E. Rattenbury, *The Conversion of the Wesleys: A Critical Study*, Epworth Press 1938, pp. 216–29.

J. H. Rigg, *John Wesley, the Church of England and Wesleyan Methodism*, WM Bookroom 1883.

J. H. Rigg, *The Churchmanship of John Wesley*, WM Bookroom 1886 edn.

J. H. Rigg, *The Living Wesley*, Kelly 1875.

A. S. Wood, 'John Wesley's Reversion to Type', *WHS* XXXV, 4, 1965, pp. 88–93.

J. Kent, 'John Wesley's Churchmanship', *WHS* XXXV, 1, 1965, pp. 10–14.

87. R. E. Davies, *John Scott Lidgett*, Epworth Press 1957 edn, pp. 79–106.

J. W. Grant, *Free Churchmanship in England 1870–1940*, Independent Press n.d.

88. Brilioth, *Evangelicalism*, p. 38.

S. Meacham, *Lord Bishop: the Life of Samuel Wilberforce 1805–1873*, Harvard University Press, USA 1970.

Gilbert, op. cit., pp. 125ff., 'The Metamorphosis of the Religious Establishment'.

89. D. M. Thompson, 'The 1851 Religious Census', *Victorian Studies* XI, No. 1, 1967, pp. 87–97.

W. S. F. Pickering, 'The 1851 Religious Census – A Useless Experiment?', *British Journal of Sociology* 2, 1967–8, pp. 382–407.

B. I. Coleman, *The Church of England in the Mid-Nineteenth Century*, Historical Association 1980.

90. Gilbert, op. cit., pp. 30ff. For statistical evidence.

91. Stranks, op. cit., pp. 42ff.

N. Yates, 'Religion', *A History of Modern Leeds* ed. D. Fraser Manchester University Press 1980, pp. 250ff.

92. Meacham, op. cit., p. 115.

93. Brown, op. cit., pp. 15ff.

94. Newton, op. cit., pp. 71ff. Lincoln – a Bishop of the Poor.

95. R. A. Soloway, *Prelates and People: Ecclesiastical Social Thought in England 1783–1852*, Routledge and Kegan Paul 1969, pp. 279–315.

Chadwick, op. cit. II, pp. 218ff.

Gilbert, op. cit., p. 130.

96. Chadwick, op. cit. II, pp. 243ff.

97. J. M. Turner (ed), *Queen's Essays*, Birmingham 1980, p. 23.

98. N. Gash, *Aristocracy and People in Britain 1815–1865*, Edward Arnold 1979, pp. 65–67.

99. *Bunting* 2, p. 171.

Cf. *Bunting* 1, pp. 208–209.

100. A. Kirk-Smith, *William Thomson: Archbishop of York, 1819–1850*, SPCK 1958, pp. 27ff.

101. P. Horn, *Labouring Life in the Victorian Countryside*, Brown, Gill and Macmillan 1976, pp. 165ff.

N. Scotland, *Methodism and The Revolt of the Field*, Allan Sutton 1981.

102. P. Horn, *Joseph Arch 1826–1919*, Kineton 1971.

M. K. Ashby, *Joseph Ashby of Tysoe 1859–1919*, Merlin Press 1974, p. 6.

103. G. Kitson Clark, *Churchmen and the Condition of England 1832–1885*, Methuen 1973, pp. 239–66.

Horn, *Arch*, p. 50.

Chadwick, op. cit. II, pp. 155, 264.

104. H. D. Rack, 'Domestic Visitation', *Journal of Ecclesiastical History*, Vol. 24, No. 4, October 1973, pp. 357–76.

H. Pelling, *Popular Politics and Society in Late Victorian Britain*, Macmillan 1968, p. 21.

105. Webb, op. cit., pp. 39, 41.

E. A. Knox, *The Tractarian Movement 1833–1845*, G. P. Putnam's Sons 1933, Chs. 3, 6.

106. J. Danielou et al., op. cit., pp. 320–21. Summary by John Kent.

Knox, op. cit., Ch. 6 'The Encircling Gloom', pp. 137–38.

107. J. H. Newman, 'Prospects for the Anglican Church', *Essays Critical and Historical*, Vol. 1, Longman 1871.

108. I owe this point to Bishop Patrick Kelly who is researching on R. I. Wilberforce.

Cf. Newsome, *Parting of Friends*, pp. 370ff.

109. E. A. Knox, *Reminiscences of an Octogenarian 1847–1934*, Hutchinson and Co. 1934, p. 112.

H. C. G. Mathew, 'Edward Bouverie Pusey', *Journal of Theological Studies*, New Series 32, 1981, pp. 101–124.

P. Butler, *Pusey Rediscovered*, SPCK 1983, Ch. 1, pp. 1–33.

110. *HMGB* III, p. 187.

111. J. S. Lidgett, *My Guided Life*, Methuen 1937, pp. 70–73.

J. Kent, *From Darwin to Blatchford*, Dr. Williams's Trust 1966, pp. 11ff.

112. Pope, *Compendium* 3, pp. 27–100.

113. Knox, *Tractarian Movement*, pp. 356–57, 364.

J. A. Froude, *Short studies on great subjects* (4 vols), Longman 1901, pp. 283, 312, 323.

Mark Pattison, *Memoirs*, Macmillan 1885, p. 210.

Bowen, op. cit., pp. 55–66, 139–54.

114. *Leeds Mercury*, 23 September 1898.

9. From Lunn to Flew

1. For this chapter cf. J. M. Turner, 'Methodism 1900–1932', *HMGB* III, pp. 341–49.

E. Barker, *Britain and the British People*, Oxford University Press 1942, p. 24 cf. p. 90.

E. Barker, *National Character*, Oxford University Press 1923, pp. 195ff.

2. P. Toon, *Evangelical Theology 1833–1856*, Marshall Morgan and Scott 1979.

3. D. M. Thompson, *Nonconformity in the Nineteenth Century*, Routledge and Kegan Paul 1972, p. 7.

Cf. J. W. Grant, *Free Churchmanship in England 1870–1940*, Independent Press n.d., pp. 114ff.

D. Bebbington, *The Nonconformist Conscience: Chapel and Politics, 1870–1914*, Allen and Unwin 1982, pp. 60–83.

G. Rupp, 'The Biblical Theologian', *John Scott Lidgett* ed. R. E. Davies, Epworth Press 1957, pp. 80–105.

The phrase about 'greatest holiness' is from Gladstone.

4. Thompson, op. cit., pp. 11ff.

5. Ibid., p. 227.

6. E. K. H. Jordan, *Free Church Unity: History of the Free Church Council Movement 1896–1914*, Lutterworth Press 1956, Ch. 2.

Bebbington, op. cit., Ch. 4.

7. R. W. W. Dale, *Life of R. W. Dale of Birmingham*, Hodder and Stoughton 1899, pp. 649–50.

8. J. Briggs and I. Sellars, *Victorian Nonconformity*, Edward Arnold 1973, pp. 168–71.

Thompson, op. cit., pp. 240–44.

G. F. A. Best, 'Popular Protestantism in Victorian Britain', *Ideas and Institutions of Victorian Britain* ed. R. Robson, Bell 1967, p. 138.

9. S. Koss, 'Wesleyanism and Empire', *Historical Journal* XVIII, No. 1, March 1975.

10. J. E. Rattenbury, 'Didsbury Fifty Years Ago', *Didsbury College Centenary 1842–1942*, ed. W. B. Brash and C. J. Wright, Epworth Press 1942, p. 98.

11. Jordan, op. cit., Ch. 4.

Gipsy Smith, *His Life and Work by himself*, Free Church Council 1902, Ch. 29.

S. Koss, *Nonconformity in Modern British Politics*, Batsford 1975, pp. 41–45.

12. B. Sacks, *The Religions Issue in the State Schools of England and Wales*, Albuquerque University, New Mexico, USA 1961.

Grant, op. cit., p. 152, quotation from Clifford, 1909.

E. A. Knox, *Reminiscences of an Octogenarian 1847–1934*, Hutchinson 1934, pp. 181–98; 238–57.

J. N. Figgis, *Churches in the Modern State*, Longman 1913, Lecture 11 'The Great Leviathan'.

J. N. Figgis, *Anti-Christ and other Sermons*, Longman 1913, p. 266.

13. Bebbington, op. cit., Ch. 7, p. 147. Bebbington gives a very clear summary of the whole issue.

14. F. C. Pritchard, 'Education', *HMGB* III.

J. Telford, *Life of J. H. Rigg 1821–1909*, Culley 1909, pp. 167–96.

15. *Free Church Year Book 1916*, pp. 1–24, Shakespeare's Presidential address.

J. H. Shakespeare, *The Churches at the Cross Roads*, Williams and Norgate 1918.

16. P. T. Forsyth, *The Church and the Sacraments*, Longman 1917, Ch. 6.

J. H. Moulton, *A Neglected Sacrament*, Epworth Press 1919, p. 20.

17. L. Newbigin, *The Household of God*, SCM Press 1953, p. 22.

18. J. S. Lidgett, *Apostolic Ministry*, Culley 1909, pp. 15–16.

J. S. Lidgett, *God, Christ and the Church*, Hodder and Stoughton 1927, pp. 244–46.

19. *Minutes* 1918, p. 82.

Jordan, op. cit., pp. 134–35.

20. B. L. Manning, *Essays in Orthodox Dissent*, Independent Press 1939, p. 148.

Manning wrote this in 1933.

21. Telford, op. cit. 1909, pp. 299ff.

22. J. H. Rigg, *The Churchmanship of John Wesley etc.*, London 1886 edn, p. 14–16.

23. B. Hellier, *His Life and Teaching* ed. by his children, London 1889, pp. 134–35. I owe this reference to Revd Norman Wallwork.

24. J. H. Rigg, *A Comparative View of Church Organizations: Primitive and Protestant with a Supplementary*, Ch. on Methodist Secessions and union, Woolmer 1887.

25. C. Wordsworth, *Miscellanies*, Vol. 3, Rivington 1879, pp. 368 ff.
    J. H. Overton and E. Wordsworth, *Christopher Wordsworth*, Rivington 1885, pp. 185–89.

26. J. A. Newton, 'Bishop King and Nonconformity', *Theology* 74, August 1971, p. 339. The phrase is from Newman, used of Pusey's *Eirenicon* in 1866.

27. *Proceedings* of Second Methodist Ecumenical Conference, 1892, pp. 125f.

28. G. F. Nuttall and O. Chadwick (eds), *From Uniformity to Unity*, SPCK 1962, pp. 280–81, 331–42.

29. Telford, op. cit., pp. 250–59.
    F. D. Maurice, *Subscription No Bondage*, Oxford 1834.

30. G. S. Rowe (ed), *Memorials of W. M. Bunting*, London 1870, p. 49.

31. J. H. Moulton, *A Neglected Sacrament*, p. 15.

32. E.g. M. K. Ashby, *Life of Joseph Ashby of Tysoe 1859–1919*, Merlin Press 1974, p. 6.
    H. Kirk-Smith, *William Thomson, Archbishop of York*, SPCK 1958, p. 150.
    E. B. Perkins, *So Appointed*, Epworth Press 1964, pp. 8–9.
    W. Fiddian Moulton, *William F. Moulton*, Isbister 1899, pp. 260–70.
    F. R. Barry, *Period of My Life*, Hodder and Stoughton 1970, p. 30.

33. T. Arnold, *Principles of Church Reform*, SPCK 1962 edn, p. 136.
    G. K. Clarke, *Churchmen and the Condition of England 1832–1885*, Methuen 1973, pp. 74–77.

34. T. A. Lacey, *Unity and Schism*, Mowbray 1917.
    T. A. Lacey, *Catholicity*, Mowbray 1914.
    T. A. Lacey, *The One Body and the One Spirit*, Clarke n.d., post 1920.
    H. H. Kelly, *The Church and Religious Unity*, Longman 1913.
    S. Mayor, 'The Ministry in late Nineteenth Century Anglicanism', *Church Quarterly*, July 1969, pp. 54ff.
    S. Mayor, 'The Anglo-Catholic Understanding of the Ministry', *Church Quarterly* 54, October 1969, pp. 152ff.

35. H. R. T. Brandreth, *The Oecumenical Ideals of the Oxford Movement*, SPCK 1947.
    C. Binfield, George Williams and the YMCA, Heinemann 1973.
    R. Rouse and S. C. Neill, *History of the Ecumenical Movement 1517–1948*, SPCK Press 2nd edn 1967, pp. 599ff.

36. C. H. Hopkins, *John R. Mott 1865–1955*, World Council of Churches 1979.

37. J. Kent, *Holding the Fort*, Epworth Press 1978, pp. 132–235. A very trenchant and critical survey.
    A. L. Drummond and J. Bulloch, *The Church in Late Victorian Scotland 1874–1900*, Saint Andrew Press 1978, pp. 9–18.
    P. C. Simpson, *Life of Principal Rainy* (2 vols.), Hodder and Stoughton 1909, pp. 408ff.

38. G. A. Smith, *Henry Drummond*, Hodder and Stoughton 1899, pp. 58ff.
    Hopkins, op. cit., pp. 29ff.
    Dale, op. cit., pp. 317ff.

Moulton, op. cit., p. 18.

39. Chadwick, op. cit. II, pp. 40ff.
40. D. Baillie and J. Marsh (eds), *Intercommunion*, SCM Press 1952, p. 95.
    G. F. Nuttall and O. Chadwick, op. cit., p. 281.
    R. T. Davidson and W. Benham, *Life of A. C. Tait*, Vol. 2, Macmillan 1891, pp. 63ff.
41. A. F. Hort, *Life and Letters of F. J. A. Hort*, Vol. 2, Macmillan 1896, p. 139.
42. Fiddian Moulton, op. cit., pp. 249ff.
43. Rouse and Neill, op. cit., pp. 338–41.
    H. S. Lunn, *Chapters from My Life with Special Reference to Reunion*, Cassell 1918.
44. Lunn, op. cit., p. 127.
45. Ibid., p. 172.
46. Ibid., pp. 380, 383, 384.
47. Rouse and Neill, op. cit., p. 340.
48. Ibid., pp. 331, 355ff.
    S. Neill, *A History of Christian Missions*, Penguin Books 1964, pp. 393–96.
    B. Gregory, *The Holy Catholic Church, the Communion of Saints*, London 1873.
49. E. Hatch, *The Organization of the Early Christian Churches*, Rivington 1882.
    E. Hatch, *The Influence of Greek Ideas and Usages Upon the Christian Church* Williams and Norgate 6th edn 1897.
    E. Hatch, *The Growth of Church Institutions*, Hodder and Stoughton 1887.
    F. J. A. Hort, *The Christian Ecclesia*, Macmillan 1898.
    J. B. Lightfoot, *St Paul's Epistle to the Philippians*, Macmillan 1883, pp. 181–269.
    T. M. Lindsay, *The Church and the Ministry in the Early Centuries*, Hodder and Stoughton 1902.
    C. Gore, *Orders and Unity*, John Murray 1909.
50. C. Gore, *The Church and the Ministry*, Longman 1902; 2nd edn 1919, revised by C. H. Turner.
    C. H. Turner, Essay on 'Apostolic Succession', *Essays on the Early History of the Church and the Ministry* ed. H. B. Swete, Macmillan 1918, pp. 95–214.
    R. C. Moberley, *Ministerial Priesthood*, John Murray 1897.
51. J. V. Bartlet, *Church-Life and Church-Order during the first four centuries* ed. C. J. Cadoux, Blackwell 1943.
52. J. S. Lidgett, *God, Christ and the Church*, p. 241.
53. W. R. Inge, *Lay Thoughts of a Dean*, G. P. Putnam's Sons 1926, p. 280.
    H. H. Henson, *Retrospect of an Unimportant Life*, Vol. 2, Oxford University Press 1943, p. 23.
54. Lacey, *Unity and Schism*.
    F. A. Rees, *Problems of Tomorrow*, Clarke 1918.
    A. Black et al., *Pathways to Christian Unity: A Free Church View*, Macmillan 1919.
55. R. C. D. Jasper, *Arthur Cayley Headlam*, Faith Press 1960, pp. 120–25.
    H. M. Smith, *Frank, Bishop of Zanzibar: Life of Frank Weston 1871–1924*, SPCK 1926, pp. 149ff.
    F. Weston, *The Case against Kikuyu*, Longman 1914.
    J. T. Willis, *The Kikuyu Controversy*, Longman 1914.
    W. G. Peel and J. J. Willis, *Steps towards Reunion*, Longman 1914.

G. Bell, *Randall Davidson*, Oxford University Press 1952, Ch. 42, 'Kikuyu 1913–14'.

56. G. Wainwright, *Eucharist and Eschatology*, Epworth Press 1971, pp. 135–41.
    O. C. Quick, *The Christian Sacraments*, Nisbet 1927.
    O. C. Quick, *Doctrines of the Creed*, Nisbet 1938, pp. 322–41.
    S. L. Greenslade, *Schism in the Early Church*, SCM Press 1953.
    Jasper, op. cit., pp. 140ff.

57. P. T. Forsyth, *The Church and the Sacraments*, pp. 45–46.
    P. T. Forsyth, *Positive Preaching and Modern Mind*, Hodder and Stoughton 1907, pp. 7, 105.

58. C. Gore, *The Church and the Ministry*, pp. 57ff.

59. Rouse and Neill, op. cit., pp. 239, 250, 264–65.
    J. E. Booty, *The Church in History*, Seabury, New York 1979, p. 26.
    W. R. Huntington, *The Peace of the Church*, 1891.
    W. R. Huntington, *The Church Idea*, E. P. Dutton and Co. 1870.

60. W. J. Woolf, J. E. Booty and O. C. Thomas, *The Spirit of Anglicanism*, T. and T. Clark, Edinburgh 1982, p. 88.
    H. G. G. Herklots, 'The Origins of the Lambeth Quadrilateral', *Church Quarterly Review*, January 1968.

61. A. G. M. Stephenson, *Anglicanism and the Lambeth Conferences*, SPCK 1978, pp. 84–86.
    Rouse and Neill, op. cit., p. 264–65.

62. Rouse and Neill, op. cit., p. 265.

63. G. K. A. Bell, *Documents on Christian Unity 1920–1924*, Oxford University Press 1924, pp. 1–5.
    Cf. J. G. Lockhart, *Cosmo Gordon Lang*, Hodder and Stoughton 1949, Ch. 23 'An appeal to all Christian Peoples'.

64. G. Stephenson, *Edward Stuart Talbot 1844–1934*, SPCK 1936, p. 261.
    Bell, op. cit., p. 158.

65. Scott Lidgett, *God, Christ and the Church*, pp. 244–46.
    Bell, op. cit., p. 5.

66. Bell, op. cit., pp. 118–42.

67. Ibid., p. 107. Primitive Methodism June 1921.
    Ibid., p. 108. United Methodism July 1921.
    Ibid., pp. 109–115. Wesleyan Methodism July 1921 July 1922.

68. Ibid., pp. 156–63.

69. Ibid., pp. 164–69.

70. G. K. A. Bell (ed), *Documents on Christian Unity*, Second Series, Oxford University Press 1930, pp. 77–86.

71. Ibid., pp. 108–10, Primitive Methodist reply, June 1926; pp. 110–12. United Methodist reply, July 1926.

72. P. Carnegie Simpson, *Church Principles*, Hodder and Stoughton 1924.
    C. A. Anderson Scott, *The Church, its Worship and Sacraments*, SCM Press 1927.
    For a typical Wesleyan statement of this period cf.
    J. Scott Lidgett, 'New Testament Principles', *The Lambeth Joint Report on Church Unity* ed. J. G. Simpson, 1923, pp. 86–104.
    W. F. Lofthouse, 'Wesleyan Methodism and the Anglican Church', *The Anglican Communion, Past, Present and Future* ed. H. A. Wilson, John Murray 1928, pp. 422–34.

Summary in J. T. Wilkinson, *1662 and After*, Epworth Press 1962, pp. 179–88.

73. A. S. Peake, *Plain Thought on Great Subjects*, Allenson n.d., pp. 25–50.

R. N. Flew, 'Methodism and the Catholic Tradition, *Northern Catholicism* ed. N. P. Williams and C. Harris, SPCK 1933, p. 528.

74. P. Carnegie Simpson, *Recollections – Mainly ecclesiastical but sometimes human*, Nisbet 1943, p. 91.

Jordan, op. cit., Ch. 13, 'The Free Churches and the Revised Prayer Book'.

O. Chadwick, *Hensley Henson: A Study in the Friction between Church and State*, Oxford University Press 1983, Ch. 8, pp. 182–218. A brilliant summary.

75. B. L. Manning, *Essays in Orthodox Dissent*, Independent Press 1919, p. 202.

J. M. Turner, 'Bernard Lord Manning as Church Historian', *Journal of URC Historical Society* 5, May 1975, pp. 131–33.

76. A. C. Headlam, 'The Lambeth Conference and Reunion', *Church Quarterly Review* 111, pp. 205–226.

V. Taylor, 'Reunion and Nonconformity', *Hibbert Journal* 29, pp. 595–608.

F. A. Iremonger, *William Temple*, Oxford University Press 1948, p. 460.

Cf. R. C. D. Jasper, op. cit., p. 207.

77. Stephenson, op. cit., pp. 155–77, especially p. 168.

78. G. S. Wakefield, *Robert Newton Flew*, Epworth Press 1971, p. 234.

79. K. E. Kirk, *Beauty and Bands*, Hodder and Stoughton 1955, p. 134.

80. A. J. Mason, *The Relation of Confirmation to Baptism*, Longman 1893.

G. Dix, *The Theology of Confirmation in Relation to Baptism*, Dacre Press 1946.

L. S. Thornton, *Confirmation, its Place in the Baptismal Mystery*, Dacre Press 1954.

Cf. G. W. H. Lampe, *The Seal of the Spirit*, SPCK 1951.

81. C. H. Turner, *Catholic and Apostolic Collected Papers*, Mowbray 1931, pp. 273–315.

82. Jordan, op. cit., p. 173.

H. G. Wood, *Terrot Reaveley Glover*, Cambridge University Press 1953, pp. 152ff.

T. R. Glover, *The Free Churches and Reunion*, Heffer 1921.

83. Iremonger, op. cit., pp. 398–99.

The World Mission of Christianity: The complete Report of the Jerusalem Conference (8 vols.), Oxford University Press 1928.

Tambaram – Madras Series (7 vols.), Oxford University Press 1939.

H. Kraemer, *The Christian Message in a non-Christian World*, EHP 1938.

84. *COPEC Comission Reports* (12 vols.), 1924.

S. E. Keeble. *COPEC: An Account of the Christian Conference on Politics, Economics and Citizenship*, SCM Press 1924.

E. R. Norman, *Church and Society in England 1770–1970*, Oxford University Press 1976, Ch. 7, 'Christian Politics, Economics and Citizenship 1919–1924 – A critique'.

85. Typical of Lofthouse's approach are: 'Wesleyan Methodism and the Anglican Church', op. cit. ed. H. A. Wilson, pp. 422–34. and 'The Possibility of a United Christendom from the standpoint of Methodism', *Union of Christendom* 2 ed. K. MacKenzie, Religious Book Club 1938, pp. 479–502.

86. L. Hodgson (ed), *Convictions: A selection from the Responses of the Churches to*

the Report of the World Conference on Faith and Order, held at Lausanne of 1927, SCM Press 1934, pp. 43–45.

87. Ibid., p. 42.
88. B. Sunkler, *Church of South India*, Lutterworth Press 1965, pp. 154–56, 187–90, 210.
   Wakefield, op. cit., p. 209.
89. B. L. Manning, op. cit., pp. 122–39, 196–209.
   H. Bett, *The Spirit of Methodism*, Epworth Press 1937, pp. 64–99.
90. B. L. Manning, *The People's Faith in the Time of Wyclif*, 1919, new edn Harvester Press 1975, pp. 184–88.
   Turner, op. cit., *Journal of URC Historical Society*.
   D. M. Thompson, 'Proposals for Covenanting. The end of an era', *Epworth Review*, Vol. 10, No. 1, January 1983, pp. 4–11.
91. E. Routley, *Creeds and Confessions*, Duckworth 1962, pp. 151–53.
   G. K. A. Bell, *Documents* 3, p. 6. Resolution 44 of Lambeth 1930.
92. K. Kirk (ed), *The Apostolic Ministry*, Hodder and Stoughton 1946.
   T. W. Manson, *The Church's Ministry*, Hodder and Stoughton 1948.
   Cf. E. S. Abbott et al., *Catholicity*, Dacre Press 1947.
   E. R. Fairweather and R. F. Hettlinger, *Episcopacy and Reunion*, Mowbrays 1953. Two Anglican viewpoints.
   K. M. Carey (ed), *The Historic Episcopate*, Dacre Press 1954. The *plene esse* theory.
93. MacKenzie, op. cit., p. 494.
94. Wakefield, op. cit., pp. 205–207.
   Bell, op. cit. 3, pp. 71–101, 102–119. Free Church Reply 1941.
95. Bell, op. cit. 3, pp. 101–119.
   Stephenson, op. cit., pp. 178–80.
96. For an analysis cf. R. Kissack, *Church or No Church. The Development of the concept of Church in British Methodism*, Epworth Press 1964, pp. 102ff.
97. Examples of Flew's skill include:
   'The View of the Methodists', *The Ministry and the Sacraments* ed. R. Dunkerley and A. C. Headlam, SCM Press 1937, pp. 230–43.
   'Methodism and the Catholic Tradition', *Northern Catholicism* ed. N. P. Williams and C. Harris, pp. 515–30.
   'The Church of Rome', *The Nature of the Church* ed. R. N. Flew, SCM Press 1952, pp. 17–40.
98. Deed of Union, Doctrinal clause.
99. Wakefield, op. cit., p. 243, pp. 146–59, 'Analysis of Jesus and His Church'.
100. C. H. Dodd, G. R. Cragg and J. Ellul, *Social and Cultural Factors in Church Divisions*, SCM Press 1952.
   For the changes in Faith and Order thinking:
   H. E. Fey (ed), *The Ecumenical Advance: A History of the Ecumenical Movement*, Vol. 2 1948–1968, SPCK 1970, pp. 145–70.
   T. F. Torrance, *Conflict and Agreement in the Church* (2 vols.), Lutterworth Press 1959–60.
   T. F. Torrance, 'Where do we go from Lund?', *Scottish Journal of Theology*, No. 1, pp. 53ff.
   N. Goodall, *Ecumenical Progress: A Decade of Change in the Ecumenical Movement 1961–1971*, Oxford University Press 1972, pp. 59–79.
   Wakefield, op. cit., pp. 224–29.

10. 'The Walk to the Paradise Garden'

1. Report of Methodist Faith and Order Committee on 'Church Relations in England', 1952, p. 6.
2. *Church Relations in England*, SPCK 1950, pp. 5–12.
   G. S. Wakefield, *R. N. Flew*, Epworth Press 1971, pp. 230–43.
3. R. E. Davies, *Methodism*, Epworth Press 1976 edn, pp. 184–86.
4. R. Kissack, *Church or No Church: The Development of the concept of Church in British Methodism*, Epworth Press 1964, pp. 117–18.
5. Ibid., p. 3.
   'Interim Statement', 1958, p. 3.
6. Ibid., p. 41.
7. G. F. Fisher, *The Anglican-Methodist Conversations and the Problems of Church Unity*, Oxford University Press 1964.
   G. F. Fisher, *Covenant and Reconciliation*, Mowbray 1967.
8. 'Interim Statement', pp. 41–44.
9. Cf. R. E. Davies, 'Since 1932', *HMGB* III, pp. 372–80.
   R. E. Davies, *The Church in our Times*, Epworth Press 1979, pp. 48–59, 101–107.
   A. G. M. Stephenson, *Anglicanism and the Lambeth Conferences*, SPCK 1978, pp. 224–25, 249–51, 263–66.
   H. D. Rack, *The Future of John Wesley's Methodism*, Lutterworth Press 1965, pp. 39–79.
   L. Paul, *A Church by Daylight*, Chapman 1973, pp. 188–208.
   G. T. Brake, *Policy and Politics in British Methodism 1932–1982*, Edsall 1984, pp. 91–150.
10. 'Interim Statement', p. 37.
11. Stephenson, op. cit., pp. 191–92.
12. 'Interim Statement', p. 44.
13. Ibid., p. 24.
14. N. Micklem, *The Doctrine of our Redemption*, Eyre and Spottiswoode 1943, pp. v, viii.
15. *Relations between the Church of England and the Church of Scotland*, 1951.
    Relations between the Church of England and the Church of Scotland, 1957.
    'The Bishops' Report'.
    Cf. I. Henderson, *Power without Glory*, Hutchinson 1967. A salutary polemic which called 'the Bishops' Report' an 'ecclesiastical Munich'.
16. 'Interim Statement', p. 36.
17. T. W. Manson, *Ministry and Priesthood: Christ's and Ours*, Epworth Press 1958, pp. 40ff.
18. 'Interim Statement', p. 21.
19. R. D. Whitehorn (ed), *The Approach to Christian Unity*, Heffer 1951, p. 48.
    E. H. Dunkley, *The Reformation in Denmark*, SPCK 1948, pp. 70ff.
    Cf. I. Henderson, op. cit., p. 173. 'I don't think God is a bloody fool'.
20. 'Interim Statement', p. 18.
21. *The Approach*, p. 47.
22. *Conversations between the Church of England and the Methodist Church*, Church Information Office and Epworth Press 1963, pp. 43, 47.
23. Ibid., p. 52.
24. D. Jenkins, *The Gift of Ministry*, Faber and Faber 1947, p. 31.

25. *Conversations*, p. 62.

26. C. H. Dodd, G. R. Cragg and J. Ellul, *Social and Cultural Factors in Church Divisions*, SCM Press 1952.

27. W. S. F. Pickering (ed), *Anglican-Methodist Relations: Some Institutional Factors*, Darton, Longman and Todd 1961, pp. 129–73.
    R. E. Davies, *Methodists and Unity*, Mowbray 1962, pp. 32–54.
    D. B. Clark, *Anglicans and Methodists in Four Towns*, Epworth Press 1964.

28. J. I. Packer (ed), *The Church of England and the Methodist Church*, Marcham Manor Press 1963, p. 47.
    Cf. G. Rupp, *Consideration Reconsidered*, Epworth Press 1964.

29. C. K. Barrett, *LQHR*, April 1956, pp. 118–22.
    C. K. Barrett, *From First Adam to Last*, SPCK 1962, pp. 118–19.
    C. K. Barrett, *The Signs of an Apostle*, Epworth Press 1970, pp. 85–114.
    C. K. Barrett, *Church Quarterly*, October 1968, pp. 114–19.
    T. E. Jessop, *The Anglican Methodist Majority Report*, Epworth Press 1964.
    T. E. Jessop, *Expository Times*, June 1963.
    T. E. Jessop, *Not This Way: A Methodist Examination of the Union Scheme and a Plea for Integrity*, Marcham Manor Press 1969.
    T. D. Meadley, *LQHR*, January 1964, pp. 27–29; July 1965, pp. 225–33.
    N. H. Snaith, *LQHR*, July 1963, pp. 24–27.
    Cf. J. Knox, *The Early Church and the Coming Great Church*, Epworth Press 1957, pp. 83ff.

30. D. Jenkins, *The British, their Identity and their Religion*, SCM Press 1975, pp. 81, 99.

31. S. L. Greenslade et al., *Conversations between the Church of England and the Methodist Church: Comments and Criticisms*, Epworth Press 1963, p. 22.

32. B. Wilson, *Religion in Secular Society*, Watts 1966, pp. 125ff.

33. A. Cresswell, 'Unity – the Dissentient Point of View', *Methodist Recorder*, 24 August 1967.
    Dodd et al., op. cit., p. 10.
    Cf. Brake, op. cit., p. 132.

34. G. Wainwright, *Doxology*, Epworth Press 1980, p. 74.

35. *Towards Reconciliation*, 1967, p. 5.

36. Ibid., p. 16.

37. Ibid., p. 20.

38. *Anglican-Methodist Unity* I, *The Ordinal*, SPCK and Epworth Press 1968.

39. R. Hooker, *Of the Laws of Ecclesiastical Polity*, Vol. 2, Everyman edn 1907, pp. 429–30.
    Cf. The Scottish *Prayer Book* of 1637.

40. G. Leonard, *To Everyman's Conscience*, Bromley n.d., p. 21.
    M. Deanesly and G. G. Willis, *Anglican – Methodist Unity*, Faith Press 1968.

41. C. Morris, *Include Me Out!* Epworth Press 1968, p. 38, Morris spoke and voted for *The Scheme*.

42. J. J. Vincent, *Here I Stand*, Epworth Press 1967, p. 59.

43. *Anglican-Methodist Unity* II, *The Scheme*, SPCK and Epworth Press 1968.

44. Ibid., p. 64.

45. Ibid., p. 85.

46. *Intercommunion To-Day*, Church Information Office 1968.
    The Scheme, p. 53.

47. Leonard, op. cit., pp. 22–23.

48. *Scheme*, p. 118.
49. Ibid., pp. 5, 55, 107.
50. Ibid., p. 34.
51. Ibid., pp. 140–45.
52. Ibid., pp. 182–83.
53. Stephenson, op. cit., p. 263 – 1969 figures; p. 265 – 1972 figures.
    Brake, op. cit., pp. 130–31.
54. Case of Barker v. O'Gorman, 1970, Chancery Division.
    Brake, op. cit., pp. 139ff.
55. *Anglican-Methodist Unity:*
    Report of the Joint Working Group, Church Information Office 1971, p. 6.
56. Ibid., pp. 29–31. Memorandum by Mr W. S. Wrigglesworth.
57. Ibid., pp. 24–25.
58. D. L. Edwards, 'The Future of the Church of England', *Liberal Christianity
    in England* ed. A. G. M. Stephenson, Holywell Press, Oxford 1970,
    p. 134.
    J. M. Turner, 'Tentative Agenda of the Future', *Methodist Recorder*, 27 July
    1972.
59. Stephenson, op. cit., p. 283.
60. H. E. Fey, *The Ecumenical Advance*, SPCK 1970, pp. 43, 149.
    In Each Place: Towards a Fellowship of Local Churches Truly United, World
    Council of Churches 1977.
61. Cf. R. E. Davies, *The Church in our Times*, pp. 62–63.
    N. Goodall, *Ecumenical Progress: a Decade of Change in the Ecumenical Movement
    1961–71*, Oxford University Press 1972.
62. C. O. Buchanan, E. L. Mascall, J. I. Packer, G. D. Leonard, *Growing into
    Union: Proposals for forming a United Church in England*, SPCK 1970.
    Brake, op. cit., pp. 135–39.
    Cf. E. G. Rupp, 'Chaos and Old Night', *Frontier*, August 1970.
    C. O. Buchanan (ed), *Unity on the Ground*, SPCK 1972. This pleaded
    for shared buildings but failed to comprehend that Methodism is a
    connexional system.
    Cf. D. Blatherwick, *Adventures in Unity*, British Council of Churches 1974.
63. J. Huxtable, *A New Hope for Christian Unity*, Collins 1977, pp. 102ff.
64. Ibid., pp. 32–39.
    R. E. Davies (ed), *The Testing. . .*, p. 172.
    P. Morgan (ed), *Unity: The Next Step?* SPCK 1972.
    For a different view stressing diversity and 'conciliarity' cf. J. Macquarrie,
    Christian Unity and Christian Diversity, SCM Press 1975,
65. Huxtable, op. cit., p. 27.
66. *Intercommunion To-Day*, 1968, especially pp. 17–21.
    Cf. R. E. Davies, *The Church of England Observed*, Epworth Press 1984,
    pp. 21ff.
67. Churches' Unity Commission, Second Annual Report, *Ten Propositions*,
    Church Information Office January 1976.
68. M. Conway et al., *Unity: Why not Yet?*, British Council of Churches 1980,
    pp. 47–48.
    Covenanting for Union for Wales, Part II, Council of Churches in Wales 1971.
    Huxtable, op. cit., pp. 49ff.
69. Wainwright, op. cit., p. 293.

Cf. J. Coventry, 'A Roman Catholic View of the Covenant Process', *Essays on the Covenant*, British Council of Churches 1980, pp. 53–56.

D. Henschell, 'The Sixth Proposition and After', *One in Christ* XVI 4, 1980, pp. 311–28.

For an earlier Roman Catholic exploration

E. Mersch, *The Theology of the Mystical Body*, St. Louis, USA 1952, Ch. XVI.

D. Tripp, 'Covenant-Drafting and Liturgy-Making', *Epworth Review*, Vol. 10, No. 2, May 1983, pp. 35–47.

70. 10 July 1978. *Towards Visible Unity*, 1980, pp. 87–88, 97.

71. D. M. Thompson, 'Proposals for Covenanting: The End of an Era', *Epworth Review*, Vol. 10, No. 1, January 1983, pp. 4–11.

72. Cf. *Baptists and Unity*, 1967.

The diversity of views about Baptism among Baptists is not always realized.

A. Gilmore (ed), *Christian Baptism*, Lutterworth Press 1959.

A. Gilmore, *Baptism and Christian Unity*, Lutterworth Press 1966.

R. E. O. White, *The Biblical Doctrine of Initiation*, Hodder and Stoughton 1960.

G. R. Beasley-Murray, *Baptism in the New Testament*, Macmillan 1962.

N. Clark, 'Retrospect and Prospect – A Baptist View', *Essays on the Covenant* ed. J. Coventry, pp. 49–52.

G. Wainwright, *Christian Initiation*, Lutterworth Press 1969, Ch. IV.

G. Wainwright, *Doxology*, Ch. IX.

73. The 'Report of the Churches' Council for Covenanting Towards Visible Unity', 1980.

74. D. Tripp, *The Renewal of the Covenant in the Methodist Tradition*, Epworth Press 1969.

75. *Towards Visible Unity*, pp. 82–96.

76. Cf. *Epworth Review*, May 1983, p. 37.

77. A. E. Harvey, *Priest or President?* SPCK 1975, pp. 37–54.

78. Huxtable, op. cit., pp. 109–115.

79. *Agenda* of Conference 1981, pp. 55–58. *Minutes* 1981, p. 23.

80. For differing positive views cf. *Unity. Why Not Yet?*, British Council of Churches 1980.

Essays on the Covenant, British Council of Churches 1980.

J. House and T. Kingsnorth (ed), *Catholics contend for the Covenant*, Leeds 1981.

For critical views:

C. K. Barrett, 'Covenanting – an alternative Viewpoint', *Methodist Recorder*, 7 January 1982.

A Group of Free Churchmen, *The 95 Theses*, 28 January, 1982.

Voice of Methodism: A critical view, n.d.

81. J. S. Habgood, Bishop of Durham, *The Times*, 13 July 1982.

82. Huxtable, op. cit., p. 83.

83. ARCIC, *The Final Report*, Catholic Truth Society SPCK 1982.

84. D. M. MacKinnon, *The Stripping of the Altars*, Fontana 1969, p. 78.

85. Cited in G. Wainwright, *The Ecumenical Moment*, Eerdmans Grand Rapids, USA 1983, p. 216.

86. Cited from Coleridge in A. R. Vidler, *The Church in an Age of Revolution*, Penguin Books 1961, p. 82.

Cf. J. S. Habgood, *Church and Nation in a Secular Age*, Darton, Longman and Todd 1983, Chs. 6, 9.

87. G. K. A. Bell, *Documents on Christian Unity*, Vol. 2, Oxford University Press 1930, pp. 117–42.

A. J. Lewis, *Zinzendorf: The Ecumenical Pioneer*, SCM Press 1962, p. 181.

N. Sykes, *Daniel Ernst Jablonski and the Church of England*, SPCK 1950.

N. Sykes, *From Sheldon to Secker*, Cambridge University Press 1959, pp. 138–39.

'A Moravian Statement', *Essays on the Covenant*, 1980, pp. 38–42.

A. C. Headlam, *Doctrine of the Church and Christian Reunion*, John Murray 1920, p. 293.

J. Pinnington, *Colloquium*, Vol. 2, October 1967, pp. 240–49.

Bulletin of John Rylands Library, Vol. LII, pp. 200ff.

88. P. Capper and K. Woolcombe, *The Failure of the English Covenant*, British Council of Churches 1982.

89. Cf. P. Avis, *The Church in the Theology of the Reformers*, Marshall, Morgan and Scott 1981.

90. *Unity Begins at Home*, British Conference on Faith and Order, Nottingham, SCM Press 1964, p. 77.

91. J. M. Turner (ed), *Queen's Essays*, Queen's College, Birmingham 1980, pp. 19–39.

P. Brooks (ed), *Protestant Spirituality*, SCM Press 1975, pp. 317–19.

T. T. Rowe, *Methodist Recorder*, 13 January 1977.

G. Wainwright, 'An Ecumenical Experiment', *Christian World*, 11 January 1979.

T. T. Rowe in P. Morgan (ed), *Unity the Next Step*, pp. 66–70.

92. M. H. Taylor 'Training for Ministry', and W. P. Stephens, 'The Theological College as a Place for Ministerial Training', *Epworth Review*, Vol. 6, No. 1, January 1979, pp. 33–57.

93. Including the personal participation of J. S. Habgood and G. Wainwright.

94. C. H. Dodd, *The Meaning of Paul for To-Day*, Allen and Unwin 1920, p. 138.

95. Is that phrase a conflation of John Hunter's 'coming church' with P. T. Forsyth's 'great church'?

Index